Celebrating a Century of Ecumenism

Celebrating a Century of Ecumenism

Exploring the Achievements
of International Dialogue

In Commemoration of the Centenary of the
1910 Edinburgh World Missionary Conference

Edited by

John A. Radano

WILLIAM B. EERDMANS PUBLISHING COMPANY
GRAND RAPIDS, MICHIGAN / CAMBRIDGE, U.K.

Published 2012 by

Wm. B. Eerdmans Publishing Co.

2140 Oak Industrial Drive N.E., Grand Rapids, Michigan 49505 /
P.O. Box 163, Cambridge CB3 9PU U.K.

Printed in the United States of America

18 17 16 15 14 13   7 6 5 4 3 2

Library of Congress Cataloging-in-Publication Data

Celebrating a century of ecumenism : exploring the achievements of international
dialogue : in commemoration of the centenary of the 1910 Edinburgh World
Missionary Conference / edited by John A. Radano.

    p.   cm.

ISBN 978-0-8028-6705-6 (pbk.: alk. paper)

1. Ecumenical movement — Congresses.

2. World Council of Churches — History — Congresses.

3. Catholic Church — Relations — Congresses.

I. Radano, John A.

II. World Missionary Conference (1910: Edinburgh, Scotland)

BX8.3.C45 2011

280'.042 — dc23

2011040633

www.eerdmans.com

Contents

Contents

Contents

Foreword

With two world wars and two totalitarian systems, the twentieth century was a dark century. The ecumenical movement, which can now look back with gratitude on 100 years, was a light-filled countermovement to the bloody and tragic conflicts. It brought closer together once more churches and their people who had been separated and often hostile for centuries, and thus contributed to peace in the world.

It is appropriate, then, to pause and ask: What have we achieved? Where are we now? Where are we going?

This present volume shows in an exemplary manner that, on the challenging but also encouraging basis of Jesus' prayer "that they may all be one," in the 100 years since the World Mission Conference in Edinburgh in 1910 we have, with God's help, achieved far more than the participants of the conference dared to hope or were able to imagine. Therefore, in spite of all that has not yet been achieved, we still have reason to be thankful.

The numerous ecumenical documents that are expertly presented and analyzed in this volume demonstrate convincingly the high degree of commonality that already exists, in shared faith in the one God and one Lord Jesus Christ who binds us together as brothers and sisters in the community of the one Holy Spirit. We have not achieved the full visible unity of all Christians; but worldwide Christendom, with Catholic, Protestant, and Orthodox Christians, and Christians in the Anglican Communion and in the Free Churches, has drawn closer together. Despite all the barriers that still exist, it sees itself as a community of brothers and sisters in Jesus Christ, and understands its duty to bear witness to fraternity and justice and peace between all people in today's world, which despite globalization is torn between the many poor and the few rich countries.

The path to the full unity of all Christians is nowhere near its end. But what has been achieved in the ecumenical century that lies behind us can give us courage and confidence that what the spirit of God has initiated will continue in the new century in a rapidly changing world, in ways that we human beings cannot predict. Here the present volume can provide us with assistance and guidance.

To all who have collaborated in this I express my appreciation and sincere thanks. I hope that this important publication will find many attentive readers, and that they will be encouraged not to cease building bridges of understanding between Christians, and to walk the path of unity in friendship and fraternal cooperation for the peace of the world.

CARDINAL WALTER KASPER
Em. President of the Pontifical Council for Christian Unity
Rome, November 2011

Acknowledgments

The editor owes a deep debt of gratitude to The Saint Paul Seminary School of Divinity of the University of St. Thomas, in St. Paul, Minnesota, for creating the context from which this book emerged, and encouraging its publication. Invited to spend the Spring 2010 semester as Scholar-in-Residence at the Seminary, one of my major responsibilities was to organize a three-day seminar/conference for colleagues. Seminary officials readily accepted the proposal that the theme for the conference relate to the centenary of the 1910 Edinburgh World Missionary Conference being celebrated in 2010, and the century of ecumenism that followed it.

I want to express my deep appreciation to the authors of the essays in this book, all of whom have contributed in substantial ways to different aspects of the ecumenical movement, for their willingness to participate in the Conference, and now to have their essays published here. A special word of thanks is offered to Walter Cardinal Kasper, for writing the Foreword to this book. His years of ecumenical leadership are appreciated throughout the Christian world.

Gratitude is owed to many persons related to the SPSSOD, in particular to David and Barbara Koch, whose generous support makes possible the "Scholar-in Residence" program; to Msgr. Aloysius Callaghan, Rector, for inviting me to take that position; to Dr. Christopher Thompson, Academic Dean, for his continual support for the conference; to Dr. Deborah Savage, Professor of Theology, for her enormous contribution to the organizational details of the conference, and seeing to the needs of the participants, and to Alexis Theis and the many other Seminary and School of Divinity students who assisted Dr. Savage in various ways; to Nancy Utoft, Director of Community Relations, and Nancy Sannerud, Assistant to the Dean. Gratitude is extended also to those who moderated conference sessions, including SPSSOD faculty Dr. Christian Washburn, Dr. Kenneth Snyder, Deacon Joseph Michalak, Dr. John Martens, Dr. Deborah Savage, Sr. Katarina Schuth, OSF, University of St. Thomas Theology Professor Dr. Philip Rolnick, Greater Minneapolis Council of Churches executive Dr. Gary Reierson, Dr. Margaret O'Gara, and Fr. Erich Rutten, campus minister at the University of St. Thomas and Ecumenical Officer of the Archdiocese of St. Paul and Minneapolis, who also organized the ecumenical prayer service held during the conference.

Anne Glynn-Mackoul, a member of the Central Committee of the World Council of Churches, was gracious enough to participate in the conference, to read and discuss the paper written by Peter Bouteneff when he was unable to come, and also to bring perspectives from her rich experience at the WCC to the discussion.

I want to thank Dr. A. Gabriel Esteban, then Provost, now President of Seton Hall University, for supporting my leave from Seton Hall in order to accept the invitation from Saint Paul Seminary; Dr. Gregory Burton, Associate Provost, for arranging technical details in regard to it; and Msgr. James Cafone, Minister of Seton Hall's Priest Community, for his support.

I am grateful to Mr. William J. Otskey, Manager of the Computer Training Center at Seton Hall University, and to Mr. Carmine Rizzi, seminarian at the Immaculate Conception Seminary, Seton Hall University, for their generous assistance in formatting the manuscript.

I am grateful also to Norman Hjelm and William Rusch, who encouraged the publication of lectures from the conference and, especially, to Mr. William B. Eerdmans Jr. for his support and willingness to publish this book.

Abbreviations

Anthology	Michael Kinnamon and Brian E. Cope, eds., *The Ecumenical Movement: An Anthology of Key Texts and Voices.* Geneva: WCC Publications and Grand Rapids: Eerdmans, 1997.
BEM	*Baptism, Eucharist and Ministry,* Faith and Order Paper no. III (1982), 25th Anniversary Printing. Geneva: WCC Publications, 1982-2007.
Catechism	*Catechism of the Catholic Church,* 1992.
DEM2	Nicholas Lossky et al., eds., *Dictionary of the Ecumenical Movement,* 2nd edition. Geneva: WCC Publications, 2002.
GA	Harding Meyer and Lukas Vischer, eds., *Growth in Agreement: Reports and Agreed Statements of Ecumenical Conversations on a World Level,* Faith and Order Paper no. 108. New York/Ramsey, NJ: Paulist Press and Geneva: World Council of Churches, 1984.
GA II	Jeffrey Gros, FSC, Harding Meyer, and William G. Rusch, eds., *Growth in Agreement II: Reports and Agreed Statements of Ecumenical Conversations on a World Level, 1982-1998,* Faith and Order Paper no. 187. Geneva: WCC Publications and Grand Rapids/Cambridge: Eerdmans, 2000.
GA III	Jeffrey Gros, FSC, Thomas F. Best, and Lorelei F. Fuchs, SA, eds., *Growth in Agreement III: International Dialogue and Agreed Statements, 1998-2005,* Faith and Order Paper no. 204. Geneva:

WCC Publications and Grand Rapids/Cambridge: Eerdmans, 2007.

GS   Vatican II, *Gaudium et Spes: Pastoral Constitution on the Church in the Modern World,* 7 December 1965.

IS   Pontifical Council for Promoting Christian Unity, Vatican City, *Information Service.*

JDDJ   The Lutheran World Federation and the Roman Catholic Church, *Joint Declaration on the Doctrine of Justification* (1999). Grand Rapids: Eerdmans, 2000.

LG   Vatican II, *Lumen Gentium: Dogmatic Constitution on the Church,* 21 November 1964.

UUS   Encyclical Letter *Ut Unum Sint* of the Holy Father John Paul II on Commitment to Ecumenism, 1995.

WCFO5   Thomas F. Best and Günther Gassmann, eds., *On the Way to Fuller Koinonia: Official Report of the Fifth World Conference on Faith and Order, Santiago de Compostela, 1993.* Faith and Order Paper no. 166. Geneva: WCC Publications.

Perspective: With Gratitude for a Century of Ecumenism

1. The centenary of the 1910 World Missionary Conference at Edinburgh, Scotland is a time to celebrate a very significant development in modern church history. During the century since that event, many Christians have confronted together the divisions among them that started long ago. They have sought to respond to the prayer of Christ for his disciples, "that they may all be one . . . so that the world may believe" (John 17:21). It has been a century of ecumenism.

2. During the past century, the conviction has gradually taken hold in the minds and hearts of Christians that divisions are a scandal and an obstacle to the proclamation of the gospel, and that unity must characterize relationships among the followers of Christ.

3. The 1910 Edinburgh Conference was convened to address the subject of world mission, and so it did. At the same time the one and only decision taken by the conference, and passed by a resounding acclamation, was the decision to establish a continuation committee. With this decision and vote, "The conference, apparently spontaneously, began to sing the doxology in relief and jubilation." J. H. Oldham, the secretary of the conference, recalled fifty years later that this "was the turning point in the history of the ecumenical movement."[1] Shortly after,

---

1. For these citations see Brian Stanley, *The World Missionary Conference, Edinburgh 1910* (Grand Rapids/Cambridge: Eerdmans, 2009), p. 300.

This statement was developed with the collaboration of some participants in the St. Paul Conference, on a "Century of Ecumenism," June 17-19, 2010, and read by Dame Mary Tanner at the ecumenical prayer service during the conference.

some who had participated in Edinburgh 1910 began to promote the Faith and Order movement, insisting that attention to doctrinal issues was necessary if Christian cooperation was to develop, whether in matters of mission, or in service to each other and to the world. These movements of mission, service, and faith and order helped to fashion the modern ecumenical movement.

4. The movement since Edinburgh 1910 has flourished in ways too numerous to mention. It has radically changed the relationships between separated Christians. Within the World Council of Churches since 1948, and in councils of churches on the national, regional, and local levels, with all their strengths and limitations, Christians have come together to seek common cause and to give witness to the gospel for the benefit of society. During this century, there have been numerous examples of church unions. A particularly significant one was the founding of the Church of South India in 1947, which for the first time united this broad range of church traditions: Anglican, Methodist, Reformed, and Congregationalist. Countless ecumenical dialogues have taken place, especially since the Second Vatican Council. They continue to produce helpful reports, challenging the churches to reconsider and overcome the theological conflicts of the past, which were often shaped in the heat of polemics. The convergence text, *Baptism, Eucharist and Ministry* (1982), from the multilateral conversation in the Faith and Order Commission of the World Council of Churches, has influenced many other ecumenical advances. In the same way the bilateral conversation between the Lutherans and Catholics led to the signing of the *Joint Declaration on the Doctrine of Justification* (1999) and has also been officially endorsed by the World Methodist Council (2006). These are only two of the many major results of the theological dialogue.

5. At the same time, those involved in that movement would admit that there is no easy road to unity. While numerous obstacles to unity have been overcome, there are still significant obstacles that continue to keep Christians divided. But that must not detract us from celebrating the important achievements and steps towards unity that have come about through the ecumenical movement.

6. We can look back over a century of ecumenism with a sense of gratitude, being ready, like those gathered at Edinburgh one hundred years ago, to sing the doxology with a sense of "relief and jubilation." Not just for something that, like then, had just begun, but, now, for much that has been accomplished. For in this ecumenical movement,

"fostered by the grace of the Holy Spirit" (*Unitatis redintegratio* 1), we have witnessed that the Spirit has moved Christians closer to one another and therefore to Christ.

7. There are many types of ecumenical activity that contribute to the movement towards unity, and are necessary on our common journey. The conference these days focuses primarily on one specific part of the ecumenical movement: the international doctrinal conversations, both bilateral and multilateral, which have served the ecumenical movement in a very particular way. The dialogues are vital and irreplaceable instruments in the cause of Christian unity, because they have sought, and in many ways succeeded, to clarify issues at the root of historic divisions, and new issues that have emerged and continue to emerge in the course of our history of separation. Even churches that do not see the goal of visible unity as the goal of the dialogues have deepened their mutual understanding and their ability to relate with fellow Christians in common witness. The results of dialogues are assisting churches and communions, still separated from one another, in their efforts to proclaim together in our generation, the one apostolic faith which is the basis of unity. The results of dialogue need to be received more and more into the life of separated churches, so that they continue to help create bonds of reconciliation between them.

8. So, for what has already been accomplished through dialogue over many decades we give thanks. For the achievements of a century of ecumenism we make our own the words of the Psalmist: "I will give thanks to the Lord with my whole heart; . . . I will sing praise to your name, O Most High" (Ps. 9:1, 2).

Introduction

This book originated at a conference held at St. Paul Seminary School of Divinity in St. Paul, Minnesota, June 17-19, 2010, to commemorate the centenary of the 1910 World Missionary Conference in Edinburgh, Scotland. The Edinburgh Conference, though focused on mission, was also a major catalyst of the modern ecumenical movement. In that sense the centenary also marks a century of ecumenism. The book presents the papers given at the conference.

Two motivations led to commemorating the centenary and to focus on exploring the achievements of a century of ecumenism. First, Edinburgh 1910 set in motion movements that have contributed to the healing of divisions between long-separated churches and communions, a process in some way touching the whole Christian world. Commemorating this milestone would give an opportunity to review some of the major steps taken during that century toward the reconciliation of divided Christians, and to ascertain what has been achieved so as to be able to build on these developments in the continuing quest for Christian unity. Second, this century of ecumenism has produced significant results, not least through dialogue. But the reports of dialogues are too often little known, analyzed, and received into the life of the churches. This would be an opportunity to contribute to making these results better known.

The history of the ecumenical movement during that century is great and diverse, with achievements (and failures) in many areas, too many to take account of here. Therefore we focus here on just one significant ecumenical arena, namely, the international ecumenical theological dialogues. This volume treats both the multilateral dialogue of the Commission on Faith and Order of the World Council of Churches, which involves theologians of many Christian churches and traditions, and also international bilateral dialogues, co-sponsored by two churches or communions.

While many types of ecumenical contact and involvement contribute to breaking down the walls of separation between Christians, it was seen from the beginning that ecumenical theological dialogue to resolve doctrinal questions over which Christians have divided was urgent and fundamental. This was recognized by some participants at the 1910 Edinburgh Conference. That Conference itself did not include discussion of doctrinal questions on its agenda, knowing how divisive they were. But some who were there, inspired by the spirit of cooperation that the World Conference fostered, and convinced that this cooperation could develop seriously only if divisive doctrinal issues were faced, started immediately afterwards to plan for a world conference on matters of faith and order. Multilateral dialogue became a prominent and important ecumenical instrument in the first half of the century of ecumenism, though there were some bilateral dialogues during this period as well.

The Second Vatican Council (1962-65), with its Decree on Ecumenism, committed the Catholic Church to the modern ecumenical movement that had developed since Edinburgh 1910. The Decree pointed to "dialogue between competent experts from different churches and communities" (no. 4) as a main feature of ecumenism. Even during the Council, the Catholic Church began to engage in the multilateral dialogue. In cooperation with the WCC, the Secretariat for Promoting Christian Unity helped arrange for Catholic biblical scholar Raymond Brown to address one of the sessions of the 1963 Fourth World Conference on Faith and Order, in which five Catholic observers sent by Rome also participated. Also, steps were taken during Vatican II that led to the beginning of bilateral dialogue between the Roman Catholic Church and some Christian world communions shortly after the Council ended. Bilateral dialogue became an important ecumenical instrument for the churches in the second half of this century of ecumenism, and a prominent feature of the Catholic Church's ecumenical activity.

A New History

The chapters of this book convey many results of decades of ecumenical contact and dialogue. In contrast to the previous centuries of division among Christians, the ecumenical movement over the last century has spurred the beginnings of a new history in the relationships between separated churches. The results of the dialogues described herein point to some of the important chapters of this new history now developing.

The dialogues have published numerous reports over the decades, and collections of these reports published over the years provide convenient access to them. To mention just a few, in regard to multilateral dialogue two documentary histories of the Faith and Order movement have been published, one covering the period 1927-1963, and the other 1963-1993. These are mentioned in the Faith and Order essays in Part I of this book. These documentary histories show the major themes treated in that movement over decades, and many more reports have been published by Faith and Order since 1993. The reports issued by international bilateral dialogues since Vatican II have been published in thick collections such as the *Growth in Agreement* series published in 1984, 2000, and 2007, often cited in the essays in Part II. New bilateral reports produced in the last several years could already fill a fourth volume in that series if that were undertaken. And in both cases, multilateral and bilateral, one can find other volumes that have collected the results of dialogue.

Though obviously distinct, bilateral and multilateral dialogues are also interrelated. A forum on bilateral dialogues has met periodically since 1978, to assist the churches in fostering some common perspectives in the dialogues, and to help promote common directions in multilateral and bilateral dialogue, as both contribute, though in different ways, to the search for a common understanding and expression of the one Apostolic Faith. The Faith and Order convergence text, *Baptism, Eucharist and Ministry* (1982), for example, resulting from fifty-five years of dialogue, has presented a level of convergence on these three fundamental areas that has proven useful for bilateral dialogues. On the other hand, bilateral dialogues between two churches can deal directly with issues separating the two, in a way that multilateral dialogue cannot. They also can provide insights that can be useful in the multilateral dialogue.

It has often been lamented that while the dialogues have published significant reports, many church leaders and church members do not know them adequately enough, and not much has been done with them. More *analysis* of these dialogue reports, and accounts of what they have achieved, are needed in order to highlight ways in which they have addressed old theological conflicts relating to divisions that took place centuries ago and have helped to resolve them, and to show how they have contributed to increased mutual understanding among the churches, and to fostering Christian unity today. The results of dialogues can also help us to see some of the lines developing in this new history of the relationships between Christian churches. They can assist the churches in formulating the theological argumentation regarding the next steps forward as these new relationships develop.

New projects of analysis are beginning to emerge. A recent and very important analysis of dialogue results is found in Walter Cardinal Kasper's *Harvesting the Fruits: Basic Aspects of Christian Faith in Ecumenical Dialogue* (2009), to which several essays in this book refer. *Harvesting the Fruits* addresses four international bilateral dialogues, the first four undertaken by the Catholic Church after Vatican II: with the Lutheran World Federation, the World Methodist Council, the Anglican Communion, and the World Alliance of Reformed Churches. Involving a long process of study by the Pontifical Council for Promoting Christian Unity over many months, initiated and led by the Cardinal, *Harvesting the Fruits* offered an extensive analysis of the way each of these dialogues, and the four together, have treated basic issues at the center of ecumenical dialogue, and suggested implications of these results for reception.

Though its method is very different, this volume adds another effort to show the effectiveness of dialogue. It includes analyses of international dialogue, both multilateral and bilateral. The eleven bilateral dialogues involving the Catholic Church presented in this book include, in addition to those just mentioned with Lutherans, Methodists, Anglicans, and Reformed, also those with Eastern Orthodox and Oriental Orthodox Churches, with other communions of the Reformation heritage such as the Baptist World Alliance, the Christian Church (Disciples of Christ), and the Mennonites who continue the Anabaptist heritage of the Reformation and are today known as a historic peace church, as well as dialogues with those making an impact more recently, such as Pentecostals and Evangelicals. The range of dialogues analyzed here, and found in one volume, is unique.

The Structure of the Book

The book consists of two parts. Part I, "Achievements of International Multilateral Dialogue," provides two analyses of the evolution and accomplishments of Faith and Order over the century, within the context of the World Council of Churches. One is by Mary Tanner, a former moderator of the Faith and Order Commission and a current WCC President. And since Roman Catholic theologians have participated in Faith and Order as voting members from 1968, the other is by William Henn, OFM Cap, a current member of the Commission. The Faith and Order movement, which grew out of Edinburgh 1910, was a key factor, along with others, that contributed to the founding of the WCC. But since the WCC's formation in 1948, it has been the context within which Faith and Order has been based. Thus Part I begins with two analyses of the contributions and limits of the WCC. They are given by Wesley Ariarajah and Peter Bouteneff, both of whom gave years of service working at the WCC headquarters in Geneva.

Part II explores "Achievements of International Bilateral Dialogue following the Second Vatican Council." Observer-delegates and guests at Vatican II helped to relate the various churches, Christian world communions, and/or the World Council of Churches from which they came, to the Catholic Church. Good relations, which did not exist before, began to develop even at Vatican II. This soon led to the beginnings of international bilateral dialogues between some of those churches and the Catholic Church just after the Vatican Council. As already mentioned, international bilateral dialogues have been among the most notable developments in the second half of this century of ecumenism, and various churches and Christian world communions have engaged in bilateral dialogues with one another in this same period. This volume, however, concentrates only on bilaterals in which the Roman Catholic Church has participated since Vatican II. Nor does it give much attention to the many significant national dialogues over the decades, although the appendix that is part of Jared Wicks' presentation (chapter 5) illustrates, in one bilateral relationship, the fact that could also be found in others, that these dialogues have also produced important results during this century of ecumenism. Nonetheless, analyses of eleven international dialogues are presented here.

While the encounter of the observers of various churches and communions with the Catholic Church at Vatican II represented an initial step in a new relationship, the start of formal dialogue represented a major step in that new relationship, a mutual determination to deal with the theological issues over which they are divided. Each dialogue began when the co-sponsors judged that it was time to engage in dialogue. The two partners decided together on the subject matter to be followed. In some cases the decision to engage in dialogue was the first major step in the new relationship, as was the case, for example, with the first two dialogues, which began in 1967, those of the Catholic Church with the Lutheran World Federation and with the World Methodist Council. In other cases, significant events in their new relationships took place years before the beginning of formal dialogue. The Orthodox–Roman Catholic international dialogue began in 1980. But already in their 1965 common declaration, Pope Paul VI and Ecumenical Patriarch Athenagoras I took a dramatic step of canceling the historic excommunications of 1054, and, around the same time, both began to describe the other as a "sister church." The dialogue between the Catholic Church and the six families of Oriental Orthodox churches together began in 2003. But major steps fostering new relationships began decades before. The common Christological declarations of Popes and some Patriarchs of Oriental Orthodox churches, signed during the 1970s to 1990s, confessing together the same faith about Jesus Christ, already contributed to healing divisions that took place centuries earlier over the Christological language of the Council of Chalcedon (451).

The bilateral dialogues are presented here in chronological order, according to the year in which the actual dialogue began. Each dialogue is treated according to its own history and dynamics, and not in relationship to another, or others. Each author was asked to illustrate the achievements of a particular bilateral dialogue since its beginning after Vatican II. Since some dialogues continued quickly into subsequent phases, they produced more reports, while for others there was a hiatus of years before a next phase began. Each dialogue in its own way comprises a rich story, and the authors sometimes focused on particular aspects of that story as a way of giving a sense of the achievements of the whole dialogue. The achievements of the dialogues, as interpreted by these authors, provide some indication of where the partner churches are now in their mutual relationship.

Among the contributing authors, three have been co-chairs of the international bilateral dialogue of which they write, and five have served on multiple phases of the dialogue. Nine have participated also in other international and/or national bilaterals. Ten (including the presenters of Faith and Order in Part I) have served in both bilateral dialogue and Faith and Order (see the list of contributors at the end of the book). At the conference at which these essays were first given, the authors were asked to make their presentation in a framework of thirty minutes. In most cases, their presentations have been revised and sometimes amplified for this book. In important ways, but not in the order in which the essays are presented, the book follows some of the pattern of the St. Paul conference. The generous resources provided for the conference enabled it to include four presentations in Part I, and eleven bilateral dialogues in Part II, including, in the case of three bilaterals, two presentations, one from each side. The book follows this pattern as well.

New international dialogues involving the Catholic Church have begun in each decade since Vatican II, and those that began earlier have gone into multiple phases. Two began in 1967. The dialogue with the Lutheran World Federation is presented by Jared Wicks, SJ, who participated in two phases of the dialogue, and also by William Rusch, who took part in the USA Lutheran–Roman Catholic dialogue. The Methodist-Roman Catholic dialogue is described by Geoffrey Wainwright, who has been its co-chair from 1986 until now, and by Lorelei Fuchs, SA, a member of that joint commission since 2005. Two began in 1970: the Anglican–Roman Catholic international dialogue, discussed by Donna Geernaert, SC, a participant in the International Anglican–Roman Catholic Commission on Unity and Mission, and also the Reformed–Roman Catholic dialogue, presented by John Radano, co-secretary of the second and third phases of that dialogue. The Pentecostal–Roman Catholic dialogue began in 1972. Cecil M. Robeck, co-chair since 1992, and Ralph Del Colle, a member of its most recent fifth phase, analyze its achievements. Evangelical–Roman Catholic dialogue began, first with Evangelical leaders in 1977, and then in 1993 co-sponsored by the World Evangelical Alliance. Jeffrey Gros, FSC, who participated in the latter phase, shows results of both. Dialogue between the Roman Catholic Church and the Christian Church (Disciples of Christ) also began in 1977; Margaret O'Gara, a member from 1983 until now, presents its achievements. In 1980, an international dialogue between the Roman Catholic Church and the Orthodox Church began, and it is analyzed here by Ronald Roberson, CSP, a member of the USA Orthodox–Roman Catholic dialogue. Baptist-Roman Catholic dialogue started in 1984, and its results are presented by Susan Wood, SCL, a member of the recently concluded second phase of dialogue. In 1998, the Mennonite-Roman Catholic dialogue began, and Helmut Harder, a co-chair of the dialogue, assesses its achievements. In 2003 the first international dialogue began between the Roman Catholic Church and the family of six Oriental Orthodox churches; it is presented by Ronald Roberson, CSP, a participant in that dialogue.[1]

Towards Continuing Dialogue

The ecumenical dialogues have been effective instruments in fostering common understanding among Christians. We can expect the churches to continue to engage in dialogue and to address issues that, despite the dialogue that has already taken place, continue to persist as obstacles to the unity for which Christ prayed (John 17:21).

At the conference in which these papers were first presented, there was some time for discussion of each of them, but no opportunity to discuss all of them together, to see what larger picture of ecumenical insights might be drawn out of this. It is hoped that the publication, now, of these essays may provoke this discussion.

---

1. The Catholic Church has also participated in other bilaterals not given separate chapters here. These include, since 1989, dialogues, more on a regional basis, with two Malankara Orthodox churches of India, which continue today, and another, earlier one with the Coptic Orthodox Church; these three churches now participate in the dialogue with the families of Oriental Orthodox churches. There has also been an international dialogue with the Assyrian Church of the East, which is presented briefly in the presentation of the Oriental Orthodox–Roman Catholic dialogue. A recent dialogue with the Union of Utrecht Old Catholic Churches has now finished a report, but it is not yet published. During the last decade there have also been informal international conversations between the Catholic Church and the Seventh Day Adventists, with the Salvation Army, and with nondenominational Christians (which have not published reports).

I Achievements of International Multilateral Dialogue

We already have an inner unity in that we are bound together by devotion to a common Lord . . . the deep and invisible bond joining the faithful, but that is inadequate. . . . The vision that God has given us is of the manifestation in visible form of inner unity.

Bishop Charles H. Brent, *A Pilgrimage Toward Unity: Report of the Preliminary Meeting to Plan a World Conference on Faith and Order*, 1920

1 Achievements and Limits of the World Council of Churches

S. Wesley Ariarajah

Edinburgh 1910 and the Ecumenical Movement

It is appropriate that we have this assessment of the ecumenical movement, and of the achievements and limits of the World Council of Churches (WCC) within it, as we celebrate the centennial of the first World Missionary Conference of 1910 in Edinburgh, Scotland. Although Edinburgh was inspired by John R. Mott's vision of evangelization of the world in that generation, there are clear indications that the Edinburgh Conference inspired the birth of both the Faith and Order and the Life and Work movements. These two movements, alongside the International Missionary Council, constitute the core of the WCC. Charles H. Brent, the pioneer of the Faith and Order movement, was at the Edinburgh Conference. He was so impressed with the ecumenical possibility that the Edinburgh Conference demonstrated in the area of mission that on his return from Edinburgh in 1910 he spoke at the General Convention of the Episcopal Church, USA, of the need for church unity and of his own conviction that "a world conference on Faith and Order should be convened." In response to his call the Convention resolved "that a joint commission be appointed to bring about a conference for the consideration of questions touching Faith and Order." Several other churches were also encouraged to pass similar resolutions, and the work of the newly appointed commission would result in the first World Conference on Faith and Order in Lausanne in 1927.[1]

---

1. Günther Gassmann, "Faith and Order," *DEM2*, pp. 461-63. Also see Ans J. Van Der Bent, "Brent, Charles Henry," *DEM2*, p. 127.

J. H. Oldham, another pioneer of the ecumenical movement, was also at Edinburgh and served as the Executive Secretary of the Conference. At the end of the Conference he became the secretary of the Continuation Committee, and was instrumental in the creation of the International Missionary Council (IMC), which he led as its secretary. Even though the roots of the Life and Work movement lie in the early peace movements following the First World War and in the passion for unity, peace, and justice on the part of Archbishop Nathan Söderblom of the Lutheran Church of Sweden, it is not difficult to trace the ecumenical impact of Edinburgh on this movement as well. Söderblom's own early ecumenical involvement can be traced to his friendship with John R. Mott and his participation in the World Student Christian Federation (WSCF) already in the early 1900s. Oldham, the Executive Secretary at Edinburgh, got deeply involved in the Life and Work movement as well, and in 1934 became the Chairman of the research committee for the Universal Christian Council on Life and Work.[2]

The roots of the formation of the WCC itself lie in the unprecedented and visionary encyclical "Unto the churches of Christ everywhere" issued by the patriarchate of Constantinople in 1920, calling for the establishment of a "league of churches" *(Koinōnia tōn Ekklēsiōn)* in the manner of the League of Nations *(Koinōnia tōn Ethnōn)* to confront the challenges facing the churches following the war. Metropolitan Germanos, who was the prime influence in the issuing of the encyclical, was also closely associated with John R. Mott through the WSCF.

It is significant that quite independent of the encyclical, and before becoming aware of it, both Oldham and Söderblom were also feeling the need for some kind of "ecumenical council of churches" so that the Mission, Faith and Order, and Life and Work movements would have some rootedness in the life of the churches. All these sentiments would converge in the eventual decision to work towards establishing the World Council of Churches.

I have engaged in these reflections for a special reason. It is commonly assumed that the designation of Edinburgh 1910 as the "beginning of the modern ecumenical movement" has to do with the success Mott had in bringing a wide ecumenical constituency of some 1200 persons to reflect on and strategize for his vision of evangelization of the world in that generation. In fact, there are deeper reasons; all the

2. Kathleen Bliss, "Oldham, Joseph Houldsworth," *DEM2*, p. 846.

three major movements that would eventually become part of the WCC drew their inspiration and motivation from Edinburgh, making it a significant landmark in the history of the ecumenical movement.

I should now turn to the topic of examining the achievements and limits of the WCC as one of the instruments of the ecumenical movement.

Issues Related to Its Nature and Constituency

Even though only 147 churches, mainly from the Western Hemisphere, constituted the WCC at its founding assembly in Amsterdam in 1948, today the WCC includes over 350 member and associate-member churches from within the Orthodox, Protestant, and Pentecostal traditions from well over one hundred countries. It had incorporated into its programmatic life all the major global streams of the ecumenical movement: Faith and Order, Life and Work, International Missionary Council, World Council for Christian Education, and the Commission of the Churches on International Affairs (founded in 1946). It had also succeeded in gaining the full participation of the Roman Catholic Church in the Faith and Order and the Mission aspects of its work, and established a Joint Working Group with the Vatican to further, monitor, foster, and promote WCC-RCC relationships. It is in this sense that the WCC is a "privileged instrument" of the ecumenical movement. No other ecumenical expression of the church is as comprehensive in its constituency, the breadth of the issues addressed, and the network of relationships it fosters across ecclesial traditions, plurality of cultures, political ideologies, and nationalities. This is no mean achievement, and something that could never have become a reality without the faith and faithfulness, the courage and conviction, and the hope and vision that characterized the early pioneers of the modern ecumenical movement.

Yet, the WCC has some serious limitations based on the way it constituted itself. It could have been conceived as a comprehensive global ecumenical movement of movements, like Faith and Order and Life and Work; it could have become the global ecumenical family of the confessional families of churches; it could have been constituted into a World Council of the National Councils of Churches around the world. However, for theological reasons, the decision was made that it should be a council of churches, with the local/national expressions of the church universal as the constituency for its membership. In order to make it possible for the maximum number of churches to join its membership, the Council was defined simply as a "fellowship" of churches, with a minimal "basis" that defined its membership as "churches that confess Jesus Christ as God and Savior according to scriptures, and therefore seek to fulfill together their common calling, to the glory of the one God, Father, Son and Holy Spirit." Yet, despite sustained efforts from both sides, the Roman Catholic Church, which constitutes a major part of the Christian constituency of the world, chose not to become a member. Further, a number of churches in the evangelical tradition also chose to remain outside the fellowship.

With more than half of the Christian constituency outside its immediate fellowship, the WCC's claim to be the "World" Council of Churches is more notional than real, and can only be justified by the reality that it has always been and continues to be an open fellowship into which those outside could come in, if and when they decide to do so.

The second limitation has to do with the question of its "nature" and its "teaching authority." From the beginning, the Council was seen as an instrument of the ecumenical movement that serves the churches in their search for unity. The Amsterdam assembly adopted a resolution on "the authority of the Council" stating that the "Council is far from desiring to usurp any of the functions which already belong to its constituent churches, or to control them, or to legislate for them, and indeed is prevented by its constitution from doing so." It went further to say that "the Council disavows any thought of becoming a single unified church structure independent of the churches which have joined in constituting the Council."

While the statement was necessary and is in the right spirit, it still raised questions about the nature of the Council as a fellowship of churches. What is a "Council of Churches," and what is its ecclesial character? And since it does speak and act as a body, what authority do its actions and statements have for its member churches and the world?

These questions prompted the need for a more elaborate statement, referred to as the Toronto Statement, on "the Church, the Churches, and the World Council of Churches" that was received by the WCC Central Committee gathered in Toronto in 1950. Here too the Council disavowed any intention to become a "superchurch" and the tradition was established that the churches together in Council will have the authority to speak and act, but that its actions and what it says do not commit or bind the churches, and that the teachings of the Council will stand or fall based on the wisdom they carry in themselves and the power they carry to convince the churches.[3]

Given the diverse and complex understandings of the church and its teaching authority within the member churches, this was perhaps the only option that was open to enable the churches to stay within the fellowship. This, however, placed enormous limits on the WCC both in promoting the unity of the churches and in speaking on matters of faith. Thus, although the WCC over its sixty plus years has made enormous contributions in drawing the churches closer together in unity, in enabling common reflection, witness, and service, and in facilitating their capacity to speak together, it remains a body that does not possess the capacity to "implement" its mission. It has to leave the churches to draw the consequences of their life together as Council for their self-understanding and their relationship to other churches. The failure of the churches to do so is often seen as the failure of the WCC.

In the 1970s and 80s attempts were made to give some ecclesial significance to the WCC by opening up discussions on Conciliar Fellowship and to see the life of the churches together in the WCC as some kind of Pre-Conciliar life. But the nervousness on the part of some of the churches resulted in those discussions running into dry ground.

Issues Related to Its Vision of Unity

As the result of having the three primary movements of Faith and Order, Life and Work, and the IMC within its embrace, the WCC has made enormous contributions in the areas of unity, mission, and social responsibility. I am sure that in the session that follows, Mary Tanner would recount for us the great strides made within Faith and Order on the nature of the unity we seek, the convergences and consensuses that have been reached, and most importantly how the work of the WCC through this Commission has so radically changed the ecumenical scene at the local, national, and regional levels.

Following the tradition of IMC, the WCC Commission on World

---

3. See "The Church, the Churches and the World Council of Churches — WCC Central Committee, Toronto, 1950," *Anthology*, p. 463.

Mission and Evangelism has facilitated major paradigm shifts in mission thinking through its periodic World Mission Conferences and the numerous studies it has facilitated on mission and evangelism and issues related to them. Faced with the reality of resurgent religions and persistent plurality in the postcolonial era, the WCC instituted a Sub-Unit for Dialogue with People of Living Faiths and Ideologies. The sustained work of this program, also in collaboration with the Pontifical Council for Interreligious Dialogue, has again made enormous and measurable changes in the way Christians and churches relate to peoples of other religious traditions.

Perhaps the best known, because of the public face it carries, is the way the Life and Work movement flourished within the WCC in the form of programs that captured the imagination of people in all parts of the world. WCC's programs in relation to Apartheid in South Africa, racism in general, human rights, religious freedom, economic justice, poverty, indigenous peoples, sustainable development, science and technology, Christian education, theological education, environment, migration, AIDS, disability, spirituality, renewal, laity, youth, etc., animated theological reflections, debates, and disagreements and touched peoples in all parts of the world. The consultations, workshops, conferences, convocations, and assemblies that the WCC facilitated among its member churches number in the thousands and have touched hundreds of thousands of people over the last sixty years. The WCC, as the largest NGO attached to the organs of the United Nations, is active in the areas of peacemaking, disarmament, conflict resolution, advocacy for human rights, etc., and is one of the major voices of the churches on international affairs. It has also mediated interchurch aid to meet emergencies and for development work in poorer countries in billions of dollars over these decades. I am resisting here the temptation to list some of the highlights because of time constraints, and also because you are aware of this aspect of its work. The achievement of the WCC in this respect is very impressive indeed.

From the very beginning, already at its first assembly in Amsterdam, the WCC decided to set up desks that would later become programmatic emphases on issues related to women in church and society and on the place and role of youth in the church. The Council also took courageous decisions on the levels of participation of women and youth in its own structures, including its staff levels at its headquarters in Geneva, in its decision-making committees, commissions, conferences, and assemblies. It instituted a four-year study process on the "Community of Women and Men in the Church" within the Faith and Order Secretariat to take up such subjects as scripture, tradition, language, and leadership as they relate to women in the traditions of the church and a special exploration of the question of Ordination of Women. These culminated in a major conference in Sheffield, U.K., in 1981. It also devoted a Decade for Churches in Solidarity with Women.

Yet, looking back at this impressive history one also sees a serious limitation that continues to plague the Council to this day. The early pioneers of the ecumenical movement were troubled by the reality of Faith and Order, Life and Work, and the missionary movement developing as separate movements independent of each other. The missionary movement was sowing the seeds of the European divisions of the church all over the world by planting denominational churches in the mission fields. Already in 1910 at Edinburgh, the two Chinese delegates at the Conference challenged the missionary movement for disregarding the Chinese culture and for transplanting denominations into China. The disquiet over this reality led the Chinese churches to launch the Three-Self Movement of Self-Governance, Self-Support, and Self-Propagation.[4]

Again, the work of the Faith and Order movement tended to look at divisions of the church on doctrinal matters in isolation from social and ethical church-dividing issues, and the role of the churches in human affairs. The Life and Work movement, for its part, concentrated on social, political, and ethical issues without the recognition of the deep divisions in the church on doctrinal questions. The primary purpose of bringing the three movements together was to integrate the three movements for mission, unity, and social concerns so that they would be seen as part of the one obedience to Jesus' prayer that "they may all be one so that the world may believe."[5]

The most serious limitation of the WCC is that it was unable to integrate these three movements in any meaningful way. Each of these

4. For an account of the speeches made by the Chinese delegation at Edinburgh 1910, see Brian Stanley, *The World Missionary Conference, Edinburgh 1910* (Grand Rapids/ Cambridge: Eerdmans, 2009), pp. 102-11.

5. Interesting discussion on the need and possibility of the three movements coming together to form the WCC is recounted by W. A. Visser 't Hooft in his memoirs. See the chapter "Preparing for a World Council of Churches," in W. A. Visser 't Hooft, *Memoirs* (Geneva: WCC Publications, 1973), pp. 76-83.

movements made some gestures from time to time that indicated their awareness of this issue and the presence of the others. The Faith and Order Commission, for instance, instituted studies such as "Unity of the Church and the Renewal of Humankind," "Giving an Account of the Hope That Is in Us," "Confessing the Faith around the World," etc., which were intended to broaden the base of Faith and Order culturally and on issues. However, they did not sufficiently serve the purpose of bringing some of the Life and Work agenda into the concern for church unity. In the early periods some of the same leaders participated in all three movements in their attempt to shepherd them into the same fold.

As someone who served on the staff of the WCC for sixteen years and worked with three of the six former General Secretaries, I have watched several attempts to restructure the programs of the WCC to bring about this desired integration, but none of them succeeded. The constituencies of the three movements, as also their visible representation in the structure of the Council as separated entities, could not be changed — a reality present to this day. This is a limitation that the Council has had to live with for the past six decades. Happily, its patience and flexibility have enabled the three emphases, if not united, to at least cohabit under the WCC umbrella without too much dissension.

Issues Related to Diversity

One of the significant achievements of the WCC has been its capacity to relate to, hold on to, and to support both the institutional churches and a great variety of people's movements. Some would say that over the decades the WCC has lost its own "movement character" and has become overly institutionalized. Others hold that it has been "clericalized" and has ceased to be the lay movement that it was in its pioneering days. Still others hold that the WCC, by catering primarily to the movements in some of the past decades and by placing its primary emphases on the Life and Work agenda, has lost its vocation and calling to enable the churches towards visible unity. It depends on whom one talks to!

A dispassionate examination of WCC's record would show that on the whole it has managed to not abandon the church and its concern for unity and to not neglect the demands of the movements. But it has had serious limitations in enabling a meaningful dialogue between its two constituencies. On the one hand, the churches of the Orthodox and the mainline Protestant denominations in the West kept the pressure on the Faith and Order agenda. On the other hand, as member churches from the "third world" increased, the agenda of the movements and Life and Work concerns pressed upon the WCC, and it had to make adequate responses. Again one of the limitations of the Council had been its inability to sufficiently negotiate these pressures in ways that bring out the vision of the One Ecumenical Movement in its legitimate diversity.

Again, one of the achievements of the WCC has been its success in enabling the full participation of constituencies that were neglected in the earlier periods of the ecumenical movement. As mentioned earlier, the WCC made enormous strides in enabling the participation of women and youth in the ecumenical movement, in spite of the fact that the ecumenical youth movement, represented by the World Student Christian Federation, chose not to become part of the WCC when it was founded. It also has an impressive record in bringing into the movement peoples with disabilities and socially marginalized groups in different parts of the world.

While this was remarkable and most welcome, it also came with the price of losing the participation of part of the academy in the varied programs of the WCC. The loss of a substantial part of the academy, and with it the essential link to the theological schools and seminaries, has seriously limited not only the participation of a constituency that played a key role within the movement but also the dissemination of the WCC's vision, ideas, work, and goals to future pastors and church leaders. Here WCC was faced with the serious limitation of its human and material resources, and had to make difficult choices on the nature of the constituencies that would participate in its ministry, but these choices have had their impact on its life and the life of the churches.

Another main achievement of the WCC has been its commitment to the Orthodox family of churches, some of which were among the founding churches of the Council. As mentioned earlier, the original vision of the "league of churches" had come out of the Ecumenical Patriarchate, and from the third assembly in New Delhi in 1961, all the Orthodox churches were part of the WCC. During the Cold War years, the WCC paid an enormous price in order to maintain contact and solidarity with the churches behind the Iron Curtain; the political right, especially in the United States, consistently engaged in propaganda that the WCC was "Communist," and it was opposed to the contact WCC was having with the Orthodox churches within the Soviet Union that had made accommodations with the Communist regime for their survival.

After the fall of the Berlin Wall, however, inter-Orthodox and WCC-Orthodox relations have undergone a difficult period, including the pain of some churches withdrawing or threatening to withdraw from the Council. The possibility of more active participation of the Orthodox churches of Eastern Europe has exposed another limitation of the WCC, namely, its predominantly Western Protestant ethos. The Council, while making all the room needed for participation of very diverse churches from all parts of the world, had never been able to negotiate a cultural ethos in which the diverse communities could equally be "at home." While this may be too much to expect of the WCC, one needs to recognize this as a serious limitation that threatens to injure the fellowship in the long run. In recent years it has instituted a Special Commission to study the Council's decision-making processes, its worship life, its policies on participation, etc. to meet some of the Orthodox reservations, but the challenge of full and meaningful participation of the Orthodox churches in the Council in their new context remains a serious issue to be resolved.

A Victim of Its Own Success?

Some are of the opinion that the WCC in some ways is a victim of its own success. The hard work done over many decades on the unity of the church has resulted in member churches launching their own Faith and Order initiatives, often with little reference to the WCC. There came, for instance, a moment in the search for unity when churches that had come closer together through the multilateral conversations of the WCC's Faith and Order Commission began to give greater priority to bilateral conversations that deal with issues that affected their mutual relationships. Following the Second Vatican Council, the Roman Catholic Church began its own bilateral conversations with WCC member churches that run parallel to the WCC's Faith and Order agenda. While these conversations have yielded much good fruit, we have yet to find effective ways of bringing the benefits of these conversations to the wider search within the multilateral conversation. The attempt to hold Forums on bilateral conversation has had only a limited success.

Similarly, as someone who struggled to promote the Dialogue program of the WCC in the 70s and 80s in the context of stiff opposition from many churches, I am aware that today the dialogue concern has been embraced by the churches to the point of making a program at the WCC somewhat irrelevant, unless it is able to reframe the issue in ways that speak to the new challenges of the day. Much of the humanitarian work that the churches undertook in the postwar context has been taken over by thousands of NGOs and specialized agencies. In the context of the technological revolutions in travel, information, communication, and the fall of the Berlin Wall, the WCC has also ceased to be the primary instrument that created networks of relationships and communication between the churches. The churches have changed, the world has changed, and the ecumenical imperatives have changed.

The WCC has, therefore, been involved with others in the search for a wider ecumenical Forum that would include the WCC member churches, the Roman Catholic Church, and the Evangelical, Pentecostal, and Charismatic churches so that a truly global body could be created to represent the Christian constituency of the world. How far such a diverse group of ecclesial expressions will be able to grow together, develop an agenda for common thinking and action, and agree on ways of addressing the world remains to be seen. While some see hope in this new development, others are bewildered by the myriad of issues that have to be resolved in order for it to become an effective instrument of unity and ecumenism.

The WCC has also had a few rounds of study and discussion to restate its vision and purpose and to identify what the WCC needs to do today that others cannot do, so that it can restructure its program life to meet those priorities. These too appear to have not resolved some of the fundamental problems facing the WCC. Among them is also the financial question. As churches begin to function independently, define their own priorities, and relate to one another without the mediation of the WCC, and as more and more NGOs take on the tasks earlier done by the WCC, the financial support that WCC could depend on in the past has been decreasing, with serious impact on its programmatic life. As the influence of the churches on their societies and on their governments continues to decline there is also a corresponding decline of the influence of the voice of the WCC in international affairs. Some have begun to speak of an "ecumenical winter."

Today the WCC has reached a point at which its post-world war mandate, which it is unable to shake away, has itself become a serious limitation. Sometime back I was asked to write an article on ecumenism for a volume to honor the former General Secretary of the WCC, Dr. Konrad Raiser. The WCC as an instrument of the ecumenical movement cannot be reformed or revitalized, I wrote, "It needs to be re-invented." I was careful not to say that it has done its job and it can now fold up. The challenges the world and the churches are facing today are no less complex, less urgent, or less demanding than those that faced the early pioneers of the ecumenical movement. Addressing these challenges again calls for all the faith and faithfulness, conviction and courage, and the vision and hope that we can muster. It has been said, that if the WCC should cease to exist, something like it would have to be invented. We need, however, to reinvent the WCC as a *new instrument* so that it can help us *today,* in a new world with new challenges, problems, and possibilities, to "fulfill together our common calling" to the glory of the one God — who creates, redeems, and sanctifies all life.

2 The World Council of Churches: An Orthodox Perspective

Peter C. Bouteneff

Addressing the relationship between the Orthodox and the World Council of Churches, I could begin by taking note of a fundamental and pivotal similarity between it and the Roman Catholic–WCC relationship: both the Orthodox Church and the Roman Catholic Church effectively see their own churches as the *Una Sancta*, the "One Holy Catholic and Apostolic Church" of the creeds, from which other Christian bodies have separated. We both struggle with ways to define the boundaries of the church: these borders are porous, the church "subsists" here but a bit less over there, and we know where the church is but not where it isn't. We are familiar with these formulations, which are attempting to articulate the same complex conviction: "The Church is us, but we're not 100 percent sure about the rest of you." And that means that, while we take unity very seriously, and recognize deep bonds of communion, we are not comfortable with the idea, the structure, or even the *name* of the World Council of Churches.

Sometimes I muse that, if we Orthodox had it all to do over again, and if we were a more organized, coherent body, we would approach the WCC as the Roman Catholics have: on our terms, as deeply committed observers, relying on our own mechanisms for ecumenical work. This would spare us the perennially awkward situation of an involvement that is alternately engaged and estranged (as I will be describing it below), while at the same time removing a large and cumbersome wrench from the workings of the WCC. But then again, had we approached the WCC in this way we would have missed a very great deal. And who is to say that "smoother workings" are the ideal? We are

Christians who know that the way forward is the way of the cross, which in turn entails countless crosses along the way, whose victories are not always immediately apparent.

But enough speculative generalizations. The main focus of this essay will be the work of the Special Commission on Orthodox Participation in the WCC.[1] Orthodox-WCC involvement has a rich history, and I could just as easily be highlighting for example the crucial work of the Faith and Order Commission. But the Special Commission is my chosen focus because it is the most recent, and the most significant and far-reaching process in the history of Orthodox-WCC relations. Moreover, the process and its aftermath are emblematic of these relations for the past century, both in their achievements and their limitations.[2] The Special Commission has yielded some gains that could only be called amazing, yet it has been in many ways both difficult and disappointing. As such, it can be seen as a cross-section of the factors that have accompanied us since the very outset. On my way to speaking of this Commission, I offer a few words to set out the historical context of Orthodox involvement with the WCC.

Prehistory

With hindsight, it may have been possible to predict from very early on that at some stage down the line, the Orthodox-WCC relationship was going to need some concerted and sustained attention. Significantly, the Orthodox Church was a presence in the most important formative stages of the modern ecumenical movement. A 1920 encyclical of the Ecumenical Patriarchate, "To the Churches of Christ Everywhere,"[3] took its place among other high-level church statements that urged specific steps towards Christian rapprochement, including the forma-

---

1. The work of the Special Commission is well documented on the WCC website. See http://www.oikoumene.org/en/resources/documents/wcc-programmes/ecumenical -movement-in-the-21st-century/member-churches/special-commission-on-participation -of-orthodox-churches.html.

2. See also my essays "The Report of the Special Commission on Orthodox Participation in the WCC: An Introduction," *The Ecumenical Review* 55 (2003): 49-55, and "A Broader and Deeper Fellowship? Orthodox Participation in the WCC and Its Implications for the Roman Catholic Church," *One in Christ* 38, no. i (2003): 3-15.

3. See *Anthology*, pp. 11-14.

tion of a "league of churches" along the pattern of the League of Nations. An important Orthodox delegation was present at the inaugural conference on Faith and Order at Lausanne in 1927, but this group tellingly felt compelled to begin what would become a long tradition of separate Orthodox statements issued at ecumenical gatherings. The Orthodox statement at Lausanne[4] established a pattern that was to be repeated in its main contours for subsequent decades: an engagement of hope, love, and enthusiasm, together with disappointment that the underlying organizational and de facto theological principles of the gathering run counter to Orthodox self-understanding.

The Ecumenical Patriarchate, with other local Orthodox churches, was among the founding members of the World Council of Churches in 1948. Within two years, the newly formed WCC produced an important and far-reaching policy statement aimed at clarifying ecclesiological presuppositions. The so-called "Toronto Statement,"[5] which counted among its chief drafters the great Orthodox theologian Georges Florovsky, was of great importance especially bearing in mind Orthodox self-identification with The Church, which, as mentioned above, closely follows Roman Catholic ecclesiology. Toronto makes it clear that, while the WCC does indeed represent the coming together of church bodies into a fellowship, it is not to be understood as, itself, a Church or a Superchurch — even if some of its members may indeed see it that way. It states explicitly that some of the members will not even consider other members to be "churches" in the full sense of that word.

The "Toronto Statement" technically ought to have quelled Orthodox ecclesiological misgivings. Yet for a great many people "on the ground" in our churches, the "optics" of the situation, despite all the policy statements that rule out such a perception, smack too much of a superchurch model to which Orthodox could never subscribe. An anti-ecumenical, and specifically anti-WCC spirit, sometimes more and sometimes less informed, runs hot within the Orthodox Church, not only within isolated pockets but at nearly every level of its organization.

4. See Gennadios Limouris, ed., *Orthodox Visions of Ecumenism* (Geneva: WCC Publications, 1994), pp. 12-14.

5. See *Anthology*, pp. 463-68.

Peter C. Bouteneff

The Genesis and Composition of the Special Commission

A pan-Orthodox meeting in Thessaloniki in May 1998[6] sounded an alarm in the ecumenical world: it showed that WCC-Orthodox relations, which (as we have seen above) had been plagued by a kind of chronic malaise, had reached a critical point. When the WCC decided to launch a Special Commission to explore the issues and make proposals, the manner of its organization and configuration was important — and telling. The intention was that 50 percent of the delegates would be Orthodox, so that the playing field would be level. This balance was important: owing to the realities of ecclesiastical organization, the Orthodox churches numbered only around twenty-five of the 330 WCC member churches at the time, despite constituting nearly half of its constituent demographic. A huge body of churches (namely the Orthodox) was consigned to a small minority — something that would not suit a commission charged with exploring the Orthodox-WCC relationship.

So the Commission had two "sides": one was "the Orthodox," consisting of Eastern and Oriental Orthodox delegates, and the other side — well, it was difficult to know what to call it: "non-Orthodox" sounded rather infelicitous and negative; "Protestant" wasn't amenable to the Anglicans and other bodies not self-identifying as Protestants. But effectively the commission had two sides: Orthodox and Protestant/Anglican.[7]

The next telling feature was the way the delegates were selected. The Orthodox delegates were all appointed by the synods of the Orthodox churches, while the "Protestant" delegates were selected by the WCC Central Committee. This aspect testified to a powerful ecclesiological culture for the Orthodox that is not consistently shared by the broadly diverse other member bodies of the WCC.

A third feature on this score was the composition of each side.

6. The "Thessaloniki Statement" is available on the WCC website at http://www
.oikoumene.org/en/resources/documents/wcc-programmes/ecumenical-movement-in
-the-21st-century/member-churches/special-commission-on-participation-of-orthodox
-churches/first-plenary-meeting-documents-december-1999/thessaloniki-statement
.html.

7. It was periodically tempting to call the two sides "Orthodox" and "WCC," nomenclature that was rejected because the Orthodox are of course *part* of the WCC. Yet the temptation was indicative. By contrast, for example, one rarely thinks of "Methodist-WCC relations."

Partly owing to the appointment process, the Orthodox side was profoundly, one might say unsettlingly, uniform. Aside from one female delegate it was all male and highly clerical, with a preponderance of bishops. (Viewed positively, this very clericalism indicated the seriousness with which Orthodox churches took the process — sending a bishop being a sign of the highest respect.)

Another factor that will surely resonate with many of you who have attempted to secure a qualified and enthusiastic Orthodox representation in your respective ecumenical endeavors: it was difficult to identify, mobilize, and motivate the Orthodox side. At many points, the non-Orthodox (as well as many of us Orthodox staff) were deeply frustrated that, in the face of an enormous show of graciousness and goodwill on the side of the WCC, it was very difficult, in the initial run, to stir Orthodox interest in the process. It almost seemed that we Orthodox were happier complaining than finding a constructive solution. Or perhaps there were few that had hopes for far-reaching change.

Ecumenical Breakthrough: Common Solutions

As relationships came to be established — rather quickly, I might add — the issues were not difficult to identify. These could be broadly categorized using a familiar rubric: *faith*, and *order*.

At the level of *faith*, there were issues stemming from the basic ecclesiological presuppositions of WCC member churches. The Orthodox constitute a communion of churches that understand themselves as *the Church*, thus distinguishing itself from the majority of WCC members who see themselves in some way as a *part* of the church. These "faith" issues extend also into the matter of common prayer or worship, something that lies at the heart of the ecumenical experience, and is held dear by many participants in ecumenical gatherings.

At the level of *order*, the Special Commission sought to redress the problem of balance alluded to above: the perpetual "minority status" of the Orthodox churches endemic to the WCC's principles of membership. This in turn spelled itself out in how the WCC accepted and categorized new member churches, and more significantly, in the ways that the Council deliberated and took decisions, most especially on social and ethical issues.

Now, on to the solutions. I will focus for now on the second constellation, the "order" ones, because these were the most dramatic in every way. Here, very broadly, is what happened:

Increasingly, both "sides" came to realize that almost none of the concerns put forward by the Orthodox were unique to the Orthodox. Many churches and church families felt similarly marginalized by the WCC's structure and decision-making ethos. Many felt uncomfortably implicated in decisions — and more so in public statements — issued on behalf of the whole Council. To add to this, both sides came to see the work of the Special Commission as a logical extension of a landscape shift that had been established through the WCC's Common Understanding and Vision (or "CUV") process not long before the Commission began its work. That shift was expressed in a constitutional change that identified the member churches, and not the council, as the main actors in the life and work of the WCC. The WCC, therefore, came increasingly to be seen as an instrument rather than an actor. The WCC should not "do" anything, nor should it "think" anything, much less should it "pontificate" about anything. It is the churches that do, think, and speak, through the WCC.

By the grace of God — and I do not use this phrase lightly — all the planets aligned and effected a solution that was so clear that it seemed inevitable. The Council (or rather, "the churches *through* the Council") would take no more decisions by vote. Instead, the churches would deliberate and decide by *consensus.* In this way the problem of minority-majority was largely defused. With the promise that no voice would be stifled, churches could deliberate and discuss even the most controversial issues without the threat of being implicated in statements that they could not stand behind. And, significantly, here was a solution that went beyond a "fix-it" for only the Orthodox concerns. Still more importantly, it was a solution with theological, ecclesiological grounding. After all, what better befits a gathering of *churches* — politicking and voting, or consensual deliberation? The latter is founded on the accounts we read in the book of Acts and the Pauline epistles, wherein the early Christian community was able to say "It seemed good to the Holy Spirit and to us . . ." (Acts 15:28).[8]

---

8. See Eden Grace, "Guided by the Mind of Christ — Yearning for a New Spirituality of Church Governance," *Ecumenical Trends* 32, no. 4 (April 2003): 1-7, as well as the series of short essays at http://www.oikoumene.org/en/news/news-management/eng/a/browse/23/article/1634/the-special-commission-on.html.

This solution struck many people as ideal. A comment I recall from the Central Committee floor, by one of the WCC's elder statesmen, summarized the reaction of many: "You've taken lemons, and you've made lemonade!" But in the complex ecumenical landscape, nothing is either simple or perfect. While the solution of consensus remains hugely significant and positive, there have been significant slowdowns and disappointments.

Some frustrations with the trajectory of the Special Commission were perhaps easy to foresee: many of the Protestant partners were deeply suspicious of the consensus idea, fearing that it would dull the prophetic edge of the WCC. They feared that the council would no longer be able to pronounce anything more than bland platitudes that represent the lowest common denominator.

What may have been more difficult to foresee was the disappointment on the part of many of the Orthodox, because the *communal* nature of the commission's flagship solutions entailed giving up on the "sole victim" narrative as well as "sole beneficiary" status. In other words, many Orthodox were finding it difficult to share with others their identity as the WCC's disenfranchised body. Moreover, many Orthodox who had expected that the Special Commission would yield a more identifiably "Orthodox" WCC were disappointed that the resulting culture shift could scarcely be identified with Orthodoxy *per se.*

Thus, the crucial problem for nearly all of the Commissioners was that their collective work was difficult to "sell" to some of their respective constituencies. This situation has compounded the immense difficulties experienced within the council in the full implementation of a consensus method, and more significantly, a genuine consensus *ethos.* People either did not understand it or were not sufficiently committed to it.

Ecumenical Breakdown?

As the years have progressed since the implementation of the Special Commission's recommendations, the journey has come to emblematize not only Orthodox-WCC relations, but the achievements and limits of the WCC as a whole. Not only have there been ongoing fits and starts in the implementation of consensus ethos, but more generally speaking, it feels as if within about a year of its acceptance, the Special

Commission's report began to fade into oblivion, becoming just another one of the processes of "reimagining the ecumenical movement," the myriad reconfigurations of staff and committees, the Decades on Women, and on Violence, and so on. The feeling among many seemed to be, "The Orthodox have gotten their bit, now let's move on."

The lack of full-scale reception is evident. Despite the CUV and the Special Commission, both of which stood behind the constitutional change that identifies all actions and opinions with *the churches* and not the Council, WCC statements continue to say that "the WCC promotes" or "supports," or "condemns," even though the WCC was supposed to have stopped being a personal subject, an "I," altogether. One similarly disenfranchised former WCC president commiserated with me on this issue, saying, "The leopard cannot change its spots."

The Special Commission's recommendations on common prayer in ecumenical settings were probably based on an overly subtle and abstract set of principles, principles that needn't detain us here. But in the end, they continue to baffle those who organize and experience the prayer life of ecumenical meetings, and either go unheeded or misunderstood.

This may be a somewhat cynical take on the matter, but I doubt that it is entirely inaccurate. The ecumenical movement does, perhaps by necessity, involve itself in processes that, by their sheer number, are difficult to sustain in a lasting way. Furthermore, the ecumenical movement is most seriously hindered by the fact that, by virtue of being a movement of *people* and of their *relationships* in specific meetings, it has its most significant effect upon the people who are actually involved in the processes. I point here to the perennial problem of *reception*.

The final report of the Special Commission is the result of some of the most fascinating and inspiring meetings I can recall, and am ever likely to attend in my life. The report represents some highly nuanced thinking. Many of us who were involved in the process cherish their memories of the project, and came away from it changed men and women — I count myself among their number. And yet it seems to me that, like much that we do in the ecumenical movement, the bulk of its work remains within the hearts of its participants, rather than finding a broad and lasting reception. Many of us who are ecumenically engaged find it as difficult as ever to carry this work to our church constituencies in such a way that they find it compelling or convincing.

Conclusions

The Special Commission exemplified many features of the ecumenical journey. It showed how marvelously creative and unpredictable the movement can be. It brought together amazing configurations of Christian people. (Imagine Clifton Kirkpatrick [then president of the World Alliance of Reformed Churches] teaming up with the Coptic theologian Metropolitan Bishoy to convince the Evangelischen Kirche in Deutschland delegation of the merits of the consensus method. Picture Eden Grace drawing on both her Quaker experience and Orthodox sources to promote the consensus ethos.) It gave an opportunity both for a genuine and self-emptying process of listening and for a fresh and thorough self-examination, one that included self-criticism (something that does not come easily to us Orthodox). This combination of listening and self-examination both fostered and was enabled by the deep mutual trust built through the Commission.

At many points, the Special Commission also exemplified the obstreperous and otherwise frustrating character of us Orthodox, as well as a different kind of unyielding nature we might associate with mainline Protestants! It emblematized at the same time the WCC's ability to change, its fickleness (tossed to and fro with every wind of realignment), and its obstinate refusal to yield a certain *de facto* superchurch pretension.

And yet, as I look back on my own involvement in the process, I wouldn't have given it up for anything. I see in it the work of God's hands, and count myself richly blessed for what it continues to give me. But this isn't about just me, for among ecumenically involved Orthodox Christians, I am far from alone in feeling this way about the encounter. Yet the depth of its effect upon us, the engaged ones, seen against the relief of the apathy or antipathy within the Orthodox churches, is sobering. Much work lies ahead, and we can only have faith that the continued efforts to know each other, and to walk in each other's shoes, will surely bear incalculable fruit.

3 Faith and Order: Achievements of Multilateral Dialogue

Mary Tanner

> *O God, holy and eternal Trinity,*
> *We pray for your Church in all the world.*
> *Sanctify its life; renew its worship;*
> *empower its witness; heal its divisions;*
> *make visible its unity.*
> *Lead us with all our brothers and sisters,*
> *towards communion in faith, life and witness*
> *so that, united in one body by the one Spirit,*
> *we may together witness to the perfect unity of your love.*
> *Amen*[1]

I am grateful to the Saint Paul Seminary School of Divinity for its generous invitation to take part in this important conference. It is a special delight to share these days with dear friends with whom I have worked around ecumenical tables of conversation for many, many years in the Faith and Order Commission of the World Council of Churches and in the Anglican–Roman Catholic bilateral conversation. As a long-time member of the Faith and Order Commission and its Moderator from 1991 to 1998, I am delighted to have been invited to speak about the achievements of Faith and Order.

---

1. Santiago Prayer in *WCFO5*, p. xii.

This is a revised form of a paper given at the Plenary Meeting of the Faith and Order Commission, Crete, October 2009.

There is something very special about reflecting on Faith and Order in these days as we celebrate the centenary of the Missionary Conference of Edinburgh 1910, for it is usually acknowledged that it was at Edinburgh that the Faith and Order movement was born. At the conference Anglicans met daily to celebrate the eucharist. It was at one of those services that Bishop Charles Brent of the Philippines came up with the idea of holding a world conference on faith and order issues to begin to explore honestly points of agreement and points of difference that were the original causes of division and continued to keep churches apart from one another. Conceived in a moment of prayer, Faith and Order's work has been grounded in prayer ever since. The sessions of the First World Conference in 1927 were punctuated by prayer, and I remember how the Commission prayed its way to the Fifth World Conference in Santiago de Compostela in 1993 with the prayer with which I began this essay. Very often people recall the experience of being together in that pilgrim city in a spirit of attentive waiting together upon God. It is not possible to read through the pages of Faith and Order's history without being struck by a deep spirituality, grounded in prayer, which blossoms in friendships and inspires the doctrinal conversations. The faith and order enterprise is not an arid academic exercise in the production of texts of clever compromise, whatever some critics may say. Listen to this from "The Call to Unity" from the First World Conference in Lausanne:

> God desires unity . . . our desire [is] to bend our wills to his. . . .
> God's Spirit has been in the midst of us. . . . His presence has been
> manifest in our worship, our deliberations, and our whole fellow-
> ship. He has discovered us to one another. We have dared and God
> has justified our daring. We can never be the same again.[2]

So, the inspiration for the First World Conference on Faith and Order came in a moment of prayer, and prayer has been foundational for the Commission ever since.

In every pamphlet Bishop Charles Brent wrote between 1910 and 1927 to convince others of the need for work on faith and order issues, he wrote in Greek and Latin — "may they all be one, so that the world might believe." The *raison d'être* of the Faith and Order movement was,

2. H. N. Bate, ed., *Faith and Order: Proceedings of the World Conference, Lausanne, August 3-21, 1927* (London: SCM Press, 1927), pp. 460ff.

and remains, unity for God's sake and the world's sake, in obedience to Christ's prayer. Its agenda is to study and find convergence in areas that were the cause of division. The search for agreement in faith which is "sufficient and required" for unity, as well as the patient search for an agreed "picture" of the unity we seek, or rather, as we would say today, the unity that is God's gift and our calling, lie at the heart of the faith and order endeavor.

Two years before the First World Conference in Lausanne in 1927, the Life and Work movement met in a World Conference in Stockholm. There were those then, and I think there still are, who were convinced that the way for Christians to get together was to cooperate on social, industrial, and political issues, while agreeing to disagree on matters of faith and order. "Service unites but doctrine divides" was the unhelpful slogan that was bandied around. Thankfully, the two movements in 1948, and later the missionary movement in 1961, came together in the formation of the World Council of Churches, providing the appropriate and potentially enriching context in which the multilateral faith and order conversation could flourish and our understanding of unity be enriched by the other ecumenical activities.

In its Constitution, the first of the functions of the World Council is described as: "to call the churches to the goal of visible unity in one faith and in one eucharistic fellowship expressed in worship and in common life in Christ." The aim of Faith and Order is "to proclaim the oneness of the church of Jesus Christ and to call the churches to the goal of visible unity in one faith and eucharistic fellowship, expressed in worship and in common life in Christ, in order that the world may believe."[3] So, the Faith and Order Commission is to be "the conscience" of the World Council — to keep it focused on its own primary task — "to call the churches to the goal of visible unity."

If only we had oceans of time to travel together from that First World Conference in Lausanne in 1927 to the most recent gathering of the Commission in Crete last October, with time to ponder the rich resources of documents and to meet some of the giants on the faith and order journey: Charles Brent, William Temple, Patriarch Athenagoras, Nikos Nissiotis, Letty Russell, Peggy Way, Christian Howard, Max

---

3. Thomas F. Best, ed., *Faith and Order at the Crossroads: Kuala Lumpur 2004, the Plenary Commission Meeting,* Faith and Order Paper 196 (Geneva: WCC Publications, 2005), p. 450.

Thurian, Jean Tillard, Desmond Tutu, Lukas Vischer, Wolfhart Pannenberg, a young Bartholomew, now the Ecumenical Patriarch, and a young Joseph, now Pope Benedict. We would see how the community around the multilateral faith and order table has expanded: more church traditions gathered, with the Roman Catholic Church joining the conversation after Vatican II; a shift from north to south; and a more just representation of women and younger ecumenical theologians. Each new presence around the table has brought new perspectives and depth to the work. So, what has been achieved in more than eighty years of this multilateral conversation?

Let me consider first how successful we have been in wrestling with those issues that were the causes of division. The agenda was set for what needed to be studied right at the beginning in 1927, and most of Faith and Order's work since has been in continuity with what Lausanne began: work on the common confession of the faith; the ministry; the sacraments; the structures of authority; the nature of the church; and the call to unity.[4] Conversations around the table were at first comparative in approach, with each church explaining its own understanding and practice to others. This was appropriate when churches were coming out of their isolations and getting to know one another. Some very important advances in understanding were made at Lausanne, not least of all, perhaps surprisingly, in the fruitful discussions on bishops, councils of presbyters, and councils of the faithful, many agreeing that each must have a place in a re-united church.

A dramatic change of approach and method was made at the Third World Conference in Lund in 1952 when it was proposed to abandon the theological method of listing and analyzing the varying beliefs of different churches, the comparative method, and to seek for those common convictions that underlay them. The breakthrough was made possible by the advances in biblical scholarship, the renewed interest in the patristic period, as well as the contribution of the liturgical movement. The Fourth World Conference on Faith and Order in Montreal in 1963 helped the churches to understand that the one Tradition (with a capital T) is witnessed to normatively in scripture and transmitted, by the Holy Spirit, in and through the traditions of each

4. Bate, ed., *Faith and Order: Proceedings of the World Conference, Lausanne, August 3-21, 1927.*

of the churches.[5] Churches were able to overcome the old divide between those who held all was given in scripture, *sola scriptura,* and those who looked to both scripture and tradition for guidance. Theologians from very different traditions discovered that it was possible to go back together to scripture, to the earliest common tradition of the undivided church, to consider together the traditions of separated churches and then move to restate together afresh their common faith, "the faith of the Church through the ages." This opened the way for the production of a new type of ecumenical agreed statement, the convergence-consensus statement.

By the 1970s the Commission had identified three requirements for the visible unity of the church: Christians should make common confession of the apostolic faith; celebrate common sacraments and be served by one ministry; and have ways of deciding together and teaching with authority.[6]

It was work on the second of those requirements that reached maturity first and resulted in the publication of the convergence document, *Baptism, Eucharist and Ministry,* often referred to as the Lima Document, because it was in Lima, Peru that the Commission voted the text "mature enough to go to the churches." (*BEM* and *Ut Unum Sint* are surely the two most important ecumenical texts of the ecumenical century.) In *BEM* the theologians were able to set down what they could now agree together about the sacraments and the ministry and, in accompanying commentaries, record honestly areas of remaining difference. The most remarkable thing was the discovery of just how much agreement there was in areas of difference once considered intractable. This was particularly true in the areas of baptism and eucharist, but there were significant advances too in the area of ministry.

It was not only the document itself that marked an impressive achievement but the dynamic process set in motion with its publication. The churches were invited to respond to the document at "the highest level of authority." *BEM* captured the imaginations of the

5. P. C. Rodger and L. Vischer, eds., *The Fourth World Conference on Faith and Order, the Report from Montreal, 1963,* Faith and Order Paper 42 (London: SCM Press, 1963), pp. 50-61.

6. The triad first appeared in the Plenary Meeting in Bangalore as "Consensus in the Apostolic faith; mutual recognition of baptism, the eucharist and the ministry; and structures making possible common teaching and decision-making." *Sharing in One Hope: Commission on Faith and Order, Bangalore, 1978,* Faith and Order Paper 92 (Geneva: WCC Publications, 1978), p. 243.

churches. The six volumes of responses of the churches, together with the Commission's own response to the responses, have given us an extraordinarily rich ecumenical resource.[7] More than that, the responses provide a fascinating case study of how different churches go about responding, whom they consult in the process, and who speaks the authoritative response for the churches. In some ways it was remarkable that certain churches found it possible to respond at "the highest level of authority" to a document co-authored by those they did not recognize as "church."

What was remarkable was that a convergence document proved also to be a convergence instrument. Faith and Order's challenge to the churches was not only to see whether churches could recognize in the text "the faith of the Church through the ages," but with that came even more demanding challenges. They were invited to consider what implications the text might have for their own worship, for their educational, ethical, spiritual life, and witness, and what reforms were required of them. And they were asked to consider what closer relations might be forged with those who could also recognize in *BEM* "the faith of the Church." *BEM* did, and still does for some, act as a convergence instrument inspiring churches to renewal in their internal lives. And *BEM* was used, and still is, by some churches as "building blocks" to establish new relationships of closer fellowship, in a committed stage on the way to visible unity. Using *BEM* as a major resource my own church, the Church of England, for example, has entered new relations of closer fellowship with Lutherans, Reformed, Moravian, and Methodist churches, which have led to increased sharing in life and mission. The convergence in faith expressed in *BEM* has not remained as empty words on a library shelf, but is now woven into our lives and relationships. The progress made on the basis of *BEM* is one of the miracles of the ecumenical movement.

It was time now to turn to one of the other requirements for unity: the common confession of the apostolic faith — but how to approach it? In 1927 the World Conference talked of "the Christian Faith which is proclaimed in the Holy Scriptures and witnessed to and safeguarded in the Ecumenical Creed, commonly called the Nicene, and in

---

7. Max Thurian, ed., *Churches respond to BEM, official responses to the "Baptism, Eucharist and Ministry" text*, vols. 1-6 (Geneva: WCC Publications, 1986-88). And, *Baptism, Eucharist and Ministry, 1982-1990, Report of the Process and Responses*, Faith and Order Paper 149 (Geneva: WCC Publications, 1990).

the Apostles' Creed, which Faith is continuously confirmed in the spiritual experience of the Church."[8] The Commission decided in the early 1980s to take the Nicene-Constantinopolitan Creed as a prism through which it would first look back to the faith grounded in scripture and then consider, in light of that scriptural faith, the present challenges to the faith in different ecclesial and cultural contexts. From this exploration the Commission then offered an explication of the apostolic faith.[9] The object was never to browbeat all into saying the words of the Creed but, rather, much more imaginatively, to help us recognize the common faith, expressed in our own lives and in the lives of other Christian communities, so that we might move to confess together, in our words and in our living, "this is the faith of the Church through the ages: this is our faith!" There was a romantic hope that our leaders might gather in Jerusalem to sing together our common faith focused in the creed — the symbol of our unity in faith.

Perhaps the churches were suffering now with an overload of ecumenical tasks — responding intensively to *BEM,* as well as to the many bilateral agreed statements that were being published in the 1980s. Or maybe it was a lack of imagination, a failure to understand the dynamic and potential of the apostolic faith study. Sadly, what might have proved a vital text for the fellowship of churches in the World Council never got the attention that *BEM* had received. I'm glad that it has recently been republished. On any reckoning it is a significant achievement.

Although a start was made as early as the 1970s on the third requirement for visible unity — namely, common ways of deciding and teaching with authority — the work never reached the state of maturity of the other two items.[10] One disappointment I have about my time as Moderator was my failure to get the Commission to do substantive work on this third requirement.[11] However, a look through Faith and

8. Bate, ed., *Faith and Order: Proceedings of the World Conference, Lausanne, August 3-21, 1927,* Section IV, Para. 28.

9. *Confessing the One Faith: An Ecumenical Explication of the Apostolic Faith as It Is Confessed in the Nicene-Constantinopolitan Creed (381),* Faith and Order Paper 153 (Geneva: WCC Publications, 1991).

10. "How Does the Church Teach Authoritatively Today?" Faith and Order Paper 91, in *Ecumenical Review* 31 (1971): 77ff.

11. Report of the Moderator, *Minutes of the Meeting of the Faith and Order Standing Commission 1994, Crêt-Bérard, Switzerland,* Faith and Order Paper 167 (Geneva: WCC Publications, 1994), pp. 7-16.

Order documents would show that there is important material there to build upon.

Something happened in the 1970s that was to radically change the ethos of Faith and Order's work and enrich its motivating vision. The Commission was more and more drawn into collaborative studies with other parts of the Council's agenda — studies on racism, the handicapped, and the community of women and men. These studies had a profound effect on all of the work of Faith and Order and ultimately on its view of the visible unity of the church. For many of us they breathed new life and credibility into our work. The Program to Combat Racism in the 70s, for example, showed clearly that if the church was to be a "prophetic sign" and an "effective instrument" in the struggles of this world, then churches had not only to overcome doctrinal differences but were required to overcome all forms of apartheid and discrimination in their own internal lives. This was not a secular agenda but a profoundly ecclesiological agenda. We began to see that divisions in human community insidiously affected the community of the church and were often reinforced by language we used, by liturgical practice, and by the way the church was ordered.[12] Faith and Order came to see that unity and the renewal of the human community of the church cannot be separated: they belong together. We have to be "renewed together into unity in the deepest fabric of our lives." The same lesson was seen in the study "The Community of Women and Men in the Church."[13] What at first seemed to be a women's liberation struggle, taken over from the secular women's movement, was shown to be a profoundly ecclesiological matter with implications for our understanding of God, of men and women created and redeemed in the image of God, our language, symbols, and imagery, our ways of doing theology and celebrating the sacraments, our ministry and our exercise of authority. It was an ecclesiological issue. In a similar way, more recently, the program on Justice, Peace, and the Integrity of Creation resulted in new thinking on the church as "moral community," and unity came to be understood as "costly unity," and "costly commitment" together to the gospel.[14] The renewal studies

12. A. van der Bent, ed., *Breaking Down the Walls: Statements and Actions on Racism, 1948-85* (Geneva: WCC Publications, 1986).

13. C. Parvey, ed., *The Community of Women and Men in the Church: The Sheffield Report* (Geneva: WCC Publications, 1983).

14. T. Best and M. Robra, eds., *Ecclesiology and Ethics* (Geneva: WCC Publications, 1997).

produced insights that breathed new life into the understanding of the unity God is calling us to live in and for the world. And when this was recognized the language and interests of the faith and order documents began to live in a new way. One of the most frequently quoted passages from *BEM* illustrates this well:

> The eucharistic celebration demands reconciliation and sharing among all those regarded as brothers and sisters in the one family of God and is a constant challenge in the search for appropriate relationships in social, economic and political life. . . . All kinds of injustice, racism, separation and lack of freedom are radically challenged when we share in the body and blood of Christ. . . . As participants in the eucharist, therefore, we prove inconsistent if we are not actively participating in this ongoing restoration of the world's situation and the human condition.[15]

The integration of these studies wasn't easy and was often resisted, even by some Commission members, but the unity and renewal studies did help the Commission to understand what sort of church would be "a more convincing prophetic sign" and "effective instrument" in the world. All of this work of relating the church to the human community, the church to the world, was drawn together in the report with that title.[16] It still repays study. It was a significant achievement.

All of this was symbolized for me at the Lima meeting when our Orthodox Moderator, Nikos Nissiotis, asked the Commission if *Baptism, Eucharist and Ministry* was "mature" enough to go to the churches. Everyone raised their hands in agreement and the whole meeting rose silently, giving thanks for reaching that special moment in the ecumenical movement. I don't think any of us could have known then just how important that text would prove to be. That moment of prayer was, for me, a moment of disclosure. As we stood in silent prayer I looked out of the window and saw the barren hills going up around us, and where the scrub gave way to desert there were some half-built shacks where the poor of Lima, unimaginably poor, eked out some sort of existence. I remember thinking that unless what we were doing enclosed in our comfortable oasis, safeguarding our life-giving traditions of baptism

---

15. *BEM,* Eucharist, no. 20.

16. *Church and World: The Unity of the Church and the Renewal of Human Community,* Faith and Order Paper 151 (Geneva: WCC Publications, 1990).

and eucharist, had something — no everything — to do with that world of poverty and starvation, we might as well give up and go home. I understood in that moment that the unity of the church and the unity and renewal of human community belong together.

So, what has Faith and Order achieved in studying those areas of division? I think we can say much was achieved. But to assess Faith and Order's achievements we need also to consider how successful Faith and Order has been in carrying out its mandate that requires it to hold before the fellowship of churches the goal of visible unity. One of the great achievements of Faith and Order has, I believe, been the patient search for an agreed picture, or portrait of the unity God calls us to live together in and for the world. We are not talking about a model of unity — "organic union," or "reconciled diversity," or even "united not absorbed." Nor are we talking of the various forms of Christian cooperation as a goal, however important these are on the way. Faith and Order has offered the World Council at its Assemblies statements on the unity we believe God is calling us to live. New Delhi, 1961, remains inspirational with its formulation in a sentence of Pauline length and complexity. It describes as the goal, "all in each place" united with the "all in every place" and "in all ages," so they can act and speak together as occasion requires.[17]

In 1991 Faith and Order prepared a statement for the Canberra Assembly, *The Unity of the Church as* Koinonia: *Gift and Calling,* which in one picture, painted in words, brings those insights of the renewal studies together with those three requirements for unity. It emphasizes the rich diversity that necessarily belongs to unity and makes a valiant attempt to respond to the pressing question that emerged at Canberra: "What are the limits to diversity?"[18] The most recent Assembly State-

---

17. "We believe that the unity which is both God's will and his gift to his Church is being made visible as all in each place who are baptized into Jesus Christ and confess him as Lord and Saviour are brought by the Holy Spirit into one fully committed fellowship, holding the one apostolic faith, preaching the one Gospel, breaking the one bread, joining in common prayer and having a corporate life reaching out in witness and service to all, and who at the same time are united with the whole Christian fellowship in all places and all ages in such wise that members and ministries are accepted by all, and that all can act and speak together as occasion requires for the tasks to which God calls his people." *New Delhi Speaks* (London: SCM Press, 1962), p. 55.

18. Michael Kinnamon, ed., *Signs of the Spirit, Official Report, Seventh Assembly, World Council of Churches* (Geneva: WCC Publications, 1991), pp. 172-74.

ment from Porto Alegre, *Called to Be the One Church,* is important but not scintillating and not without its ambiguities![19] In it the outline of unity remains — a visible *koinonia* expressed in faith and sacraments, reconciled ministry and common life, linked together in each place through a conciliar fellowship of churches.

These Assembly statements, prepared by Faith and Order but influenced by Assemblies, have been ways in which Faith and Order has been faithful to its mandate to keep the goal of visible unity before the fellowship of churches. How to draw the churches into transformative conversations around these statements remains a challenge. But without that conversation the question will remain: "Do we at this stage of the ecumenical movement share a common understanding of the goal of the ecumenical movement?"

Faith and Order has done more than produce short portraits in words, important as these markers have been for the goal of visible unity. The Commission began preparing for the Fifth World Conference in 1993, in Santiago, by asking, "Where are we, where are we going in the ecumenical movement in the search for visible unity?" The title of the Conference was Faith and Order's answer to its own question: "Towards *koinonia* in faith, life and witness."[20] This title enabled the Conference to harvest the work it had done on faith and sacraments, and embryonic as it was, on bonds of communion (structures of grace), together with the inspiration from the renewal studies, into its picture of visible unity grounded in the divine Trinitarian life. The concept of *koinonia,* not a model of unity, but the very essence of divine/human unity, the very foundation and nature of the church, was seen to breathe new life into the portrait of visible unity. So long as we were firmly grounded in our trinitarian faith, the communion of God's own life and love, there could be no doubt about the goal of visible unity. The message from Santiago was clear: "There is *no turning back* either from the goal of visible unity or from the single ecumenical movement that unites concerns for the unity of the Church and concern for the engagement in the struggles of the world."[21]

It was from this harvesting at Santiago that work on ecclesiology

---

19. Luis N. Rivera-Pagán, ed., *God, in your grace . . . Official Report of the Ninth Assembly of the World Council of Churches* (Geneva: WCC Publications, 2007), pp. 255-61.

20. *WCFO5.*

21. *WCFO5,* p. 225.

became the central task of the Commission in the next years, issuing in the document *The Nature and Purpose of the Church,* now revised as *The Nature and Mission of the Church.*[22] Notice that both are subtitled: *a stage on the way to a common statement,* a modest claim for the work. The latest statement continues to harvest the work on faith, sacraments, ministry, and to deepen thinking significantly on that third requirement of unity with its reflections on personal, communal, and collegial oversight; conciliarity; and for the first time, a bold reflection on the ministry of primacy at the world level. The document includes strange "boxes," in which are highlighted remaining issues requiring transformative conversations. The vision is large — the church in the purposes of God: its order of priority — God, the world, the church. The process of engaging the churches in conversation around the statement has begun but has not yet sparked anything like the energy or enthusiasm that *BEM* was met with in the 1980s. So far of eighty responses received only twenty-four are from churches, not very impressive when we consider that there are 349 member churches of the WCC. Does this say more about the times we live in, the other pressing agendas before our churches? Or does it perhaps suggest that there is little commitment to unity — to the visible unity of the church? We are content with cooperating when it suits us.

So, what has Faith and Order achieved? I dare to answer with thankfulness for all those who have contributed over many years: "Faith and Order has achieved much." Churches do understand one another and the original causes of separation better because of Faith and Order's work.[23] Significant convergence, even consensus, has been reached on some issues that seemed intractable. Faith and Order work has both contributed to the bilateral conversations and learned from them. Some churches have renewed their own liturgical and catechetical lives on the basis of the insights of the documents. Some new partnerships of closer communion have been formed, using as building blocks the documents and the vision of unity articulated by Faith and Order. The ecclesial landscape has changed in response to Faith and

22. *The Nature and Purpose of the Church: A Stage on the Way to a Common Statement,* Faith and Order Paper 181 (Geneva: WCC Publications, 1998). *The Nature and Mission of the Church: A Stage on the Way to a Common Statement,* Faith and Order Paper 198 (Geneva: WCC Publications, 2005).

23. Thomas F. Best and Tamara Grdzelidze, eds., *BEM at 25: Critical Insights into a Continuing Legacy,* Faith and Order Paper 205 (Geneva: WCC Publications, 2007).

Order's work. We live beyond the limits of the landscape our grandparents knew.

As we celebrate the centenary of Edinburgh 1910 this is not the time to give up. Faith and Order must pursue its work with continuity and freshness. Faith and Order must help the World Council of Churches as institution, and as a fellowship of churches, to be centered on its primary aim to call the churches to the visible unity of the church — a unity in faith, sacraments, ministry, and connected life for the sake of effective service and credible mission. Faith and Order must continue in the broadest ecumenical forum, to offer a motivating vision of visible unity. That means that Faith and Order needs to be more intentional about nurturing transformative conversations around *The Nature and Mission of the Church,* and the Porto Alegre statement.

Secondly, to be faithful to its mandate Faith and Order will need to go on working at those neuralgic issues that still keep us apart. It will need to help the churches explore once more what is illegitimate diversity in relation to the ministry of oversight and apostolicity and help us to think more deeply about the relation of the local to the universal, what living a connected life entails and how, when deep differences divide the Christian community, we might stay together and discern together the mind of Christ. I am glad that Faith and Order is now working on this agenda, approaching it in a new way by reflecting on case studies on moral discernment in our churches today and asking what their different ways tell us about the sources used and the ecclesial structures and the processes through which discernment takes place. In this study Faith and Order will need to face hard questions about the place of prophetic witness and the place of restraint in discerning the mind of Christ for the church.

And there is a third thing: "reception." Faith and Order needs to discover more effective and sustained ways of challenging both the World Council of Churches as institution and the member churches in the fellowship, as it did in the *BEM* process, to receive the fruits of its work into changed lives and relationships.

My sense from being at the Crete Assembly of Faith and Order in 2009 is that Faith and Order has entered a new, more focused phase of its work. A new generation is taking up the mantle and working with continuity and freshness. We can expect more achievements from Faith and Order in the future. The question is: Will our churches respond and receive those achievements in reformed lives and new relationships, and will they respond to the call to the visible unity of the church? There are both achievements to celebrate and challenges to face as we celebrate this hundredth anniversary of Edinburgh 1910, the place where the Faith and Order movement began.

4 The Achievements of Faith and Order: A Catholic Perspective

William Henn, OFM Cap

I. Beginnings

In the account of the First World Conference on Faith and Order that appears in the famous Rouse/Neill history of the ecumenical movement, Tissington Tatlow uses the following anecdote to illustrate something of the tone of that meeting and of the challenges it faced:

> Section IV dealt with "The Church's Common Confession of Faith." There were 115 members — Americans and Europeans, drawn from countries as different as Ireland, Russia, Sweden, Portugal, and France. There was one Oriental — a Japanese. A few members — for example, Bishop Brent and Dr. Peter Ainslie — had long taken a lead in the movement . . . but the majority were strangers to each other. Some vigorously-worded opinions were heard during the first meeting and a good deal of heat was generated. "We must declare our loyalty to the Nicene Creed," said an Orthodox, to which a Congregationalist replied, "Well, I think we should clear all that old lumber out of the way."[1]

That was at Lausanne, in a meeting that lasted from August 3 to 21, 1927. It is perhaps no coincidence that one of the most significant Catholic interventions concerning ecumenism to appear in the first

---

1. Tissington Tatlow, "The World Conference on Faith and Order," in Ruth Rouse and Stephen Charles Neill, eds., *A History of the Ecumenical Movement*, vol. 1: *1517-1948* (Geneva: WCC Publications, 2004) [first published in 1954], pp. 403-41 at 422-23.

half of the twentieth century was the short encyclical letter of Pius XI, *Mortalium animos,* dated January 6, 1928, less than five months after the close of the meeting in Lausanne.[2] On its surface, *Mortalium animos* seems very negative in its assessment of the ecumenical movement. It forbids Catholic participation and insists in rather uncompromising terms that the only hope for the unity of all Christians is the "return" of all to the Catholic Church and submission to the teaching authority of the pope. Pius XI's somewhat simple and straightforward argument went like this: God had revealed and accomplished the salvation of human beings through the missions of Christ and the Holy Spirit, missions that established and sustained the church as the effective instrument to proclaim revealed truth and lead human beings to salvation. The church's unity required unity in faith, and the community was furnished with a magisterial teaching office precisely for the purpose of promoting and maintaining such unity. Official teaching was not to add anything to the original deposit of revealed truth; any doctrine had to be contained at least implicitly in the revelation given fully in Christ at the beginning. In that way, Pius emphasized the authority of God as the ultimate foundation of Christian doctrine. But this implied at least two consequences concerning unity in faith. First, the church does not have the authority simply to select a certain number of so-called "fundamental articles" that could serve as a kind of "least common dominator" around which all Christians could unite. The whole of revelation, since it comes from God, must be embraced by all believers. Second, it followed logically that ecclesial unity must not be conceived as a merely charitable fellowship rooted in Jesus' command to love one another, which would countenance, within the reestablishment of full unity, the coexistence of contradictory doctrinal beliefs. Pius XI illustrated this by mentioning five specific questions about which Christians, then involved in the nascent ecumenical movement, seemed to hold contradictory opinions: whether tradition is a true fount of revelation; whether a hierarchy of bishops, priests, and deacons has been divinely constituted; whether Christ is really present in the eucharist; whether the eucharist has the nature both of a sacrament and a sacrifice; and whether it be good and useful to invoke the

2. An English version of the complete text of thirteen numbered paragraphs can be found in http://www.vatican.va/holy_father/pius_xi/encyclicals/documents/hf_p-xi_enc_19280106_mortalium-animos_en.html [accessed December 19, 2010].

saints by prayer. One wonders whether he had heard and was thinking of the just-mentioned disagreements at Lausanne when he compiled that list![3]

I cannot say whether Pius XI's rather sharply negative encyclical was timed precisely to indicate the Catholic Church's initial assessment of the Faith and Order movement, which he does not mention by name. But if his comments were occasioned mainly by its founding world conference in 1927, then perhaps it can be attributed to divine irony that, in point of fact, the Faith and Order movement ended up pursuing precisely the two fundamental values about unity in faith that were the basis of *Mortalium animos,* that is, first, the concern to listen to the authoritative, revealed Word of God as the ultimate source of Christian faith, and second, the attempt to overcome contradictory doctrinal convictions.

One of Faith and Order's most important achievements from a Catholic perspective is precisely that it has persistently sought convergence and consensus about questions concerning doctrine and ecclesial order. Its contribution is particularly valuable because of its multilaterality, as Msgr. John Radano, one of the most authoritative Catholic commentators about the commission, has pointed out: "The Catholic involvement with Faith and Order is very important especially because the Faith and Order Commission is the most diverse ecumenical body fostering dialogue among a broad multilateral range of Christian communions, on issues which need to be dealt with to reach the goal of visible unity (the goal stated in the Constitution of the Commission on Faith and Order, as well as in the constitution of the World Council of Churches)."[4] Such wide inclusivity carries with it disadvantages as well as advantages. The principal disadvantage shows up in the requirement to satisfy the expectations of such a wide constituency. It stands to reason that a bilateral dialogue would be able to move ahead with greater speed and precision. On the other hand, the process of responding to the Lima text of 1982, titled *Baptism, Eucharist and Ministry,*

---

3. It is remarkable, even if disconcerting, that the various issues mentioned by *Mortalium animos* still seem divisive today, after so many years. John Paul II's list of topics requiring further dialogue in paragraph 79 of his encyclical *Ut unum sint* of 1995 echoes some of the themes mentioned by his predecessor back in 1928. UUS can be read at: http://www.vatican.va/edocs/ENG0221/_INDEX.HTM [accessed on December 19, 2010].

4. John A. Radano, "The Catholic Church, Faith and Order, and BEM," *Centro pro unione Semiannual Bulletin* 73 (Spring 2008): 3-14, at 4.

which resulted in the publication of six volumes of official responses, demonstrates the principal advantage of Faith and Order.[5] It represents a high percentage of the world's Christian communions and, thus, when its work results in convergence, even those churches that were at first reticent about the content of such convergence find themselves more willing to rethink their earlier positions and to consider the possibility of revision or reform. Great Christian thinkers from Augustine to John Henry Newman saw wide-ranging consensus as a sign of the activity of the Holy Spirit, and Faith and Order provides a forum where such wide-ranging ecumenical consensus can occur.

2. Achievements from the First Decades up to Montreal (1963)

In reflecting upon the achievements of Faith and Order, the documentary histories provided by two of the commission's past directors — Lukas Vischer for the years 1927-1963 and Günther Gassmann for the years 1963-1993 — offer a helpful framework. From a Catholic perspective, the great achievement of the first three decades of the life of the commission, in addition to its seminal role in actually establishing the World Council of Churches, was Faith and Order's move "from the comparative method to a form of theological dialogue which approaches controversial issues from a common biblical and Christological basis," a shift that can be situated at the Third World Conference held in Lund, Sweden, in 1952.[6] That methodological shift made "convergence" and "consensus," rather than the mere "comparison" of the doctrines of the different communities, the goal of this most widely representative dialogue group.

Using this method, the Fourth World Conference held in Montreal in 1963 made a momentous breakthrough on the relation between scripture and tradition.[7] In my estimation, this is the most significant,

5. See below, note 11, on the reception of *BEM*.

6. Günther Gassmann, "Faith and Order," in *DEM2*, pp. 461-63. The Lund Conference as well as many other details from the first thirty-six years of its life are told in Lukas Vischer, ed., *A Documentary History of the Faith and Order Movement 1927-1963* (St. Louis: Bethany Press, 1963).

7. This document is reprinted in Günther Gassmann, *Documentary History of Faith and Order 1963-1993*, Faith and Order Paper 159 (Geneva: WCC Publications, 1993), pp. 10-18.

groundbreaking achievement of the first half of the history of Faith and Order. Without downplaying the many other issues treated in those early decades, Montreal's statement overcame the inadequate and simplistic view that held scripture and tradition to be in opposition to one another; as such it provided a more promising point of departure for returning to those sources. Montreal could not yet resolve the question of the relative authority of these means of transmission of the Word of God, in particular the question of how to discern the authenticity of specific traditions. But in principle the playing field was changed. Scripture itself was seen as a product of tradition, and tradition, for its part, was seen as the process of handing on the Word of God whose inspired form is found in scripture. While some have questioned the durable value of Montreal, it seems to me that its insight about the complementarity of these two means of the transmission of revelation is, on the whole, irrefutable. Montreal's achievement has been further developed in the Faith and Order text *A Treasure in Earthen Vessels* of 1998, which explores how the variety among traditions is related to cultural diversity and how discernment concerning the gospel authenticity of any given tradition takes place within the church conceived as a hermeneutical community, in which the guidance of ordained ministers has an irreplaceable role.[8]

Faith and Order's work on scripture and tradition was accompanied by some significant developments in Catholic thinking that were sparked by Pius XII's 1950 proclamation of the Assumption of the Virgin Mary. Because this doctrine could not draw upon explicit biblical support, it was incumbent upon Catholic theologians to reflect upon the role of tradition in the way Catholics come to understand revealed truth. This led to the reconsideration of what the Council of Trent (1545-1563) had proposed in response to the theme of *sola scriptura,* associated with the Protestant Reformation. This rethinking eventually made possible the view of revelation proposed by the bishops of Vatican II. While in no way contradicting *Mortalium animos* on the authority of revealed truth and the need to overcome contradictory interpretations of it, *Dei verbum* describes the event of revelation as an

8. This text is reprinted in P. Bouteneff and D. Heller, *Interpreting Together: Essays in Hermeneutics,* Faith and Order Paper 189 (Geneva: WCC Publications, 2001), pp. 134-60. This volume also contains nine studies that contributed to the preparation of *A Treasure in Earthen Vessels,* which was also published as a separate Faith and Order Paper in 1998 and presented at the Harare general assembly of the WCC that year.

encounter between God and human beings in history. This encounter brings people into communion with the triune God, Father, Son, and Holy Spirit, and at the same time gives birth to that communion of believers which is the church. Such a view of revelation makes it easier to overcome an inadequate opposition between scripture and its transmission through tradition, since both are means by which this encounter takes place. At the same time seeing revelation as "encounter" coheres nicely with the fundamental activity of ecumenism — that is, the Holy Spirit's work of reestablishing full communion between those who have encountered Christ yet remain divided from one another into separate Christian communities. Thus Faith and Order's landmark statement on "Scripture, Tradition and Traditions" of 1963 was contemporaneous with important developments in the way Catholics think about scripture and its relation to tradition. I cannot help seeing the activity of the Holy Spirit in such a coincidence.

3. Achievements from Montreal to Santiago (1993)

Günther Gassmann's *Documentary History of the Faith and Order Movement 1963-1993* allows one to take up the story from there. He nicely sketches out the work of the commission in two long chapters that constitute 300 of the 325 pages of his history. The first of these, titled "Main Faith and Order Themes 1963-1993," identifies these themes as four: first, the visible unity of the church; second, baptism, eucharist, and ministry; third, the unity of the church and the renewal of the human community; and fourth, confessing the one faith. A second extensive chapter lists seven projects on such topics as the interpretation of scripture, councils, teaching authority, and worship, which "were not pursued continuously throughout this period, but were on the agenda for a limited space of time only."[9] For the sake of simplicity I will use Gassmann's four main themes as an outline for identifying some of the achievements of Faith and Order during this period.

First, a general comment about the four of them together. The work on each of these themes ultimately led to the publication of some significant ecumenical texts. The first resulted in the brief statements on visible unity that were received by the general assemblies of the

9. G. Gassmann, ed., *Documentary History of Faith and Order 1963-1993*, p. 201.

WCC at New Delhi, Nairobi, Canberra and, we may add, Porto Alegre.[10] The work on the second theme produced the famous Lima text *Baptism, Eucharist and Ministry* of 1982.[11] Work on the unity of the church and the renewal of the human community resulted in the study titled *Church and World* of 1990,[12] while the apostolic faith project produced the commentary *Confessing the One Faith* of 1991.[13] Anyone familiar with the reception of these texts will immediately notice a rather striking disparity. The introduction to the thirty-ninth printing of *Baptism, Eucharist and Ministry* on its twenty-fifth anniversary in 2007 noted that there were at that time 180,000 English copies in print and translations in about forty other languages; that more than 180 churches had officially responded to *BEM*, not to mention many other responses, such as from councils of churches or individuals; and that many communities had received *BEM* in a deep sense by taking it into the life and practice of their churches. That did not happen in the case of publications concerning the other three themes, and the temptation to compare them unfavorably with *BEM* can be almost irresistible. But I think that such a temptation should be resisted. The purpose of each project is quite distinct; each can yet make a significant contribution to the ultimate goal of visible unity, as I would like to argue now.

The major Unity Statements of the general assemblies insist that the unity for which Christ prayed is not a kind of amicable federation of independent and autonomous communities. The bonds of faith,

10. Cf. Gassmann, ed., *Documentary History of Faith and Order 1963-1993,* pp. 35-80. The three general assembly unity statements that had been completed by that time — those of New Delhi, Nairobi, and Canberra — are printed on pages 3-5 of the same book.

11. Cf. H. E. Metropolitan Vasilios (Moderator) and Thomas F. Best (Director), "Introduction" to *Baptism, Eucharist and Ministry:* 25th Anniversary Printing (Geneva: WCC Publications, 2007), Faith and Order Paper 111, pp. vii-viii. This document has also generated the six volumes of M. Thurian, ed., *Churches Respond to BEM: Official Responses to the "Baptism, Eucharist and Ministry" Text,* vols. 1-6; Faith and Order Papers 129, 132, 135, 137, 143, and 144 (Geneva: WCC, 1986-88); and occasioned two other volumes: *Baptism, Eucharist and Ministry 1982-1990: Report on the Process and Responses,* Faith and Order Paper 149 (Geneva: WCC, 1990); and Thomas F. Best and Tamara Grdzelidze, ed., *BEM at 25: Critical Insights into a Continuing Legacy,* Faith and Order Paper 205 (Geneva: WCC Publications, 2007).

12. *Church and World: The Unity of the Church and the Renewal of the Human Community,* Faith and Order Paper 151 (Geneva: WCC Publications, 1990).

13. *Confessing the One Faith: An Ecumenical Explication of the Apostolic Faith as It Is Confessed in the Nicene-Constantinopolitan Creed (381),* Faith and Order Paper 153 (Geneva: WCC Publications, 1991).

sacraments, ministry, and service are too deep for such a loose unity. Moreover, the series of statements from New Delhi through Nairobi and Canberra to Porto Alegre expresses a genuine progression, filling out a vision of church that includes some profound common ecclesiological convictions. If one were to compare Porto Alegre's "Called to Be the One Church" of 2006 with Toronto's "The Church, the Churches and the World Council of Churches" of 1950, one can see how the Faith and Order dialogue on unity has gradually allowed the churches to speak with serenity about issues that fifty years ago were a source of great tension and even to arrive at a considerable degree of convergence on some ecclesiological themes. For its part, Catholic ecclesiology in the last fifty years has affirmed with repeated and growing emphasis that the church is a communion of disciples who believe the same faith, celebrate their sharing in the life of God sacramentally and liturgically, and dedicate themselves to service both within and without the Christian community so as to cooperate in bringing about God's design for the human family through proclaiming the gospel and promoting the values of the Kingdom. The three basic elements of faith, worship, and service are well integrated into the unity statements of the general assemblies of the WCC, statements prepared by Faith and Order. They are thus one of its important achievements, from a Catholic perspective.

I have already mentioned the remarkable success of *Baptism, Eucharist and Ministry* in generating a very wide discussion of the issues it treated. But, of course, if it is honest, such a wide discussion will reflect the differences and contradictory convictions that currently divide Christian communities. The responses verified this. At the same time, however, *BEM* opens several doors that offer hope for eventual convergence and reconciliation. For example, the way in which the section on baptism speaks about the relation of individual faith to the faith of the community and about the lifelong process of Christian formation reconfigures the discussion of disagreements about the baptism of infants and adults. Commonly shared insights in *BEM* about the biblical meaning of "memorial" *(anamnēsis)* and the invocation of the Holy Spirit *(epiclesis)* have given a new framework for considering the real presence of the risen Christ in the eucharist and the relationship of its celebration to the unique sacrifice of Jesus on Calvary. Finally, *BEM* situates a necessary and biblically founded ministry of oversight or *episkopē* within the active engagement of the whole priestly people of

God in the life of the community and qualifies that ministry as personal, collegial, and communal. Most responses seem to accept these affirmations about ministry. As such, they provide a new common framework for addressing points that have proved divisive in the past. Obviously, on none of these issues has *BEM* achieved full consensus. Nevertheless, the wide and generally positive reception of *BEM* has made it a platform from which further convergence can be sought.

Church and World does several very important things from a Catholic perspective. First of all, it relates the nature and mission of the church to the kingdom of God. It would be very interesting to compare this document with Vatican II's *Gaudium et spes,* with John Paul II's *Redemptoris missio,* and with a number of the synodal or papal writings about the church's responsibility in the areas of justice, peace, and the protection of the environment. Second, a key ecclesiological concept woven into this study document was that of the church as "mystery" and "prophetic sign." Perhaps a sample of this regrettably little-known text would not be out of place:

> As the body of Christ, the church participates in the divine mystery. As mystery, it reveals Christ to the world by proclaiming the gospel, by celebrating the sacraments (which are themselves called "mysteries"), and by manifesting the newness of life given by him, thus anticipating the kingdom already present in him. . . . [A]ll talk of the church as "sign" is possible only if it is directly connected with the "mystery" of Christ, the "mystery revealed" (cf. Col. 1:26-27) of God's saving purpose to unite all things and people in Christ through the preaching of the gospel and the response to it (cf. Eph. 1:10, 3:5). It is Christ, present and active in the church through the Holy Spirit, who makes the church through its life, witness and service a sign of judgment and salvation to all humankind.[14]

Language about mystery and sign is the natural ambiance for a theology of sacraments. In *Church and World* such language is being applied to the community as a whole. From a Catholic point of view, a sacramental understanding of the church is of central importance, as is clear from the first chapter of *Lumen gentium* — "The Mystery of the Church" — and its first paragraph: "the Church is like a sacrament, that is, a sign and instrument of communion with God and of unity

14. *Church and World,* paragraphs 21 and 31, pages 27 and 30.

among all human beings" (*LG* 1). Finally, directly addressing the relation of women and men in society and within the Christian community gave *Church and World* occasion to present Mary, the mother of Jesus, as a model of discipleship.

As a Catholic commentator I would like to recall merely two among the many achievements of *Confessing the One Faith*. First, it proves the presence of a remarkable harmony among Christians regarding the heart of the faith as expressed in the creeds and professed today by the vast majority of believers. The creeds are widely understood as products of the tradition, which developed in relation to the sacraments of Christian initiation. The methodology of *Confessing the One Faith* opted to look back to the Bible in order to show the rootedness of each article of the creed in scripture and to look to the present to attempt a contemporary, credible explanation written by theologians from various still-divided ecclesial communities. The first step — looking back to scripture — demonstrates the fundamental harmony between scripture and tradition (the creeds being products of tradition) as well as the fact that we are not divided on the foundations of the Christian faith. One of the more important Catholic teachings pertinent to ecumenism is Vatican II's affirmation of a hierarchy of truths; all Christian doctrine is organically related to the foundations of Christian faith. *Confessing the One Faith* shows that there is substantial consensus about these foundations. Secondly, the attempt to address our contemporaries together, even in our currently divided state, in a way that could show the relevance and meaning of traditional Christian beliefs for the existential questions that face human beings today, underlines forcefully the common mission that we all share even now. Ecumenism began among missionaries one hundred years ago in Edinburgh. *Confessing the One Faith* is a missionary and catechetical document. It is less a document to be "received" so as to foster unity among churches than a document to be "used" so as to form old and new believers in the relevance of faith for people today.

4. Into the Future

Günther Gassmann's *Documentary History* ends in 1993, on the eve of the Fifth World Conference, held in Santiago de Compostela. John Paul II had a high estimation of that World Conference, whose theme was "Towards Koinonia in Faith, Life and Witness."[15] Santiago set the direction that the commission has pursued since then, and because the new phase of the work of Faith and Order is still in the process of unfolding it is perhaps too early yet to talk of achievements.[16] Three plenary commission meetings at Moshi, Tanzania (1996), Kuala Lumpur, Malaysia (2004), and Kolympari, Crete (2009) each assessed and promoted work on a range of ongoing studies. Probably it is fair to say that ecclesiology has been the principal unifying theme in the recent work of Faith and Order. The plenary meeting held in Crete from October 6 to 14, 2009, may serve to illustrate this. It was structured so as to maximize the input of the 120 plenary commission members on its current projects concerning the three themes of (1) the nature and mission of the church, (2) the authority of tradition, especially patristic literature, within the church, and (3) moral discernment in the church. From a Catholic point of view, all three of these topics are of great significance for the reestablishment of full communion.

In particular, the Pontifical Council for Promoting Christian Unity responded in a very thorough way to requests by Faith and Order for contributions to its ongoing ecclesiology work. Earlier, the carefully produced Catholic response to *BEM* had already called upon Faith and Order to give special attention to three broad ecclesiological themes: sacrament/sacramentality, authority, and tradition. The commission's current work on ecclesiology is clearly seeking to do this. Moreover, Santiago de Compostela's "Report of Section II" had signaled that multilateral dialogue had reached a point of maturity such that the topic of a ministry in service to the universal unity of the church — what Catholics refer to as the Petrine or primatial ministry — could now be taken up.[17] Pope John Paul was attentive to that signal and opened his beautiful and humble nine-paragraph exposition in *Ut unum sint* of his ministry as Bishop of Rome with an acknowledgment

---

15. J. A. Radano, "Pope John Paul II's Reflection on the Fifth World Conference on Faith and Order," *Midstream* 33 (1994): 463-70. See also J. A. Radano, "The Catholic Church, Faith and Order, and BEM," pp. 5-6. The official report of this conference appeared as T. F. Best and G. Gassmann, eds., *On the Way to Fuller Koinonia: Santiago de Compostela 1993*, Faith and Order Paper 166 (Geneva: WCC Publications, 1994).

16. This estimation, however, is not meant to take anything away from the fine work on tradition and hermeneutics already produced in *A Treasure in Earthen Vessels* of 1998.

17. See *WCFO5*, p. 243.

of Faith and Order's willingness to discuss the primacy.[18] The latest version of the ecclesiological study does in fact take up the question of the primatial ministry within the context of the conciliarity and synodality of the church as a whole and of the ministry of *episkopē* as personal, collegial, and communal. From a Catholic point of view these are very promising developments.

The principal achievements celebrated at the Fifth World Conference on Faith and Order in 1993 and that were commented upon above, following Gassmann's four-point outline, can each be integrated into the current work on ecclesiology. It has already been said that *BEM* lives on in the ecclesiology project.[19] The same should happen with the unity statements of the general assemblies and with the study documents *Church and World* and *Confessing the One Faith*. These materials, along with the responses to *The Nature and Mission of the Church* and the current efforts by the Faith and Order commission to develop that statement in light of those responses, give reason to hope that important work can still be done in seeking more convergence and even consensus in this crucial ecumenical area of ecclesiology.

At the first plenary meeting of that Pontifical Council for Promoting Christian Unity that took place after the publication of BEM, Cardinal Johannes Willebrands took the occasion "to acknowledge the work of the Holy Spirit and give thanks for it" and "to realize the complexity of the task and the need for the Catholic Church through her theologians to take a full part in this common search for unity."[20] He added that, from a Catholic perspective, the success of the World Council of Churches in achieving its aim of calling the churches to visible unity will depend largely upon the importance given to its Faith and Order Commission. On the occasion of the fortieth anniversary of the WCC in 1988, Cardinal Willebrands noted: "In my opinion, the World Council of Churches [needs] to study once again the nature and meaning of what the Church is, the meaning of the 'communio' *(koinonia)* between the Churches, both in the communion of faith and sacraments and in the institution as it has evolved in the theological

---

18. See *UUS*, nos. 88-96, for John Paul's description of his primatial ministry and invitation to other Christians to dialogue about the form of its exercise; the citation of Santiago is in no. 89, footnote 148.

19. See H. E. Metropolitan Vasilios and T. F. Best, "Introduction," *BEM*, p. viii; and J. A. Radano, "The Catholic Church, Faith and Order, and BEM," pp. 13-14.

20. Text reprinted in *IS* 101 (1999/II-III): 129.

discussion."[21] It seems to me that Faith and Order has focused precisely on these issues ever since Santiago in 1993.

The ultimate aim of Faith and Order — visible unity — has, of course, not been achieved. But we have come a long way from Lausanne. At a formal level, Faith and Order has achieved a sustained multilateral theological dialogue involving the participation of a very wide constituency. It has touched the lives of the majority of Christian communities for the better and has drawn them closer to one another. It has shifted the method of dialogue from comparison to convergence and consensus on the basis of the Word of God. On specific doctrinal issues, Faith and Order has achieved a significant breakthrough on the inseparability of scripture and tradition; it has progressively fleshed out the fundamental ecclesial elements of communion in the statements it has developed for the WCC general assemblies; it has provided a new field of play where common ground can contextualize further dialogue about divisive issues regarding baptism, eucharist, and ministry; it has situated the Christian social commitment within the context of the kingdom of God and proposed the church as a mystery and prophetic sign of the Kingdom; it has illustrated the harmony of scripture and tradition in its exposition of the creed and provided thereby a credible tool for the common mission of proclaiming the truth of the gospel to people of today. These may not yet constitute the ultimate achievement hoped for — something that is really the work of the Holy Spirit in the hearts of the people and their ministers. But, from a Catholic perspective, these achievements are certainly important steps along the way. Moreover, the current course, as illustrated in the three themes currently being explored by the Faith and Order Commission, is, from a Catholic point of view, right on target.

We have not yet arrived at the goal of full communion. But looking at the achievements of Faith and Order, I believe that we have every right to join our brothers and sisters who, one hundred years ago at Edinburgh, when the voice vote to establish a continuation committee resulted in a thunderous acclamation to the call for "ayes" and total silence to the call for "nays," spontaneously rose to their feet and began to sing the hymn known affectionately as "The Old Hundredth" — "Praise God from Whom All Blessings Flow." These words of praise and

---

21. J. Willebrands, "40 Years of the World Council of Churches," in *IS* 70 (1989/II): 64-65.

thanks to God reflect what may rightly be called the Catholic estimation of the achievements of Faith and Order. These achievements are blessings from the God who is the principal architect of the unity of the church; they inspire hope because they are fruits of the Holy Spirit, the principle of the church's unity; and they reinforce the irrevocable Catholic commitment to participate fully in the work of seeking the unity for which Jesus Christ prayed. Catholics thank God for the good that has been achieved through Faith and Order and look forward in hopeful anticipation to what yet may be accomplished.

II Achievements of International Bilateral Dialogue following the Second Vatican Council

[T]he ultimate purpose of all bilateral dialogues is not theological consensus merely for the sake of theological consensus or general agreement, but theological consensus for the sake of church unity.

Harding Meyer and Lukas Vischer, Introduction to
*Growth and Agreement: Reports and Agreed Statements of
Ecumenical Conversations on a World Level,* 1984

5 Lutheran–Roman Catholic World-Level Dialogue: Selected Remarks

Jared Wicks, SJ

The Appendix at the end of this essay begins by listing ten documents produced by world-level Lutheran-Catholic dialogue commissions in over forty years of work. I hope to convey fresh perspectives on these texts by going back to consider the basis and background of the dialogue, before treating the *Joint Declaration on the Doctrine of Justification* of 1999 (= *JDDJ*), and then offering considerations on key parts of the recent work of the world-level dialogue, "The Apostolicity of the Church," completed in 2006.

1. Foundation and Initial Proposal of a Lutheran–Catholic World-Level Dialogue

In mid-1964, before Vatican II's third working period, the revised draft of the dogmatic schema *De ecclesia* listed in no. 15 the "elements" of sanctification and truth shared in common by the Catholic Church and other Christians. The elements include Holy Scripture as the norm of belief and life, apostolic zeal, faith in God and in Christ as Son of God and Savior, and baptism, by which Christians, both Catholics and others, are united with Christ. At this point, a new phrase had been inserted into the mid-1964 draft about believers in the non-Catholic bodies, namely, that ". . . they acknowledge and receive other sacraments *in their own churches or ecclesiastical communities.*" This statement gained the approval of the Vatican II full assembly in the votes of the third period in autumn 1964, with the result that this acknowledgment of the separated churches and communities is part of the Dogmatic Constitution *Lumen gentium,* promulgated by Pope Paul VI on November 21, 1964.

Before the bishops voted on the text in autumn 1964, it came to them in a booklet that also gave the Doctrinal Commission's *Relatio,* explaining the modifications over the previous draft that the bishops had discussed in 1963. On no. 15, this explanation listed several inter-ventions by Council members who called for adding a reference to the ecclesial venue in which the elements become formative of individual and communal Christian life, prayer, and service. This then was done to show that the elements affect not only individual Christians but also communities that cherish and celebrate them. The Commission also said that here one has what is the principle of the ecumenical move-ment *(principium motionis oecumenicae).*[1] Thus, Catholic dogmatic eccle-siology grounds the church's ecumenical engagement with Lutherans and others in the recognition that their communities take scripture and creedal dogmas as normative and these communities administer to their members the sacramental means of saving grace.

I note in this connection that the same *Relatio* of the Doctrinal Commission made no major claim, comparable to its evaluation of the insertion in no. 15, about the term "subsists in," which entered the draft *De ecclesia* in no. 8 at the same time that no. 15 on the "elements" was revised in recognition of the communities. No. 8 says that the church of Christ *subsists in* the Catholic Church, although several of the elements are present elsewhere. Explaining this, the Commission's *Relatio* says simply that "subsists in" has replaced the earlier wording *(est),* in order to fit better with recognition of the elements in other bodies (as no. 15 lists them).[2] This suggests that the interpreters who

---

1. *Acta synodalia,* III/1, 204. This was not totally new in the *Relatio* of mid-1964. The earlier 1963 schema had also treated the elements or *vincula* which constitute connec-tions between non-Catholic Christians and the Catholic Church in no. 9. Gérard Philips, the lead drafter, wrote in his explanation for the bishops of the 1963 text that recognition of the elements is the *"fundamentum theologicum Oecumenismi."* AS II/1, 231.

2. The *Relatio* on no. 8 is given in *Acta synodalia,* III/1, 177, commenting on the text given on p. 167. In the work of the Doctrinal Commission on no. 8, *"subsistit in"* entered the text on November 26, 1963, at the suggestion of Fr. Sebastian Tromp, the Commis-sion Secretary. This occurred at a plenary meeting of the Commission, at which the subcommission for revision of chapter 1 presented the results of its work, during which the *"est"* of simple identity between the Church of Christ and the Catholic Church had already been changed to *"adest in"* to take better account of the elements of the church present in other bodies. At the November 26 Commission meeting, the *peritus* Heribert

have recently debated the meaning of "subsists in" have dealt with what was only a minor adjustment of *De ecclesia.* The Doctrinal Commission did not even offer a particular account of "subsists in" in its *Relatio,* but let stand what had been prepared to explain the intermediate formulation, "is present in" *(adest in),* even though this had given way to "subsists in."[3] The latter formulation is not the basis of ecumenism in the Catholic Church. The foundation lies instead in the modification made in the mid-1964 text of no. 15, a change that recognizes the significance of the separated Christian bodies in which members receive the elements that foster truth in faith and holiness of heart and living. This is the reason for the intensive engagement of the Catholic Church in the bilateral dialogues.

Another event of 1964 was significant for our topic. The Vatican II observer Prof. George Lindbeck, representing the Lutheran World Federation (LWF), was proposing to the Federation that, in concert with the Secretariat for Promoting Christian Unity (SPCU), the Federation should undertake a dialogue with the Catholic Church. Exchanges at Vatican II between the observers and the members and theologians of the Secretariat had been so profitable that they should continue in a structured way after publication of the Council's documents. Lindbeck showed his proposal to the SPCU Secretary, Msgr. Johannes Willebrands, on June 11, 1964, who wrote telegraphically in his diary, "Visit to the Secretariat by G. Lindbeck. His report on the topic of further evolution of dialogue. A very interesting conversation."[4]

The world-level dialogue, first proposed by Lindbeck, took its initial shape through meetings in 1965 and 1966 of an LWF-SPCU planning commission and then began its first phase in 1967, proving to be

---

Schauf raised an objection to *"adest in,"* since he preferred the earlier *"est."* In response, Tromp proposed *"subsistit in,"* which was quickly inserted without any discussion. Since the change was made so quickly, theological scholarship has only a minimal objective basis in the records of Vatican II for interpreting *"subsistit in,"* which is why interpretations of the term differ so widely. The development of this passage of *Lumen gentium* is presented by Alexandra von Teufenbach, in *Die Bedeutung des* subsistit in *(LG 8). Zum Selbstverständnis der katholischen Kirche* (Munich: H. Utz Verlag, 2002), pp. 375-88.

3. A. von Teufenbach, *Die Bedeutung des* subsistit in *(LG 8),* p. 389. The explanation refers clearly to the "elements": *"dicitur 'subsistit in', ut expressio melius concordat cum affirmatione de elementis ecclesialibus quae alibi adsunt"* (Acta synodalia, III/1, 177).

4. *Les agendas conciliaires de Mgr. J. Willebrands, Secrétaire du Sécretariat pour l'Unité des Chrétiens,* ed. and trans. Leo Declerck (Leuven: Maurits Sabbebibliotheek & Peeters, 2009), p. 131.

remarkably fruitful, as is shown by the catalogue given below of the
Lutheran-Catholic documents.

2. The Singular Status of the *Joint Declaration on the Doctrine of Justification (JDDJ)*

Our Appendix of Lutheran-Catholic dialogue documents gives first the
texts worked out by world-level commissions. These extend from "The
Gospel and the Church" of 1972 to the study-document "The Apostolicity of the Church," completed in 2006. Further on, the Appendix lists
the texts of Lutheran-Catholic dialogue in particular locales. These extend from "The Status of the Nicene Creed as Dogma of the Church," a
work of 1965 in the United States, to the Swedish-Finnish study *Justification in the Life of the Church,* completed in 2009. But the catalogue highlights with bold characters the *JDDJ,* because of its singular standing
amid all these reports and statements. The *JDDJ* is singular because of
its high level of official reception by the churches, expressed when it
was formally signed on behalf of the churches in Augsburg on Reformation Sunday 1999.

The status of the documents other than the *JDDJ* was clarified in
1971. At that time Cardinal Willebrands, President of the SPCU, and
Pope Paul VI had to make a decision about two dialogue documents
then being finalized, namely, the Anglican–Roman Catholic International Commission I's Windsor Statement on Eucharistic Doctrine
and the Lutheran-Catholic Commission's "The Gospel and the
Church." Their decision was to permit publication of the studies, while
clearly stating that the churches were not officially approving and receiving the contents. The partners agreed to this, and so the first
Lutheran-Catholic statement

> is being offered to the churches with a recommendation for thor-
> ough study. It is hoped that the work of the Study Commission will
> contribute to further clarification and improvement of relation-
> ships between the Lutheran churches and the Roman Catholic
> Church. This report has no binding character for the churches.[5]

5. Preface to "The Gospel and the Church," co-signed February 8, 1972, by André
Appel, General Secretary of the LWF, and Jan Willebrands, President of the SPCU, *GA,*

This same withholding of official approval, along with the denial of "binding character," affects the standing of all the documents I have catalogued below — with the huge exception of the *JDDJ*. All the other documents are, in truth, study documents, even if they do not say this in their self-designation.[6] But the *JDDJ* is not affected by this reservation, for it has become a text *of* the churches, and among Catholics it has even entered the body of texts of reference in theological education.[7]

3. Major Ecumenical Gains in the *JDDJ*

Beyond its official character, I believe that its content gives the *JDDJ* "landmark status" in the long ecumenical effort that began a century ago at the 1910 Edinburgh Conference on World Mission. I would place the *Joint Declaration* alongside three other brief but theologically weighty statements of this century of ecumenism. These are:

- The World Council's Basis (1948, 1961) as "a fellowship of churches which confess the Lord Jesus Christ as God and Savior according to the scriptures and therefore seek to fulfill their common calling to the glory of one God, Father, Son and Holy Spirit."
- Vatican II, Decree on Ecumenism, *Unitatis redintegratio* (1964), which had a climate-changing impact on both the Catholic Church and the wider ecumenical movement.

---

p. 168. Similarly, ARCIC's Windsor Statement is being presented to the Anglican and Catholic authorities, "but obviously it cannot be ratified by them until such time as our respective Churches can evaluate its conclusions." *GA,* p. 68.

6. The recent work to be presented below, "The Apostolicity of the Church" (2006), is thus not innovating in its subtitle "Study Document of the Lutheran–Roman Catholic Commission on Unity." It is only making explicit what is true of the other texts of this dialogue, but is not true of the *JDDJ*.

7. *JDDJ* nos. 15-41 are now included in J. Neuner and J. Dupuis, eds., *The Christian Faith in the Doctrinal Documents of the Catholic Church,* 7th edition (Bangalore: Theological Publications in India, 2000, and New York: Alba House, 2001), pp. 844-52 (in ch. 19, "The Life of Grace"). In addition, the "Official Common Statement" signed on October 31, 1999, is given on p. 413 (in ch. 9, "The Church and the Churches"). Also, nos. 14-18 of the *JDDJ* is now in the German "Denzinger," *Enchiridion Symbolorum,* 40th edition, ed. Peter Hünnermann (Freiburg: Herder, 2009), nos. 5073-74, with the *JDDJ*'s "Gemeinsame Offizielle Feststellung" also given as no. 5081.

- WCC Commission on Faith and Order, *Baptism, Eucharist and Ministry* (1982), which engaged a large number of churches in a fundamental clarification of their doctrine, worship, and life.

The *JDDJ*, now affirmed officially by the Catholic Church, the Lutheran World Federation, and the World Methodist Council, will, I suggest, rank with such major texts, because it unites Christians precisely at a point where longstanding controversy and division had reigned for centuries. But the three ecclesial bodies are now one, without reservation, on three tenets that the *Declaration* makes explicit in nos. 14-18, making up its all-important Part 3, "The Common Understanding of Justification." (1) The three bodies together hold that justification is the work of the triune God, based on the incarnation, death, and resurrection of Christ (no. 15). (2) They confess together, "By grace alone, in faith in Christ's saving work and not because of any merit on our part, we are accepted by God and receive the Holy Spirit, who renews our hearts while equipping and calling us to good works" (no. 15). And (3) they share "the conviction that the message of justification directs us in a special way toward the heart of the New Testament witness to God's saving action in Christ" (no. 17). This profession and witness of *JDDJ* Part 3 give to Catholics, Lutherans, and Methodists a profound enrichment of their life in the Lord. Such a text is surely a theological landmark of the first century of ecumenical engagement — a text of obligatory reference in Western ecumenical efforts.

Beyond these substantive agreements in central doctrines, the *JDDJ*'s Part 4, "Explicating the Common Understanding of Justification," offers an exemplary lesson on working through a set of particular doctrines, which seem to make the churches quite different in their teaching, in order to show through careful study that the differences do not in fact have the divisive impact generally ascribed to them.

The singular importance of the *JDDJ* receives confirmation in *Harvesting the Fruits*, published by Cardinal Walter Kasper in 2009 after intensive work in the Pontifical Council for Promoting Christian Unity.[8] Chapter 2 of *Harvesting*, on "Salvation, Justification, Sanctifica-

---

8. W. Kasper, *Harvesting the Fruits: Aspects of Christian Faith in Ecumenical Dialogue* (London and New York: Continuum, 2009). I introduced this work in "*Harvesting the Fruits*: Taking Stock of Catholic-Reformation Dialogues and Charting New Directions," *Ecumenical Trends* 39, no. 11 (November 2010): 5-8 and 11.

tion," takes the *JDDJ* as its initial source for showing "essential points" of the basic consensus on justification now existing between Catholics, Lutherans, and Methodists, the signatories of the *JDDJ*, and which is further attested in documents of the Catholic-Reformed and Catholic-Anglican dialogues. *Harvesting* calls the *JDDJ* both "an important step on the road to full communion" and "a milestone in ecumenical relations."[9] Reflection on this agreement also points the way to further issues our dialogues have to face, the most urgent of which is that of Christian moral practice, e.g., of sexuality and marriage, as the fruit of justification.[10]

4. The Vatican II Basis of the *JDDJ*

Now for three particular observations on the *JDDJ*, starting with an indication of how it rests, in an important aspect, on the teaching of the Second Vatican Council.

Among the particular doctrinal solutions offered in *JDDJ*, Part 4 treats the long-controverted issue of "assurance of salvation" in nos. 34-36. The shared confession is that the faithful can rely on the mercy and promises of God (34). What is specifically Lutheran is to insist that believers not look to themselves but "solely to Christ and trust solely in him" — with full assurance (35). Catholics do not speak this way, but they do hold, in accord with Vatican II, that "to have faith is to entrust oneself totally to God, who liberates us from the darkness of sin and death and awakens us to eternal life." Here, for Catholics, Vatican II's Constitution on Revelation, *Dei verbum* (DV), proves to be part of the solution of a serious ecumenical problem.[11]

The passage from DV 4, on God's liberating work leading to eternal life, is central to Vatican II's revision of what the First Vatican Council of 1870 had said on God's revelation. Vatican I stated that God has made known, for our instruction in faith, "himself and the eternal decrees of his will," doing this in a supernatural manner exceeding the reach of our reason. Here Vatican I gave a quite terse account of the

9. Kasper, *Harvesting the Fruits,* pp. 44-45.

10. Kasper, *Harvesting the Fruits,* pp. 46 and 203.

11. English translations of the *JDDJ*, note 20 (e.g., Eerdmans edition, p. 24), should be corrected to refer not to DV 5 on faith, but to DV 4 on Christ's revelation of God as our liberating savior from sin and death.

content of revelation, namely, God's self and his will's decrees.[12] But Vatican II transformed this in *Dei verbum* by attending to revelation in salvation history, to revelation as christocentric, and, especially, to revelation as focused in its soteriological content.[13] This Vatican II account of God's word to humans provides an essential conviction for Catholics that advances notably their agreement with Lutherans, with whom they confess together Christ as their salvation, as in *JDDJ,* no. 15.

5. Justification as Criterion:
The Problem and the *JDDJ*'s Solution

One of the "hardest nuts" that had to be cracked in coming to the *JDDJ* concerned the Lutheran conviction that correct teaching on justification is *the* criterion that must be applied critically to all Christian teaching and life.

The 1972 study, "The Gospel and the Church," stated the issue:

> Although a far-reaching agreement in the understanding of the doctrine of justification appears possible, other questions arise here. What is the theological importance of this doctrine? Do both sides similarly evaluate its implications for the life and teaching of the church? According to Lutheran understanding, and on the basis of the confession of justification, *all traditions and institutions of the church are subject to the criterion* which asks whether they are enablers of the proper proclamation of the gospel and so do not obscure the unconditional character of the gift of salvation.[14]

---

12. Vatican Council I, Dogmatic Constitution *Dei Filius,* given in Heinrich Denzinger and Adolf Schönmetzer, eds., *Enchiridion symbolorum, definitionum et declarationum de rebus fidei et morum,* 33rd ed. (Barcelona: Herder, 1965), nos. 3000-45, treating revelation itself in nos. 3004-05, which are given in English in Neuner and Dupuis, eds., *The Christian Faith in the Doctrinal Documents of the Catholic Church* (as in note 7 above), 43 (nos. 113-14).

13. The 2006 study document, "The Apostolicity of the Church," presented in no. 107 the connection of DV, in its major account of revelation in nos. 2-4, and the *JDDJ.* My article, "Toward Vatican II on Revelation — From Behind the Scenes," in *Theological Studies* 71, no. 3 (Sept. 2010): 637-50, tells how Vatican II *periti* such as Pieter Smulders, Joseph Ratzinger, Karl Rahner, and Jean Daniélou went to work early in the Council with the aim of transforming the Catholic account of God's revelation.

14. "The Gospel and the Church," nos. 28-29 (emphasis added). The peculiar ca-

Thus, the correct account of justification serves to delimit what is true and proper throughout the church's teaching and life. It has a critical and restrictive effect across a wide range of topics in the churches.

The U.S. dialogue, "Justification by Faith" (1983), spoke of justification-doctrine from the Lutheran perspective "as a criterion or corrective for all church practices, structures, and theology," adding that "[a]ll aspects of Christian life, worship, and preaching should lead to or flow from justifying faith in this gospel, and anything which opposes or substitutes for trust in God's promises alone should be abolished" (no. 28). But the Catholic side was wary about using one doctrine as a principle whose "abolishing" impact might erode the catholic heritage. "Catholics insist that the gospel cannot be rightly interpreted without drawing on the full resources available within the church" (no. 118). Although the U.S. dialogue did point out certain shared concerns in this matter, it admitted that "some consequences of the different outlooks seem irreconcilable, especially in reference to particular applications of justification by faith as a criterion of all church proclamation and practice" (no. 121).[15]

Naturally, this problematic surfaced in the 1990s during the preparation of the *JDDJ*. The *Declaration*'s formulation became a target of criticism by German Lutheran professors, for example, Eberhard Jüngel, who protested against rendering innocuous the critical function of justification by calling it only *"an* indispensable criterion."[16]

---

reer, in German Protestant academic theology, of the idea of justification-as-criterion is sketched by Risto Saarinen in "Die Rechtfertigungslehre als Kriterium. Zur Begriffsgeschichte einer ökumenischen Redewendung," *Kerygma und Dogma* 44 (1988): 88-103. The term "criterion," regarding justification, does not come directly from the sixteenth-century Lutheran confessional texts, but emerged in the 1930s, in influential interpretations of Luther advanced by Hans Joachim Iwand and Ernst Wolf.

15. Illustrative of this Catholic insistence is the paper of Carl J. Peter from the years of work on "Justification by Faith," "Justification by Faith and the Need of Another Critical Principle," *Justification by Faith*, ed. Paul Empie, T. Austin Murphy, and Joseph A. Burgess (Minneapolis: Augsburg, 1985), pp. 304-15, 376-78. The biography of Avery Dulles takes us behind the scenes of the U.S. Lutheran-Catholic dialogue from 1971 to 1996, with details on the round treating justification. Patrick W. Carey, *Avery Cardinal Dulles: Model Theologian* (New York and Mahwah, NJ: Paulist, 2010), pp. 349-90, especially 364-73 on the dialogue on justification by faith.

16. E. Jüngel, "Um Gottes willen — Klarheit! Kritische Bemerkungen zur Verharmlosung der kriteriologischen Funktion des Rechtfertigungsartikels — aus Anlaß einer ökumenischen 'Gemeinsame Erklärung zur Rechtfertigungslehre,'" *Zeitschrift für*

The *JDDJ* states in no. 18 the Catholic-Lutheran agreement that the doctrine of justification "is more than just one part of Christian doctrine. It stands in an essential relation to all truths of faith. . . . It is an indispensable criterion that constantly serves to orient all the teaching and practices of our churches to Christ." On this Lutherans and Catholics agree, but the accents remain different, as the text continues. However, the different outlooks or approaches are, most importantly, not exclusive of each other:

> When Lutherans emphasize the unique significance of this criterion, they do not deny the interrelation and significance of all truths of faith.

> When Catholics see themselves as bound by several criteria, they do not deny the special function of the message of justification.

Here is movement toward reconciling a difference, for the dialogue has brought out certain considerations that had been quietly presupposed on both sides, but only through ecumenical conversation and exchange have become explicit ("they do not deny"). The effect is to qualify bare statements of positions ("unique significance"/"several criteria"). Both positions are richer than short formulae give one to understand, for the partners have come to discover, in the movement of dialogue, that neither of them denies outright the relevant central concern of the other. The fears caused by all-too-simple formulations should be allayed. Furthermore, *JDDJ* 18 continues:

> Lutherans and Catholics share the goal of confessing Christ in all things, who alone is to be trusted above all things as the one Mediator (1 Tim. 2:5) through whom God in the Holy Spirit gives himself and pours out his renewing gifts.

Still, a difference remains between "the unique significance" that justification has as *the* supreme criterion and critical norm for Lutherans, and a "special function" among "several criteria" that Catholics envisage when they use the potent term "criterion." A real difference

---

Theologie und Kirche 94 (1997): 394-406. Not only was the indefinite article problematic, but also the term "indispensable" (German, *unverzichtbar*), since for Jüngel it makes no sense to speak of a "dispensable" criterion when the issue is the truth or authenticity of a position or reality.

has been, it seems, only partially reconciled.[17] But we have also to add that, most likely, this is not a church-dividing difference. Nonetheless, we have here a remaining issue, which is also a point that both Lutheran and Catholic opponents of the *JDDJ* can raise in framing their objections.[18]

6. Beyond the *JDDJ*: Do Binding Norms Shape Moral Living in the Grace of Justification?

I will return below to the criterion-issue, but only after one more consideration relevant to the *JDDJ*. This concerns the question whether Lutherans and Catholics agree in holding, beyond their consensus on the unmerited gift of justification, that they are bound to transmit in catechesis a biblically based "moral corpus" that states norms of living that have an imperative character in shaping the lives of persons justified gratuitously through Christ.[19]

Raising this question is not to posit observance of the law as a condition for receiving forgiveness of sins, reconciliation and communion with God, being a new creation, and the Holy Spirit's renewal of heart for good works, as *JDDJ* describes justification from the New Testament

17. *Harvesting the Fruits* speaks of an "ongoing tension" arising from *JDDJ* 18 and of possible misinterpretations of what it states (pp. 45-46).

18. Such opponents, to be sure, must also deal with recent scholarly treatments of justification-doctrine as "criterion," such as André Birmilé's *La communion ecclésiale. Progrès oecuménique et enjeux méthologiques* (Paris: Éditions du Cerf, and Geneva: Labor et Fides, 2000), pp. 140-49 and 192-221. The Munich *Habilitationsschrift* of Birgitta Kleinschwärzer-Meister is an ample (643-page) study of *JDDJ* 18, *In allem auf Christus hin. Zur theologischen Funktion der Rechtfertigungslehre* (Freiburg: Herder, 2007).

19. The existence of a body of such norms mediated ecclesially, based on the Council of Trent, is affirmed by Pieter De Witte in "Doctrine, Dynamic and Difference: A Critical Study of the Emergence of a Differentiated Consensus between Lutherans and Roman Catholics on the Doctrine of Justification and of Its Official Reception in the *Joint Declaration*" (Ph.D. diss., Catholic University of Leuven, 2010), pp. 89-90.

It is also obvious that the Catholic magisterium of official teaching takes responsibility for articulating and further specifying moral norms of individual and social practice. A dialogue on this topic would clearly draw as well on classic Lutheran sources, such as Luther's catechisms. At the world level, only one bilateral ecumenical dialogue has treated moral matters, namely "Life in Christ: Morals, Communion and the Church," of 1993 by the Anglican-Roman Catholic International Commission (ARCIC II), given in *GA II*, pp. 344-70.

in nos. 8-11. God gives these gratuitously. Rather the issue concerns the "good works," or their opposite, which justified and reborn persons must observe or avoid. I am suggesting the need of dialogue on how Lutherans and Catholics understand and practice, especially in their catechesis, what *JDDJ* indicates, also from the New Testament, about the justified having to "be exhorted to live righteously in accord with the will of God" (no. 12). More specifically, we have to clarify whether we hold and teach norms of "living righteously" which Scripture and our churches' doctrinal traditions give to us as binding in positive and negative norms. If a "moral corpus" has in fact come from these sources, then we need a further Lutheran-Catholic dialogue about the "post-justification" behavior of those whom God renews in their hearts and calls to good works (cf. *JDDJ*, 15, central common confession).[20]

7. A First Report on "The Apostolicity of the Church" (2006)

I pass on now to present several considerations based on the work of the fifth phase of the world-level dialogue that produced in 2006 the study-document "The Apostolicity of the Church."[21] The self-description as a "study document," as I showed above, does not give it a lower status than its predecessor texts of world-level Lutheran-Catholic commissions, but only makes explicit what is true of all of these commission texts, except of course the officially adopted *JDDJ*.

"The Apostolicity of the Church" is singular in its length, with its four Parts extending through no fewer than 463 numbered paragraphs. One reason for this length is the inclusion *in* the text itself, and not in appended papers, of extended exegetical and historical expositions. For example, Part 1 gives the "New Testament Foundations" of apostolicity

20. The recently completed dialogue in Sweden and Finland, "Justification in the Life of the Church," in the midst of its treatment of "The New Life of the Baptized Person," pp. 67-73 (nos. 189-208), does speak of the justified person as now "able to will that which is God's will," on p. 70 (no. 196), but does not take up what might be the next question, that is, just how God's will for our behavior is communicated in the church. Cardinal W. Kasper states the need for further dialogue on ethics and its anthropological basis in *Harvesting the Fruits,* pp. 46 and 203.

21. The study came out in English as a book from Lutheran University Press of Minneapolis and in German as *Die Apostolizität der Kirche* (Paderborn: Bonifatius, and Frankfurt am Main: Otto Lembeck, 2009). Both the English and German versions come from the Commission and are both official texts of the Commission.

in sixty-four paragraphs of careful exegesis, which Parts 2, 3, and 4 complement by further sections of "Biblical Orientations" (sections 2.2, 3.2, and 4.2), comprising a further thirty-nine paragraphs of biblical exposition on specific components of apostolicity. The study also lays out early and medieval developments on the ordained ministry (nos. 184-93) and on the rule of faith, creeds, the biblical canon, councils, and tradition (nos. 314-54). The Commission accepted these texts from its drafters, but did not examine them critically in their details, so as to arrive at a declaration of consensus. It simply agreed to include these passages as competently written parts of the study-document. Similarly, nos. 355-89 cover the Lutheran development, beginning amid early Reformation controversy, of standards and instances of true teaching. The section worked out by the drafters gives accounts from Luther on scripture interpretation and the ministry of teaching, which most Commission members found enlightening in its details and promising in clarifying aspects of Lutheran church life. But again, the Commission trusted the accuracy of the account without a concentrated study of its content in view of formally agreeing to its argumentation.

Thus the new study of apostolicity is singular among the dialogue documents by its length and great amount of detailed biblical interpretation and historical presentations of how Catholic and Lutheran doctrine and life have come to their present-day configuration and emphases.[22]

8. The Lutheran Reformation and the Faith-Creating Practices of Church Life

Amid all the contents of "The Apostolicity of the Church," an important section presents the Lutheran position on the criterion of what is authentic in the church. Here the Lutheran position, already treated in the dialogues on justification and in the *JDDJ*, is formulated in a manner not stated earlier. The most recent dialogue treats justification and church life in a manner with which I think Catholics can substantially agree.

We read in the study that Luther understood the church's conti-

---

22. "The Apostolicity of the Church" appears in *Harvesting the Fruits*, in chapter 3 on the church in its section treating the "Sources of Authority in the Church," on pp. 80, 84, 88-89, 95, and 98.

nuity with the apostles as consisting not only in preaching the apostles' message of gratuitous forgiveness and personal renewal, but also "as continuity in practicing baptism, the Lord's Supper, the office of the keys, the call to ministry, public gathering for worship in praise and confession of faith, and the bearing of the cross as Christ's disciples." These are the marks "by which the Holy Spirit creates faith and the church" ("The Apostolicity of the Church," no. 95).[23] Thus, while the correct doctrine of justification was the key part of the Lutheran renewal of preaching and life, the reform was also inclusive of essential elements, ecclesial elements, of the apostolic and catholic heritage.

The apostolicity study explains that the Reformers aimed "to regather the elements of apostolicity around their proper center" (no. 127). The elements are multiple, but with a center which is itself complex and has its own pattern.

> The center is . . . the holy gospel that promises forgiveness and salvation given freely by God's grace, for Christ's sake, received by faith alone. The preached gospel is linked inseparably with baptism and the Lord's Supper in articulating the grace given to believers. For the good news of salvation to be communicated in its depth and saving power, the preached gospel must be joined with the sacraments, along with the ministry of the keys. This is the vital center of the church's life, the central cluster of authentic continuity with the apostles, by which their mission continues. (no. 128)

Other elements concern the church community as socially embodied, with offices and institutions, doctrines, liturgies and church orders, and an ethos and spirituality animated by the message of God's grace (no. 130). A crucial clarification in the midst of this passage is most revealing for a Catholic reader: "The concern here . . . is not reduction through the exclusion of other elements, but the concentration of everything in the community on the central communication of God's life-giving forgiveness" (no. 129).

---

23. Luther describes these practices in his 1539 treatise, *On the Councils and the Church,* calling them the "possessions by which to recognize the Christian holy people remaining on earth" and "the true seven principal parts of the great holy possession whereby the Holy Spirit effects in us a daily sanctification and vivification in Christ." *Luther's Works,* 41, 148-66. A work of 1541, *Against Hanswurst,* gave a similar list of essential Christian practices (194-99).

Justification as "criterion" is therefore not only critical and potentially erosive of the heritage, but also constructive in giving a shape
and pattern to ecclesial life. This concern for communal life centered
on the gospel was, I think, largely absent in the academic arguments
over the *JDDJ*. But now the apostolicity study has drawn on later works
of Luther to make explicit what for him were the essential instituted
means of conveying to needy and sinful humans the saving graces of
Christ.

Furthermore, this account, drawn from the apostolicity study of
2006, illustrates quite well Vatican II's account of "elements," which I
sketched at the beginning of this paper. Hearing about justification as
a constructive criterion also goes a long way toward calming Catholic
fears that the central Reformation conviction may well erode the catholic heritage. It also opens for Catholics a promising avenue for approaching the coming Reformation commemorations of 2017 with new
appreciation.

9. Catholics and Lutherans Acknowledging
Each Other's Ecclesial Apostolicity

Part 2 of "The Apostolicity of the Church" treats the apostolic gospel
and the church's mark or attribute of apostolicity. After a set of "Biblical Orientations" to this topic in nos. 70-81, a historical section presents in nos. 82-92 the relations between the apostles and the church as
these were expressed and developed from the early church through the
Middle Ages, down to late medieval calls for reform, e.g., in appeals by
Wycliffe and Jan Hus for renewed biblical preaching, in the penitential
message of Savonarola, and the promotion of the New Testament by
Erasmus for the transformation of theology, preaching, and spirituality. A section then relates the reforms of the Lutheran reformation with
its centering of practices on the message of unmerited justification
and its combination of continuity in elements of truth and practice
with critique of perceived deformations (nos. 93-102), followed by a report on the Council of Trent and its aftermath in Catholic life (nos.
103-5).

The important Section 5 of Part 2 describes recent "developments
toward resolution and consensus" among Catholics and Lutherans.

Teachings of Vatican II, e.g., on the many strands of particular traditions making up the Tradition of church life and teaching, laid a basis for considering how separated communities, such as the Lutheran churches, preserve and foster the "elements" of sanctification and truth, which "are not meteorites fallen from heaven into the churches of our time, but have come from Christ through the ministry of his apostles and are components of the apostolic tradition" (no. 121). The ecumenism decree of Vatican II made it explicit that bodies outside the Catholic communion, by their apostolic faith and practices, "have by no means been deprived of significance and importance in the mystery of salvation. For the Spirit of Christ has not refrained from using them as means of salvation . . . (*Unitatis redintegratio,* 3, cited in no. 120). Here is a Catholic recognition of the separated ecclesial communities. This still stands when the acknowledgment is qualified by contrast with the full complement of sacramental and ministerial "elements" of the Catholic Church (no. 122).

Then, an elaborated "ecumenical Lutheran account of apostolicity," developed in nos. 124-43, includes a Lutheran statement on the apostolicity of the Roman Catholic Church (nos. 139-43). On this, just as in the Catholic development, there has been movement, especially in the culminating moment of the signing of the *JDDJ.* The agreement on justification is momentous for the Lutheran outlook on its dialogue partner. It entails a recognition by Lutherans that,

> despite continuing differences, the teaching of the Roman Catholic Church on justification is compatible with faithful proclamation of the good news of Jesus Christ in accord with the apostolic witness. This is for Lutherans the recognition that the basic reality which makes a church apostolic is present in the Roman Catholic Church. (no. 142)

To be sure, this recognition has to be qualified by what Lutherans perceive, in Roman Catholic church life, as factors in tension with basic apostolicity. The Roman Catholic insistence on historical apostolic succession in episcopal ministry, as well as the doctrine of papal primacy, constitute obstacles to "an unrestricted recognition" by Lutherans of Roman Catholic apostolicity (no. 142).

Thus, "The Apostolicity of the Church" has arrived in its Part 2 at grounded statements on both sides of the Lutheran–Roman Catholic relationship in which each partner recognizes genuine apostolicity in the other, while qualifying or restricting that recognition. However, the qualifications do not lead to resignation, but instead to further work. In the study, Part 3 treats the apostolicity of the ordained ministry and the issue of apostolic succession in ministry, while Part 4 presents the means and instances of authoritative teaching by which, in each body, believers and their communities are kept in the truth of the apostolic gospel of salvation.

10. Further Points of Consensus Made Manifest in the Apostolicity Study

Parts 2, 3, and 4 of "The Apostolicity of the Church" each contain concluding sections that draw together what has emerged from the preceding accounts of biblical topics and the historical developments of the Roman Catholic and Lutheran churches.[24] Here I offer a sample, from the conclusion of Part 2, while leaving to other venues a report on the conclusions of Parts 3 and 4.

In Part 2, "The Apostolic Gospel and Apostolicity of the Church," Section 2.6 begins its account of "Conclusions on Ecclesial Apostolicity" with "Shared Foundational Conclusions of Faith" (nos. 146-48), which move from the *JDDJ*'s consensus on justification to articulate a shared confession of the Holy Spirit, "the Lord and Giver of Life," to whom both Lutherans and Catholics ascribe, in the third major section of their common creed, the work of creating communities of believers by the instrumentality of the gospel. The biblical sections of the study yield the shared perception of Christ's apostles as heralds of the gospel that witnesses to his resurrection, gathers believers, and imparts forgiveness of sins (no. 147). This apostolic witness is for Lutherans and Catholics "both a normative origin and an abiding foundation" of their churches, which thus confess themselves to be "apostolic" in every age by reason of the gospel coming from the apostles and received as both saving grace and the center of the task of ongoing transmission (no. 148).

---

24. These three sections of "Conclusions" are laced with cross-references to earlier paragraphs of the study. By these indicators these sections become places at which an otherwise sprawling mass of data comes to serve a limited yet important set of ecumenical conclusions.

The concluding section of Part 2 then moves on to set forth a set of "shared understandings" on the gospel and apostolicity that the dialogue commission has come to discover. These concern, first, the gospel which is the true center of Lutheran ecclesial life, but which on the Catholic side was singled out as "the source of all saving truth and norms of practice," in a key statement of the Council of Trent (no. 153).[25] The further concentration of revelation in its soteriological center by Vatican II's *Dei verbum*, chapter 1, only confirms the accord on "the Gospel" (no. 154). The second point of discovered agreement is "that the apostolic legacy, by which faith is instilled, nurtured, and embodied, is a manifold and many-faceted heritage" (155). Vatican II spoke of the apostolic tradition as "comprising everything that serves to make the people of God live their lives in holiness and increase their faith" (DV 8.1, cited in no. 156). But this "everything" includes the "elements of sanctification and truth" also present and operative in the other communities (no. 157) and corresponds to a large extent with the "practices" of the gospel, singled out by Luther, which the Holy Spirit is using to embody and communicate Christ's mercy and renewing grace (no. 158).

At the end, Part 2's concluding section points ahead to treatments to come in Parts 3 and 4 of "significant reservations" that set limits to the acknowledgment of ecclesial apostolicity in the partner church of the dialogue. These limitations arise, first, from "differences in understanding ordination to the pastorate, ministry in apostolic succession, and the office of bishop in the church" (no. 163), which is then treated at length in Part 3 of "The Apostolicity of the Church" (nos. 165-293). Second, there exist "differences over how the teaching office is constituted and how Scripture functions as the source and apostolic criterion of all that our churches believe and teach" (no. 163), which is then the topic, again at no little length, in Part 4 (nos. 294-460) of "The Apostolicity of the Church."

Limits of space available make it imperative to end this presentation here and so to forego a report on the extensive narrowing of Lutheran–Roman Catholic differences on ordained ministry (Part 3) and

25. This word about the gospel of Christ preached by the apostles occurs in Trent's "Decree on Reception of the Sacred Books and Apostolic Traditions" (April 8, 1546), treated in no. 103 of "The Apostolicity of the Church" and found in Norman Tanner, ed., *Decrees of the Ecumenical Councils* (London: Sheed & Ward, and Washington, DC: Georgetown University Press, 1990), pp. 2, 663.

on "Church Teaching That Remains in the Truth" (Part 4). But I conclude with a dose of hope that these pages have "shown the solid basis of mutual recognition of apostolic continuity," which no. 163 claims for Part 2 of "The Apostolicity of the Church." The contents of Part 2 are, of course, much richer than this presentation, but these pages are enough to suggest how "The Apostolicity of the Church" clarifies in fresh ways the central reality of the Lutheran–Roman Catholic relationship of real but incomplete ecclesial communion, which is true communion notwithstanding certain limitations, from both sides, of the recognition of apostolicity in the other body.

APPENDIX:
THE DOCUMENTS OF LUTHERAN–CATHOLIC DIALOGUE

World-Level Dialogues (LWF & SPCU/PCPCU)

The Gospel and the Church, 1972 (*GA*, 168-89)

The Eucharist, 1978 (*GA*, 190-214)

Ways to Community, 1980 (*GA*, 215-40)

All Under One Christ: Statement on the Augsburg Confession, 1980 (*GA*, 241-47)

The Ministry in the Church, 1981 (*GA*, 248-75)

Martin Luther: Witness to Jesus Christ, 1983 (*GA II*, 438-42)

Facing Unity, 1984 (*GA II*, 443-84)

Church and Justification, 1993 (GA II, 484-565)

Joint Declaration on the Doctrine of Justification, signed by the LWF President and Vice-Presidents and by Cardinal Edward Cassidy for the Catholic Church, Augsburg, October 31, 1999 (*GA II*, 566-82 and in a booklet, Grand Rapids: Eerdmans, 2000)

The Apostolicity of the Church, 2006 (Minneapolis: Lutheran University Press)

Dialogues in the USA (Series: *Lutherans and Catholics in Dialogue*)[26]

    I   The Status of the Nicene Creed as Dogma of the Church, 1965

   II One Baptism for the Remission of Sins, 1966

  III The Eucharist as Sacrifice, 1967

  IV Eucharist and Ministry, 1970 (New York: USA National Committee of the LWF, and Washington, DC: U.S. Bishops' Committee for Ecumenical and Interreligious Affairs)

   V Papal Primacy and the Universal Church, 1974, ed. Paul Empie and T. Austin Murphy (Minneapolis: Augsburg, n.d.)

  VI Teaching Authority and Infallibility in the Church, 1978, ed. Paul Empie, T. Austin Murphy, and Joseph A. Burgess (Minneapolis: Augsburg, 1980)

 VII Justification by Faith, 1983, ed. Paul Empie, T. Austin Murphy, and Joseph A. Burgess (Minneapolis: Augsburg, 1985)

VIII The One Mediator, the Saints, and Mary, 1990, ed. H. George Anderson, J. Francis Stafford, and Joseph A. Burgess (Minneapolis: Augsburg, 1992)[27]

  IX Scripture and Tradition (only the "Common Statement"), ed. Harold C. Skillrud, J. Francis Stafford, and Daniel F. Martensen (Minneapolis: Augsburg, 1995)[28]

   X The Church as Koinonia of Salvation: Its Structures and Ministries, 2004, ed. Randall Lee and Jeffrey Gros (Washington, DC: U.S. Conference of Catholic Bishops, 2005)[29]

  XI The Hope of Eternal Life, ed. Lowell G. Almen and Richard J. Sklba (Minneapolis: Lutheran University Press, 2011)

---

26. The published volumes include papers by the participants along with a Joint Statement of conclusions from the dialogue. Rounds I-III, ed. Paul Empie and T. Austin Murphy, came out in a single volume from Augsburg Press.

27. Also in *Growing Consensus: Church Dialogues in the United States, 1962-1991*, ed. Joseph A. Burgess and Jeffrey Gros (New York/Mahwah, NJ: Paulist, 1995), pp. 374-484.

28. Partial publication also in *Growing Consensus II: Church Dialogues in the United States, 1992-2004*, ed. Lydia Veliko and Jeffrey Gros (Washington, DC: Bishops' Committee for Ecumenical and Interreligious Affairs, USCCB, 2005), pp. 135-51.

29. Also in *Growing Consensus II*, pp. 152-280.

Dialogues in Germany

Kirchengemeinschaft in Wort und Sakrament, 1984 (Bilateral Working
  Group of the German National Bishops' Conference and the
  Church Leadership of the United Evangelical Lutheran Church of
  Germany; Paderborn: Bonifatius, and Hannover: Lutherisches
  Verlagshaus)

Communio Sanctorum. Die Kirche als Gemeinschaft der Heiligen, 2000 (Bilat-
  eral Working Group; Paderborn: Bonifatius, and Frankfurt: Otto
  Lembeck. In English as *Communio Sanctorum: The Church as the
  Communion of Saints,* trans. Mark W. Jaske, Michael Root, and
  Daniel R. Smith; Collegeville, MN: Liturgical Press, 2004)

Lehrverurteilungen — kirchentrennend? 3 vols., ed. Karl Lehmann and
  Wolfhart Pannenberg, Dialog der Kirchen, 4-6 (Freiburg: Herder,
  and Göttingen: Vandenhoeck & Ruprecht, 1986-1990). Vol. 1,
  *Rechtfertigung, Sakramente und Amt im Zeitalter der Reformation und
  heute,* is translated as *The Condemnations of the Reformation Era: Do
  They Still Divide?* (Minneapolis: Fortress Press, 1990).

NB The Ecumenical Working Group of Evangelical and Catholic Theologians, which produced the condemnations study, has continued to
publish papers and reports on doctrinal positions in the series Dialog
der Kirchen, from Herder and Vandenhoeck & Ruprecht:

— *Verbindliches Zeugnis,* 3 vols., ed. Theodor Schneider and Wolfhart Pannenberg, Dialog der Kirchen, 7, 9, 10 (1992-98), on the
   biblical canon, tradition, the teaching office, and the understanding and use of scripture
— *Antwort auf kirchliche Stellungnamen,* ed. Wolfhart Pannenberg
   and Theodor Schneider, Dialog der Kirchen, 8 (1994), concerning the condemnations study
— *Gerecht und Sünder zugleich? Ökumenische Klärungen,* ed. Theodor
   Schneider and Günther Wenz, Dialog der Kirchen, 11 (2001),
   clarifying *JDDJ,* nos. 28-30, on *simul iustus et peccator*
— *Das kirchliche Amt in apostolischer Nachfolge,* 3 vols., ed. Theodor
   Schneider, Dorothea Sattler, and Günther Wenz, Dialog der
   Kirchen, 12-14 (2004-2008)

Jared Wicks, SJ

Dialogues in Australia

Agreed Statement on Baptism, 1977 (*Stages on the Way. Documents from the Bilateral Conversations between Churches in Autstralia,* ed. Raymond K. Williamson [Melbourne: Joint Board of Christian Education, 1994], 57-59).
Sacrament and Sacrifice, 1985 (*Stages on the Way,* 60-101).
Pastor and Priest, 1989 (*Stages on the Way,* 102-29).
Communion and Mission, 1995 (*Stages on the Way,* II, *Documents from the Bilateral Conversations between Churches in Australia 1994-2007* [Strathfield NSW: St. Pauls Publications, 2007], 172-208).
Justification, 1999 (*Stages on the Way,* II, 209-26).

Dialogue in Scandinavia

Justification in the Life of the Church. A Report from the Roman Catholic–Lutheran Dialogue Group for Sweden and Finland, 2009, in English, 2010. Accessed May 24, 2010 at http://www.svenskakyrkan.se/Webbplats/System/Filer/b30f0f74-747a-444d-b974-9533206e3ed7.pdf

6 The History, Methodology, and Implications for Ecumenical Reception of the Apostolicity Study of the Lutheran–Roman Catholic International Dialogue

William G. Rusch

Under the general theme of "A Century of Ecumenism: What has been achieved? What are the next steps forward?" I have been asked to address the topic: "The Achievements of the International Lutheran-Catholic Dialogue." I am going to limit this title somewhat and speak about *one* achievement of this dialogue, which I believe has not received the attention it deserves.

My intention here is to offer some comments on the latest report from the international Lutheran–Roman Catholic dialogue, titled *The Apostolicity of the Church: Study Document of the Lutheran–Roman Catholic Commission on Unity (ApC)*.[1] Specifically I propose to look at this document in terms of its history and methodology.

It seems to me that such an examination is in keeping with the overall theme of this conference: to note what has been achieved ecumenically over the last one hundred years and to explore what future steps may be taken in the light of those achievements. I believe that such a process can be especially informative in regard to the ongoing challenge and opportunity before both the Lutheran and Roman Catholic churches to engage in ecumenical reception in this second century of the modern ecumenical movement.[2]

---

1. *The Apostolicity of the Church: Study Document of the Lutheran–Roman Catholic Commission on Unity — The Lutheran World Federation and the Pontifical Council for Promoting Christian Unity* (Minneapolis: Lutheran University Press, 2006). Hereafter *ApC*.

2. On the topic on ecumenical reception see William G. Rusch, *Ecumenical Reception: Its Challenge and Opportunity* (Grand Rapids: Eerdmans, 2007).

William G. Rusch

1. The Prehistory of *The Apostolicity of the Church* in the Lutheran–Roman Catholic Dialogue

The origins of the international Lutheran–Roman Catholic dialogues lie in discussions that took place in the closing days of the Second Vatican Council in 1965.[3] The dialogue itself began meeting in 1967 with a mandate to study the topic of "the gospel and the church." It issued its first document in 1972, *The Gospel and the Church,* commonly referred to as the Malta Report.[4] This text included a considerable number of topics: tradition and scripture, justification, gospel and the world, ordained ministry, and papacy. This report noted progress in overcoming doctrinal disputes and the structural issues that divided the churches. It called for a mutual recognition of the ordained ministry and occasional intercommunion between Lutherans and Roman Catholics. The report was not unanimously approved by the dialogue participants, and none of the churches involved through the Pontifical Council on Promoting Christian Unity (then the Secretariat for Promoting Christian Unity) and the Lutheran World Federation took any official action in regard to it. Such a situation gives an indication of the limits of the Malta Report, and also of this period of ecumenical history.

Nevertheless, *The Gospel and the Church* because of both its accomplishments and limits resulted in the authorization of a second series of international Lutheran–Roman Catholic dialogue. This series produced two texts dealing with special anniversaries: *All Under One Christ* in 1980 on the 450th anniversary of the Lutheran confessional document, the Augsburg Confession, and *Martin Luther — Witness to Jesus Christ* on the 500th anniversary of Luther's birth in 1983. This phase of the dialogue also published texts dealing with doctrinal issues in dispute between Lutheran and Roman Catholics: *The Eucharist* in 1978 and *The Ministry in the Church* in 1981. The first text concluded that differences over presence and sacrifice in the Lord's Supper should no longer be regarded as church-dividing. The second document affirmed an agreement that a special ministry in the church is constitutive and a high degree of agreement has been reached on ministry, which raises

---

3. For an overview of the international Lutheran-Roman Catholic dialogue, see Michael Root, "Lutheran-Roman Catholic Dialogue," in *DEM2*, pp. 720-21.

4. The documents from the first and second series of the dialogue appear in *GA*, pp. 167-275; and *GA II*, pp. 438-84.

the question of mutual recognition as part of a process in which the churches reciprocally accept each other.

The second series concluded its work by releasing two texts that described what a process of mutual acceptance would look like. These are *Ways to Community* in 1980 and *Facing Unity* in 1984. All these publications received no official response from the churches.

The third series of the international dialogue issued a lengthy text on the subject *Church and Justification* in 1993.[5] This document is the result of seven years of dialogue work. *Church and Justification* sets forth certain basic convictions that Lutherans and Roman Catholics share about justification and the church in such a way that excludes a fundamental conflict or opposition between the church and justification. Thus the dialogue was probing the perceived consensus on justification by looking at its implications for ecclesiology. The dialogue in this report declared that it was quite compatible with the role of justification to see that all the church's institutions contribute to the church's abiding truth in the gospel, which alone creates and sustains the church.[6]

It is this history and collection of dialogue-texts that form the context for the international dialogue's most recent publication, *ApC*.

2. *The Apostolicity of the Church:* Its History and Contents

2.1. *General Comments*

ApC represents the work of the fourth series of Lutheran–Roman Catholic dialogue on the world level, i.e., from 1995 to 2006. As its introduction makes clear, although the mandate of the dialogue was wider, the participants in the conversations made the decision to concentrate on apostolicity in view of its complexity and importance ecumenically.[7] This dialogue text is to be viewed as a further step along the process begun in 1972 with *The Gospel and the Church*.

Yet two particular features stand out in the introductory material

---

5. This text is published in *GA II*, pp. 485-565.

6. See Heinz-Albert Raem, "The Third Phase of Lutheran-Catholic Dialogue (1986-1993)," in *One in Christ* 29 (1994): 310-27.

7. *ApC*, p. 7.

to *ApC*. First, it is self-described as a "study document of the Lutheran–Roman Catholic Commission on Unity." This specific term has not been used with early publications from this dialogue. The three most recent dialogue reports before *ApC, The Ministry in the Church, Facing Unity,* and *Church and Justification,* are not identified as "study documents." The new nomenclature does raise the question of whether this text is to be viewed in a lower status than other reports coming from this dialogue. *ApC* itself does not speak to this question. The rationale for the use of this new description should have been given, especially since it carries the implication that *ApC* could be less significant than earlier texts.

This question takes on an added complexity when *Growing Together in Unity and Mission* from the International Anglican–Roman Catholic Commission for Unity and Mission is considered.[8] This text is described as "an agreed statement." Still, *Growing Together in Unity and Mission* itself makes clear that because of internal developments within the Anglican Communion, the present time is not appropriate for Anglicans and Roman Catholics to enter a new formal stage of relations.[9] The question presents itself: Why is *ApC* a "study document" and why is *Growing Together in Unity and Mission* an "agreed statement"? Perhaps both texts provide evidence for the need for some standardization of ecumenical terminology about such reports.

Second, the introduction of *ApC*, although signed by the two chairpersons, but presumably with the endorsement of the participants of the commission, is less urgent in its call for the churches to respond and receive this text. The introduction speaks of reports and analyses of *ApC*'s contribution toward hastening the recognition of greater communion between the Catholic and Lutheran churches of the world.[10] On the other hand, the foreword of *Church and Justification* asks whether this text along with the other earlier documents from the dialogue does not constitute the sufficient consensus that would allow the churches to embark upon concrete steps toward visible unity.[11] The tone seems quite different between the two documents at this point.

8. *Growing Together in Unity and Mission: An Agreed Statement of the International Anglican–Roman Catholic Commission for Unity and Mission* (London: Society for Promoting Christian Knowledge, 2007).

9. *Growing Together in Unity and Mission,* p. 10.

10. *ApC,* p. 12.

11. *Church and Justification* in *GA II,* pp. 486-87.

These two factors could suggest that the ultimate goal of this dialogue as visible unity between the Roman Catholic Church and the Lutheran Communion is less urgent than it once was in some circles. If this interpretation is accurate, it is regrettable.

The participants of the Commission were approximately eight or nine Lutherans and an equal number of Roman Catholics from several continents. To this group of eighteen were added two or three consultants from both the Lutheran and Roman Catholic side, plus staff and interpreters.[12]

The members of the dialogue recognize that during the period of their work a major ecumenical achievement occurred with the production and the signing of the *Joint Declaration on the Doctrine of Justification (JDDJ)* in 1999.[13] It will become apparent in the course of this presentation how the *JDDJ* and its methodology were contributing factors of major proportions in the creation of the *ApC* itself.

ApC exists in both an English and German text. Both stand on the same level of authority. For this presentation, the English edition of *ApC* has been used. The introduction to the text makes clear that there are two critical limits in its contents: *ApC* does not address the ordination of women to the pastoral office or episcopal office, nor does it in a comprehensive way offer an ecumenical examination of the papacy.[14]

As dialogue texts go, *ApC* is a long document of some 200 pages.

---

12. *ApC*, pp. 197-98.

13. The *Joint Declaration* was published in English as *Joint Declaration on the Doctrine of Justification* (Grand Rapids: Eerdmans, 2000). The official German text of the *JDDJ*, the *Official Common Statement* and the annex can be found in *Gemeinsame Erklärung zur Rechtfertigungslehre: Gemeinsame offizielle Feststellung, Anhang (Annex) zur Gemeinsamen Feststellung* (Frankfurt am Main: Otto Lembeck, and Paderborn: Bonifatius, 1999). The *JDDJ* in English had been published earlier in *Origins* 28, no. 8 (July 1998): 120-27. The English text of the *Common Statement* and annex appeared in *Origins* 29, no. 6 (July 1999): 85-87. Studies that contributed to the production of the *JDDJ* included among others: H. George Anderson, T. Austin Murphy, and Joseph A. Burgess, eds., *Lutherans and Catholics in Dialogue VII: Justification by Faith* (Minneapolis: Augsburg, 1985); Karl Lehmann and Wolfhart Pannenberg, eds., *The Condemnations of the Reformation Era: Do They Still Divide?* (Minneapolis: Fortress Press, 1990), especially pp. 1-69 [the original report appeared as *Lehrverurteilungen-kirchentrennend?* (Freiburg im Breisgau: Herder, and Göttingen: Vandenhoeck & Ruprecht, 1986)]; Pierre Duprey, "The Condemnations of the 16th Century on Justification: Do They Still Apply Today?" with response by Harding Meyer, *Occasional Papers Contributing to 1997 Decisions* (Chicago: Department for Ecumenical Affairs, ELCA, 1995).

14. For all of these introductory matters, see *ApC*, pp. 7-12.

In light of the formidability of its subject and the importance of agreement about it for ecumenical progress, a text of this size is not unexpected. *ApC* is divided into four major sections after a short introduction. These divisions deal with the following aspects of the general topic of apostolicity: The Apostolicity of the Church — New Testament Foundations; The Apostolic Gospel and the Apostolicity of the Church; Apostolic Succession and Ordained Ministry; and Church Teaching That Remains in the Truth.

2.2. *"The Apostolicity of the Church — New Testament Foundations"*

ApC acknowledges the critical nature of the first section on the New Testament for all of its work.[15] It declares that its desire is to avoid prooftexting and to allow the writings of the New Testament in all of their complexity on this subject to speak for themselves. In this portion of text, some twenty pages are devoted to an examination of the New Testament witness to the apostles and their mission on behalf of the gospel of Jesus Christ. The diversity of the books of the New Testament is acknowledged, as is the difference of interpretation of these texts. Yet *ApC* is clear that Lutherans and Roman Catholics share the conviction that scripture is normative for both of them. The New Testament is fundamental as a witness to the Word of God; it is an invitation to examine critically the dogmatic tradition. Attention is given to the mission of the Twelve during Christ's earthly ministry, the commission of the risen Christ, and promise of the Spirit. It is the Spirit who unites the church for its mission. A long section is devoted to the apostolicity of the church and apostles in which the diversity of the New Testament is stressed.

The topic of ecclesial structures and patterns of ministry is taken up. *ApC* speaks of the emergence of a threefold order in the church in the context of the early church's diversity. It sees the influential role of the Pastoral Letters in this regard. Finally the New Testament section speaks of the living tradition of the church and its desire to remain faithful to the apostolic witness. It sees the eventual canon of the Bible as the normative exposition of this concern. The conclusion of this first part is: "No human authority is able to guarantee the truth of the

15. The New Testament section of *ApC* is pp. 13-38, nos. 1-64.

gospel. . . . On the other hand, however, faithfulness of the church requires certain forms of traditioning and a particular ecclesial ministry of proclamation, reconciliation, and teaching in order to ensure the orderly transmission of the apostolic teachings."[16]

The pages of *ApC* describing the New Testament witness contain no footnotes. They seek to have the New Testament speak for itself. Yet the overall view presented is one in harmony with contemporary biblical scholarship, especially in recognition of the diversity of New Testament witnesses and the unfolding of a structured life of the church. This material also is in agreement with other ecumenical texts on ministry. This is certainly true when *ApC* and *Baptism, Eucharist and Ministry* are compared.[17]

2.3. *"The Apostolic Gospel and the Apostolicity of the Church"*

ApC in its second part deals with the apostolic gospel and the apostolicity of the church.[18] This portion of the text addresses two questions: What makes the church apostolic, and what are the resources of the Lutheran and Roman Catholic churches to acknowledge in dialogue their apostolic character as partner churches that are not in full communion? It builds on its work in the first section to offer material on biblical orientation to speak of the apostolic gospel and the apostolicity of the church. Then this section offers a historical overview of how the apostles and the church were treated in early and medieval interpretations. Here *ApC* covers the special apostolicity of the Church of Rome, and how apostolicity is portrayed in the lifestyle, art, and liturgy of these historical periods. Apostolicity and the church are reviewed in the Lutheran reformation and in the developments within the Roman Catholic Church at Trent and later, including the twentieth century and the Second Vatican Council. A renewed understanding of tradition in Catholic theology is pictured along with its ecumenical import and

16. *ApC,* pp. 37-38, no. 64.

17. See for example, *BEM,* pp. 20-32. At one point *Baptism, Eucharist and Ministry* states, "The Church has never been without persons holding specific authority and responsibility" (p. 21). *ApC* indicates, "The church has never been without persons holding specific responsibilities and authority, and functions and tasks make sense only when persons carry them out" (p. 27, no. 35).

18. *ApC,* pp. 39-71, nos. 64-164.

implications. A parallel subsection offers an ecumenical Lutheran understanding of apostolicity of the church. This understanding includes an appreciation of diversity and of a differentiated consensus.[19]

This second part of *ApC* concludes by describing three areas: (1) Foundational convictions about ecclesial apostolicity that Lutherans and Roman Catholics share. Here the *JDDJ* is a critical resource. (2) Shared understandings about apostolicity and the church, which this dialogue has discovered. These common understandings include the centrality of the gospel and an agreement on a manifold and many-faceted apostolic legacy. (3) Differences that require deeper examination to achieve reconciliation or to clarify if they still have a church-dividing character.

2.4. *"Apostolic Succession and Ordained Ministry"*

Part Three of *ApC* is titled "Apostolic Succession and Ordained Ministry."[20] It addresses such themes as the role of witness for testimony, and the place of institutions and structures. Ministry in its doctrinal and institutional aspects is seen of great significance for the apostolicity of the church. Two critical questions are identified: Can one office of ministry manifest itself in different structures? And what belongs to the substance of ministry and what belongs to structures, which within limits are variable? A subsection takes up biblical orientation, stressing diversity, the universal priesthood, special ministry, and issues of succession. Then a historical review follows on ordained ministry in the early church and in the Middle Ages. This survey is followed by a discussion of ordained ministry in the Lutheran reformation and at the Council of Trent. Attention is given to the problem of the episcopate and the tension of being faithful to the gospel and to transmission of the office in traditional forms. It is pointed out that Trent's concern was to preserve traditional teaching on ministry; it did not present a total and coherent ecclesiology. The historical material concludes with an examination of ordained ministry according to the Second Vatican Council and in contemporary Lutheran teaching.

This major section of *ApC* ends by describing both agreements

---

19. On the precise meaning of this expression, *ApC*, p. 64, no. 138. See also 3.3 below.
20. *ApC*, pp. 73-134, nos. 165-293.

and differences between Lutherans and Roman Catholics on these two topics. It notes that there is an asymmetry in the situation. Lutherans recognize the Roman Catholic Church as apostolic; the converse is not presently true. But both Lutherans and Roman Catholics agree that the church is apostolic. They further acknowledge together that Christ gives himself to humans in word and sacrament. They agree there are a universal priesthood of all believers and an ordained ministry, instituted by God, with specific functions. Lutherans and Roman Catholics also are of one voice in the recognition that induction into this special ministry is by ordination.

Yet Lutherans and Roman Catholics differ about a number of aspects of ordained ministry. Roman Catholics hold a view that the threefold hierarchy of ordained ministry is by divine institution; Lutherans do not. There is a difference over what makes a person a rightful holder of a regional ministry, and there are differing views about the local church and its relation to the universal Church. *ApC* speaks of the Catholic view of *defectus* in Lutheran ministry.

In the light of these differences, *ApC* offers an ecumenical perspective. It builds this perspective on the *JDDJ*. *ApC* states that for apostolic succession, succession in faith is an essential aspect. It continues that the signing of the *JDDJ* implied the acknowledgment that ordained ministry in both churches has by the power of the Holy Spirit fulfilled its service of maintaining fidelity to the apostolic gospel. It notes that in history the relation between offices of priest and bishop has been defined in different ways, and ministries have undergone structural changes. Again basing its argument on the *JDDJ*, *ApC* declares that there are many individuals in Christendom who exercise an office of supervision, which in the Roman Catholic Church is done by bishops. These persons bear special responsibility for the apostolicity in their churches, and the Roman Catholic Church recognizes this in the *JDDJ*.

Therefore *ApC* asks the question of whether a differentiated consensus is not possible for Lutherans and Roman Catholics in the doctrine of ministry or ministries.[21] It notes that such a differentiated consensus could appeal to the various agreements on ministry in *ApC*. This approach would follow on the path taken by the *JDDJ*. It would recognize the possibility of differing structures of ministry, which

21. See 3.3 below.

would not be church-dividing, because they would realize and serve the same fundamental intention of ministerial office. *ApC* acknowledges such a step would be a risk taken while trusting in the support of the Holy Spirit.[22]

2.5. *"Church Teaching That Remains in the Truth"*

The last major section of *ApC* follows a pattern that has been observable in the previous three divisions of the work.[23] In the setting of agreement on the gospel that makes the church apostolic and the fundamental role of the ordained ministry of word and sacrament, this fourth part is centered on how the church remains in the truth revealed in the gospel of Jesus Christ. It notes that since the Reformation, and especially the First Vatican Council, there have been differences on the structure of ministries and how these ministries function in relation to scripture between Lutherans and Roman Catholics. A subsection deals with the New Testament orientation to the truth of doctrine, teaching ministries, and the resolving of doctrinal conflicts. The conviction of *ApC* is that scripture bears witness to the truth of the gospel and also gives account of disputes over the gospel. Such conflicts must be settled on the basis that all teaching must serve the truth of the gospel. In this regard the canon of scripture has a function to exercise. This fourth part discusses doctrine and truth in early and medieval developments. Here it gives attention to the function of the rule of faith and the creeds, and to the significance of the councils of the first eight centuries. It mentions the various approaches to interpreting scripture in the early and medieval churches. Detailed attention is provided to how in accord with the Lutheran reformation the church was maintained in truth, including the place and function of the Lutheran Confessions in this task.

Then the fourth portion of the text turns to Catholic doctrine about the biblical canon, interpretation of scripture, and the teaching office, including Catholic biblical interpretation from the Council of Trent to the Second Vatican Council. When the Catholic doctrine about the teaching office is presented, *ApC* points out several areas of

---

22. See *ApC,* especially pp. 133-34, nos. 292 and 293.
23. *ApC,* pp. 135-95, nos. 294-460.

Lutheran–Roman Catholic agreement. They agree that correct doctrine is essential in shaping a right relation of faith with God and Christ's saving work. There is also agreement on the importance of a ministry of regional oversight of teaching. Lutherans and Roman Catholics are of one mind that it is the Holy Spirit who effectively maintains the church in the truth of the gospel and in the correct celebration of the sacraments.[24]

The final pages of this section offer conclusions to be drawn from the dialogue's work. It states that the dialogue's intention is to contribute to bringing about full communion between the Catholic Church and the Lutheran churches of the world. Here *ApC* presents its results in two steps. First, there are three foundational convictions that are held in common. The report declares this is an area of full communion. Second, there are three topics where a differentiated consensus has been discovered so that on these issues the remaining differences are not church-dividing. The report indicates this is an area of reconciled diversity.

In regard to the foundational convictions, they are the following. First, Lutherans and Roman Catholics fully agree that God has issued in human history a message of grace and truth, by word and deed. The *JDDJ* is referred to in this common affirmation. This is the gospel of God's grace in Christ. Second, Lutherans and Roman Catholics fully agree that God's revelation of himself in Jesus Christ for human salvation continues to be announced in the gospel that the first apostles preached and taught, and that the church of every age stands under the imperative to preserve God's word in continuous succession. Third, Lutherans and Roman Catholics agree that the scriptures are the source, rule, guideline, and criterion of correctness and purity of the church's proclamation, of its doctrine, and of its sacramental and pastoral practice.

The area of reconciled diversity includes the topics of the canon of scripture and the church, scripture and tradition, and the necessity and context of the teaching office in the church. In regard to canon and church, *ApC* states that Lutherans and Roman Catholics are in such an extensive agreement on the source of the Bible's canonical authority that their remaining differences over the extent of the canon are not of such weight to justify continued ecclesial division. Likewise regarding scripture and tradition, Lutherans and Roman Catholics are of such an extensive agreement that their different emphases on their relation do not of

---

24. See *ApC,* especially p. 180, no. 412.

themselves require maintaining the present division of the churches. Finally, concerning the necessity and context of the teaching office, Lutherans and Roman Catholics agree in spite of their different configurations of teaching ministries that the church must designate members to serve the transmission of the gospel. Therefore, the teaching office, or ministry, is a necessary entity by which the church is preserved in the truth of the gospel according to Lutherans and Roman Catholics.

3. *The Apostolicity of the Church:* Its Methodology

There are three aspects of the methodology employed by *ApC* that deserve special attention. They are the use of scripture, of the *JDDJ,* of the concept of differentiated consensus.

3.1. *The Use of Scripture in* The Apostolicity of the Church

The use of scripture in *ApC* is conspicuous. Approximately one quarter of the entire text is devoted to New Testament foundations or biblical orientation. Scripture is prominent and a controlling element in all four major divisions of the text. The document seeks to build on a common biblical basis shared by Lutherans and Roman Catholics to find an approach to move beyond the sixteenth century and later disputes. The novelty of this method becomes apparent when other reports from this dialogue are considered. *The Gospel and the Church* contains neither a scriptural section nor scriptural references in the text. *The Eucharist* has a section on scripture, and references to scripture in the text and in footnotes. *Ministry in the Church* refers to scripture in certain parts of the text. *Church and Justification* has no initial section setting forth a scriptural foundation. References to scripture run through the text. They tend to cluster in certain parts of the text, chapters 1 and 2, and a specific portion of chapter 5.

The three documents, *Ways to Community, Facing Unity,* and *All Under One Christ,* have relatively few scriptural references. In these three cases the particular subject matter may well not lend itself to copious quotations from the Bible.[25] Nevertheless the general impression

---

25. For all these dialogue reports, see the references in footnote 4 above.

gained from these dialogue reports is that scripture is often employed in a prooftexting manner.

Admittedly the use of scripture in ecumenical texts is a complex subject.[26] *ApC* by its explicit comment in the introduction and in the body of its report is seeking a different procedure: "The investigation of the New Testament witness to the apostles and their mission on behalf of the gospel of Jesus Christ contributes extensive and important results to our document."[27] This methodology is quite similar to that utilized by the *JDDJ*, and may be another indication of the direct influence of that text on *ApC*.[28] It is an approach that should be welcomed in future ecumenical texts.

3.2. The Use of the Joint Declaration on the Doctrine of Justification *in* The Apostolicity of the Church

The *JDDJ* was signed during the course of the work of this fourth series of Lutheran–Roman Catholic dialogue. The participants in the dialogue recognized the notable weight and authority possessed by the *JDDJ* as a result of this signing. The *JDDJ* is referred to and quoted on numerous occasions in *ApC*.[29] The implications of the *JDDJ* for other areas of agreement in addition to justification are expressed.[30]

This use of the *JDDJ* is one example of its ecumenical reception by participants in an official dialogue. This practice should encourage official and practical reception of the *JDDJ* in both churches. As the churches begin to struggle with the question of an initial response to

26. See for example the discussion in Matthias Haudel, *Die Bibel und die Einheit der Kirchen: Eine Untersuchung der Studien von "Glauben und Kirchenverfassung"* (Göttingen: Vandenhoeck & Ruprecht, 1993).

27. *ApC*, p. 9.

28. See *JDDJ*, "1. Biblical Message of Justification," nos. 8-12.

29. For example, see *ApC*, p. 65, no. 142; p. 66, nos. 146-47; p. 74, no. 167; pp. 130-31, no. 288; pp. 133-34, no. 293; p. 187, no. 432.

30. For example, see *ApC*, pp. 130-31, no. 288. Here it is stated "[t]he signing of the *JDDJ* implies an acknowledgment that ordained ministry in *both* churches [italics mine] has by the power of the Holy Spirit fulfilled its service of maintaining fidelity to the apostolic gospel" in terms of justification. See also *ApC*, p. 134, no. 293, where it is argued on the basis of the *JDDJ* that an approach may be followed to recognize the possibility of differing structures of ministry that realize and serve the fundamental intention of the ministerial office.

ApC, they will have the opportunity to acknowledge their ongoing reception or nonreception of the *JDDJ*.[31]

The fact that *ApC* draws out further implications of the *JDDJ* for ministry and maintaining the church in truth will challenge both churches to reflect on the wider significance of the *JDDJ* for agreement in other areas. Until now this is a largely unknown topic, and immediate consensus on the larger connotations of the *JDDJ* should not be assumed. The acceptance and signing of the *JDDJ* placed both the Lutheran and Roman Catholic churches in a new situation that will require further exploration.

3.3. The Use of "Differentiated Consensus" in the Joint Declaration on the Doctrine of Justification and in The Apostolicity of the Church

An examination of dialogue reports on various levels has recently offered clear evidence that the dialogues have created a definite way of working, which was neither foreseen nor developed in advance. This method is now generally denoted by the term "differentiated consensus."[32] Its chief characteristic is the recognition of a double structure. This trait is viewed in terms of two levels: there is a first or fundamental level; this is a level of consensus. Here there is real and essential agreement that is neither a general, loose agreement nor a compromise. Yet in addition, there is a second level. Here there are remaining differences. These differences are also real and essential. But the critical point is that all these differences do not challenge the agreement or consensus on the first level. This schema provides for unity and diversity. It does not require the churches in dialogue to either convert to one or the other, or to achieve a synthesis of their differing positions.

It is precisely and explicitly this methodology of differentiated

---

31. See William G. Rusch, *Ecumenical Reception: Its Challenge and Opportunity*, pp. 77-80.

32. Fundamental for an understanding of differentiated consensus is Harding Meyer, "Die Prägung einer Formel: Ursprung und Intention" in *Einheit — Aber Wie? Zur Tragfähigkeit der ökumenischen Formel vom "differenzierten Konsens,"* in *Quaestiones Disputatae* 184, ed. Harold Wagner (Freiburg: Herder, 2000), pp. 36-58. See also William G. Rusch, "Structures of Unity: The Next Ecumenical Challenge — A Possible Way Forward," *Ecclesiology* 2, no. 1 (September 2005): 107-22, and in *Ecumenical Trends* 34, no. 9 (October 2005): 2-8; William G. Rusch, *Ecumenical Reception: Its Challenge and Opportunity*, pp. 118-30.

consensus that made the *JDDJ* possible.[33] The *JDDJ* was not the first dialogue report to employ this method, but the signing on the highest level of appropriate authority of the *JDDJ* moved differentiated consensus in Lutheran–Roman Catholic relations out of the realm of theory and into the areas of practice and acceptance.

Therefore, it is extremely significant that *ApC* in reaching its areas of agreement between Lutherans and Roman Catholics on apostolicity utilized differentiated consensus. *ApC*'s uses of differentiated consensus are extensive. It employs the Roman Catholic application of "apostolic" to other churches.[34] It affirms reconciled diversity between churches that can only be recognized on the basis of differentiated consensus.[35] In several sections *ApC*, when dealing with the "apostolic gospel and apostolicity of the church," names differentiated consensus and approves its use.[36] It concludes this major section by claiming that there is a fundamental agreement between Catholics and Lutherans on apostolicity and that the remaining differences do not call into question that agreement. The term "differentiated consensus" does not appear, but the idea is obviously expressed and affirmed.[37] In the section on "apostolic succession and ordained ministry," *ApC* offers a list of fundamental agreements between Lutherans and Roman Catholics. Its language is similar to the *JDDJ*, where the expression "we confess together" is used (in *ApC*, "Together, Catholics and Lutherans affirm"). Then the differences are given. The conclusion is that this combination of agreements and differences can be described as differentiated consensus.[38] In the section of *ApC* on "church teaching that remains in the truth" agreement on the basis of differentiated consensus is reached in regard to ministry and the teaching office, the canon of scripture, and the relation of scripture and tradition.[39]

---

33. See, for example, *JDDJ*, nos. 17, 18, 19-24. See also William G. Rusch, *Ecumenical Reception: Its Challenge and Opportunity*, pp. 123-25.

34. *ApC*, p. 59, no. 122.

35. *ApC*, p. 63, no. 135.

36. *ApC*, pp. 63-65, nos. 136-38, 142; pp. 66-67, nos. 146-47, 149, and 150. The last two paragraphs especially mention fundamental agreement between Lutherans and Roman Catholics.

37. *ApC*, p. 70, no. 160.

38. The agreements are given on *ApC*, pp. 123-25, nos. 271-75; the differences on pp. 127-33, nos. 281-92; the differentiated consensus is articulated on pp. 133-34, no. 293.

39. *ApC*, pp. 180-81, nos. 412-13; p. 190, no. 441; p. 192, no. 448.

This use of differentiated consensus in *ApC* is a further example in Lutheran–Roman Catholic dialogue of the validity and acceptance of the methodology and concept. It offers evidence that ecumenical reception between Lutherans and Roman Catholics, i.e., the process by which a church under the guidance of God's Spirit makes the results of a bilateral or multilateral conversation a part of its faith and life, and thus moves to greater visible unity with another church, will be possible by means of differentiated consensus.[40] Thus the implications of *ApC* for ecumenical reception can only be unmistakable — with one stipulation: the sponsoring churches take seriously the document's challenge and opportunity.

If this insight is accurate the implications for ecumenical reception are enhanced by the outstanding work accomplished by *ApC*.

---

40. See William G. Rusch, *Ecumenical Reception: Its Challenge and Opportunity*, p. 61.

7 Methodist–Roman Catholic International Dialogue: Mutual Reassessment in a New Context

Geoffrey Wainwright

If the modern ecumenical movement be conventionally reckoned to date from 1910, that chronology may justify my beginning these Methodistical reflections in a rather personal way. I may consider myself to have been part of that movement for half its history so far. In 1960 I began my theological studies at the University of Cambridge. Two events remain of striking importance to me. First: I attended a celebration of the Lord's Supper that was led by a presbyter on furlough from the Church of South India who conducted the service according to the rite of that body, which in 1947 had brought into union the fruits of mainly British-based missionary labors: Anglican, Methodist, Church of Scotland (Reformed), and the Congregationalist London Missionary Society. The liturgy was a weave of elements from the constitutive traditions, drawing in also litanies from the Syrian Orthodox long present in India and even the lovely "Adesto" invocation from Mozarabic Spain: "Be present, be present, O Jesus, thou good High Priest, as thou wast in the midst of thy disciples, and make thyself known to us in the breaking of the bread." The second event, on a different occasion, was saying the Lord's Prayer as Protestants together with Roman Catholics — a rather recent concession for the latter, and of course we never then knew whether to continue on through "For thine is the kingdom, the power, and the glory forever and ever. Amen." My next sustained contacts with Roman Catholics came while I was a graduate student at the Ecumenical Institute in Geneva, Switzerland, and the initiative for mutual visits and conversations came from a number of English Benedictines who were studying at the nearby University of Fribourg. Come 1966-67 I was awarded a fellowship for study on the European continent, and I chose to spend the time in Rome, where the Second Vatican Council was still fresh in everyone's mind. At that time, the international dialogue was just getting under way as the World Methodist Council (WMC) — on whose behalf several senior figures had been present at Vatican II as delegated observers — from its London sessions in August 1966 responded enthusiastically to the Roman invitation to set up a "bilateral dialogue" of the kind to which the Catholic Church was also inviting other "Christian world communions." The first meeting of the Methodist–Roman Catholic dialogue, in fact, took place at Ariccia, near Rome, in October 1967. Skipping over the intervening years (which certainly contained — in my case also — continuing engagements of various kinds with Roman Catholics, and notably among theologians), I was in 1983 appointed by the WMC as a member of its Joint Commission for Dialogue with the Roman Catholic Church, and in 1986 I became the Commission's chairman on the Methodist side.

I will begin my account of the Commission's work with what in fact is its eighth report, coming at the end of the fourth decade of its existence: the Seoul Report of 2006. That is already the occasion for me to explain the working procedures of the Joint Commission. From the start the Commission has operated in periods of five years in order to be able to present a report of its work simultaneously to the Holy See and to the World Methodist Council according to the quinquennial rhythm of the latter body's plenary sessions. That last procedure has led to the practice of citing the documents (also on the Catholic side!) by the venue and date of their presentation to the WMC. Typically, the WMC "receives with gratitude" the reports and authorizes the continuation of the dialogue. In Rome, the reports are examined by the Congregation for the Doctrine of the Faith and then are published by the Pontifical Council for Promoting Christian Unity in company with an essay by a respected theologian who summarizes their strengths and weaknesses from a Catholic point of view. Over the years, there has naturally been some renewal in the Commission's composition, but the general sense is that of consistency in the work done, and I hope to convey that in the present outline account.

I begin with the Seoul Report — *"The Grace Given You in Christ": Catholics and Methodists Reflect Further on the Church* — because the Commission considered that the time had at last come for a "mutual reassessment" in the "new context" set by the ecumenical movement. Attention to the opening chapter of the Seoul Report allows us therefore to go back to the beginnings of modern ecumenism, considering even the earlier history of attitudes and relations between Methodists and Roman Catholics that began very gradually to change for the better in the first half of "the ecumenical century."[1]

In a sense, we must undertake a big leap backwards in time. Already in its first report — "Denver 1971" — the Joint Commission called attention to a most remarkable document from the hand of John Wesley himself, the principal founder — under God — of the Methodist movement. That was his *Letter to a Roman Catholic,* written from Dublin in July 1749 in an effort to allay Catholic opposition to the evangelistic work of the Methodists in Ireland. Wesley begins with the "tenderest regard" in which he must hold his addressee on account of their being creatures of the same God and their both being redeemed by God's own Son and "studying to have a conscience void of offence towards God and towards man." In the two main sections of the Letter, Wesley then sets out "the belief of a true Protestant" and "the practice of a true Protestant," making the most of the commonalities between Protestants and Catholics. The *fides quæ creditur* is presented in terms of an expansion upon the Nicene-Constantinopolitan Creed, bringing out the Chalcedonian teaching concerning the person and natures of Christ and the traditional understanding of Christ's "threefold office" as

---

1. On the Roman Catholic side, there was in the 1920s the substantial Louvain study of Maximin Piette, *La réaction de John Wesley dans l'évolution du protestantisme* (by neglecting the nuance of "réaction," the title of the published English translation — *John Wesley in the Evolution of Protestantism* [1937] — forfeited the work's thesis of the "catholic" swing represented by Wesley). On the Methodist side, the Briton Robert Newton Flew (1886-1962) highlighted the "catholic" profile of Methodism in a number of ecclesiological writings, including a chapter in *Northern Catholicism* edited by N. P. Williams (1933); and at a time when Roman Catholics were still officially forbidden to take part in ecumenical gatherings, Flew wrote the chapter on Roman Catholic ecclesiology for the volume *The Nature of the Church* that was produced in connection with the Third World Conference on Faith and Order held at Lund, Sweden, in 1952. The American Albert Cook Outler (1908-1989), a WMC observer at Vatican II, was ready to describe Methodism as "une église manquée" — a movement needing "a catholic church within which to function as a proper evangelical order of witness and worship, discipline and nurture" (see Albert C. Outler, "Do Methodists Have a Doctrine of the Church?" in Dow Kirkpatrick, ed., *The Doctrine of the Church* [Nashville: Abingdon Press, and London: Epworth Press, 1964], pp. 11-28).

prophet, priest, and king. The *fides quâ creditur* gets embodied in love towards God and neighbor, "works of piety," and "works of mercy." Together these constitute "the old religion," "true, primitive Christianity." And on that shared basis, Wesley says to his Catholic reader: "If we cannot as yet think alike in all things, at least we may love alike"; and so they should be kind to one another in thought, word, and deed, and finally "endeavour to help each other on in whatever we are agreed leads to the Kingdom": "So far as we can, let us always rejoice to strengthen each other's hands in God." That irenic letter — remarkable for its own time and for any time — has been held aloft by the Joint Commission for Dialogue.[2] It may certainly be hoped that not only the "union in affection" but even the "entire external union" that Wesley — in a related sermon titled "Catholic Spirit" (1750) — deemed unattainable in his own day on account of "smaller differences" in theological "opinions," "modes of worship," and "church government," has been brought closer by the agreements and convergences recorded by the Joint Commission; but two and a half centuries have elapsed since Wesley's time, and the way has not been easy. So we must now at least acknowledge with the Seoul Report that for the longest time, mutual "evaluations" were indeed sometimes "based on genuine understandings of each other's faith and life," but "more often they were coloured by the religious, social and political conflicts which have generally characterized relationships between Protestants and Catholics, and they were fed by mutual ignorance, defective understandings or partial views of the other." The sad story is sketched in chapter one of the Seoul Report as necessary background to the "mutual reassessment" made possible, as that same chapter outlines, by the "new context" set by ecumenism and the "new hermeneutical perspectives" that have been developed.

Let me now, therefore, offer a chronological and thematic account — as concise as possible — of the work of the Joint Commission for Dialogue between the WMC and the Roman Catholic Church as it has found expression in the quinquennial reports.

The first report offered more of a narrative than a systematic account of the opening round of the dialogue. Besides calling attention

---

2. Attention to Wesley's epistle was enhanced by a substantial edition of it at the hands of the Irish Jesuit Michael Hurley, himself a member of the Commission in its first two rounds: Michael Hurley, SJ, ed., *John Wesley's Letter to a Roman Catholic* (Nashville: Abingdon, 1968).

to John Wesley's letter to a Roman Catholic, "Denver 1971" called attention to: (a) a significant historical factor in relations between the two parties; (b) a shared emphasis in the spiritual life; and (c) another feature of liturgical, and even doctrinal, import. Thus first, "a singular advantage" was claimed in that "there is no history of formal separating between the two Churches, none of the historical, emotional problems consequent on a history of schism" (no. 6). Then, recognition was given to "the central place held in both traditions by the ideal of personal sanctification, growth in holiness through daily life in Christ" (no. 7; cf. nos. 49-56). Third, the hymns of Charles Wesley were appreciated as "a rich source of Methodist spirituality," that at least find "echoes and recognition" among Catholics: "This is not least true of the eucharistic hymns, which we saw as giving a basis and hope for discussion of doctrinal differences about the nature of the Real Presence and the sense of the 'sacrificial' character of the Eucharist. Methodists on their side were candid in considering Roman Catholic questions on how far the Wesleys remain a decisive influence in contemporary Methodism" (no. 9; cf. nos. 19, 79-84).

The "Dublin 1976" report showed the Joint Commission to have been tackling questions that were being treated around that time in other bilateral dialogues (notably in the Anglican–Roman Catholic International Commission's Windsor Statement on the Eucharist and its Canterbury Statement on Ministry and Ordination) and in World Council of Churches circles (notably in the Faith and Order process leading up to the Lima Statement on Baptism, Eucharist and Ministry, and in the Bangkok conference of Mission and Evangelism on Salvation Today). The themes of eucharist and ministry would continue to recur along the course of the Methodist–Roman Catholic dialogue.

The "Honolulu 1981" report was chiefly devoted to the person and work of the Holy Spirit, where the scriptural and creedal doctrine was expounded "with one voice" (no. 7). The doctrinal agreement on the Holy Spirit was pursued into the realms of "Christian experience," from which consequences were drawn for "authority in the Church." It was observed that "the old oppositions of Scripture and Tradition have given way to an understanding which we share, that Scripture in witness to the living tradition from which it arose has a normative role for the total tradition of the Church as it lives and is guided still by the Spirit of Truth" (no. 34). The Report strikingly declared: "We believe that emotions surrounding such relatively modern terms as infallibility and irreformability can be diminished if they are looked at in the light of our shared doctrine concerning the Holy Spirit. The papal authority, no less than any other within the Church, is a manifestation of the continuing presence of the Spirit of Love in the Church or it is nothing" (no. 35). The pneumatological thrust of the Honolulu Report came to be integrated into a fully rounded trinitarian pattern in all the subsequent reflection and writing of the Commission.

It was with "Nairobi 1986" — "Towards a Statement on the Church" — that ecclesiology began to establish itself as henceforth the governing theme of the Methodist–Roman Catholic dialogue. Facing the issues of schism and the concrete location of the church, the Joint Commission frankly declared that "we cannot expect to find an ecclesiology shaped in a time of division to be entirely satisfactory" (no. 22). It was, however, possible to set the "goal" of the dialogue — in a phrase that would be consistently maintained in all subsequent rounds — as "full communion in faith, mission and sacramental life" (no. 20). In the second half of its report, the Commission took on — no doubt prematurely — the question of "the Petrine office," or the special ministry of a universal primacy in teaching and jurisdiction, which Roman Catholics see as devolving from the apostle Peter through the New Testament and the patristic period to the Bishop of Rome. Methodists stated that they "accept that whatever is properly required for the unity of the whole of Christ's Church must by that very fact be God's will for his Church" (no. 58). In that light, "a universal primacy might well serve as focus of, and ministry for, the unity of the whole Church." And, in a gently apophatic mode, "it would not be inconceivable that at some date in a restored unity, Roman Catholic and Methodist bishops might be linked in one episcopal college and that the whole body would recognize some kind of effective leadership and primacy in the bishop of Rome" (no. 62).[3] Certainly, the Nairobi Report ended with the assertion that "Catholics and Methodists are agreed on the need for an authoritative way of being sure, beyond doubt, concerning God's action insofar as it is crucial for our salvation" (no. 75).

3. Or did the double negatives ("it would not be inconceivable") anticipate already a curial mode of speech? Certainly the linguistic style was rather different from that adopted by His Grace the Archbishop of Canterbury, Dr. Rowan Williams, in an interview reported in *The New Yorker* of April 26, 2010: "In the long run, it would be nice to have some sort of [Roman] primacy, but not the way things are — and that's not about the present Pope" (p. 47).

With the ecclesiological goal in place — distant as it might yet be — the Commission determined that progress would require attention to issues in "fundamental theology" *(Fundamentaltheologie),* and the next three rounds were devoted to such matters. Thus "Singapore 1991" treated "The Apostolic Tradition" in a way intended to enable Catholics and Methodists to see their own and each other's teaching and claims concerning the church in a broad historical and theological perspective that was "consistent with the doctrinal positions of both churches" and allowed convergences between them to be discerned. The report registered that "Methodists have become more willing to recognize the Roman Catholic Church as an institution for the divine good of its members," while "for its part, the Roman Catholic Church since Vatican II certainly includes Methodists among those who, by baptism and faith in Christ, enjoy 'a certain though imperfect communion with the Catholic Church'; and it envisages Methodism among those ecclesial communities which are 'not devoid of meaning and importance in the mystery of salvation'" (no. 100, citing *Unitatis redintegratio,* 3). As far as "the pattern of Christian faith," "the pattern of Christian life," and "the pattern of Christian community" were able to find matching delineations between Catholics and Methodists, the more recent positive evaluations of each other could be reckoned justified, and a basis existed for progress towards mutual recognition, reconciliation, and a more complete ecclesial communion. "Singapore 1991" included, in paragraph 94, a bold proposal that has been recalled also in some more recent reports, even though the details still necessarily remain imprecise:

> As we continue to consider remaining differences over the sacramental nature of ordination and the forms of succession and oversight, we rejoice in the work of the Spirit who has already brought us this far together, recognizing that the ecumenical movement of which we are a part is itself a grace of the Holy Spirit for the unity of Christians. When the time comes that Methodists and Catholics declare their readiness for that "full communion in faith, mission and sacramental life" toward which they are working, the mutual recognition of ministry will be achieved not only by their having reached doctrinal consensus but it will also depend upon a fresh creative act of reconciliation which acknowledges the manifold yet unified activity of the Holy Spirit throughout the ages. It will involve a joint act of obedience to the sovereign Word of God.

Pursuing the track of fundamental theology, "Rio de Janeiro 1996" offered — under the title "The Word of Life" — a "statement on revelation and faith"; and then "Brighton 2001" treated "teaching authority among Catholics and Methodists" under the title "Speaking the Truth in Love." Progress made in the intervening years pointed to a more expressly sacramental understanding of the church. A paragraph from Nairobi 1986 opened up a vision that remains crucial: "The Mystery of the Word made flesh and the sacramental mystery of the eucharist points towards a view of the Church based upon the sacramental idea, i.e. the Church takes its shape from the Incarnation from which it originated and the eucharistic action by which its life is constantly being renewed" (no. 10). That theme was renewed in "Rio de Janeiro 1996" (nos. 94-107) and in "Brighton 2001" (nos. 52-61).

"Seoul 2006" has already been cited for its opening chapter on the "mutual reassessment" that has been made possible by the "new context" of ecumenism. Chapter two then offers a thoroughly trinitarian and generally sacramental ecclesiology: the church is understood as "People and Family of God the Father," "Body and Bride of Christ, God the Son Incarnate," "Living Temple of God the Holy Spirit"; it is "marked with signs of Christ's life, cross and resurrection," "marked with signs of Pentecost," "sharing the mission of the Son and of the Spirit in the world." The church "is indeed a visible reality; its visibility is essential to its nature and mission. But there is more to the Church than meets the eye, and only the eye of faith can discern its deepest reality, its invisible mystery. . . . The invisible and the visible come together, and the former is made known through the latter. This holding together of the invisible and the visible is essential to our understanding of the Church as Catholics and Methodists. It is rooted in Christ himself, the invisible Word made visible in the flesh, fully divine and fully human" (nos. 47-48). However, Catholics and Methodists also both "confess that the life and actions of the pilgrim Church have at times made it particularly difficult to look beyond its visibility to the invisible presence of God. The Church is a community of weak and vulnerable human beings who often fail and fall, alone and together"; it is "always in need of purification and renewal" (no. 50). Yet in the journey "from sinfulness to holiness, God in his grace leads us forward": "We are confident of Christ's promises and the transforming presence of the Holy Spirit. We place our trust in Christ who says to his Church, 'My grace is sufficient for you, for my power is made perfect in weakness' (2 Corinthians 12:9)" (no. 95).

In "Seoul 2006" the Joint Commission worked with the conceptuality employed by Pope John Paul II in his encyclical of Ascension Day 1995, *Ut unum sint*: ecumenical dialogue, as a dialogue of both truth and love, entails both an exchange of ideas and an exchange of gifts. In light of the "very considerable" (no. 97) or "extensive" (no. 141) agreement on the nature and mission of the church established through the exchange of ideas in a dialogue of truth, the Joint Commission considered the moment had come to face directly the question of the church's identity and concrete location. The Report declares in paragraph 97:

> It is time now to return to the concrete reality of one another, to look one another in the eye, and with love and esteem to acknowledge what we see to be truly of Christ and of the Gospel, and thereby *of the Church,* in one another. Doing so will highlight the gifts we truly have to offer one another in the service of Christ in the world, and will open the way for an exchange of gifts which is what ecumenical dialogue, in some way, always is (cf. *Ut unum sint,* 28). In our striving for full communion, "we dare not lose any of the gifts with which the Holy Spirit has endowed our communities in their separation" [cf. United Methodist-Roman Catholic Dialogue, USA, *Through Divine Love: The Church in Each Place and All Places* (2005), §178]. The Holy Spirit is the true giver of the gifts we are seeking to exchange.

The Joint Commission summed up the potential benefits of reconciliation between Methodists and Catholics in terms of the creedal "notae Ecclesiae" as "the mutual enhancement of each other's oneness, holiness, catholicity and apostolicity" (no. 137). That third chapter on "deepening and extending our recognition of one another" thus concludes that, "in an important sense, two uniting churches [would] give to one another the gift of *unity,*" reinforce their shared sense of *holiness* in the church, augment the desire for ever-greater *catholicity,* and gain a vital sign of *apostolicity* in providing Methodists with the apostolic succession of bishops and Catholics with a rich Methodist sense of apostolic mission.

It was chiefly in the area of the "instrumentality" of grace that "divergences" between Methodists and Catholics "require further exploration and discussion": "There remain aspects of teaching and ecclesial elements which Catholics regard as essential to what we must hold in common in order to have full communion and to be fully the church of Christ. These include a precise understanding of the sacramental nature of ordination, the magisterial role of the episcopate in apostolic succession, the assurance asserted of certain authoritative acts of teaching, and the place and role of the Petrine Ministry" (no. 92). Some, at least, of those matters are occupying the Joint Commission as it works towards the report for "Durban 2011," which is provisionally titled "Encountering Christ the Saviour: Church and Sacraments."

Meanwhile the Joint Commission has also been engaged on a rather different kind of task. Following a meeting in 2005 between the co-chairmen of the Methodist–Roman Catholic dialogue and Cardinal Walter Kasper, then president of the Pontifical Council for Promoting Christian Unity, it was agreed that there was a need to synthesize the achievements of the near half-century of dialogue so far, in order that a consolidated statement might be offered to the sponsoring bodies with a request for their official approval. By Easter 2010, such a "synthesis statement" had been framed under the title "Together to Holiness." As far as possible, the statement sticks with the formulations used in the original reports of the Joint Commission, thus instantiating the consistency of the Commission's work over the decades. The Preface signed by the co-chairmen runs in part thus:

> The order of the document is thematic rather than chronological. It makes clear those doctrinal matters about which consensus appears to have been achieved between the Churches of the Wesleyan or Methodist Tradition and the Catholic Church. There has also been an attempt to indicate where convergence has been achieved to varying degrees on matters that might have been viewed in the past as divisive, even though this convergence falls short of full agreement. Finally, attention has been drawn to matters that clearly need further dialogue and which are more resistant to consensus or convergence; the most significant of these are indicated by italics in the text.
>
> The text is now submitted to the World Methodist Council and the Pontifical Council for Promoting Christian Unity with the hope that it might provide the grounds for a more formal discussion between the Catholic Church and the World Methodist Council about the Dialogue and its achievements to date. It is hoped the

synthesis will witness to the consensus and convergence that has been achieved and point to the further steps needing to be taken which would allow the convergence to be deepened and those issues which are resistant to resolution to be dealt with in succeeding phases of dialogue.

The first main section of the synthesis text is devoted to "God Revealed and Redeeming" (6-48): "The Holy Trinity" (6-10); "Creation and Salvation" (11-15); "Revelation and Faith" (16-26); "Justification and Sanctification" (27-34); "Scripture and Tradition" (35-40); "Christian Experience" (41-44). In all that, very few passages require the problematizing italic format — except to state under "Hierarchy of Truths" (45-48) that "though Catholics and Methodists share to a great extent a common faith, they are not yet fully agreed on what further doctrinal accord is necessary for the full communion of faith which would unite our traditions" (45), there being "need for further discussion on the identity and order of what are considered essential doctrines" (48). When the second main section deals with "The Church" (49-164), the same rarity of italics holds with regard to its first half, "The Nature and Mission of the Church" (49-82): "The Mystery of the Church" (50-55); "Koinonia: Connection and Communion" (56-62); "Abiding in the Truth" (63-65); "Cooperation and Participation" (66-68); "Called to Mission" (69-76) — until we come to the penultimate paragraph under "Gifts of the Spirit" (77-82): "Methodists and Catholics are not yet fully agreed on what constitutes the essential gifts, in the areas of doctrine, sacraments and structures. For Catholics, the essential gifts of the Spirit include the historic episcopate in the apostolic succession, and the Petrine ministry of the Bishop of Rome. For Methodists, the essential gifts include Christian conference" (81). With that, readers are prepared for the second half of the section on the church, where use of the italic font steadily increases: "Means of Grace and Sacraments" (83-88); "Baptism" (89-94); "Eucharist" (95-107); "Other Means of Grace" (108-13), where some rapprochement is noted in the fact that "Methodists, while using the term 'sacrament' only of the two rites for which the Gospels explicitly record Christ's institution, do not thereby deny sacramental character to some other rites," for which the characteristic Wesleyan term would be "prudential means of grace"; and then "Authority and Ordained Ministry" (114-58), where the problematic passages multiply: "Ordained

Ministry" (114-28); "Authority" (129-37); "Teaching Authority" (138-50); "Petrine Ministry" (151-58).

In matters concerning "The Christian Life," the synthesis records that "Catholics and Methodists subscribe to the teaching on Christ's will for matrimonial permanence and fidelity," though having "different views on the possibility of divorce and re-marriage when a marriage irrevocably breaks down" (164). Moreover, the two churches "are confronted with complex moral issues relating to abortion," which require further attention (173). There is agreement that "social concern is a fruit of faith" and belongs in the context of "God's purpose for the whole of creation" (176-81). As to the "communion of saints," there is agreement that "the 'cloud of witnesses' transcends denominational barriers" (182-83). There is "much in common at the heart of Methodist and Catholic prayerful devotion," with at its core "a desire to grow in holiness as perfect love in intimate union with the Risen Christ" (185-88). And on an italicized topic that has scarcely yet surfaced in the dialogue: "For Roman Catholics, devotion to Mary is an integral and important part of their Christian experience and of 'Life in the Spirit.' For Methodists, the dogmatic status of Catholic doctrines concerning the Mother of the Lord remains an issue of serious disagreement between the two traditions. Mary and the saints remain a topic for future dialogue between Catholics and Methodists" (184).

8 Church as Koinonia in the Methodist–Roman Catholic International Dialogue

Lorelei F. Fuchs, SA

Introduction

Neither polemical history nor mutual condemnation taints the Methodist–Roman Catholic past — no schism, only the reality of four centuries of separate ecclesial living. This living apart, however, is checkered with unpleasantness between the people called "Protestants" and those known as "Papists" — suspicion of each other, misunderstanding of each other's doctrine — the "unkindness" of which John Wesley in his *Letter to a Roman Catholic* "endeavour[ed] to remove."[1] No existing dissension at any time, however, eroded Methodist-Catholic consensus on essential elements of Christian faith.[2] Cultivating this consensus, the Joint Commission for Dialogue between the World Methodist Council and the Roman Catholic Church has enjoyed from its outset an honest and open exchange.[3] In what was perceived as a *kairos* moment for ecu-

---

1. "A Letter to a Roman Catholic," in Michael Hurley, SJ, ed., *John Wesley's Letter to a Roman Catholic* (London: Geoffrey Chapman, 1968), p. 49, n. 5.

2. On the Methodist side these were recently articulated in "Wesleyan Essentials of Christian Faith" (1996), available at http://worldmethodistcouncil.org. On the Catholic side, see Part One, "The Profession of Faith," nos. 26-1065 in the *Catechism of the Catholic Church*, prepared by the Interdicasterial Commission for the Catechism of the Catholic Church (Washington, DC: United States Catholic Conference/Libreria Editrice Vaticana, 1994).

3. The official name of this international dialogue is the Joint Commission for Dialogue between the World Methodist Council and the Roman Catholic Church. In this paper the name of the dialogue will also be cited as Joint Commission, Methodist–

menism, unexpected agreement was recognized.[4] The "growth in understanding" of one another's tradition led dialogue partners to believe that there is more that unites Methodists and Roman Catholics than divides them — a surprising awareness from two traditions that seemingly held little in common and from a dialogue that often goes unnoticed in the ecumenical world.[5]

In three parts this paper focuses on the concept of *koinonia* (communion) in the dialogue.[6] Doing so, it discloses what is perhaps the most consequential finding in Methodist-Catholic exchange: seeing the church of the Lord Jesus Christ in each other's church. Part I considers the language sources of dialogue in general and introduces the foundation of koinonia language in the Methodist–Roman Catholic international dialogue in particular. Part II traces themes through which the koinonia concept shapes the dialogue's understanding of the church. Part III looks to the future harvest of this Joint Commission. It refers to

---

Roman Catholic Joint Commission, and MRCJC. A sketch of its development is given in *DEM2*, pp. 758-60. As indicated above (p. 94), dialogue reports of this commission are named after the cities in which the World Methodist Conferences are held. During these conferences they were received by a plenary meeting of the World Methodist Council: Denver (1971), Dublin (1976), Honolulu (1981), Nairobi (1986), Singapore (1991), Rio (1996), Brighton (2001), Seoul (2006). These reports appear in the following sources: Reports from 1971-1982 in *GA*. Reports from 1982-98 in *GA II* (volume based on Harding Meyer, H. G. Urban, und Lukas Vischer, eds., *Dokumente wachsender Übereinstimmung II: 1982-1990* [Paderborn: Bonifatius, and Frankfurt am Main: Otto Lembeck, 1992]).

All reports are posted on the Vatican website, http://www.vatican.va/roman _curia/pontifical_councils/chrstuni/ and the Centro Pro Unione website, http://www .prounione.urbe.it/dia-int/e_dialogues.html. Each report is also published in pamphlet form by the World Methodist Council, POB 518, Lake Junaluska, NC 28745.

4. Denver 2. Unless otherwise indicated, numbers indicate paragraphs in reports.

5. From the dialogue's outset the notion of "growth in understanding" emerges as a foundational theme of this Joint Commission and became the unofficial title of its second report. See *Dublin Report, 1976*, in "Methodist-Roman Catholic Conversations," in *GA*, pp. 340-66, especially Dublin 43, 117; see also Brighton 64, where footnote 63 cites the Dublin Report as *Growth in Understanding*. The same can be said with "growth in agreement." This became the unofficial title of the commission's first report, which outlines key areas of agreement on issues such as Christology, scripture, theistic worldview, the crisis of faith in the modern world, human dignity, and Christian spirituality; see Denver 34-50.

6. For a broader overview of the concept of koinonia and the ecclesiology of communion, see Lorelei F. Fuchs, SA, *Koinonia and the Quest for an Ecumenical Ecclesiology: From Foundations through Dialogue to Symbolic Competence for Communionality* (Grand Rapids and Cambridge: Eerdmans, 2008).

the current round, and tenders an approach to issues that remain unresolved as well as issues thus far not approached by the dialogue.

May MRCJC's ecumenical findings find reception among Methodists and Catholics in their daily living of Christian discipleship.

Part I: The Language of Dialogue

Language Sources

A dialogue's language is crafted essentially from two sources. First, it is intrachurch language. That is, the language of each tradition — in this dialogue, of Methodism and Catholicism. One of the fruits of ecumenical cooperation and conversation is becoming aware that the languages of the traditions sometimes say the same or similar things, but say them differently. Second, it is interchurch language. That is, it is language the churches share, a language shaped and nurtured by the ecumenical movement. A fruit of both "denominational language" and "ecumenical metalanguage" is the mutual informing and forming that takes place as Christians seek together unity in the church's faith in apostolic tradition, the church's life in word and sacrament, the church's mission in witness and service.

Foundations of Koinonia Language in the
Methodist–Roman Catholic International Dialogue

The koinonia concept comes to the Methodist–Roman Catholic fore in the fourth series of the dialogue (1982-86), which initiates a study of ecclesiology. It is in its report, *Towards a Statement on the Church,* that the Joint Commission states for the first time the "aim and objective" of this bilateral relationship: "fullness of fellowship and communion":[7]

> In obedience to him who will bring about this unity, we are committed to a vision that includes the goal of full communion in faith, mission, and sacramental life. Such communion, which is the gift of the Spirit, must be expressed visibly.[8]

7. Nairobi Preface 8 (unnumbered).
8. Nairobi 20, 21.

With this as the dialogue's goal, understanding the church as koinonia (communion) emerges as fundamental to Methodist-Catholic unity, as the Joint Commission explored "ways of being one church."[9] Its labor wrought particular fruition with the sixth series on revelation and faith, and the eighth on ecclesiology, in which the Joint Commission asserts that koinonia (communion) lies at the heart of the way Catholics and Methodists understand the nature and mission of the church.[10]

Thereby the koinonia concept serves as the organizing principle of the dialogue and as an expression of Christian experience. As such, the multivalence of *koinōn*-language discloses the richness of the "elements and endowments" that Methodists and Catholics recognize in each other and, in some sense, share with each other.[11] *Koinōn*-language prevalent in MRCJC is the Greek word κοινωνία used in transliteration as "koinonia," and in translation, in particular, as "communion," "community," "fellowship."[12] In MRCJC's reports these terms are used in various ways, i.e., as complementary, as mutual qualifiers, as interchangeable. Yet there is a certain recourse to the transliterated "koinonia" as possessing the plethora of meaning whereas other *koinōn*-terms reflect a certain facet thereof:

> We have found that *koinonia,* both as a concept and an experience, is more important than any particular model of Church union that we are yet able to propose. *Koinonia* is so rich a term that it is better to keep its original Greek form than bring together several English words to convey its meaning. For believers it involves both **communion** and **community**. It includes **participation** in God through Christ in the Spirit by which believers become adopted children of the same Father and members of the one Body of Christ **sharing** in the same Spirit. And it includes deep **fellowship** among participants, a **fellowship** that is both visible and invisible, finding expression in faith and order, in prayer and sacrament, in mission

9. Nairobi 22-28.

10. See Seoul 51-53.

11. The words "elements and endowments" were used by the Second Vatican Council to express the gift of exchange that different traditions can recognize in each other and even exchange with each other. MRCJC used these words in its last round; see Seoul 9, 87, 97, 100, 110, 111, 114, 115, 120, 141, 146, 151, 152, 156, 157, 161, 162, where in places reference is made to Vatican II documents.

12. Words such as "participation" and "sharing" also appear in MRCJC.

and service. Many different gifts have been developed in our traditions, even in separation. Although we already **share** some of our riches with one another, we look forward to a greater **sharing** as we come closer together in **full unity** (cf. Vatican II, Decree on Ecumenism, *Unitatis redintegratio,* 4).[13]

Part II: A Thematic Look at Koinonia in the Dialogue

Five *koinōn*-themes emerge in the reports of the Joint Commission as foundational to its understanding of koinonia. The degree of their overlap is remarkable, often expressed in conjunction with ecclesial models of unity, particularly that of "organic unity in the *koinonia* of the one Body of Christ."[14] Also notable is the sense of the already-but-not-yet character of Methodist-Catholic unity. Communion with God and with one another is lived and experienced by word and sacrament in the worship of the Christian community.[15] "Despite our inability to manifest it perfectly, the fruit of the Spirit (Gal. 5:22-23) is ever a potent factor in drawing others into Christian fellowship."[16]

The Trinitarian Roots of Koinonia and the Creedal Faith of the Church

Methodists and Catholics believe that the mystery of the church is rooted in the mystery of the Trinity.[17] "As God's people (1 Peter 2:9-10) the Church is the setting of fellowship in which one hears and responds to the divine call of Father, Son and Holy Spirit."[18] The report, which states the dialogue's goal, opens with the trinitarian source of Christian koinonia in terms of the church's identity and mission:

> Because God so loved the world, he sent his Son and the Holy Spirit to draw us into communion with himself. This sharing in God's life, which resulted from the mission of the Son and the

13. Nairobi 23 (bold added).
14. Nairobi 24.
15. Rio 117.
16. Honolulu 24.
17. See Seoul 51.
18. See Honolulu 27, 31, 40.

Holy Spirit, found expression in a visible koinonia[1] of Christ's disciples, the church.[19]

"Communion with the Triune God is the very life of the church; communion with the mission of God's Son and Spirit is the very mission of the Church."[20]

There is particular appeal to the Holy Spirit as the agent of koinonia. "The Holy Spirit is the prime artisan of our Christian experience,"[21] "source and distributor of the diversity of gifts for the good of the koinonia," and "the inner power of new life in Christ."[22] "Full communion between Catholics and Methodists 'will also depend upon a fresh creative act of reconciliation which acknowledges the manifold yet unified activity of the Holy Spirit throughout the ages.'"[23]

The creedal faith of the church as one, holy, catholic, and apostolic is rooted in koinonia's trinitarian foundation.[24] These four marks "derive from its creation by and its communion with the Triune God...."[25] Noting the faith of the church in the Nicene Creed, MRCJC refers to the already-but-not yet: "it constrains us to take very seriously the degree of communion that Catholics and Methodists already share."[26] Unity, holiness, catholicity, and apostolicity are already God's gifts to the church, but they are not yet fully realized.[27] The dialogue urges that proclamation of the creed "be an occasion for giving thanks and a stimulus to deepen our unity in Christ."[28]

Biblical Foundations of Koinonia

Because MRCJC places each series of dialogue under a scriptural theme and cites biblical passages frequently, the biblical foundations of

---

19. Nairobi 1; footnote 1 in the quotation reads: "Cf. no 23. Paragraph 23 is on the meaning of the word koinonia and is quoted next."
20. Seoul 74.
21. Honolulu 27.
22. Singapore 27.
23. Seoul 144 (12), quoting Singapore 94.
24. See Brighton 12.
25. Seoul 65.
26. Singapore 38.
27. Seoul 66.
28. Singapore 38; see also Brighton 28.

koinonia are seemingly assumed. Accompanying this assumption, however, are insights into the multivalence of the concept, in particular two: the relationship of scripture and tradition, and the symbol competence of biblical images and metaphors of the church.

Concerned that scripture and tradition have been "notionally separated," the dialogue considers it imperative that they be reunited.[29] It asserts that: "Scripture was written within Tradition, yet Scripture is normative for Tradition." Evident here is the interplay between "tradition in scripture" and "scripture in tradition."[30] Essential for the church's growth is fidelity to the word of God by listening and acting. Thereby the living tradition of Christ and his apostles is continued and the faith handed on through the Holy Spirit.[31]

A clear warrant of the assumed biblical foundations of koinonia appears in the Rio Report issued from MRCJC's study of revelation and faith. It looks to the trinitarian basis in the First Letter of St. John as the "most complete statement of what the New Testament writers understand by the Greek word *koinonia* (communion)." The letter is addressed to "those whose discipleship of Christ is to bring them, throughout the ages and in union with the apostles, into an intimate sharing in the communion in love of the three Persons of the Trinity: 'that which we have seen and heard we proclaim also to you, so that you may have fellowship [*koinonia*] with us; and our fellowship [*koinonia*] is with the Father and with his Son Jesus Christ' (*1 John* 1:3)."[32]

Elsewhere the commission looks to the biblical images and metaphors that shed light on understanding the church as communion.[33] The church as the body of Christ is the favored image. It is prevalent in St. Paul who relates it to the eucharistic body of Christ in 1 Corinthians 10:14-17, and to the body and its members in 1 Corinthians 12:12-30 and Romans 12:4-6. The dialogue takes as exemplar the intimate bond of ecclesial communion of the baptized members of the early church:

29. Singapore 21.

30. See Singapore 18.

31. See Singapore 31.

32. Rio 108.

33. What follows draws on Brighton Report 13 and 15; article 13 is accompanied by a footnote detailing sources in the two traditions and in the British Methodist-Catholic bilateral dialogue.

"Baptized into the faith and proclaiming the crucified and risen Lord, the members were united to one another by the Spirit in a life marked by the apostolic teaching, common prayer, the breaking of bread and often by some community of goods; and those who were converted and drawn to them became part of this *koinonia*." This life-bringing communion with the Risen Lord is so profound that we call the church "the bride of Christ" and "the body of Christ."[34]

Methodist Koinonia

Following the inspiration of John Wesley, three terms emerge in Methodism to describe ecclesial relationship as central: *community, covenant,* and *connection.* A dynamic relationship exists among these terms, with "connection" being the foundational descriptor of what it means to be church. Methodist theologians have exposed the notion of connection as "Methodist koinonia."[35]

Connectionalism expresses the relationship among Methodist Christians, preachers and people with each other, and together with John Wesley. It is relationship of covenantal commitment that bespeaks their identity and mission. Christian conferencing structures this.[36] Joined together in Christ, they are interdependent and mutually accountable to one another, in local Christian community as well as in the wider Christian community. As a renewal movement, Methodism's vocation is to "spread scriptural holiness throughout the land."[37] Who they are calls them to do what they do. That is, they gather to confer about their spiritual identity and are sent forth on a scripture-based mission.

"Community" and "covenant" serve as qualifiers of each other, and they describe this identity and mission. Reports of the dialogue weave them together, often with images of the church:

34. Seoul 56; quoting Nairobi 2.

35. For example, see Bruce Robbins and David Carter, "Connexionalism and Koinonia: A Wesleyan Contribution to Ecclesiology," *One in Christ* 34, no. 4 (1998): 320-36.

36. See Rio 70.

37. See Denver 7; Rio 55, 60; Brighton 86 (which cites "Large Minutes," *The Works of John Wesley,* Jackson Edition, 8:299), 90; Seoul 17, 30, 41, 42, 69, 114. See also ch. 12, "Connection and Connectionalism" by Russell E. Richey in William J. Abraham and James E. Kirby, eds., *The Oxford Handbook of Methodist Studies* (Oxford/New York: Oxford University Press, 2009), pp. 211-28; this book is also cited in this paper as Abraham and Kirby, *OHMS.*

The chief mark of the post-Easter Church is that God gives to it the Spirit and thus creates the community of the New Covenant. The risen and exalted Lord takes possession of the world through his body, the Church, into which members are baptized in the Spirit.[38]

This community of faith is God's people, who by their baptism are a new creation in Christ and incorporated into his body.[39] It is a covenantal relationship of Christ's faithful love.[40] Covenantal community describes the connection the people of God have with him and with each other. It is a relationship rooted in the Holy Trinity, as Elmer M. Colyer notes:

> Connexion, in Wesley's Trinitarian understanding of salvation and the church, is invitation to communion, deepening communion, and full communion with the Triune God and one another. The Triune God builds up Christ's followers towards full salvation within particular forms of community that manifest certain kinds of relations or "connexion."[41]

This is the way to ". . . constant communion with the Father and His Son Jesus Christ through the Holy Spirit. . . ."[42] "Theirs is the fellowship of the new creation, of which they have received a foretaste by the gift of the Holy Spirit."[43]

Methodist understanding of community, covenant, and connection has thus informed and formed the commission as it unfolds the meaning of its goal of full communion in faith, mission, and sacramental life.

Catholic Koinonia

Catholic understanding of koinonia (communion) follows the vision of the Second Vatican Council. Two aspects emerge as foundational to

38. Honolulu 19.
39. Rio 50.
40. See Brighton 56.
41. Ch. 29, Elmer M. Colyer, "Trinity," in Abraham and Kirby, *OHMS,* p. 512.
42. Honolulu 18, citing John Wesley's sermon on the new creation.
43. Rio 79; see also Rio 101.

the council's focus on the church: the church as communion and the church as mission. As we have seen in Methodism, so in Catholicism the referent concerns what the church is and what the church does. Two documents ground the council's ecclesiology, and they are foundational to other conciliar and postconciliar documents. Concerning communion, it is the ecclesiology of *Lumen gentium;* concerning mission, it is the ecclesiology of *Gaudium et spes.*[44]

Catholicism brings to dialogue an overt communion ecclesiology. It is a sacramental ecclesiology, which is structured by episcopal oversight. MRCJC expresses this thusly:

> In a Catholic understanding the Church is united through its unity in faith and sacramental communion. The teaching of a common faith by the college of bishops in union with the successor of Peter ensures unity in the Truth. The succession of bishops through the generations serves the continued unity of the Church in the faith handed on from the apostles.[45]

> . . . the baptized and believing community is a communion. Holding in common the faith in which they are baptized and all the things that are God's gifts, they grow into a communion of the people who are made holy by God's grace and power.[46]

Following a reference to John Wesley's awareness that "the Holy Spirit is ever at work, bonding the exercise of particular spiritual gifts into unity with the exercise of complementary gifts in all the other mem-

---

44. The documents of the council may be found in Norman P. Tanner, SJ, ed., *Decrees of the Ecumenical Councils,* Volume Two: *Trent to Vatican II* (Original Text Established by G. Alberigo and Others) [in Latin and English] (London: Sheed & Ward, and Washington, DC: Georgetown University Press, 1990). They are also on the website of the Vatican, www.vatican.va. In addition to the council's other documents, two postconciliar documents in particular draw on these ecclesiologies in articulating the Roman Catholic Church's commitment to and engagement in the ecumenical movement: John Paul II's encyclical, *Ut unum sint,* and the Pontifical Council for Promoting Christian Unity's *Directory for the Application of Principles and Norms of Ecumenism.* See Johannes Paulus II, *Ut unum sint,* and Pontificium Consilium ad Christianorum Unitatem Fovendam, *Directory for the Application of Principles and Norms on Ecumenism* (Vatican City: Vatican Press, 1993). These documents are also on the Vatican website.

45. Singapore 93.

46. Singapore 66, which concludes referring to the "communion of saints" among whom the "cloud of witnesses" transcends denominational barriers.

bers of the body of Christ, the Church,"[47] the Rio Report on authority states the Catholic understanding:

> In the perspective of Vatican II, this action of the Spirit brings about an interdependence in communion between the spiritual instinct of the whole body of the faithful and those who are empowered to make normative acts of discernment of what is, or is not, faithful to Christian Tradition. "Thus the remarkable harmony of bishops and faithful comes into being in the preservation, the practice and the confession of the traditional faith" (*Dei verbum*, §10).[48]

These are among the "elements and endowments which build up and give life to the Church (*UR* no. 3)," which serve "the communion and mission of the Church."[49] So too with the Word of God and the sacraments. "By baptism and the faith in Christ which it signifies," "Catholics and Methodists already enjoy a certain measure of ecclesial communion."[50] This baptismal koinonia will find fulfillment when Methodists and Catholics can sit together at the eucharistic table of the Lord.

Catholicism speaks of the church as being "in Christ as a sacrament . . . ,"[51] which the dialogue refers to in this way:

> Christ works through his Church, and it is for this reason that Vatican II speaks of the Church as a kind of sacrament, both as an outward manifestation of God's grace among us and as signifying in some way the grace and call to salvation addressed by God to the whole human race (cf. Vatican II, *Lumen gentium*, I, 1).[52]

The divine call to salvation implies mission. As a sacrament, the church is the continuing presence of Christ in the world and thereby participates in *missio Dei*. The dialogue finds "considerable convergence in its understanding of the church's mission in the world":[53]

47. Rio 57.
48. Rio 58.
49. See Seoul 87.
50. Rio 10.
51. *Lumen gentium* 1.
52. Nairobi 9.
53. Rio 125.

Christian communion as *koinonia* necessarily includes communion in mission. It is communion with God, who sent his Son to reconcile the world and sent his Spirit to restore in human beings the image of God. Communion in mission is at the same time the fellowship of those who are sent . . . to be witnesses of God's love and peace throughout the world.[54]

Communion and mission, therefore, are inseparable. The church gathers as *communio* and scatters in *missio.* In the words of John Paul II, ". . . communion represents both the source and the fruit of mission: communion gives rise to mission and mission is accomplished in communion."[55] The sacramental life of the church, says MRCJC, nurtures this communion and sustains this mission.[56]

Expressions of Koinonia: Methodist Connection and Catholic Communion

Each of the themes considered here mirrors the koinonia concept as both descriptor of the Methodist-Catholic goal of full visible unity, and organizing principle by which the dialogue seeks to manifest that goal. To this end Methodism shares its charism of connection, and Catholicism shares its ecclesiology of communion. The Joint Commission recognizes in the two concepts correlative meanings. An example that elucidates this is the discussion on the church local and the church universal.[57]

First, each term, *connection* and *communion,* is a referent that is both diachronic and synchronic. That is, "Christian communion is more than the fellowship of the members of the same congregation or the same local community. . . . Communion means therefore also communion with the church of those who preceded us in the faith throughout the ages."[58] Methodism recognizes the continuity of the apostolic tradition preserved by the faithfulness to the apostolic teach-

---

54. Rio 123.

55. *On the Vocation and the Mission of the Lay Faithful in the Church and in the World* (*Christifideles laici* 1988), 32, available on the Vatican website, www.vatican.va.

56. See Singapore 67-69.

57. While looking at "connection" and "communion," MRCJC employs other *koinōn*-terms, in particular, "community" and "fellowship."

58. Rio 126; see 127-30.

ing, and the necessity of oversight in this preservation, and the role of the conferences. Connectional structures bind local churches in relationship to the whole church.[59] Catholicism relies on the promise given to St. Peter and the apostles, which has been fulfilled throughout history in the apostolic succession and the episcopal college together with its head, the Bishop of Rome as the successor of St. Peter. The hierarchical structure of the church is an important means and guarantee given by God's grace to preserve the continuity and universality of the Catholic Church.[60]

So described, the connectional/communional interrelationship of local churches within the church universal indicates considerable convergence, yet not without divergence. Catholics and Methodists agree that *episkopē* is essential to the ordained ministry.[61] They share a common concern regarding the church universal as an expression of communion in Christ. "But," warns the Rio Report, "they differ widely in their beliefs about the means which God has given to attain or preserve this goal. These differences may be the greatest hindrances on the way to full communion."[62]

Second, connection and communion refer to the nature and the mission of the church as inseparable: "Jesus' call to communion with his life (Come to me) is inseparable from his call to communion with his mission (Go in my name)."[63] In its consideration of "visible communion as sign of invisible koinonia," the 2006 Seoul Report develops the communion/connection matrix of koinonia by viewing the church as "connectional society," "a vital web of interactive relationships."[64] It claims that Methodists and Catholics have an essentially "connectional" understanding of Christ's call to discipleship, to holiness, and to mission. This call is God's gift, rooted in sharing in the invisible koinonia that is the life of the Holy Trinity. To be called is to be gathered, in communities of local churches that belong to the one communion of the church universal. The life of communion includes "deep fellowship among participants, a fellowship which is both visible and

---

59. See Rio 130.
60. See Rio 129.
61. See Dublin 88.
62. Rio 130.
63. Seoul 57.
64. See Seoul 60-62.

invisible, finding expression in faith and order, in prayer and sacrament, in mission and service."[65]

This dynamic of connection and communion belongs to disciples gathered in local community and to the worldwide community as the body of Christ. Both Methodists and Catholics hold that Christ wills one visibly united, universal church, even though they may differently identify the structures needed for such unity.[66] Mutual discernment of structures of koinonia is therefore essential for Methodist-Catholic unity.[67] "Our connection and communion with one another serve our growth towards holiness and our sharing in God's mission."[68]

Part III: The Dialogue's Ecumenical Findings for a Future Harvest

MRCJC 9

"Encountering Christ the Saviour: Church and Sacraments" is the current thematic topic of the Methodist–Roman Catholic Joint Commission. Drawing on the fruits of previous findings, our exploration is taking us to deeper probes of ecclesiology and sacramentality. Doing so, it follows the "BEM sequence" — baptism, eucharist, ministry — within the thematic context of the "paschal mystery of the death and resurrection of Christ."[69]

The study opens with the question: How do Christians live in union with Christ's death and resurrection? This the dialogue identifies as a fundamental question to which Catholics and Methodists must be able to give a united answer if the "full communion of faith, mission and sacramental life" that they seek is to be realized. Full communion must necessarily be a full communion in Christ and in the "paschal mystery."

Within this context, baptism, eucharist, and ministry are then being considered.[70] Concerning baptism, three questions have been

---

65. Nairobi 23.
66. Seoul 61.
67. See Singapore 7.
68. Brighton 48.
69. The sequence is that of the milestone study *BEM*.
70. The sources for what follows are working drafts of the round's report.

raised: the relationship between baptism and faith; between baptism and new life; and between baptism and church. Concerning eucharist, two issues identified as unresolved are addressed: the precise meaning of the eucharist as the sacramental "memorial" of Christ's saving death and resurrection; and the particular way in which Christ is present in Holy Communion. Concerning ministry, five areas are being considered: apostolic ministry, the nature of ordained ministry, ministerial priesthood and the common priesthood of the faithful, ordination as an effective sign, the ministry of oversight. Characteristic of this Joint Commission, this round looks for guidance from the Holy Spirit, the "Remembrancer Divine" and the "True Recorder of His Passion" (from *Hymns on the Lord's Supper* 16, v. 1).

Future Considerations

In the course of its ecumenical advance, MRCJC has found a certain largesse in the ecclesial model of unity in diversity.[71] The strength of this model lies in its capacity to embrace the wondrous diversity of our God-given unity. Its weakness lies in its tendency to become a least common denominator of how believers live, pray, and minister together in Christian fellowship. This model has, so to speak, borne fruits that the commission has harvested. As each dialogue round takes a step towards its goal of full communion, the commission also identifies those issues that have been treated yet remain unresolved and those issues that have yet to be taken up in dialogue. These are, so to speak, fruits yet to be harvested. Perhaps fresh consideration of the unity-in-diversity model might help surmount the impasse on these tabled matters and ready the dialogue for addressing new matters that still await.

To nurture a future harvest of ecumenical findings, it might be productive for this Joint Commission to engage in a study that would consist of two components. First would be an analytical study of the model and its functions vis-à-vis Methodist-Catholic relations. This would entail probing together the meaning of "unity" and "diversity"; the breadth and the limits of "unity" and of "diversity"; and what is meant by "legitimate diversity" and "reconciled diversity," which often

71. See Nairobi 5; Singapore 27; Brighton 25, 45, 50-51; Seoul 43.

qualify the model. Second would be an application of the model to issues that the commission has discussed but remain unresolved and issues that have yet to be studied. This would perhaps entail preparing "synthesis papers," similar to the one produced on prevalent themes in MRCJC — one reporting what the dialogue has already said on unresolved issues and another identifying issues the commission has yet to study and should. In a sense this effort would respond to the concern stated in the Rio Report: "While we are agreed on the existence of a common faith between us . . . , problems arise when we seek to define the distinctive teachings which are necessary to constitute the full communion of faith which would unite our churches."[72] To come to the full communion that is our goal, certain "distinctive teachings" need further clarification if ecumenical findings are going to be received in our churches. Nine series of this Joint Commission have paved the way for this to happen.

Concerning unresolved issues, a possible point of departure might be to frame these within a structure similar to *BEM,* drawing on the work of the current round and the principles and proposals in the last round's Seoul Report for "a mutual exchange of gifts, of ecclesial elements and endowments."[73] Among the issues awaiting this Joint Commission's direct attention, four emerge as timely considerations: scripture and tradition as sources of authority; the *communio sanctorum:* the place of Mary and the saints; apostolic succession: *episkopē* and Petrine ministry; Christian koinonia as moral community. None of these issues is completely uncharted territory for the commission. However, each represents "distinctive teachings" that might present obstacles to the goal of full visible unity of Methodists and Catholics. Engaging in such an "exchange of gifts" may risk facing the fact that not all gifts given are received. Seemingly the discernment of this Joint Commission is that in faith such risks are worth taking.

Conclusion

In the getting-to-know-you stage that characterizes the first phase of the dialogue, 1967-1970, the perspectives were: "how a Roman Catholic

72. Rio 114.
73. See Seoul, ch. 4, 139-62.

looks at Methodism" and "how a Methodist looks at Roman Catholicism."[74] The view was from a member of one tradition looking not at a member of the other tradition but at the tradition itself. Forty years later Methodists and Catholics are still looking. But the vision has grown. "It is time now to return to the concrete reality of one another, to look one another in the eye, and with love and esteem to acknowledge what we see to be truly of Christ and of the Gospel, and thereby *of the Church,* in one another."[75] Our traditions have real faces. There are people behind the documents.

The urgency in this Joint Commission concerns reception: What do we do with what we know? The urgency calls for harvesting its ecumenical findings so that by their "exchange of gifts" Methodists and Catholics will grow in mutual recognition and mutual accountability, and thereby enter into "full communion in faith, mission and sacramental life."

To continue being fruitful, the exchange of gifts between our churches must be ongoing. In "search of the catholic spirit," may we "bear fruit with patient endurance" (Luke 8:15).[76]

---

74. Denver 6.
75. Seoul 97.
76. Regarding the phrase "catholic spirit," see pp. 450-52 in ch. 26, David M. Chapman, "Methodism and the Future of Ecumenism," in Abraham and Kirby, *OHMS.*

9 Achievements of ARCIC and IARCCUM

Donna Geernaert, SC

Introduction: Anniversaries

The year 2010 was a time of anniversaries: one hundred years since the 1910 Edinburgh Missionary Conference usually identified as the beginning of the twentieth-century ecumenical movement, forty-five years since the close of the Second Vatican Council, and forty years since the beginning of formal Anglican–Roman Catholic bilateral dialogue in 1970. Anniversaries provide an opportunity both to look back to assess what has been accomplished, and to look forward to projected hopes for the future. With this in mind, these anniversaries are being marked by a number of conferences internationally, in Edinburgh and Rome, and locally, in such places as Victoria, British Columbia and St. Paul, Minnesota. In reviewing past achievements, however, it is important to do more than to engage in a kind of nostalgia. In fact, a certain *anamnesis* provides an opportunity for an active remembering that will allow the energy of past actions to inform and shape future events.

Bilateral Dialogue

While a number of bilateral dialogues were initiated at the time of the Reformation, the 1960s saw a renewed emphasis and sudden surge of these conversations between two parties seeking to address and overcome divisive issues. Two factors especially contributed to this development: (1) multilateral dialogues, especially through the World Council of Churches' Faith and Order Commission, and (2) the official entrance of the Roman Catholic Church into the ecumenical movement. With its strong sense of identity and universality, the Catholic Church developed a natural preference for bilateral dialogues. Other churches, particularly those that also have a strong sense of identity and worldwide coherence in doctrine, worship, and practice, took up dialogue with the Roman Catholic Church and subsequently among themselves. Much has been said, as is evident in the publication of reports of the dialogues held between 1972 and 2005 in three volumes of *Growth in Agreement*.[1] Thus, our gathering of participants from so many of these dialogues for this conference at the Saint Paul Seminary School of Divinity offers a unique opportunity to identify common themes, to reflect on what has been achieved, and to explore new ways of integrating these dialogue results into the life of our churches as well as the broader search for Christian unity "so that the world may believe" (John 17:21).

ARCIC

The private visit of the Archbishop of Canterbury, Dr. Geoffrey Fisher, to Pope John XXIII in 1960 — the first such meeting since the Reformation — marked the beginning of a new relationship between the Anglican Communion and the Catholic Church.[2] In March 1966, the Archbishop of Canterbury, Dr. Michael Ramsey, paid an official visit to Pope Paul VI in Rome. They signed a *Common Declaration* and decided to set up an official international dialogue whose work might lead to the unity in truth for which Christ prayed. The joint preparatory commission, which was established to organize the dialogue, held its first meeting in January 1967. In 1968, this preparatory commission published its findings in the Malta Report.[3] The report begins by referring

---

1. Hereafter *GA, GA II,* and *GA III*. Analogous collections of agreed dialogue texts and common declarations exist in Italian, German, French, and Spanish.

2. This new relationship is highlighted in the Second Vatican Council's *Decree on Ecumenism*, which states: "Among those [communions separated from the Roman See in the sixteenth century] in which some Catholic traditions and institutions continue to exist, the Anglican Communion occupies a special place." *Unitatis redintegratio,* 13 in Walter M. Abbott, ed., *The Documents of Vatican II* (New York: America Press, 1966). Hereafter cited as *UR*.

3. The Malta Report, in *GA,* pp. 120-26.

to a sense of urgency to respond to God's will, penitence for shared responsibility for harboring prejudices, thankfulness for the degree of unity that is already given in baptism, and a determination to bring this work of reconciliation to fulfillment within the context of the wider unity of all Christians. It moves on to suggest how progress could be made by stages. Each new stage of relationship would be entered into on the basis of agreements in faith, which would form the foundation for recognition from the highest authority, and lead to binding commitments to live closely together in many practical ways.

The Anglican-Roman Catholic International Commission (ARCIC I) held its first meeting in 1970. In 1981, its Final Report was published and forwarded to both Anglican and Catholic authorities for official response. It included agreed statements on: "Eucharistic Doctrine" (1971), "Elucidation" (1979), "Ministry and Ordination" (1973), "Elucidation" (1979), "Authority in the Church I" (1976), "Elucidation" (1981), and "Authority in the Church II" (1981).[4] The Anglican Communion gave its official response at the Lambeth Conference in 1988 and the Catholic Church gave its official response in 1991.[5] In 1993, ARCIC II published *Clarifications on Eucharist and Ministry,* which answered specific questions raised in the Roman Catholic response to the Final Report.[6] In light of these *Clarifications,* Cardinal Cassidy wrote to the co-chairmen in 1994 saying that the agreement was "greatly strengthened and no further study would seem to be required at this stage."[7]

In 1982, Pope John Paul II and the Archbishop of Canterbury, Dr. Robert Runcie, signed a *Common Declaration* which authorized the formation of a new international commission (ARCIC II).[8] Following a mandate to examine issues of grace and justification in relation to ecclesiology and Christian life, ARCIC II published agreed statements on *Salvation and the Church* (1986), *Church as Communion* (1990), and *Life in Christ: Morals, Communion and the Church* (1993).[9] In 1998, ARCIC II

4. The Final Report, in *GA,* pp. 62-118.

5. Resolution 8, Lambeth Conference of 1988; "Catholic Response to the Final Report of ARCIC I," published in *L'Osservatore Romano,* December 6, 1992, reprinted in *IS* 82 (1993/I): 47-51.

6. *IS* 87 (1994/IV): 239-42.

7. *IS* 87 (1994/IV): 237.

8. *GA II,* pp. 313-14.

9. *Salvation and the Church,* in *GA II,* pp. 315-25, *Church as Communion,* in *GA II,* pp. 328-43, and *Life in Christ: Morals, Communion and the Church* in *GA II,* pp. 344-70. Unlike

continued its reflection on ecclesial authority with the publication of *The Gift of Authority: Authority in the Church III*. In 2004, its dialogue on the place and understanding of Mary in Christian life and devotion was published as *Mary: Grace and Hope in Christ*.[10]

Following a meeting at the Vatican in November 2006, Pope Benedict XVI and the Archbishop of Canterbury, Dr. Rowan Williams, signed a *Common Declaration* which stated: "It is a matter of urgency . . . that in renewing our commitment to pursue the path towards full visible communion in truth and love of Christ, we also commit ourselves in our continuing dialogue to address the important issues involved in the emerging ecclesiological and ethical factors making that journey more difficult and arduous."[11] Meeting again on November 23, 2009, they reaffirmed their desire to strengthen ecumenical relations between Anglicans and Catholics. At this time, a preparatory committee met to plan the third phase of dialogue. ARCIC III will begin within the year and will address fundamental questions on the relationship of the local church to the universal church. More specifically, the dialogue will consider the authority of local bishops and local churches to make decisions on matters of church practice and moral issues.[12]

Published over a forty-year period, the ARCIC texts show a remarkable degree of consistency and coherence. The theology of communion *(koinonia)* runs through and unifies all of the agreed statements. The world's need for salvation explains the urgency of the call to Christian unity: "Only a reconciled and reconciling community, faithful to its Lord, in which human divisions are being overcome, can speak with full integrity to an alienated, divided world, and so be a credible witness to God's saving action in Christ and a foretaste of God's Kingdom."[13] The ARCIC agreements were reached by a method of attempting "to discover each other's faith as it is today and to appeal to history only for enlightenment, not as a way of perpetuating past

---

the ARCIC I Final Report, the ARCIC II documents (apart from the CDF's 1988 "Observations on *Salvation and the Church*") have not yet received official responses from the churches.

10. *The Gift of Authority: Authority in the Church III*, in *GA III*, pp. 60-81, *Mary: Grace and Hope in the Church*, in *GA III*, pp. 82-112.

11. *Common Declaration of the Archbishop of Canterbury Rowan Williams and Pope Benedict XVI*, November 23, 2006, in *IS* 123 (2006/III-IV): 86, para. 4.

12. *IS* 132 (2009/III/IV): 76.

13. *Salvation and the Church*, 30, *GA II*, p. 324.

controversy."[14] This method of dialogue, grounded in scripture and the ancient common traditions, has led to the discovery of common faith that can be expressed in doctrinal agreements.[15]

Mississauga Consultation

A *Common Declaration* signed by Pope John Paul II and the Archbishop of Canterbury, Dr. George Carey, on December 5, 1996, reaffirms their commitment to the quest for Christian unity and encourages ARCIC "to continue to deepen our theological dialogue, not only over issues connected with our present difficulties but in all areas where full communion has still to be reached." At the same time, the *Declaration* asks if "[i]t may be opportune at this stage in our journey to consult further about how the relationship between the Anglican Communion and the Catholic Church is to progress."[16] Since both churches are hierarchical in structure, it seemed that the primary responsibility for promoting unity should go first and foremost to the bishops of the two communions. It was therefore decided to hold an episcopal consultation to review and evaluate the accomplishments of thirty years of ecumenical dialogue between the two traditions and to reflect on how the special relationship between them has been developing in different parts of the world.

This decision was implemented in May 2000 when, at the invitation of the Archbishop of Canterbury, Dr. George Carey, and Cardinal Edward Cassidy, President of the Vatican's Pontifical Council for Promoting Christian Unity, pairs of Anglican and Catholic bishops from thirteen regions around the world gathered at a retreat house in Mississauga, Ontario.[17] Making use of a theological reflection model

14. The Final Report, Preface, *GA*, p. 62.

15. In a symposium on *Harvesting the Fruits* held in Rome, February 8-10, 2010, Bishop N. T. Wright of Durham expressed appreciation for this ARCIC method of dialogue, which he noted is "not always (it seems) easy to imitate." *IS* 133 (2010/I): 13-17.

16. *Common Declaration: George Carey, Archbishop of Canterbury and Pope John Paul II, December 1996,* in *GA II,* pp. 371-72.

17. Bishops attending this meeting were not a self-selecting group but were chosen by their fellow bishops to represent their Province or Episcopal Commission. Representatives came from countries where Anglicans and Catholics were in significant relations with each other: Antilles, Australia, Brazil, Canada, England and Wales, India,

based in experience, the consultation was designed with a minimum of input. Among the goals identified by the planning committee, it was hoped that the bishops would have an experience of exercising *episkopē* together, which might encourage commitment to a more regular exercise of shared *episkopē* locally. The importance of shared experience was reflected as well in the results of a four-point questionnaire forwarded to the countries of the participating bishops prior to the conference. Responses to the questionnaire provided a kind of "map" of the nature and state of current relationships, the strengths and weaknesses of these relationships, significant examples of ongoing joint witness and work, and current issues and challenges that should be addressed together.[18]

Grounded in prayer, the meeting began with a time of retreat, a shared meditation on conversion, communion, and a renewal of baptismal promises. The eucharist, and morning and evening prayer, were celebrated on alternate days according to the tradition of each communion. This experience highlighted both the closeness of our common liturgical inheritance and the pain of division at the eucharist. At the midpoint of the meeting, the bishops joined in ecumenical evening prayer with the local Christian community. To the surprise of many, the church was full and the congregation enthusiastic — perhaps an expression of a true and ongoing desire for unity among clergy and laity of both churches and of the wider Christian community as well.

The dialogue began with reflection on communion in life, a re-

---

Ireland, New Zealand, Nigeria, Papua New Guinea, South Africa, Uganda, and the United States of America. The presence of pairs of bishops was important, allowing for opportunities to discuss future possibilities realistically and to report back to their fellow bishops so that new relationships might be developed.

18. Responses to the questionnaires report close and cordial relations between the two churches, particularly at the level of episcopal sharing, with an end to old hostilities and suspicions. Relations are closest at the local (diocesan) level but do not seem to be matched by collegial sharing at a regional or national level. In places of social, tribal, or political tensions and hostilities, joint witness becomes an important sign of the possibility of reconciliation. The reports identify a number of current issues and challenges that should be addressed together. There appears to be a general agreement about the importance of joint Christian witness to gospel values in an increasingly secular society. Various forms of joint action, often involving members of other churches, are common, but a process for ecumenical accountability is lacking. Ecumenical consultation prior to major policy changes is unusual, and decision-making bodies often do not seem to consider the ecumenical consequences of an individual church's actions.

view of the mapping of Anglican and Roman Catholic relationships in thirteen countries around the world, and a panel outlining specific issues in two areas: Papua, New Guinea and Northern Ireland. Participants were then invited to consider agreement in faith as outlined in the ARCIC documents and including the experience and challenge of reception at the local level. A paper by Jean-Marie Tillard provided input on the vision of unity emerging from the ARCIC dialogue: "a eucharistic *communion* of Churches demonstrating by their harmonious diversity the richness of faith, unanimous in the application of the principles governing moral life, served by ministries that the grace of ordination unites *together* in an episcopal body, grafted to the group of the Apostles, and which is at the service of the authority that Christ exercises over his Body with the Spirit of Truth for the Salvation of the World and the glory of the Father. In one Word, it is the communion of the Body of Christ, here and now on earth."[19] And, a panel with participants from India, Nigeria, and New Zealand strongly asserted that the church's mission would be enhanced by its unity. It was noted that there is a need to be clearer about the shape of full visible unity, and to identify principal marks of the goal in order to take appropriate interim steps. Further, the interim steps are not a settling for second best, but have their own integrity and contribute positively towards attainment of the goal of full visible unity.

The final two days of the consultation looked toward the naming of elements for a common commitment. A concluding statement, *Communion in Mission,* and an Action Plan were adopted on the last day of the meeting. In this statement, the bishops claim their communion together is no longer to be viewed in minimal terms. Not just formally established by sharing a common baptism in Christ, it is, they affirm, "even now a rich and life-giving multifaceted communion." Further, the bishops say they have discerned that "[w]e have moved much closer to the goal of full visible communion than we first dared to believe." While unresolved differences and challenges (the understanding of au-

---

19. J. M. R. Tillard, "Our Goal: Full and Visible Communion," *One in Christ* 39, no. 1 (January 2004): 43. Involved in ARCIC dialogue from its inception until his death in 2000, Tillard here makes reference to a definition developed at a subcommission meeting in preparation for the 1973 Canterbury statement. The text does not appear to have been quoted in that or subsequent statements. In "Unity and Ecclesial Communion," *Church as Communion* 42-48, *GA II,* pp. 338-40, ARCIC offers a more detailed description of the "*constitutive elements* essential for the visible communion of the church."

thority and the way it is exercised, the precise nature of the future role of the universal primate, Anglican Orders, the ordination of women, moral and ethical questions) are recognized, these "are not to be compared to all we hold in common." In fact, the communion already shared has an "inner dynamic which, animated by the Holy Spirit, impels us forward toward the overcoming of these differences." In this context, the bishops see that they have embraced "a new stage of 'evangelical *koinonia*.' By this we mean a communion of joint commitment to our common mission in the world (John 17.23)."[20]

The marks of this new stage of communion in mission are identified as:

> our trinitarian faith grounded in the scriptures and set forth in the catholic creeds; the centrality of Christ, his death and resurrection, and commitment to his mission in the Church; faith in the final destiny of human life; common traditions in liturgy and spirituality; the monastic life; preferential commitment to the poor and marginalised; convergence on the eucharist, ministry, authority, salvation, moral principles, and the Church as communion, as expressed in agreed statements of ARCIC; episcopacy, particularly the role of bishop as symbol and promoter of unity; and the respective roles of clergy and laity."[21]

This list, much longer than that given in the Malta Report, includes convergences discovered through the work of ARCIC I and II. Thus, even without an official response to the ARCIC II statements, the bishops seem ready to acknowledge that progress has been made.

Called together to evaluate the state of Anglican–Roman Catholic relations and to chart a course for the future, the bishops maintain that their experience at the meeting "encourages us to believe that we have reached a very significant new place on our journey."[22] And, they agree: "Now is the time for the authorities of our two Communions to recognise and endorse this new stage through the signing of a Joint Declaration of Agreement."[23] Significantly, the experience of the meeting seems to have engendered in its participants an increasing aware-

20. *Communion in Mission,* in *GA III,* pp. 113-15.
21. *Communion in Mission,* 9, in *GA III,* p. 114.
22. *Communion in Mission,* 5, in *GA III,* p. 114.
23. *Communion in Mission,* 10, in *GA III,* p. 114.

ness "that as bishops we ourselves have a responsibility to guide, promote, and energise the ongoing work of unity in our churches."[24] They commit themselves "wholeheartedly to this task" and draw up an action plan as a means of translating their commitment into visible and practical outcomes.

As a first step in their action plan, the bishops recommend the establishment of a Joint Unity Commission, which will oversee the preparation of a Joint Declaration of Agreement and plan for its signing and celebration. Among other tasks, this new commission will prioritize the ongoing work, promote and monitor the formal response and reception of the ARCIC agreed statements, examine ways of dealing pastorally with situations of interchurch marriages, and encourage cooperation locally on clergy formation, education, and other pastoral matters. Other items in the action plan make reference to follow-up by the pairs of bishops from the thirteen participating countries, future agenda for ARCIC, the annual Informal Talks, and the Pontifical Council for Promoting Christian Unity as well as the Anglican Communion Office.[25]

IARCCUM

Established in January 2001, this International Anglican–Roman Catholic Commission for Unity and Mission (IARCCUM) is comprised of bishops from a variety of countries, assisted by a few specialists. Officially launched at Lambeth Palace and Rome in November 2001, IARCCUM received strong encouragement for its work from both the Archbishop of Canterbury and the Pope. At this meeting, three subcommittees were set up. One began to prepare a first draft of a common declaration that would formally express the degree of agreement in faith that already exists between Anglicans and Catholics, consolidate the results of more than thirty years of dialogue, and commit the dialogue partners to a deeper sharing in common life and witness. A second agreed to focus on practical recommendations for facilitating the ongoing reception of ecumenical texts, especially those of ARCIC; and the third would identify pastoral and practical strategies to help the two

24. *Communion in Mission*, 11, in *GA III*, p. 115.
25. *Action Plan to Implement Communion in Mission*, in *GA III*, pp. 116-18.

communions, particularly in local contexts, to do together whatever is possible in this current stage of real but imperfect communion.[26]

A second meeting took place in Malta in 2002. Draft texts were carefully reviewed, and practical proposals were made with regard to the local reception of ARCIC texts through mutual study and understanding rather than by formal response. In the following year, 2003, the churches of the Anglican Communion entered into a period of dispute occasioned by the authorization of a rite of blessing for same-sex couples and the episcopal ordination of a priest living in a same-sex union. The Vatican expressed concern over these developments, which it saw as not of a merely disciplinary nature but of vital importance to the preaching of the gospel in its integrity. The work of IARCCUM was put on hold to allow for a period of discernment. In this context, the Archbishop of Canterbury, Dr. Rowan Williams, invited the PCPCU Prefect, Cardinal Walter Kasper, to join him in setting up an IARCCUM subcommission to reflect on what the ARCIC agreements might contribute to this discernment process. Its Report, titled "Ecclesiological Reflections on the Current Situation in the Anglican Communion in the Light of ARCIC,"[27] proceeded to identify some of the ecclesiological implications of the moral decisions taken. With the October 2004 publication of *The Windsor Report*[28] and the Primates' communiqué of February 2005,[29] the Anglican Communion addressed these difficulties and IARCCUM was able to resume its work. Its agreed statement was published early in 2007.[30] With the original vision of the

26. *IS* 111 (2002/IV): 230; the work of the three groups is also reported in *IS* 115 (2004/I-II): 50-51.

27. "Ecclesiological Reflections on the Current Situation in the Anglican Communion in the Light of ARCIC," *IS* 119 (2005/III): 102-15. The Pontifical Council for Christian Unity praised Archbishop Williams's initiative as an affirmation of the strength of the mutual relationship, as an acknowledgment that the actions of one church have a significant impact on the other, and as an important step towards the reception of the results of dialogue.

28. Available at: www.anglicancommunion.org/windsor2004/downloads/index .cfm.

29. Available at: www.anglicancommunion.org/communion/primates/resources/ downloads/communique%20_english.pdf.

30. *Growing Together in Unity and Mission: Building on 40 Years of Anglican–Roman Catholic Dialogue. An Agreed Statement of the International Anglican–Roman Catholic Commission for Unity and Mission* (London: SPCK, 2007). Also published in *IS* 124 (2007/I-II): 44-66. Hereafter cited as *GTUM*.

Malta Report in mind, the IARCCUM bishops hoped to reinstate and promote a broad practical program of engagement between the two churches, not just in relation to one another but primarily in view of joint witness and common mission in the world. As stated in *Growing Together in Unity and Mission,* the document is "a call for action, based upon an honest appraisal of what has been achieved in our dialogue."[31] Affirming the concept of unity by stages and acknowledging the need to grow gradually into the full communion that Christ desires, the authors of this statement nevertheless believe "that it is the time to bridge the gap between the elements of faith we hold in common and the tangible expression of that shared belief in our ecclesial lives."[32] The text is structured in two main parts: (I) The Achievements of Anglican–Roman Catholic Theological Dialogue, and (II) Towards Unity and Common Mission.

The first part of the text includes a large section on "The Faith We Hold in Common" with topics presented under nine headings: "Belief in God as Trinity," "Church as Communion in Mission," "The Living Word of God," "Baptism," "Eucharist," "Ministry," "Authority in the Church," "Discipleship and Holiness," and "The Blessed Virgin Mary." In all but two of these ("Belief in God as Trinity," "Baptism"), the text clearly indicates in boxed paragraphs topics that require further exploration. Frequently used in other bilateral and multilateral dialogues, this formatting invites reflection on unresolved issues within the framework of already-recognized agreements. Identified in this way, areas of divergence are not minimized but placed within a broader context that may allow for new interpretations. Through the past forty years of ecumenical dialogue, Anglicans and Catholics have, IARCCUM affirms, "grown closer together and have come to see that what they hold in common is far greater than those things in which they differ."[33]

Consistent with the conviction expressed at Mississauga, the IARCCUM text sees a logical, theological, and intrinsic relationship between the developing experience of ecclesial communion and the imperative to engage step by step in forms of shared life and mission.

31. *GTUM,* Preface, p. 4.
32. *GTUM,* 10, p. 11.
33. *GTUM,* 2, p. 7. In his encyclical on commitment to ecumenism, Pope John Paul II stresses the importance of avoiding facile agreement. "Serious questions must be resolved, for if not, they will reappear at another time, either in the same terms or in a different guise." *UUS,* no. 36, p. 43.

"The Commission has become more profoundly aware of how intimately connected are understanding and co-operation, faith and mission. It is our conviction that, as we grow towards full, ecclesial communion and respond afresh to the common mission entrusted to his Church by our Lord, the remaining Church-dividing issues will be resolved more effectively."[34] In brief, the agreements reached in theological dialogue are to have an impact on interchurch relations, to encourage Anglicans and Catholics to do together whatever is possible to express the degree of agreement that has been achieved. And, these practical steps are intended to become a means not only of consolidating the gains that have been made but also of leading to new depths of communion on the way to that fullness of unity which is the will of Christ.[35]

While acknowledging that the time may not be right to initiate "a formal new stage in our relations," the second part of *Growing Together in Unity and Mission* "proposes some specific steps to deepen our fellowship in life and mission which we believe are responsibly open for us and would be appropriate for us to take in the present context."[36] The text states: "Genuine faith is more than assent: it is expressed in action"; "the extent of common faith described in this statement compels us to live and witness together more fully here and now."[37] Because "the context and dynamics of relationships between Anglicans and Roman Catholics differ widely across the world,"[38] appropriate action must be determined locally. Taking up and expanding the Malta Report's proposals, however, the text makes numerous practical recommendations under four headings: "Visible expressions of our shared faith," "Joint study of our faith," "Co-operation in ministry," and "Shared witness in the world."[39]

---

34. *GTUM,* 94, p. 48.

35. In a private audience with the members of the Commission in November 2001, Pope John Paul II noted that as an international group of bishops, they are "especially well qualified to consider the next practical steps." *IS* 115 (2004/I-II): 51.

36. *GTUM,* 10, p. 11.

37. *GTUM,* 96, p. 50. As is evident in the "Survey of Anglican–Roman Catholic Relations" presented at the Mississauga meeting, what is appropriate, even commonplace, in some areas may be misunderstood in others. Local tensions may place real limitations on joint action. See *One in Christ* 39, no. 1 (January 2004): 7-22.

38. *GTUM,* 99, pp. 50-51.

39. *GTUM,* 100-125, pp. 51-58.

Prepared by an episcopal commission, *Growing Together in Unity and Mission* is addressed primarily to bishops. It encourages bishops around the world to exercise their episcopal role and responsibility to guide, promote, and energize the ongoing search for Christian unity, especially in their own dioceses. The action steps in the second part of the text, as Bernard Longley points out, are based on ARCIC agreements, many of which have not been formally recognized by either of the two churches.[40] Yet, much of what is contained in this section is already within the framework of what other officially approved texts, such as the Pontifical Council for Promoting Christian Unity's *Directory for the Application of Principles and Norms on Ecumenism* (1993) and *The Ecumenical Dimension in the Formation of Those Engaged in Pastoral Work* (1997), agree can be implemented. In their 2006 *Common Declaration,* moreover, Pope Benedict XVI and Archbishop Rowan Williams call for closer cooperation in a wide range of areas of witness and service, including pursuit of peace in the Holy Land, promotion of respect for life from conception until natural death, outreach to the poor, care for the environment, commitment to interreligious dialogue, and addressing the negative effects of materialism.[41]

Where regional meetings of Anglican and Catholic bishops can and do occur, discernment of appropriate practical initiatives will be facilitated.[42] Joint action in mission is not only an expression of the degree of faith already shared but also an invitation to deepen the communion yet to be shared. Over the past forty years, increased interaction has led to greater mutual understanding, setting Anglicans and Catholics free to witness more effectively together. While rejoicing in what has been accomplished, the bishops of IARCCUM call on all bishops to encourage their clergy and people "to engage in a searching exploration of new possibilities for co-operation in mission."[43] "In addi-

---

40. Bernard Longley, "A Commentary on *Growing Together in Unity and Mission,*" in *IS* 124 (2007/I-II): 71, 76.

41. *IS* 123 (2006/III-IV): 87.

42. *GTUM,* 109, p. 54, notes the example of Anglican and Roman Catholic bishops in the Sudan who have met regularly over the past four years to jointly address important social issues.

43. *GTUM,* 126, p. 58. Reception of dialogue results, the bishops affirm, is not merely a theoretical and theological process but must involve the life of the churches. Ecumenical texts need to be studied and understood at a local level so that the implications of agreements reached can be reflected in appropriate action.

tion to all we can and must do," the bishops say, "we trust the Holy Spirit that the One who initiated our pilgrimage to unity and common mission will bring it to fulfilment."[44]

At the end of the Mississauga Consultation, the bishops confidently asserted that a new stage in Anglican and Catholic relations had been reached and that this should be marked by the signing of a Joint Declaration of Agreement. In line with recommendations of the Malta Report and the consensus on basic truths of the doctrine of justification formally acknowledged by the Lutheran World Federation and the Catholic Church in 1999, such a Declaration would acknowledge the consensus in faith that had been reached and give new impetus to a sharing in common life and witness. Yet, *Growing Together in Unity* identifies its work as an Agreed Statement, the same phrase used to identify the ARCIC texts. Like ARCIC's work, the text is published under the authority of the commission members. The Co-Chairmen's Preface states clearly that the text "is not an authoritative declaration by the Roman Catholic Church or by the Anglican Communion. What is offered here by IARCCUM is a statement which is intended to foster discussion and reflection."[45] Well aware that they have "not answered the full challenge extended by the bishops at Mississauga," the IARCCUM bishops have "sought to undertake what is appropriate in the present context."[46] Asked to initiate a process leading towards an authoritative joint declaration, commission members found themselves only able to develop an agreed statement that they see as a significant step towards such a declaration. In what will necessarily be a longer process, the text is now submitted to the sponsoring bodies for study and reflection. Responses to it will assist the Catholic Church and the Anglican Communion to discern whether it provides a sound basis for a formal agreement that could be affirmed, officially signed, and celebrated in the future.

In his "Commentary on *Growing Together in Unity and Mission,*" Bernard Longley identifies the IARCCUM text as a new genre of ecumenical document.[47] The majority of dialogue documents, including those of ARCIC, focus on identifying and resolving church-dividing is-

---

44. *GTUM,* 8, p. 11.
45. *GTUM,* Preface, pp. 3-4.
46. *GTUM,* 8, pp. 10-11.
47. Longley, "Commentary," p. 67.

sues specific to the dialogue partners. In a process more reflective of that employed in producing the 1999 *Joint Declaration on the Doctrine of Justification,* however, the IARCCUM text offers a review and synthesis of the work of ARCIC directed toward identifying those results of the dialogue that Anglican and Catholic authorities might affirm as areas of shared faith. This responds to a frequently expressed concern about the fact that many years of dialogue have produced good results, which now need to be consolidated and officially recognized so they can shape ecclesial lives and action in appropriate ways. In his "Commentary," Longley expresses appreciation for IARCCUM's careful reading of ARCIC's Agreed Statements but also questions its apparent lack of attentiveness to official or authoritative responses to ARCIC's work. "If the reception process is understood to include a refining of a text in the light of responses from the churches," he notes, "IARCCUM could have been more deliberate in addressing concerns raised there."[48] Following a careful analysis of the text's content and methodology from a Roman Catholic doctrinal and pastoral perspective, Longley concludes that "[i]t deserves to be welcomed and further studied by our two Communions so that the present reality of our ecumenical relations may be more clearly understood and the real though partial communion we enjoy may become more visible in effective witness and mission."[49]

At a symposium honoring Cardinal Willebrands in November 2009, the Archbishop of Canterbury, Dr. Rowan Williams, raises some interesting questions.[50] Beginning with Vatican II's "re-theologizing" of the church and taking account of the "ethos and idiom" of the ecumenical dialogues that have taken place since the Council, he finds "an integral connection between what is said about the nature of God and what is said about the Church, its mission and ministry."[51] With reference to Cardinal Kasper's recently published *Harvesting the Fruits,* he affirms that "the issues between Christians in the historic Churches are *not* about the essential shape of our language concerning God and God's action in Christ . . . the self-definitions of the churches remain solidly anchored in the Nicene faith, understood precisely as the faith

48. Longley, "Commentary," p. 71.

49. Longley, "Commentary," p. 81.

50. "Ecclesiological Foundations and the Ecumenical Agenda since Cardinal Johannes Willebrands," *IS* 132 (2009/III-IV): 46-50.

51. "Ecclesiological Foundations and the Ecumenical Agenda," 1, para. 2, p. 46.

that makes sense of the experienced reality of communion in Christ."[52] In terms of sacramental forms and doctrines, moreover, "the links from trinitarian doctrine straight through to the meaning of the Lord's Supper are strongly affirmed on all sides."[53] When so much agreement about the identity and mission of the church has been firmly established, he inquires, "is it really justifiable to treat other issues as equally vital for its health and integrity?"[54] "Are they *theological* questions in the same sense as the bigger issues on which there is already clear agreement?"[55] In brief, he asks whether the unfinished business between us "is as fundamentally church-dividing as our Roman Catholic friends generally assume and maintain. And if it isn't, can we allow ourselves to be challenged to address the outstanding issues with the same methodological assumptions and the same overall spiritual and sacramental vision that has brought us thus far?"[56]

Ongoing Challenges

While official reception of the ARCIC agreements is crucial to the growing rapprochement between Anglican and Catholic churches, two issues — one in a more specifically Anglican context and the other more specifically Catholic — present particular challenges to both communions. What has become clear through the experience of dialogue over the past number of years is, in the words of Archbishop Rowan Williams, that "no part of the Christian family acts without profound impact on our ecumenical partners."[57]

52. "Ecclesiological Foundations and the Ecumenical Agenda," 2, para. 1, p. 47.

53. "Ecclesiological Foundations and the Ecumenical Agenda," 2, para. 2, p. 47.

54. "Ecclesiological Foundations and the Ecumenical Agenda," Introduction, 4, p. 46.

55. "Ecclesiological Foundations and the Ecumenical Agenda," Introduction, 3, p. 46.

56. "Ecclesiological Foundations and the Ecumenical Agenda," 6, para. 3, p. 50.

57. Address given in the papal private library on November 23, 2006. *IS* 123, p. 86. This thought is echoed in Cardinal Kasper's address to the PCPCU's plenary meeting of 2003: "It should be borne in mind that as ecumenical partners we are not simply observers, but active participants; indeed, the ecumenical fabric has become very closely woven, and the decisions of one partner impinge upon relations with all the others, and therefore these decisions should be taken in solidarity with one another." *IS* 115 (2004/I-II): 28.

Within the Anglican Communion, differing responses to questions about human sexuality and women's ordination have given rise to decisions within some of the Provinces that appear to seriously threaten the unity of the Communion. Cardinal Kasper's address to the Lambeth Conference in July 2008 highlights some of the challenges as seen from a Catholic perspective.[58] In brief, he says: "We hope we will not be drawn apart, that we will be able to remain in serious dialogue in search of full unity so that the world may believe."[59] Reflecting more specifically on the *Windsor Report,* he notes: "While the Report stresses that the Anglican provinces have a responsibility towards each other and towards the maintenance of communion, a communion rooted in the Scriptures, considerably little attention is given to the importance of being in communion with the faith of the Church through the ages."[60] Further, he says: "It also seems to us that the Anglican commitment to being 'episcopally led and synodically governed' has not always functioned in such a way as to maintain the apostolicity of the faith, and that synodical government misunderstood as a kind of parliamentary process has at times blocked the sort of episcopal leadership envisaged by Cyprian and articulated by ARCIC."[61] Throughout this period of controversy and discernment, the Anglican Communion's commitment to take seriously the concerns of its ecumenical dialogue partners has been clearly evident. Close communications and friendly relations have been maintained, and a number of consultations have taken place. In this context, ecumenical partners "have been able to speak with an openness and directness which in the past would have been impossible."[62]

Within the Roman Catholic Church, the publication of the Apostolic Constitution *Anglicanorum coetibus* raises another series of ques-

---

58. *IS* 129 (2008/III): 143-49. More than 200 of the 880 Anglican bishops worldwide refused to attend the 2008 Lambeth Conference because of differences over responses to same-sex relationship in the USA and Canada. There was a significant ecumenical presence at this Conference, including a Catholic delegation of ten who were invited to take part in discussions and to address the assembly on the difficulties within the Communion.

59. *IS* 129, Introduction, para. 4, p. 143.

60. *IS* 129, II, para. 19, p. 147.

61. *IS* 129, II, para. 20, p. 147.

62. Cardinal Walter Kasper, "Message to the 13th Anglican Consultative Council Meeting," *IS* 119 (2005/III): 101. Cf. *IS* 123 (2006/III-IV): 107.

tions. Announced on October 20, 2009 by the Prefect of the Congregation for the Doctrine of the Faith (CDF), Cardinal William Levada, and signed by Pope Benedict XVI on November 4, 2009,[63] this Apostolic Constitution allows for the establishing of personal ordinariates for groups of individuals who wish to retain an Anglican identity in full communion with the Roman Catholic Church. In spite of some rather sensational media reactions, both churches have stressed that this is a pastoral response to requests from some Anglicans and not a betrayal or alternative to ecumenical dialogue. Timed to coincide with Cardinal Levada's October 20th announcement of the imminent publication of *Anglicanorum coetibus,* a press conference held in London by the Archbishop of Canterbury, Rowan Williams, and the Archbishop of Westminster, Vincent Nichols, affirms: "The Apostolic Constitution is further evidence of the overlap in faith, doctrine and spirituality between the Catholic Church and the Anglican tradition. Without the dialogues of the past forty years, this recognition would not have been possible. . . . In this sense, this Constitution is one consequence of ecumenical dialogue between the Catholic Church and the Anglican Communion." "With God's grace and prayer we are determined that our ongoing mutual commitment and consultation . . . should continue and be strengthened."[64] On January 15, 2011, the CDF published a Decree erecting the first Personal Ordinariate for groups of Anglicans and their pastors wishing to enter into full communion with the Catholic Church. An Ordinary was appointed to oversee the catechetical preparation of those groups who will be received into the Catholic Church at Easter. The newly appointed Ordinary issued a statement in which he expresses his gratitude for his life and ministry in the Anglican Communion and his appreciation for the patience and support of the Archbishop of Canterbury during the time of discernment. A press release from the Holy See again states: "The provision of this new structure is consistent with the commitment to ecumenical dialogue, which continues to be a priority for the Catholic Church."[65]

In both of these cases as well as in the painful sexual abuse scandals that have rocked the Catholic Church, the strength of ecumenical

---

63. See: www.vatican.va/holy_father/benedict_xvi/apost_constitutions/documents/hf_ben-xvi_apc_20091104_anglicanorum-coetibus_en.html.

64. Available at: www.catholic-ew.org.uk/catholic-church/media-centre/.

65. Available at: www.catholic-ew.org.uk/catholic-church/media-centre/. The Ordinariate will be known as the Personal Ordinariate of Our Lady of Walsingham.

dialogue becomes apparent. Dialogue is not an easy task. It is always hard to keep an open mind, to try to enter into another's way of thinking and seeing things, to persevere when disagreements arise. And, the difficulties are compounded when dialogue touches on matters of faith. The constant commitment to seek and do God's will provides a sound basis for dialogue, while at the same time dialogue with others who are seeking the face of God will stimulate and strengthen this commitment. In the words of Cardinal Kasper: "We have begun to learn — and let me hasten to say this is a reciprocal learning — what it means to walk with each other amidst difficulties, to carry the burdens of the other."[66]

Conclusion: A God of Surprises

As Christians, our commitment to ecumenism is a response to our understanding of Christ's prayer and will for the church. As the Second Vatican Council's *Decree on Ecumenism* declares, discord among Christians "openly contradicts the will of Christ, provides a stumbling block to the world and inflicts damage on the most holy cause of proclaiming the good news to every creature."[67] Yet, this same *Decree* affirms that the Spirit of God alone has the power to create or restore the one church of Christ. Very specifically, "the reconciliation of all Christians in the unity of the one and only church of Christ — transcends human powers and gifts."[68] In a meditation given one morning at the Missis-

---

66. Homily given at vespers service at Santa Maria Sopra Minerva, November 24, 2006. *IS* 123 (2006/III-IV): 90. The Report of the Third Phase of WARC-Catholic dialogue, *The Church as Community of Common Witness to the Kingdom of God,* has a section on "Ecumenical Dialogue as Common Witness," which relates the dialogue process to the paschal mystery and asserts: "Dialogue purifies its participants so that each can approach the other with the freedom that comes from taking on the mind of Christ." *IS* 125 (2007/III): 246, no. 201.

67. *UR,* 1.

68. *UR,* 24. In his address to participants in the PCPCU's plenary meeting of 2010, Pope Benedict XVI reiterated this point: "We do not know the time that the unity of all Christ's disciples will be achieved, and we cannot know it because we do not 'make' unity, God 'makes' it; it comes from on high, . . . it is a participation in divine unity. Yet this must not diminish our commitment; quite the contrary, it must make us ever more attentive to recognising the signs and times of the Lord, knowing how to recognise with gratitude what unites us and working to ensure it . . . grows." Vatican Information Service, November 18, 2010.

sauga Consultation, the words of Cardinal Kasper struck a chord: "God will always surprise us. [God] cannot be understood through our human system or correspond to our positive or negative predictions for the future. Faith means to be open to God. . . . A faith that does not take account of wonder is meaningless and ineffective. Hence our expressions of faith transcend themselves in the greater mystery of God. In our ecumenical efforts we should keep in mind that one day we will rub our eyes and be surprised by the new things that God has achieved in his Church. It is true that in the course of history we have done much against love and unity, but God — and this is our hope — will make things good again."[69]

69. "Meditation on Acts 13:30-33," *One in Christ* 39, no. 1 (January 2004): 53-55.

10 Perspectives on Christ, the Church, and Christian Social Witness

John A. Radano

Introduction

Since Vatican II, there have been three phases of international dialogue co-sponsored by the World Alliance of Reformed Churches and the Catholic Church (through the Pontifical Council for Promoting Christian Unity). The first phase (1970-77) produced a report titled "The Presence of Christ in Church and World."[1] The second phase (1984-1990) produced a report titled "Towards a Common Understanding of the Church."[2] The third phase took place 1998-2005 and its report is titled "The Church as the Community of Common Witness to the Kingdom of God."[3]

The purpose of the conversations "has been to deepen mutual understanding and to foster the eventual reconciliation of our two communities" (TCUC, no. 1).

---

1. "The Presence of Christ in Church and World: Final Report of the Dialogue between the World Alliance of Reformed Churches and the Secretariat for Promoting Christian Unity, 1977," in *GA*, pp. 433-63. Hereafter PCCW.

2. "Towards a Common Understanding of the Church. Second Phase, 1984-1990," in *GA II*, pp. 780-818. Hereafter TCUC.

3. "The Church as the Community of Common Witness to the Kingdom of God: Report of the Third Phase of the International Theological Dialogue between the Catholic Church and the World Alliance of Reformed Churches 1998-2005," in *IS* 125 (2007/III): 110-56. Hereafter CWKG.

Ecumenical Challenges

As this dialogue began, both partners experienced ecumenical challenges. The Catholic Church was receiving the new perspectives of the Second Vatican Council into many aspects of its life. The ecumenical mandate given to the church by the Council was relatively fresh, even though significant ecumenical events had already taken place, and it had begun other dialogues.

The Reformed partner in this dialogue was evolving ecumenically when the dialogue began, and has continued to do so over the decades during which this dialogue has been taking place. The World Alliance of Reformed Churches came into existence in 1970, the year this dialogue began, as a merger of two previous international bodies: the Alliance of Reformed Churches throughout the World holding the Presbyterian System (1875) and the International Congregational Council (1891). Its membership during the years of this dialogue has included Congregational, Presbyterian, Reformed, and United churches. It has roots in the sixteenth-century reformation led by John Calvin, John Knox, Ulrich Zwingli, and others, as well as the earlier reforming movements of Jan Hus and Peter Waldes.[4] While there are numerous Reformed confessions of faith, the World Alliance has been a federation of churches without a specific common confession.[5] It has counted some 75 million Christians in some 215 member churches in 107 countries.[6] During this period it has also welcomed into membership the Church of South India and the Church of North India, both of which include Anglican heritage as well as Reformed and Congregationalist and other protestant heritage. This is especially interesting, because both of those churches have bishops in the Anglican tradition, while for the Reformed tradition in general, episcopacy has been problematic.

And another major development took place in 2010. Churches of the World Alliance and those of the Reformed Ecumenical Council, a smaller international Reformed body consisting of about 5 million persons in some thirty-five member churches, joined together to form a new body, the World Communion of Reformed Churches, including

---

4. Cf. World Alliance of Reformed Churches website, http://warcjalb.de/warcajsp/side.jsp?news_id=2&part2_id=19&navi=8.

5. Paraic Reamonn, "World Alliance of Reformed Churches," in *DEM2*, pp. 1217-18.

6. See http://warcjalb.de/warcajsp/side.jsp?news_id=2&part2_id=19&navi=8.

some 80 million persons in about 230 churches (some churches had previously held joint membership in WARC and REC).[7] The fourth phase of International Reformed-Catholic Dialogue, then, for which initial preparations have already been made, will be between the Catholic Church and the World Communion of Reformed Churches.

Priorities of This Dialogue

In the preparatory stage of the dialogue, the planners chose as the theme, "The Presence of Christ in Church and World" because "it seemed to have a bearing not only on the ultimate salvation of man but also on his life and happiness here and now" (PCCW, no. 5). They also thought that the discussion on this theme, and especially on the meaning of Christ's saving humanity, would bring to light the differences between them, and an honest appraisal of these differences could help the two traditions to overcome them and "discover together what they must do in order to become more credible in the eyes of the world" (Joint Report, Vogelenzang, April 17-19, 1969)(PCCW, no. 5).

Furthermore, they also uncovered the need "to attend to three traditional problems related to the central one of understanding the Lordship of Christ today: Christology, ecclesiology, and the attitude of the Christian in the world" (PCCW, no. 6). And they recognized that though these are traditional problems "the church confronts them in a new form today: the historical conditions which shaped their earlier formulations have radically changed, developments in the secular world cry for urgent attention, and the findings of the historical sciences and biblical exegesis demand new perspectives on inherited positions." These three issues have been addressed in the dialogue, over its three phases.

Facing Classical Divisive Issues

From the start, the dialogue began to face some of the classical issues over which Christians have been in conflict, finding significant areas

---

7. J. J. Bauswein and Lukas Vischer, *The Reformed Family Worldwide* (Grand Rapids: Eerdmans, 1999), indicate that there are more than 700 Reformed churches. Thus many do not even belong to the new Reformed body.

of convergence. Three examples from the report of the first phase illustrate this. First, PCCW includes a substantial treatment of the
eucharist. Reformed confessions of the sixteenth and seventeenth centuries condemned the Catholic Mass, charging, for example, that it is
"most contradictory" to Christ's one only sacrifice (Westminster Confession, XXIX).[8] But PCCW, while pointing to significant differences
needing further study, indicates that the discussions "have resulted in
a greater appreciation of the richness in our respective Eucharistic
doctrines and practices. We believe we have reached a common understanding of the meaning and purpose and basic doctrine of the Eucharist, which is in agreement with the Word of God and the universal
tradition of the Church."[9] Second, concerning the relationship of
Scripture and Tradition, the same report states that the difference between Catholics and Reformed has always focused on the alternative:
"Scripture and Tradition" and "Scripture only" (no. 24). But on both
the Catholic and on the Reformed side today, "the problem is no longer presented in terms of the battle lines of post-Tridentine polemic.
Historical researches have shown not only how the New Testament
writings are themselves already the outcome of and witness to traditions, but also how the canonization of the New Testament was part
of the development of tradition" (no. 25). Third, concerning ministry,
PCCW affirms that there is a "special ministry to which administration of Word and Sacrament is entrusted" (no. 97) and that the "continuity of this special ministry of Word and Sacrament is integral to
that dimension of Christ's sovereign and gracious presence which is
mediated through the Church" (no. 99). It affirms that "[t]he liturgical validation at the time of the act of ordination includes the invocation by the Holy Spirit ('epiclesis') with the laying on of hands by
other ordained ministers" (PCCW, no. 98). Further dialogue made
clear that the nature of ordination is still a difficulty between them.
For example, "Is the laying on of hands a sending on a mission, a passing on of a power, or an incorporation into an order?" (TCUC, no. 141).

8. See also the Scots Confession (1560) ch. XXII, and the Heidelberg Catechism
Q&A 80.

9. PCCW, no. 91. It continues, "Reformed and Roman Catholics hold to the belief
in the real Presence of Christ in the Eucharist; and both hold at least that the Eucharist
is, among other things: (1) a memorial of the death and resurrection of the Lord; (2) a
source of loving communion with him in the power of the Spirit (hence the epiclesis in
the liturgy), and (3) a source of the eschatological hope for his coming again."

More must be said about each of these three issues, but what has been said illustrates that from the beginning, the dialogue began to face questions concerning which Reformed and Catholics have had conflict, and to produce initial convergences.

There has been no official reception by the Catholic Church and the World Alliance of Reformed Churches of the results of their dialogue. But three phases of dialogue have addressed issues important for Reformed and Catholic reconciliation and produced results that can contribute to their reconciliation.

In this paper, I will outline four areas in which the dialogue has made significant contributions, under the headings: (1) *affirming the trinitarian faith of the church, and Christ as the unique mediator; (2) some important convergences/agreements on the church; (3) Christian witness in the world; (4) steps toward a reconciliation of memories.*

I. Affirming the Trinitarian Faith of the Church, and Christ as the Unique Mediator

A trinitarian thread runs throughout the three reports. TCUC indicated that Reformed and Catholics have discovered anew that they are bound by manifold ties, among them that they "confess Jesus Christ as Lord and Saviour [and] affirm the trinitarian faith of the apostolic church through the ages" (no. 4). While this might have been already known, the three reports document this affirmation.[10] The image that comes to me is that, even though Reformed and Catholics have been separated for centuries, in our time they are meeting each other once again in proclaiming the mystery of the Trinity.

Reformed and Catholics together affirm the *role of each person of the Trinity.* The first report, which includes sections on "Creation and Redemption" and "Church and World," speaks of the Father as "the absolutely primary principle, for he is 'source, guide and goal of all that is' (Rom. 11:36; cf. 1 Cor. 8:6)" (PCCW, no. 46). "The Creator of the world does not want mankind to destroy itself through lack of liberty, peace and justice (cf. Ezek. 18, 32). Rather, through the revelation of his will,

---

10. Agreement on the Trinity in this and other dialogues is documented in W. Kasper, *Harvesting the Fruits: Basic Aspects of Christian Faith in Ecumenical Dialogue* (London and New York: Continuum, 2009).

he leads mankind onto the road of salvation and in Jesus Christ offers it the gift of final redemption from all ungodly ties and participation in his divine life and thus in his freedom" (PCCW, no. 51).

While each of the three reports speaks significantly of Christ, the person and work of Christ the Son are featured especially in the second report, "Towards a Common Understanding of the Church," in particular within chapter II, "Our Common Confession of Faith." A number of qualities of the Son are confessed, among them that he is "at once true God and true human being" (TCUC, no. 73) whose death and resurrection is "the event which saves humanity" (no. 68), the mediator who "achieves our reconciliation" (no. 71). (More on this below.)

Each of the three speaks significantly of the Holy Spirit. While TCUC (no. 75) already states that "[t]he Holy Spirit is present and active throughout the history of salvation," the third report, "The Church as Community of Common Witness to the Kingdom of God" (CWKG), features more the role of the third person. "The Spirit is a principal agent in establishing the Kingdom and guiding the church so that it can be a servant of God's work in this process (chapter I). It is the spirit who plays the decisive role in leading believers to discern what they should do to serve the fuller realization of the Kingdom in particular situations (chapter III). . . . The Spirit is the basis both of the efficacy of Word and sacrament, and of the emerging presence of the reign of God" (CWKG, no. 195). And then this statement of convergence: our previous report referred to the Holy Spirit, "reflecting both the 'more Reformed' emphasis upon the freedom of the Spirit and the more Roman Catholic appreciation of the presence of the Holy Spirit in the historical existence of the Christian community. When we consider the role of the Spirit in relation to the Kingdom, it becomes clear that these two confessional perspectives require one another and are complementary and mutually informative. The Spirit who blows freely . . . (cf. John 3:8) also guides and equips the community of faith (cf. John 16:13, 14; 1 Cor 12:4-13)" (CWKG, no. 195).

The reports profess *the trinitarian basis of the church* and the role of each person therein. "The church's calling is set within the Triune God's eternal plan of salvation for humankind. In this sense, the church is already present at creation (Col. 1:15-18). . . . Even more the church is present at the establishment of the people of the covenant. Through the law and the prophets, God calls this people and prepares them for a communion which will be accomplished at the sending of

Emmanuel, 'God with us' (cf. Matt. 1:23)."[11] There is "full agreement in presenting the church as the Body of Christ" (PCCW, no. 16), that Jesus Christ, "the foundation of the church,"[12] "is present in the church and through his Lordship over the church . . . exercises his Lordship over the world."[13] The church is the Temple of the Holy Spirit. "Just as the Spirit came upon Jesus at . . . his baptism, so the Spirit descends upon the disciples gathered in the upper room (Acts 2:1:12), and on the gentiles who listen to his word (Acts 10:44-48). These three closely linked 'Pentecosts' belong to the foundation of the church and make it the temple of the Holy Spirit" (TCUC, no. 76).

The Trinity is central in sacraments and ministry. Reformed and Roman Catholic churches say that they "are bound by manifold ties. Both communions confess Jesus Christ as Lord and Savior, affirm the Trinitarian faith of the apostolic church through the ages, and observe the one baptism into the threefold name."[14] Concerning the eucharist, "Christ himself is present, who 'gave himself up on our behalf as an offering and sacrifice . . .' (Eph 5:2). Sanctified by his Spirit, the Church, through, with, and in God's Son, Jesus Christ, offers itself to the Father. It thereby becomes a living sacrifice of thanksgiving, through which God is publicly praised (cf. Rom 12:1; 1 Pet 2:5). The validity, strength, and effect of the Supper are rooted in the cross of the Lord and in his living presence in the Holy Spirit."[15] "The specific mode of Christ's real presence in the Eucharist is thus to be interpreted as the presence of the son who is both consubstantial with us in our human and bodily existence while being eternally consubstantial with the Father and the Holy Spirit in the Godhead (Jn 17:21-23)."[16]

Concerning ordination to ministry, "The liturgical validation at the time of the act of ordination includes the invocation of the Holy Spirit ('epiclesis') with the laying on of hands by other ordained ministers. The invocation of the Holy Spirit is a reminder of the essential role which the doctrine of the Trinity must fulfill in any balanced understanding of the ministry. It gives proper weight both to Jesus

---

11. TCUC, no. 81. This passage also calls attention to the continued existence of the chosen people as an integral part of the history of salvation.

12. TCUC, no. 83.

13. PCCW, no. 43.

14. TCUC, no. 4, cf. PCCW, nos. 79 and 96.

15. PCCW, no. 81, cf. nos. 69, 75.

16. PCCW, no. 84, cf. nos. 82, 85.

Christ's historical and present action and to the continual operation of the Holy Spirit" (PCCW, no. 98).

"Our Common Confession of Faith": Jesus Christ, the Unique Mediator

In the first chapter of the 1990 report TCUC, titled "Towards a Reconciliation of Memories," Reformed and Catholics each explain their interpretation of the events in the sixteenth century that led to division, and events that happened afterwards. Given the chief Christ-centered affirmations of early Reformed ecclesiology (TCUC, no. 19), the Reformers rejected all in the life of the church that, in their understanding, obscured the unique mediatorship of Jesus Christ and seemed to give to the church an excessive role alongside him. The emphasis placed in the ensuing controversy on the authority of the church and its hierarchy led them to question the value of episcopal succession as an expression of the continuity of the church in the apostolic truth through the centuries (TCUC, no. 20).

In this framework, the second chapter of TCUC, titled "Our Common Confession of Faith," addresses this primary concern of the mediatorship of Christ with a strongly stated confession. Although it is made clear that this "is neither a confession in the ecclesial sense, nor a complete statement of faith. . . . the importance of what we are able to say together merits such a title" (TCUC, no. 64). Furthermore, they understand that "[t]his confession involves . . . the recognition of the authority of the Scriptures" and that "[t]he teaching of the Church ought to be an authentic explanation of the Trinitarian and Christological affirmations of the early confessions of faith and the early councils" (TCUC, no. 67).

With this explanation there are six statements of confession, under three interrelated categories, in which, together, they highlight the role of Jesus as unique Mediator:

First, *Christ, Mediator and Reconciler:*

1. "We announce the death of the Lord (cf. 1 Cor. 11:26) and proclaim his resurrection from the dead (cf. Rom. 10:9; Acts 2:32; 3:15). In that mystery of death and resurrection *we confess*[17] the event which saves human-

17. The emphasis given to *we confess* in numbers 1-6 is added.

ity . . ." (no. 68). "*We therefore confess together* that Christ, established as Mediator, achieves our reconciliation in all its dimensions" (no. 71).

2. "*We confess together* that just as God is unique, the Mediator and Reconciler between God and humankind is unique and that the fullness of reconciliation is entire and perfect in him. Nothing and nobody could replace or duplicate, complete or in any way add to the unique mediation accomplished 'once for all' (Heb. 9:12) by Christ . . ." (TCUC, no. 72).

Second, *The work of Christ reveals that he is the Son within the Trinity.*

3. "[W]ith the church of every age, *we confess* Jesus Christ as at once true God and true human being, at once God and joined in solidarity with humankind, not an intermediary between God and humanity but a genuine Mediator, able to bring together God and humanity in immediate communion" (no. 73). They say together that "the work of Jesus, the Son, reveals to us the role of the Spirit of God who is common to him and to the Father: it reveals to us that God is triune" (no. 74).

Third, *justification by grace, through faith:*

4. They say together that "[b]ecause we believe in Christ, the one Mediator between God and humankind, we believe that we are justified by the grace which comes from him, by means of faith which is a living and life-giving faith. . . . We recognize that our justification is a totally gratuitous work accomplished by God in Christ. *We confess* that the acceptance in faith of justification is itself a gift of grace. By the grace of faith we recognize in Jesus of Nazareth, established Christ and Lord by his resurrection, the one who saves us and brings us into communion of life with God" (no. 77).

5. "*Together we confess* the Church, for there is no justification in isolation. All justification takes place in the community of believers, or is ordered toward the gathering of such a community. Fundamental for us all is the presence of Christ in the church, considered simultaneously as both a reality of grace and a concrete community in time and space" (no. 80). Furthermore, "The church's calling is set within the Triune God's eternal plan of salvation for humankind" (no. 81).

6. "[W]e believe that the people of God gathered together by the death and resurrection of Christ does not live solely by the promise. Henceforth it lives also by the gift already received through the mystery of the event of Jesus, Christ and Lord, who has sent his Spirit. *We therefore confess* Jesus Christ as the foundation of the church (1 Cor. 3:11)" (no. 83).

This confession not only outlines our shared faith in Christ. In contrast to the anathemas arising from polemics of the past, today Reformed and Catholics are beginning to confess together the apostolic faith for the benefit of the world. It is one way in which they are trying to leave behind the previous history of conflict, and to write a new history reflecting the growing degree of reconciliation they are fashioning together.

II. Convergences/Agreements on the Church

The confession just seen states: "Together we confess the church, for there is no justification in isolation" (point 5 above). But how do we understand the church? This dialogue, while considering various topics, gives extensive consideration to developing common views of the church. This is seen in each report. To illustrate, the first report explored Christ's relationship to the church, and the teaching authority of the church. The second report explored important concepts of the church, comparing a Reformed view of the church as *Creatura Verbi* (the creation of the Word), and a Catholic concept of the church as *Sacramentum Gratiae* (Sacrament of Grace). The third report treated extensively the biblical notion of the kingdom of God to see whether consideration of this might help to foster further common understanding of the church. And, while each phase of dialogue has been separated by seven or eight years, the participants in a subsequent phase have consciously sought to build on the previous report. Members of the third phase worked in close continuity with the previous two reports and especially with the second. We will highlight just two important ecclesiological themes.

The Church: An Instrument of the
Salvific Activity of Jesus Christ

The dialogue makes clear our common view of Christ's relationship to the church, the basis of the church's role as an instrument of salvation. According to the first report, "There was complete agreement in presenting ecclesiology from a clear Christological and pneumatological perspective in which the church is the object of declared faith and cannot be completely embraced by a historical and sociological description. There was an agreement in presenting the church as the 'body of Christ' (cf. 1 Cor. 12:12, 27; Eph. 5:30). . . . The church exists . . . as the body of Christ essentially by the Holy Spirit, just as does the exalted Lord" (PCCW, no. 16). "The mission and task of Jesus . . . are authoritative for the church of every age and culture" (PCCW, no. 14).

The second phase is more explicit. "The church's calling is set within the triune God's eternal plan of salvation for humankind" (TCUC, no. 81). It is called into being "as a community of men and women to share in the salvific activity of Christ Jesus" (TCUC, no. 85). The church "is at once the place, the instrument, and the minister chosen by God to make heard Christ's word and to celebrate the sacraments in God's name throughout the centuries." When it "faithfully preaches the word of salvation and celebrates the sacraments, obeying the command of the Lord and invoking the power of the Spirit . . . it carries out in its ministry the action of Christ himself" (TCUC, no. 86). It explains further that "[t]he ministerial and instrumental role of the church in the proclamation of the gospel and in the celebration of the sacraments in no way infringes the sovereign liberty of God. If God chooses to act through the church for the salvation of believers, this does not restrict saving grace to these means. The sovereign freedom of God can always call anyone to salvation independently of such actions." At the same time it is also "true to say that God's call is always related to the church, in that God's call always has as its purpose the building up of the church, which is the body of Christ (1 Cor. 12:27-28; Eph. 1:22-23)" (no. 87).

The third phase, exploring the biblical notion of the kingdom of God, goes still further. It states that "the church is meant to serve the establishment of the Kingdom as a prophetic sign and an effective instrument in the hands of God" (CWKG, no. 64). But also, through exploring in this context the theme of common witness to the Kingdom, "Reformed and Catholics have thus been able to discern a further fundamental agreement about the church. We can affirm that the church is a kind of sacrament of the kingdom of God, with a genuine role of mediation, but only insofar as it is utterly dependent upon God" (CWKG, no. 197).

And the report holds out the hope that by "speaking about the church as 'sacrament of the kingdom of God,' past tensions regarding differing convictions about the continuity, ministry and order of the church through the ages may prove to be complementary and even creative in shared reconstruction." And further, "We hope that our articulation of the church's ministerial and instrumental role, in total dependence on the Spirit of Christ and directed toward God's kingdom, can make a contribution to Christian unity that reaches beyond our own communities" (CWKG, no. 197; cf. 191, 194).

Creatura Verbi and *Sacramentum Gratiae:*
Two Images of the One Church

Another particularly important contribution of the dialogue, over two phases, was to illustrate, after intense study, that two visions or conceptions of the church, as *creatura verbi* (a Reformed emphasis) and as *sacramentum gratiae* (a Catholic emphasis), are complementary.

In the first phase, in a section focusing on "The Teaching Authority of the Church" and dealing with the relationship of scripture and tradition, agreement on one of these notions is expressed. "We are agreed," they say, "that as *creatura verbi* the Church together with its Tradition stands under the living Word of God and that the preacher and teacher of the Word is to be viewed as servant of the Word (cf. Lk 1:2) and must teach only what the Holy Spirit permits him to hear in the Scriptures. This hearing and teaching take place in a living combination with the faith, life and, above all, the worship of the community of Christ" (PCCW, no. 26).

In the second phase, these two concepts are studied together. After the second chapter says that "together we confess the Church" (TCUC, no. 80), a third chapter titled "The Church We Confess and Our Divisions in History" takes into account both areas about the church where there are *differences* of perspective such that the position of the partner is complementary, and on the other hand, other positions that seem to diverge, and appear mutually incompatible (TCUC, nos. 91, 92). They explore both types. Here we give attention to the dialogue's findings in only one.

They choose to explore, as an example of the first, two conceptions of the church, the more Reformed view of the church as *creatura verbi* and the more Catholic view of the church as *sacrament of grace*. They do it in the context of what they have already affirmed: the ministerial and instrumental role of the church in the proclamation of the gospel and the celebration of the sacraments (TCUC, nos. 85-86); they show that these two different conceptions provide two different ways of understanding the church, and the way it fulfills its ministerial and instrumental role (TCUC, no. 94). After a lengthy treatment of both concepts[18] they conclude that these two conceptions "can in fact be seen as expressing the same instrumental reality under different aspects, as complementary to each other or as two sides to the same coin. They can also become the poles of a creative tension between our churches" (TCUC, no. 113).

The importance of confirming and deepening this complementarity led the two partners, in the third phase of dialogue, to see if they could go even further through an investigation of the biblical notion of the kingdom of God. The report of the third phase affirms a deepening of the convergences concerning the church as *creatura verbi* and *sacrament of grace* in two ways. First, precisely because

> we can now position those insights in the broader, more dynamic continuum required by our exploration of the kingdom of God — e.g. the biblical, patristic, and more recent theological perspectives, including the results of ecumenical dialogues ... [which] illustrates that both concepts are integral to the notion of the kingdom of God and should serve the establishment of the kingdom of God in this world. Second, our exploration of the patristic material illustrated that the themes of the Word of God and the grace of God were of great significance in the ecclesiological reflection of the early Christian writers, even if they did not use the specific terminology used later in TCUC. Those writers certainly would have considered the church to be both a creation of the Word of God, and a sacrament of grace. Both factors help us affirm that neither of these visions of the church can wholly exclude the other, but are mutually dependent. Both are basic to an understanding of the nature of the church. (CWKG, no. 230)

"A 'sacramental' church that does not give proper place to the Word of God would be essentially incomplete; a church that is truly a creation of the Word will celebrate that Word liturgically and sacramentally."[19]

18. TCUC, nos. 95-101 and 102-11.

19. CWKG, no. 193. Concerning the argumentation, having explored biblical, patristic, and historical perspectives on the kingdom of God, each of these two expressions conveys something about the way in which the church should serve the establishment of the kingdom of God in the world. First, the church is the community created by the Word of God as it hears and responds to it. Jesus, the Word made flesh, proclaimed that the kingdom is at hand and the community of disciples consists of that group which, under the influence of grace, has responded in faith. In turn, their response of saving

In this matter, then, the dialogue makes a particular contribution to a recovery, between Reformed and Catholics, of a common view of the one church established by Christ.

The Need for Further Dialogue on the Church

The dialogue makes clear that we still differ on questions such as the nature of sin in the church, the interpretation of the continuity of the church in the division of the sixteenth century, the identification of the church with its visible aspects and structure, and, on questions concerning ministry.[20] Relating to the exercise of the authority of Christ in the church through ministry, there is agreement on the need of *episkopē* in the church on the local, regional, and universal levels. But there is disagreement concerning who should be regarded as *episcopos* at different levels of the church, and what is the function or role of the *episcopos* (TCUC, no. 142). Dialogue on this and other aspects of the church must continue.

III. Christian Witness in the World: Relating Orthodoxy and Orthopraxis

The Reformed-Catholic dialogue, in all three phases, has been concerned with questions of Christian witness to the world. A section in the first report titled "Church and World" (PCCW, nos. 51-59) states

---

faith impels them to proclaim the Word of salvation, and to witness to the kingdom values that Jesus taught. In these two ways, in its mission as servant to the kingdom, the church shows itself to be the *creatura verbi* (no. 190).

Second, the kingdom is envisioned in Scripture as the effect of God's powerful acting through Christ in the Holy Spirit, in history and beyond history. It is not the result of human efforts but of grace to which humans are privileged to respond. To the extent that the church is an instrument intended by God to serve in bringing about the kingdom, it must therefore be an instrument of grace (e.g., *sacramentum gratiae*). Furthermore, Christians believe the transformation of the world that the kingdom of God will bring is realized now in an anticipatory way in that communion between God and human beings which takes place in the church especially through the proclamation of the Word and the celebration of sacraments. "As a sacrament of the kingdom the church is and must be both creation of the Word and sacrament of grace" (no. 191).

20. TCUC, nos. 122, 123, 129, 142.

that "[i]f the Church goes out into the world, if it brings the gospel to men and endeavors to realize more justice, more conciliation and more peace, then . . . it is only following its Lord into domains that, unbeknown to men, already belong to him and where he is already anonymously at work" (PCCW, no. 53). The church "is called to be the visible witness and sign of the liberating will of God, of the redemption granted in Jesus Christ, and of the kingdom of peace that is to come. . . . It belongs to the nature of the church to proclaim the word of judgement and grace, and to serve Christ in the poor, the oppressed and the desperate (Mt. 25:31-40)" (PCCW, no. 54).

Going further, the report of the second phase calls for common witness. It indicates that a new situation exists between the Roman Catholic Church and Reformed churches. They share much in common and can therefore "enter into a living relationship with one another" (TCUC, no. 145); they "should no longer oppose each other or even simply live side by side. Rather, despite their divergences, they should live for each other in order to be witnesses to Christ" (TCUC, no. 149). Living for each other must also mean "bearing common witness" and making "every effort to speak jointly to the men and women of today" (TCUC, no. 157). "Every opportunity for taking common stands with regard to contemporary issues should be taken and used." For example, both agree that "every form of racism is contradictory to the Gospel and must therefore be rejected" and in particular, that apartheid must be condemned (TCUC, no. 158). The most profound convictions of their faith "oblige both churches to render decisive witness" on issues of justice, peace, and the integrity of God's creation (TCUC, no. 159).

The report of the third phase, "The Church as Community of Common Witness to the Kingdom of God" (2007), gives the most extensive and intense discussion on Christian witness. It arrived at a unique methodology for taking into account both theological reflection and Christian experience in facing conflicts, for relating orthodoxy and orthopraxis. The report reflects the mutual concern of matters of peace and justice, as well as the fact that during the period of the 1980s and 1990s, WARC was focusing more and more on issues of social justice as its main priority.[21] There was also a tension among the participants concerning the degree of attention to be given within the dialogue to systematic theological reflection as compared with questions of com-

21. The theme of its 1997 General Council was "Breaking the Bonds of Injustice."

mon witness, as a way of achieving unity between Reformed and Catholics. In fact, considerable attention was given to both.

In their effort to explore how Christians in difficult situations give common witness to the values of the kingdom of God in difficult situations, chapter II of its report describes three case studies, each of considerable length, concerning (1) "Advocating Aboriginal Rights in Canada" (CWKG, nos. 70-81), (2) "Facing Apartheid in South Africa" (CWKG, nos. 82-101), and (3) "Struggling for Peace in Northern Ireland" (CWKG, nos. 102-22).[22] After chapter I treats "The Kingdom of God in Scripture and Tradition," chapter II highlights the correlation between the gospel as heard, and the gospel as lived (CWKG, no. 124). The dialogue held meetings in each of the three locations, requested and heard accounts by local people of the various conflicts there, and reflected, through the papers delivered, theologically and empirically on the situation. The case studies illustrate the growing significance of ecumenical relations between Reformed and Catholics. In each context, although Reformed and Catholics began to face the conflicts separately, eventually both moved towards witnessing together. Each also illustrated the ways in which the universal expression of the church made an impact on the local church and vice-versa, and the importance of the interrelationship of these two aspects of the church (CWKG, no. 232). The narratives show that common witness by Reformed and Catholics is happening in various places all over the world. This coming together around issues of peace and justice in concrete situations happens in spite of historic issues that continue to divide us. Common witness makes life between us spiritually richer, is based on shared faith, and contributes to the fullness of unity that we seek (cf. CWKG, no. 233).

While the analysis in the case studies themselves started this process, it became clear that, in struggling with the role of the churches in three different and complex situations, further reflection was necessary concerning how these two communions discern God's will for their service to the Kingdom within contemporary situations throughout the world. Therefore, after chapter II in which these case studies are found, chapter III focuses on "Discerning God's Will in the Service of the Kingdom" (CWKG, nos. 124-58). Positive aspects and difficulties of discernment are shown. Discernment is described "as a process of listening to

---

22. Together the three comprise fifty-two of 235 paragraphs, or a little less than one-fourth of the report.

the Holy Spirit in order to discover the presence of God, the signs of God's activity in human history and God's will or call in any situation" (CWKG, no. 125). It is admitted that it is not always easy to discover the true nature of particular situations, their causes and solutions. At times, political, economic, racial, or other factors can be "disguised under the garb of religion or 'justified' by appeal to Scripture or tradition" (CWKG, no. 129). Common sources for discernment are mentioned. These include the Word of God as "the primary source by which the Holy Spirit guides the discernment of the church." But while both our communities affirm the ultimate authority of the Word of God in discerning God's will for the church, "the paths by which we claim to have access to that Word can be quite different" (CWKG, no. 130). Another source comprises Christian voices from the patristic era that provide a common heritage for both, since they date from prior to our divisions (CWKG, no. 131). And among "indicators essential for discerning God's will for the church's witness in society is the voice of the poor." Evidence is presented with biblical support from Old and New Testament such as Matthew's depiction of the last judgment, where Jesus identifies himself with those in need (cf. Matt. 25:31-46) (CWKG, no. 132).

Efforts at discernment recognized that there are differences between Reformed and Roman Catholics in the use of sources, relating to our different ecclesiologies, and our distinctive understandings of authority and of the role of experience in our traditions.[23] Still it is possible for our two traditions "to learn from the strengths of each other's discernment processes and thus to enrich one another" (CWKG, no. 147). The fundamental parallel between the approaches of our two communities to discernment "lies in our common desire to know God's will and to respond to grace as disciples of Jesus Christ in specific situations" (CWKG, no. 148).

This combination of systematic theological and biblical reflection on the kingdom of God, the use of case studies to determine how Christians in particular contexts tried to give witness to the values of the kingdom of God, and theological reflection about the way Reformed and Catholics discern God's will in the service of the Kingdom (taking into account lessons drawn from the case studies), provides a unique methodology within international bilateral dialogue, for analyzing the relationship between theological reflection and "lived theology."

23. CWKG, no. 144.

IV. Steps towards a Reconciliation of Memories

In Catholic-Reformed relations over the decades, significant attention has been given to the healing and reconciliation of bitter historical memories. This is reflected in the international dialogue, in specific statements and gestures of Pope John Paul II, and also in specific actions taken by some member churches of WARC.

TCUC's first chapter, titled "Toward a Reconciliation of Memories," sought mutual understanding of the issues at stake in the sixteenth-century conflict by presenting a Reformed perspective (nos. 17-20) and then a Catholic perspective (nos. 33-47) of ecclesiological and reforming concerns at that time. Unable to write that history together, initial versions were done by each separately; the final versions were the result of reading and reviewing the drafts together, learning from one another, and, because of this, modifying what had been written separately. The two admit that "over the centuries our forebears had often misunderstood each other's motives and language.... [O]ur histories were sometimes a matter of action and reaction, but at other times we followed separate paths" (no. 15). All of this, it says, has contributed now to a "certain reassessment of the past, clearing away misunderstanding." It urges that the next step be to move toward "a reconciliation of memories" in which we begin to share "one sense of the past rather than two" (no. 16). But more than that, besides the respective concerns in the sixteenth century, each side outlines important developments since then, and the way attitudes towards the other have changed, especially in recent times (nos. 21-32 and 48-61 respectively). This too contributes to a healing of memories.

Picking this theme up again in chapter IV ("The Way Ahead"), TCUC cites John Paul II's address to members of the Swiss Evangelical Church federation in 1984: "Remembrance of the events of the past must not restrict the freedom of our present efforts to eliminate the harm that has been triggered by these events. Coming to terms with these memories is one of the main elements of ecumenical process. It leads to frank recognition of mutual injury and errors in the way the two communities reacted to each other, even though it was the intention of all concerned to bring the church more into line with the will of the Lord" (no. 154). The report states that while much has been accomplished, much remains to be done (no. 155). One suggestion is that the mutual anathematizations of the past still have impact today, and need to be faced (no. 156b).

In fact, the dialogue has been accompanied by important healing gestures on both sides. Pope John Paul II has made other important statements and gestures over the years fostering a healing of memories in meetings with Reformed Christians, for example, in France in 1980,[24] in Switzerland in 1984,[25] in Czechoslovakia in 1990,[26] and in Debrecen, Hungary, December 1991.[27]

Concerning anathemas, the Council of Trent never mentioned a single Reformer by name, even though it condemned what it thought were Protestant errors (TCUC, no. 44). Reformed confessions of the sixteenth and seventeenth centuries, however, include strong anti-papal statements, because of the polemics of that time. Some member churches of the WARC have taken actions recently in regard to the anti-Catholic condemnations in Reformed confessions. For example, the

24. Addressing French Protestants in Paris, the Pope urged that "[f]irst and foremost, and in the dynamics of the movement towards unity, our personal and community memory must be purified of the memory of all the conflicts, injustice and hatred of the past . . . through mutual forgiveness from the depths of our hearts" (*IS* 44 [1980]: 84).

25. On the same 1984 visit to Switzerland just cited in TCUC, when the Reformed were celebrating significant anniversaries of the Reformers Calvin and Zwingli, the Pope, in the same address mentioned above, expressed the hope that Swiss Catholics and Protestants would "write the history of that troubled and complex period together with objectivity rooted in charity" (*IS* 55 [1984]: 47).

26. Addressing leaders of the cultural and intellectual world, and other Christian church authorities in Prague on April 21, 1990, acknowledging the importance of John Hus in the religious and cultural history of the Bohemian people, and past conflicts in relationship to him, the Pope challenged experts, especially Czech theologians, to "define more precisely the place which John Hus occupies among the reformers of the Church" (*IS* 75 [1990]: 139). A joint Catholic and Reformed commission to study Hus was set up there shortly afterwards. In 1999, addressing a symposium on John Hus held in Rome, John Paul II stated that their work "means that a figure like Jan Hus, who has been such a point of contention in the past, has now become a subject of dialogue, of comparison and shared investigation." He expressed his "deep regret for the cruel death inflicted on John Hus, and for the consequent wound of conflict and division which was imposed on the mind and hearts of the bohemian people" (*IS* 103 [2000/I-II]: 37 and 36 respectively).

27. After addressing an ecumenical service in the Reformed church, the Pope personally visited and offered prayers at a monument on the church grounds dedicated to Reformed preachers who, during the seventeenth-century religious wars, were sold as galley slaves. Although he referred to the monument in his address, this gesture was not part of the program but done spontaneously (*IS* 80 [1992]: 4).

Assembly of the Presbyterian Church (USA) in 2004 approved a policy statement in which it distances itself from such anti-Roman Catholic language in its *Book of Confessions,* saying that it does not represent PC(USA) understanding of the Catholic Church today.[28] It indicates that the polemical statements in question will not be removed from these confessions because they are historical documents. However, this new policy statement will be inserted in the Preface to *The Book of Confessions.* Footnotes pointing to relevant sections, referring to the policy statement, will be placed in the Preface of all future editions of the *Book of Confessions.* Furthermore, hoping to broaden the impact of this action, the Assembly asked that conversations be initiated with the World Alliance of Reformed Churches, seeking a WARC statement on this issue.[29]

Thus, a healing of memory between Reformed and Catholics has been fostered through dialogue, and in other ways.

Continuing Dialogue

This presentation has illustrated developments in several important areas, showing significant points on which Reformed and Catholics have achieved common ground during the decades in which they have been in dialogue. Nonetheless, as seen already, the dialogue needs to con-

28. According to the policy statement, "Specific statements in the 16th- and 17th-century confessions and catechisms in *The Book of Confessions* contain condemnations and derogatory characterizations of the Catholic Church: Chapter XVIII and XXII of the Scots Confession; Question and Answer 80 of the Heidelberg Catechism; Chapter II, III, XVII, and XX of the Second Helvetic Confession. (Chapters XXII, XXV, and XXIX of the Westminster Confession of Faith have been amended to remove anachronous and offensive language. Chapter XXVIII of the French Confession does not have constitutional standing.) While these statements emerged from substantial doctrinal disputes, they reflect 16th- and 17th-century polemics. Their condemnations and characterizations of the Catholic Church are not the position of the Presbyterian Church (USA) and are not applicable to current relationships between the Presbyterian Church (USA) and the Catholic Church." See http://oga.pcusa.org/ga216/business/commbooks/comm06.pdf.

29. Also in 2004, the Synod of the Christian Reformed Church in North America, after dialogue with Catholic theologians, acknowledged that the description of the Catholic mass in Q&A 80 of the Heidelberg Catechism (1563), as a denial of the one sacrifice of Christ, and therefore an idolatry, does not correctly represent Catholic teaching, and declared that "Q&A 80 can no longer be held in its current form as a part of our confession."

tinue on issues related to the church, as well as on other questions that have not been treated extensively here, such as sacraments. These must be part of the future agenda of this dialogue.

To highlight one issue, of particular importance is the previously identified question of the disagreement between Reformed and Catholics about how the authority of Christ is exercised in the church through *episkopē* at the local, regional, and universal levels, and especially "about who is regarded as *episcopos* at these different levels and what is the function or role of the *episcopos*" (TCUC, no. 142). Of many issues still unresolved, one might argue that coming to agreement on these questions is one of the most difficult challenges not only within Reformed-Catholic relations, but also within the broader ecumenical movement today, and one of the keys to ecumenical progress.

In the USA, the Episcopal Church and the Presbyterian Church have initiated efforts to achieve unity on several occasions. These have not fully succeeded. The notion of a personal *episcopos* has been one of the main stumbling blocks between them. The most recent example has been the Consultation on Church Union, which began in 1960. Eventually coming to include, also, eight other mainline Protestant churches, it was able, over the decades, to agree on a solid theological basis, and more recently evolved into a new body called *Churches Uniting in Christ.* One of the main reasons keeping the participating churches in CUIC from achieving a full visible unity has been the inability, thus far, to achieve and accept a common understanding of a personal episcopacy.

On the global level, the Faith and Order multilateral dialogue, involving theologians of many traditions, has dealt with this. The Faith and Order convergence text *BEM,* developed over more than fifty years, includes extensive reflection on this and related issues, and has achieved levels of convergence that have been offered to all.[30] Its proposals, addressed to churches that have maintained the threefold pattern of ministry and claim an episcopacy within the apostolic succession, and those who have not, are still valid as a contribution to the discussion today.

The important convergences achieved in the Reformed-Catholic dialogue now challenge it to seek a theological basis for breaking the impasse between them on this issue, which is also an important question in the broader ecumenical world.

30. See *BEM,* Ministry, sections III, IV, V, VI.

11 The Achievements of the Pentecostal-Catholic International Dialogue

Cecil M. Robeck Jr.

On more than one occasion, the international Pentecostal-Catholic dialogue has been labeled "extraordinary" or "improbable."[1] What could Pentecostals and Catholics possibly have in common? Are they not on opposite ends of the theological spectrum? Catholics have a complex sacramental theological system while Pentecostals are just beginning to construct their own theology in any systematic way. The Catholic Church claims that the "Church" subsists in it,[2] while Pentecostals often view themselves more as a "movement" within the church, suggesting that the church is far larger than that which "subsists" in the Catholic Church.[3] The Catholic Church is officially hierarchical in its

---

1. Peter Hocken, "Dialogue Extraordinary," *One in Christ* 24, no. 3 (1988): 202-13; Kilian McDonnell, "Improbable Conversations: The International Classical Pentecostal-Roman Catholic Dialogue," *Pneuma: The Journal of the Society for Pentecostal Studies* 17, no. 2 (1995): 163-74; Anthea Butler, "Institutional Authority vs. Charismatic Authority: The Roman Catholic-Pentecostal Dialogue," in Christoph Dahling-Sander, Kai M. Fundschmidt, und Vera Mielke, eds., *Pfingstkirchen und Ökumene in Bewegung*, a special issue of *Beiheft zur Ökumenischen Rundschau*, no. 71 (Frankfurt am Main: Otto Lembeck, 2001): 100-114.

2. *LG* 8 reads, "The Church, constituted and organized as a society in the present world, subsists in the Catholic Church, which is governed by the successor of Peter and by the bishops in communion with him. Nevertheless, many elements of sanctification and of truth are found outside its visible confines."

3. Among the most hotly debated and highly politicized questions among Pentecostal scholars today is the definition of Pentecostalism. Should it be defined historically, and if so, from what perspective should it be done? Should it be defined theologically, and if so, from what perspective should it be done? Is it Church, Movement,

organization, while Pentecostals are often congregationally governed. Catholics function with a highly stylized ritual, while Pentecostals, who possess their own rituals, are much more spontaneous. The Catholic Church has been around for millennia, while Pentecostal churches have been around for a mere century. And sadly, in some places, there is considerable animus between these two groups. Many leaders in the Catholic Church still spit the accusation that Pentecostals are nothing more than a "sect,"[4] while Pentecostal leaders often raise their fists at the Catholic Church, accusing it of idolatry and spiritualism and of not even being Christian, let alone "the Church."[5] Yes, *extraordinary* and *improbable* may be accurate descriptions of this dialogue.[6]

Spirituality, or something else? Who makes these decisions and where does their authority lie? Increasingly, Pentecostal denominations have begun to think of themselves as churches in the same way that older churches do.

4. "Vatican Reports on Sects, Cults and New Religious Movements," *Origins: CNS Documentary Service* 16, no. 1 (May 22, 1986): 2-10; Alta/Baja California Bishops, "Dimensions of a Response to Proselytism," *Origins: CNS Documentary Service* 19, no. 41 (March 15, 1990): 666; for instance, Benjamín Bravo, "Sectas" in Benjamín Bravo, compiler, *Vocabulario de la religiosidad popular* (Mexico City: Ediciones Dabar, S.A. de C.V., 1992), p. 173, states that "[b]y sects or new religious groups, we mean those religious organizations founded in the past century which have grown progressively stronger and which reject or directly oppose the historical churches. We refer especially, to the Church of Jesus Christ of Latter-day Saints (Mormons), Jehovah's Witnesses, Seventh-day Adventists, Pentecostals in a variety of forms and others."

5. Cf. Terry Peretti, "Proclaiming the Gospel in Italy," *The Pentecostal Evangel* 4220 (March 26, 1995): 18, and Terry Peretti, "Learning from the Past, Looking to the Future," *The Pentecostal Evangel* 4220 (March 26, 1995): 19; Luisa Jeter de Walker, *Siembra y Cosecha: Las Asambleas de Dios de Argentina, Chile, Peru, Bolivia, Uruguay y Paraguay* (Deerfield, FL: Editorial Vida, 1992), 2:163-64, where she speaks of syncretism and idolatry in Bolivia. The "Regulamento Interno" of the Igreja Pentecostal Deus É Amor classifies Catholic baptism under the category Batismo — pagão. Item B 6 reads. '*O batismo Católico é sacrifício aos ídolos, o batismo bíblico é de pessoas adultas, libertas e transformadas, que prometem ser fiéis até a morte, cumprindo a justice de Deus. Assim sendo, é proibido ir a batismo Católico, por ser Sacrifício aos ídolos. 1 Cor. 8.1 a 13 = Sal. 115.1 a 18 e is. 45.20.* This rule is found in "Regulamento Interno: Igreja Pentecostal Deus É Amor," appended to *A Bíblia Sagrada* (São Paulo, Brasil: Sociedade Bíblica do Brasil, 1969), p. 4.

6. The history of this dialogue has been published in a number of works, including: Norbert Baumert and Gerhard Bially, eds., *Pfingstler und Katholiken im Dialog. Die vier Abschlussberichte einer internationalen Kommission aus 25 Jahren* (Düsseldorf: Charisma-Verlag, 1999); Arnold Bittlinger, *Papst und Pfingstler: Der römisch Katholische-pfingstliche Dialog und seine ökumenische Relevanz*, SIHC 16 (Frankfurt am Main: Peter Lang, 1978); Peter Hocken, "Dialogue Extraordinary," *One in Christ* 24, no. 3 (1988): 202-13; Veli-Matti

On the other hand, it must be asked whether these are the only adjectives that do this dialogue justice. Is the international Pentecostal-Catholic dialogue anything more than an ecumenical anomaly? If that is all that it is, then how do we explain that this dialogue has run, more or less continuously, since 1972? How is it the case that when pressure to end the dialogue has been applied by Catholics and Pentecostals alike, the dialogue continues?[7] How do we explain the apparent incongruity that within the Catholic Church today, more than 120 million people or approximately 10 percent of all Catholics worldwide identify themselves as having some kind of positive relationship with Pentecostalism through the Catholic Charismatic Renewal?[8]

Kärkkäinen, Spiritus ubi vult spirat: *Pneumatology in Roman Catholic–Pentecostal Dialogue* (1972-1989), SLAG 42 (Helsinki: Luther-Agricola-Society, 1998); Veli-Matti Kärkkäinen, Ad ultimum terrae: *Evangelization, Proselytism and Common Witness in the Roman Catholic–Pentecostal Dialogue (1990-97),* SIHC 117 (Frankfurt am Main: Peter Lang, 1999); Paul D. Lee, *Pneumatological Ecclesiology in the Roman Catholic–Pentecostal Dialogue: A Catholic Reading of the Third Quinquennium (1985-89)* (Rome: Pontifica Studiorum Universitas A.S. Thoma Ag. in Urbe, 1994); Kilian McDonnell, "Improbable Conversations," pp. 163-74; Kilian McDonnell, "Five Defining Issues: The International Classical Pentecostal-Roman Catholic Dialogue," *Pneuma: The Journal of the Society for Pentecostal Studies* 17, no. 2 (1995): 175-88; Cecil M. Robeck, Jr., "On Becoming a Christian: An Important Theme in the International Roman Catholic-Pentecostal Dialogue," *PentecoStudies: Online Journal for the Interdisciplinary Study of Pentecostalism and Charismatic Movements* 8, no. 2 (Fall 2008): 1-23; Jerry L. Sandidge, *Roman Catholic/Pentecostal Dialogue [1977-1982]: A Study in Developing Ecumenism,* SIHC 16 (Frankfurt am Main: Peter Lang, 1987); Juan Fernando Usma Gómez, "El Diálogo Internacional Católico-Pentecostal 1972-1998: Reseña História, Presentación Final de la Cuarta Fase: Evangelisación, Proselitismo y Testimonio Común, y Perspectivas," *Medellín: Theología y pastoral para América Latina* 24, no. 95 (1998): 449-70.

7. On the Pentecostal side, pressure came from the Assemblies of God, which had defrocked David du Plessis, the first Chairman of the Pentecostal team, and had passed a bylaw that made ecumenical dialogue virtually impossible. It appeared among the executives of the Pentecostal World Conference (PWC), when in Jerusalem, 1995, the Reverend Francesco Toppi, General Superintendent of the Assemblies of God in Italy and a member of the PWC executive, resigned following a failed attempt to have the dialogue condemned by the PWC executives. On the Catholic side, various Bishops from Latin America have appealed repeatedly to the PCPCU not to engage further with Pentecostals, although they have been informed by that office that their view is not in keeping with the position of the PCPCU.

8. David B. Barrett, George T. Kurian, and Todd M. Johnson, *World Christian Encyclopedia,* 2nd ed. (Oxford: Oxford University Press, 2001), 1:20, Table 1-6a. This figure is regularly used by the office of the International Catholic Charismatic Renewal Services and is available for consultation on its website at http://www.iccrs.org/about_ccr/

And is it really the case that the Catholic Church is the "Church" and that Pentecostals are no more than a "sect" or even merely a "movement," or are they both partial manifestations of the "one, holy, catholic and apostolic church"? All of these questions are enough to make one wonder whether this international Pentecostal-Catholic dialogue has achieved anything of significance over the past four decades.

Initial Achievements of the Dialogue

Unlike the dialogues that the Pontifical Council for Promoting Christian Unity (hereafter PCPCU) has held with the Orthodox and with churches that stem from the time of the Reformation in which some form of visible unity is a stated goal, the expectations of the Pentecostal-Catholic dialogue have been much more restrained. It has repeatedly excluded visible unity as an explicit goal,[9] focusing instead on concerns such as "prayer, spirituality and theological reflection,"[10] supporting "growth in mutual understanding,"[11] searching for doctrinal and pastoral areas of convergence and agreement, and lifting up issues where "further dialogue is required" between the parties.[12] It was only in the fifth round of discussions that participants dared to declare for the first time

---

ccr_worldwide/CCR%20worldwide.htm. See also "On Becoming a Christian: Insights from Scripture and the Patristic Writings with Some Contemporary Reflections. Report of the Fifth Phase of the International Dialogue Between Some Classical Pentecostal Churches and Leaders and the Catholic Church (1998-2006)," n. 260, in *IS* 129 (2008/III). All numbers used in this and subsequent reports indicate paragraphs.

9. "Final Report, Dialogue between the Secretariat for Promoting Christian Unity and Leaders of Some Pentecostal Churches and Participants in the Charismatic Movement within Protestant and Anglican Churches (1972-1976)," in *GA II,* p. 713, no. 4, stated categorically that "This dialogue has a special character. The bilateral conversations that the Roman Catholic Church undertakes with many world communions (e.g., the Anglican Communion, the Lutheran World Federation, etc.) are prepared to consider problems concerning church structures and ecclesiology and have organic unity as a goal or at least envisage some kind of structural unity. This dialogue has not."

10. "Final Report (1972-1976)," no. 4.

11. "Final Report, Dialogue between the Secretariat for Promoting Christian Unity and Some Classical Pentecostals (1977-1982)," no. 2, in *GA II,* p. 721.

12. "Perspectives on *Koinonia.* Report from the Third Quinquennium of the Dialogue between the Pontifical Council for Promoting Christian Unity and Some Classical Pentecostal Churches and Leaders (1985-1989)," no. 5, *GA II,* p. 735, and "Evangelization, Proselytism and Common Witness (1990-1997)," no. 2, *GA II,* p. 753.

their desire to resolve "those differences that keep us separated from one another, especially in light of the prayer of Jesus for his disciples 'that they may all be one . . . so that the world may believe . . .' (John 17:21)."[13]

The caution that has kept any explicit commitment to the quest for unity at bay is based on two specific concerns that no longer play much of a role in the Reformation-era churches. First, the churches that formed during or shortly after the Reformation — Anglican, Lutheran, Reformed, even Anabaptist — have a four-century head start in relating to Rome. In the interim period tensions have eased, especially since the Second Vatican Council and the establishment of the PCPCU. Thus, time has allowed these churches to mature in their relationships, and has softened many of the harder edges between them. It has become possible for them to establish official, and in some cases, close relationships. By comparison, Pentecostal churches have barely reached their adolescence. They are still finding their place and as a result, they have not yet officially established a clear ecumenical agenda of their own.

Second, from the beginning, the dialogues between the Reformation-era churches and the PCPCU have been approved by their top leaders, synods, and judicatories. This is not the case for the Pentecostal-Catholic dialogue. Each report has contained something like the following disclaimer: "This is the report of the fifth phase of the international dialogue between some Classical Pentecostal churches and leaders and the Catholic Church. . . ."[14] Fueled by concern over Pentecostal successes beginning in the mid-twentieth century in places such as Latin America where Catholic hegemony was being challenged, and further motivated by the challenge to authority that the Catholic Charismatic Renewal seemed to present at roughly the same time, the Vatican quickly became interested in speaking with Pentecostals. But the vast majority of Pentecostals were neither interested in nor prepared to meet with Catholics.[15]

These two facts point to a third dynamic, which has played an important role in this dialogue. This is not a dialogue in which all Pente-

13. "On Becoming a Christian (1998-2006)," 3.

14. "On Becoming a Christian (1998-2006)," 1.

15. In 1961, the Chairman of the Classical Pentecostal groups that belonged to the Pentecostal World Conference attempted to block all ecumenical activity apart from Pentecostal-Evangelical relationships. *Addresses Presented at the Sixth Pentecostal World Conference, Jerusalem, May 19th to 21st, 1961* (Toronto: Testimony Press, 1961).

costals are represented. It has been very carefully proscribed. It is a dialogue between the Pontifical Council for Promoting Christian Unity and what have been termed "some Classical Pentecostal churches and leaders." The elements of this limitation need further explanation.

The designation "Classical Pentecostal churches," initially defined by Fr. Kilian McDonnell, OSB, was intended to represent "those groups of Pentecostals which grew out of the Holiness Movement at the beginning of the [twentieth] century."[16] Many, though by no means all of these groups, are North American in origin. But "Classical Pentecostal churches" is a designation for which Fr. McDonnell's definition no longer does justice.

The claim that they are *churches* suggests that Classical Pentecostals have an organizational side that the term *movement* does not adequately capture. In point of fact, some of these "churches," or "fellowships," or denominations," such as the General Council of the Assemblies of God, with its headquarters in the USA and its more than 61 million members and adherents spread around the world, are both large and global in their scope.[17] Others, such as the *Verenigde Pinkster — en Evangeliegemeenten (VPE)* of the Netherlands are relatively small, with about 22,000 members. Since their formation at the beginning of the twentieth century, they have developed just like the older churches, with clear structures of governance, confessions of faith, constitutions and bylaws, cooperative programs, extensive property holdings, and memberships in umbrella organizations such as the Pentecostal World Fellowship and/or the World Evangelical Alliance.

The term "Classical Pentecostals," however, is not limited to "churches" in the sense of denominations or to those groups that amount to denominations while strongly denying that designation.[18] It

---

16. Kilian McDonnell, *Charismatic Renewal and the Churches* (New York: Seabury Press, 1976), p. 2.

17. This figure comes from the official General Council of the Assemblies of God website, accessed May 24, 2010, at http://www.ag.org/top/press/index.cfm.

18. Such groups might include such entities as much of the Scandinavian Pentecostal Movement or the Independent Assemblies of God, which views itself as an umbrella fellowship of ministers and ministry, and prides itself on its commitment to the sovereign integrity of the local congregation. It claims to exercise no control over ministry except at the local level, but the organization functions largely for purposes of fellowship and legal representation. Their website is http://www.iaogi.org/. This group is not to be confused with the General Council of the Assemblies of God.

may also be used to designate local congregations. For the most part, the international Pentecostal-Catholic dialogue has not included many of the independent Pentecostal congregations that for one reason or another have decided to function independently of such organized churches, nor does it include the many churches that have sprung up around the teachings of certain evangelists, missionaries, and preachers, who were reared within Classical Pentecostal denominations or congregations but who for one reason or another (e.g., discipline by these denominations, frustration at denominational restrictions placed on their unique ministries, disagreement over doctrines, practices, or emphases) now choose to stand on their own.[19]

Without wishing to sound triumphalistic, it is fairly easy to demonstrate that most such congregations, churches, and movements are cut from the same basic "Classical Pentecostal" cloth. Groups that use such self-designations as "Deliverance" churches, "Full Gospel" churches, "Latter Rain" churches, many of the "Sanctified" churches within the African American tradition, and churches that more recently have defined themselves or have been defined by social scientists as "neo-Pentecostal churches," like the Brazilian-born *Igreja Universal do Reino de Deus,* or *Deus es Amor,* or the Word of Faith and/or *Rhema* churches that emphasize the prosperity teachings of Kenneth Hagin and Kenneth Copeland, as well as many of the Pentecostal-type African Instituted churches that were birthed from earlier "Classical Pentecostal" denominations, are still easily able to fit under the "Classical Pentecostal" umbrella. And while the phrase "Classical Pentecostal churches" provides a sufficiently large tent to incorporate Oneness Pentecostals, they have so far been excluded from the international Pentecostal-Catholic dialogue.[20] That there are many Pentecostal

---

19. The PCPCU has recently convened a Non-Denominational Charismatic-Catholic Preliminary Conversation at the request of a group originating first in the USA, but with partners in England, Ireland, and Sweden. Their name has changed from Non-Denominational Pentecostals to Non-Denominational Charismatics as late as 2009 in their attempt to define themselves over against Classical Pentecostals, though most of these leaders were at one time members of "Classical Pentecostal churches."

20. Oneness Pentecostals do not accept the classical articulation of the Trinity, but tend to embrace a modal expression of the Godhead. See David A. Reed, *"In Jesus' Name": The History and Beliefs of Oneness Pentecostals,* Journal of Pentecostal Theology Supplement Series 31 (Blandford Forum, UK: Deo Publishing, 2008), 394 pp. Only at the 1986 session of the dialogue, meeting in Sierra Madre, CA, was a Oneness Pentecostal,

churches that would have been able to enter into official dialogue with Rome but have not done so, should not confuse us with respect to this dialogue. The Pentecostal-Catholic dialogue did not spring from them.

The other part of the boundaries surrounding Pentecostal participation in this dialogue is the designation "some Pentecostal . . . leaders." The dialogue grew out of the personal interest of one provocative Pentecostal leader, David du Plessis, who had been defrocked by the Assemblies of God for his ecumenical activities that ran back more than a decade and as such had no denominational backing, but who took it upon himself to correspond with Cardinal Bea about the possibility of opening such a conversation.[21] Thus, it was through an individual contact with the PCPCU that the dialogue, which took as its starting point a friendship between one Pentecostal, David J. du Plessis, and one Catholic, Fr. Kilian McDonnell, OSB, came into being. The significance of "some Pentecostal . . . leaders" acting in an independent capacity in this dialogue to this day, alongside some Classical Pentecostal groups, is a factor that is unique in ongoing Catholic ecumenical relations.

Whether one considers these exceptional beginnings to be the work of mavericks or as something genuinely prophetic, the international Pentecostal-Catholic dialogue has been progressively welcomed within the global Pentecostal community, first by the Pentecostal academic community and subsequently by a small but growing list of Pentecostal denominations. In the academic arena, the Society for Pentecostal Studies was the first Pentecostal group to publish all the reports of the dialogue. In 1990, *Pneuma: The Journal of the Society for Pentecostal Studies* published the reports of the first three quinquennia and included thirteen responses to "Perspectives on *Koinonia*."[22] It continued

---

Dr. Manuel Gaxiola-Gaxiola, a Bishop of the *Iglesia Apostólica de la Fe en Cristo Jesús de Mexico* invited to participate, and then only as an observer.

21. On David du Plessis's ecumenical journey see David du Plessis, *The Spirit Bade Me Go,* rev. (Plainfield, NJ: Logos International, 1970); David du Plessis, "David as told to Bob Slosser," *A Man Called Mr. Pentecost* (Plainfield, NJ: Logos International, 1977); and David du Plessis, *Simple and Profound* (Orleans, MA: Paraclete Press, 1986).

22. *Pneuma* 12, no. 2 (Fall 1990): 85-183. The issue included respondents from the American Baptist Convention, Christian Reformed Church, Roman Catholic Church, Swiss Reformed Church, Assemblies of God, Church of God in Christ, Church of God of Prophecy, International Pentecostal Holiness Church, Swiss Pentecostal Mission, and United Pentecostal Church.

this practice, publishing "Evangelization, Proselytism and Common Witness," again with responses, in 1999.[23] The Society for Pentecostal Studies has hosted and affirmed a well-attended preconference "Ecumenical Session" for issues related to the dialogue and to Pentecostal-Catholic relations at each of its annual meetings since 1996.[24] Since 2002, the Society has added a permanent Ecumenical Section, inclusive of Pentecostal-Catholic relations, but with a broader ecumenical agenda as well.[25]

On the denominational front, the Apostolic Faith Mission of South Africa in which David du Plessis grew up has been joined by the Church of God of Prophecy, *La Iglesia Mision Pentecostal de Chile,* the International Church of the Foursquare Gospel, the Open Bible Church, and the *Verenigde Pinkster — en Evangeliegemeenten (VPE)* of the Netherlands. All of them now recognize the dialogue as an official extension of their own ecumenical ministry.

23. *Pneuma* 21, no. 1 (Spring 1999): 11-168. Respondents came from the American Baptist Convention, Anglican Church, Episcopal Church, Evangelical Church in Germany [Lutheran], Orthodox Church in America, Roman Catholic, Southern Baptist Convention, Swiss Reformed, Assemblies of God, and International Church of the Foursquare Gospel. "Evangelization, Proselytism and Common Witness: The Report from the Fourth Phase of the International Dialogue 1990-1997 between the Roman Catholic Church and Some Classical Pentecostal Churches and Leaders" was also published in the *Asian Journal of Pentecostal Studies* 2, no. 1 (January 1999): 105-51.

24. In 1996, Dr. Cheryl Bridges Johns (Church of God Theological Seminary) and Fr. John C. Haughey, SJ (Loyola, Chicago) initiated the preconference Ecumenical Seminar. Dr. Frank Macchia gave the first address, "Signs of the Spirit at Pentecost: The Challenges and Possibilities of Pentecostal–Roman Catholic Dialogue." See the March 7-9, 1996 conference program, "Memory and Hope: The Society for Pentecostal Studies at 25 Years" (Wycliffe College, Toronto), p. 2 plus insert.

25. The Ecumenical Seminar at the March 2010 meeting of the Society for Pentecostal Studies included the following papers: Jeffrey Gros, "The Medieval Franciscans as a Proto-Pentecostal Movement; Peter D. Hocken, "A Catholic and Ecumenical Understanding of the Pentecostal Movement." In addition, a special two-hour session on the Roman Catholic–Pentecostal dialogue was keynoted by Fr. Kilian McDonnell, "Improbable Conversations: Personal Reflections on the Catholic/Pentecostal Dialogue." Papers in the Ecumenical section included: Jeremiah Gibbs, "Spirit Baptism and the *Ordo Diaconia:* An Ecumenical *Apologia* for the Pentecostal Doctrine of 'Subsequence'"; Charley Earp, "Pentecostal/Quaker Eschatology"; Cecil M. Robeck, Jr., "Pentecostals and the Global Christian Forum"; Wolfgang Vondey, "Denominationalism in Classical and Global Pentecostal Ecclesiology: A Historical and Theological Evaluation"; Joshua Ziefe, "Boldly Going Where No Pentecostal Has Gone Before: David J. du Plessis and the 1959 Princeton Mission Lectures"; Robert L. Brenneman, "The People of Acts 2 and Islam."

These details may seem to support the *extraordinary* and *improbable* labels given to this dialogue, but they also reveal several important achievements. As oddly conceived and as risky as it was for anyone to initiate this formal international dialogue between the most powerful church in the world and a defrocked, self-appointed, charismatic "representative" of a fairly aggressive younger "movement" that wanted no such representation at the time, the fruit of this dialogue thus far has demonstrated the wisdom of the decision to do so. First, it is the preeminent international ecumenical dialogue in which Pentecostals have participated, and it has opened up the way for other important dialogues to follow.[26] Second, the subject of ecumenism is now taken seriously by the Pentecostal scholars who are entrusted with the training of pastoral candidates for Pentecostal ministry throughout the world, as has been demonstrated by the growing reality of ecumenism in their scholarly meetings and publications. Third, this dialogue and the broader subject of ecumenism are now on the minds of Pentecostal leadership in ways that were not possible just a few years ago. Ways of speaking about ecumenism within Pentecostal circles have begun to change,[27]

---

26. Other international dialogues with a direct line of influence from the international Pentecostal-Catholic dialogue include the Pentecostal dialogue with the World Alliance of Reformed Churches, which began in 1996; the Pentecostal conversation with members of the Lutheran World Federation, which has served in a preliminary capacity for a formal dialogue that is expected to result in an official dialogue between Pentecostals and the Lutheran World Federation following the LWF Assembly in July 2010; the establishment of the Joint Consultative Group, which brings together representatives of WCC member churches and Pentecostals; and beginning in October 2010, preliminary discussions between the Ecumenical Patriarchate and Pentecostals. More recently, the Salvation Army and the Baptist World Alliance have inquired about Pentecostal interest in opening up international dialogues with them, and Pentecostals have been participating regularly in the Global Christian Forum. Pentecostals have become full or associate members or observers in National Councils of Churches in various countries around the world. Several Pentecostal groups have also joined Christian Churches Together in the USA.

27. One example of this is reflected in the recent change within the Bylaws of the Assemblies of God, which prior to 2005 disapproved of virtually all ecumenical activity on the part of its churches and pastors. Now it embraces ecumenical participation in much more positive ways. One need only compare the statement in "Bylaws of the General Council of the Assemblies of God, Article IX.B, List of Doctrines and Practices Disapproved, Section 11, The Ecumenical Movement," *Minutes of the 50th Session of the General Council of the Assemblies of God, with Revised Constitution and Bylaws, 50th General Council, Washington, D.C., July 31–August 3, 2003* (Springfield, MO: General Secretary's Office,

and the momentum continues to grow for more and deeper ecumenical involvement.[28]

Further Achievements of the Dialogue

The first two rounds of dialogue achieved little more than what has been outlined above. In the First Quinquennium, David du Plessis had difficulty gathering a team of Classical Pentecostals who were willing to sit with Catholics in dialogue. The team of twelve included six participants from Classical Pentecostal churches, supplemented by six Charismatics from the Orthodox, Anglican, Reformed, and Lutheran wings of the church with the hope that their "Pentecostal" experience would be sufficient to help make the Pentecostal case. Of the six Classical Pentecostals, only Dr. Russell P. Spittler (Assemblies of God) and Dr. François Möller, Sr., President of the Apostolic Faith Mission of South Africa (AFM) were trained theologians. David du Plessis held no ministerial credentials at the time, the Reverend F. A. Hölscher was an AFM pastor, and John McTernon and John L. Meares were pastors of independent congregations with little if any formal theological training at the bachelor's level. It quickly became apparent that such a mixed team of "Pentecostals" would never work because their educational levels and starting points were so different and their commitments, for example on baptism, were sometimes at odds with one another.

2003), pp. 131-32, with the statement found in the *Minutes of the 51st Session of the General Council of the Assemblies of God, with Revised Constitution and Bylaws, 51st General Council, Denver, Colorado, August 2-5, 2005* (Springfield, MO: General Secretary's Office, 2005), p. 125, to note the extent of this change.

28. One can see this in the growing number of Pentecostal groups that now hold membership in National Councils of Churches and in Christian Churches Together in the USA. Currently, thirty-seven hold full membership and six hold associate membership in such councils. While not immediately obvious, this information is available from Huibert van Beek, compiler, *A Handbook of Churches and Councils: Profiles of Ecumenical Relationships* (Geneva: World Council of Churches, 2006). Bishop James Leggett, former General Superintendent of the International Pentecostal Holiness Church, has encouraged other Pentecostal leaders to join him in this initiative. His denomination has been joined by the Church of God of Prophecy, the Elim Fellowship (Lima, NY), and the Open Bible Churches. The Church of God (Cleveland, TN), the Church of God in Christ, Inc., and the Pentecostal Free Will Baptist Church have sent observers to some CCT meetings.

During the Second Quinquennium, the Pentecostal team changed. It consisted solely of representatives from "Classical Pentecostal" denominations as well as some "Classical Pentecostal" leaders who led independent congregations or groups of congregations (e.g., Bishop John Meares).[29] The weaknesses during this second round of discussions were primarily three. First, of the twenty-two Pentecostals who participated over the period of five years, only five held a theological degree at the master's level or above.[30] Second, the number of topics discussed in any one year was too great to develop any substantial understanding between the two parties. Reports were frequently reduced to summaries of what was discussed. Third, at the insistence of the Pentecostals but with some Catholic resistance, the dialogue took on the subject of "Mary." That decision carried considerable negative fallout, especially within the larger Pentecostal community. It did, however, create an opening for further discussion on the *communio sanctorum,* and this issue specifically suggested the transition to the topic chosen for the Third Quinquennium, "Perspectives on *Koinonia.*"[31]

It is easy to see that the first two quinquennia of the international Pentecostal-Catholic dialogue did not look or function like most other dialogues in which the PCPCU was involved. One might wonder how it even survived those early years. Still, these discussions resulted in two Ph.D. dissertations,[32] and participants on both teams developed a level of trust that encouraged the continuation of the dialogue.[33] It

29. Bishop John Meares is an interesting case of mixed identity. He had been a minister with the Church of God (Cleveland, TN). In 1955 he founded Evangel Temple in Washington, DC. Through his influence other congregations were established, and in 1972 he became president of a consortium of related churches under the name International Evangelical Church and Missionary Association. In 1983, he was consecrated Presiding Bishop by that body. Evangel Temple is now known as Evangel Cathedral.

30. Of the five with a master's degree or higher, two of them were designated as "Observers." This meant that they had no voice in the plenary discussions.

31. "Perspectives on *Koinonia,*" nos. 7-10.

32. Arnold Bittlinger, *Papst und Pfingstler: Der römisch Katholische–pfingstliche Dialog und seine ökumenische Relevanz,* SIHC 16 (Frankfurt am Main: Peter Lang, 1978), 484 pp. The second dissertation and the most complete analysis of the early years of the international Pentecostal-Catholic dialogue is that of Jerry L. Sandidge, *Roman Catholic/Pentecostal Dialogue [1977-82]: A Study in Developing Ecumenism,* Studies in the Intercultural History of Christianity 16 (Frankfurt am Main: Peter Lang, 1987), 2 volumes.

33. Subsequent dissertations that studied the third quinquennium are Veli-Matti Kärkkäinen, *Spiritus ubi vult spirat: Pneumatology in Roman Catholic–Pentecostal Dialogue*

would be in the Third Quinquennium where a different pace would be set, a new method of working would be found, and the first substantive document would be produced.[34]

Beginning with the Third Quinquennium ("Perspectives on *Koinonia*," 1985-1989) and continuing through the fourth ("Evangelization, Proselytism and Common Witness," 1990-1997) and fifth rounds of discussion ("On Becoming a Christian: Insights from Scripture and the Patristic Writings with Some Contemporary Reflections," 1998-2006), the dialogue produced three major documents. In a sense, they moved from the general to the specific. Even though participants on both teams agreed that their churches did not enjoy full *koinonia* with one another, they did acknowledge that some level of *koinonia* between Catholics and Pentecostals already existed.[35] Once that point had been affirmed, it was easier for them to address one of the most difficult issues contributing to the breakdown of that *koinonia,* namely proselytism.[36] In the fifth round, they went more deeply into the nature of their *koinonia* by addressing the inability of both groups to distinguish between those who need to be evangelized and those whose evangelization could actually be understood as proselytism. In order to do that, the dialogue participants studied how conversion is conceived in each tradition and what it means for an individual to become fully integrated into the life of the church.[37]

"Perspectives on *Koinonia*"

From the outset, the Third Quinquennium was different from the two earlier rounds. This round of discussions would focus on a single theme, that of *koinonia,* rather than multiple unrelated themes over the

---

(1972-1989), SLAG 42 (Helsinki: Luther-Agricola-Society, 1998), 509 pp., and David Leon Cole, *"Pentecostal Koinonia: An Emerging Ecumenical Ecclesiology among Pentecostals,"* unpublished Ph.D. dissertation (Pasadena, CA: Fuller Theological Seminary, School of Theology, 1998).

34. The dissertation most directly related is Paul D. Lee, *Pneumatological Ecclesiology in the Roman Catholic–Pentecostal Dialogue: A Catholic Reading of the Third Quinquennium (1985-1989)* (Rome: Pontificia Studiorum Universitatis a S. Thoma Aq. in Urbe, 1994), 364 pp.

35. "Perspectives on *Koinonia*," 54-55.

36. "Evangelization, Proselytism and Common Witness," 68-70.

37. "On Becoming a Christian," 5-7.

five-year period. It would go more deeply into the subject by inviting a single paper from each team each year, and developing both the annual and the larger discussions around issues raised by these papers. It would also involve a greater percentage of Pentecostal scholars than in previous rounds.[38]

There were several reasons for the choice of *koinonia* as the topic for this quinquennium. First, following the Second Vatican Council, *koinonia* became an important theme in Catholic ecclesiological discussions, such as ARCIC I with the Anglican Church.[39] Second, this theme was being used in broader ecumenical discussions at the time, as an important means of approaching the unity question.[40] Third, many Pentecostals were familiar with the term *koinonia* because it was frequently used by Pentecostals to describe their relationship with one another. The earlier discussion on Mary provided an easy segue to a broader discussion on the Communion of the Saints, and with that as its lead the dialogue went on to discuss "The Holy Spirit and the New Testament Vision of *Koinonia*," and "*Koinonia*, Church and Sacrament," before studying the relationship between "*Koinonia* and Baptism."

In the end, the topic of "*Koinonia* and Baptism" played a larger role than either side anticipated. The baptism question arose for two reasons. For the Catholics it was clear that Christian *koinonia* begins at baptism (*Decree on Ecumenism* 22). For Pentecostals, the issue was more complex. For most Pentecostals, *koinonia* might begin at the time of baptism, but only if it included a profession of personal faith in Jesus Christ. The leadership of the Pentecostal team believed that it had been unable to present a unified position on baptism during the First

38. Over this five-year period, twenty-three Pentecostals attended the dialogue. Eleven of them attended at least three sessions. Of these eleven, five of them held doctoral degrees in theological fields. Among the observers who attended at least one session, four more held doctoral degrees and one held the Th.M. degree.

39. The Introduction, paragraphs 4-9 to the "Anglican–Roman Catholic Conversations: Final Report 1981 [ARCIC I]," in *GA*, pp. 64-67, makes it explicit.

40. Several other reasons are also offered in "Perspectives on *Koinonia*," 7-10. The theme was not new to the World Council of Churches, but from the Vancouver Assembly onward it took on new life, most notably in the 1987 mandate of the Central Committee of a study on "The Unity We Seek," ultimately completed and adopted as "The Unity of the Church as *Koinonia*: Gift and Calling," at the 1991 Canberra Assembly. "On the Way to Fuller *Koinonia*" subsequently became the theme of the Fifth World Conference on Faith and Order, in Santiago de Compostela, Spain, 1993.

Quinquennium because the team included "Pentecostal" participants from historic churches that practiced infant baptism. Those Pentecostals involved in the earlier discussions had assumed that all Pentecostals practiced the baptism of those who had already made a confession of faith. It came as a disconcerting surprise for most of the Pentecostal participants in the Third Quinquennium to discover that baptismal practice among Classical Pentecostal denominations around the world varied so widely, and that a number of Pentecostal groups practiced the baptism of infants.[41] Thus, one of the important achievements of this dialogue has been to educate Pentecostals about themselves.

This fact gives rise to another set of important though unexpected achievements of the dialogue. If it can be said that Pentecostals are still at the beginning stages of constructing a Pentecostal theological system, then it must also be said that the international Pentecostal-Catholic dialogue has served as an impetus to this process of theological development.[42] While it cannot be viewed as providing the *only* impetus to the current increase in theological developments within Pentecostalism, the dialogue has done two things. It has required "Classical Pentecostals" to take seriously the global character of the Movement, and it has forced Pentecostal scholars to take seriously the theological diversity that makes global Pentecostalism what it is. It is no longer possible to study Pentecostalism simply as a phenomenon born and nourished by North American or Western ways of thinking. As such, it has given Pentecostal partners around the world a voice that did not seem possible at the time the dialogue began.

The issue of baptism provided a good example of this change. Baptism had emerged as a divisive discussion item in the First Quinquennium.[43] During this Third Quinquennium, the subject was

41. The Pentecostal paper demonstrated some of this diversity. Initially, it was heavily criticized by the Pentecostal participants. By the end of the quinquennium, they had accepted the fact that this diversity on questions of baptism did, in fact, exist. A shorter version of the Pentecostal paper was subsequently published as Cecil M. Robeck, Jr. and Jerry L. Sandidge, "The Ecclesiology of *Koinonia* and Baptism: A Pentecostal Perspective," *Journal of Ecumenical Studies* 27, no. 3 (Summer 1990): 504-34.

42. Among the Pentecostal theologians who have been most influenced by the dialogue are Simon Chan, David Cole, Dale Coulter, Veli-Matti Kärkkäinnen, Harold Hunter, Cheryl Bridges-Johns, Japie Lapoorta, Wonsuk and Julie Ma, Frank Macchia, Jean-Daniel Plüss, Tony Richie, Cecil M. Robeck, Jr., Del Tarr, Cees van der Laan, Paul van der Laan, Wolfgang Vondey, Matthias Wenk, Amos Yong, and Huibert Zegwaart.

43. "Final Report (1972-76)," 9-27.

engaged more fully with the emphasis upon its meaning, its relationship to faith and to the church, the variations in baptismal practice, and the place of baptism vis-à-vis the experience of the Holy Spirit.[44] The realization that Classical Pentecostals differed among themselves on the subject of baptism ultimately allowed them to think more broadly than their own experience. Thus, the implications of the different positions taken between Catholics and Pentecostals as well as between different groups of Pentecostals became more evident than had been previously expressed. The clarity with which the differences came to be seen also made it possible for the group to express more transparently the places in which they ultimately agreed.

Together, the teams agreed that "baptism involves a passing over from the kingdom of darkness to Christ's kingdom of light, and always includes a communal dimension of being baptized into the one body of Christ."[45] Baptism was also viewed as a rite related to the initiation of a person into the Christian community, and as such as "an ecclesial event, a faith experience for the worshipping community."[46] It was noted that most Classical Pentecostals agree with Catholics that it should be performed "in the name of the Father and of the Son and of the Holy Spirit" in keeping with Matthew 28:19.[47] While it was agreed that immersion best represents the death and resurrection motif inherent in the idea of baptism, making it the most effective sign to convey baptism's meaning,[48] both communities recognized the validity of other modes of baptism (e.g., pouring) and somewhat less enthusiastically, the baptism of infants. It was observed that most Classical Pentecostals agree with Catholics that baptism is intended to be received only once, with the understanding that rebaptism is not an acceptable practice.[49]

In both communities, it was agreed that faith and conversion are necessary components of Christian initiation[50] and that faith precedes

---

44. "Perspectives on *Koinonia*," 39-69.

45. "Final Report (1972-76)," 19.

46. "Final Report (1972-76)," 19; "On Becoming a Christian," 54.

47. "Perspectives on *Koinonia*," 56. The use of such adjectives as "some," "many," and "most" became common as team members sought to be more precise in their understanding of Pentecostal diversity on this and other subjects.

48. "Perspectives on *Koinonia*," 57.

49. "Perspectives on *Koinonia*," 58.

50. "Perspectives on *Koinonia*," 43.

and is a necessary precondition for baptism to be authentic.[51] Catholics and Pentecostals affirmed together that "the church is a communion of faith whose nature is essentially missionary, impelling it to foster the profession of faith by each of its members and to invite into this communion of faith others who do not yet know the joy of believing in Jesus Christ."[52] Thus there was agreement that "instruction in the faith necessarily follows upon baptism in order that the life of grace may come to fruition" and that "a pastor should delay or refuse to baptize an infant if the parents (or guardians) clearly have no intention of bringing up the infant in the practice of faith."[53]

At the same time, the partners in this round of dialogue agreed that *koinonia* is a dynamic term, "requiring mutuality in its many dimensions."[54] They claimed that each believed in the oneness of the church, though not on how it was best manifested in the world.[55] They contended that *koinonia* is rooted in the Trinitarian life of God.[56] Both sides acknowledged their failure to achieve that same mutuality at various levels.[57] They both acknowledged that the current division that marks the church so clearly is a stumbling block to evangelization and lamented the scandal in which they participate.[58]

At the same time, both parties confessed their dependence on the Holy Spirit, the source of *koinonia*,[59] their need to invoke the Spirit, their faith — in keeping with Matthew 18:20 — that God is present whenever two or three are gathered together in Christ's name,[60] and their recognition that the unity that the Holy Spirit desires to manifest is "resplendent with diversity."[61] It was clear, however, that there were major stumbling blocks between Pentecostals and Catholics that made greater expressions of their already-existing *koinonia* sometimes difficult to see. The fourth round of discussions would take up some of these issues.

---

51. "Perspectives on *Koinonia*," 43.
52. "On Becoming a Christian," 96.
53. "Perspectives on *Koinonia*," 62.
54. "Perspectives on *Koinonia*," 73.
55. "Perspectives on *Koinonia*," 34.
56. "Perspectives on *Koinonia*," 29.
57. "Perspectives on *Koinonia*," 74-76.
58. "Perspectives on *Koinonia*," 37-38.
59. "Perspectives on *Koinonia*," 30, 77.
60. "Perspectives on *Koinonia*," 77.
61. "Perspectives on *Koinonia*," 36.

Cecil M. Robeck Jr.

"Evangelization, Proselytism and Common Witness"

Upon the completion of "Perspectives on *Koinonia*," and shortly after the beginning of the fourth round of discussions, several members of the first generation of Pentecostal participants either died or retired.[62] The Pentecostal co-chair changed in 1992, from an ecclesial leadership as had been represented by David and Justus du Plessis, to a more academic one. Fewer denominational leaders would participate, while the denominations represented were served by more participants with formal academic training in various theological disciplines.[63] The steering committee exercised considerable care to ensure that all participants were actively involved in their respective churches and that they faithfully represented the teachings of the churches of which they were a part.

Among the most difficult issues to be confronted by the church since at least the time of the Reformation have been the related questions of evangelization and proselytism. This was the case for members of this dialogue as well. It was strongly debated as to whether the Pentecostal-Catholic dialogue could address these issues without destroying the dialogue altogether.[64] The teams acknowledged that Catholics and Pentecostals held much in common,[65] but there was consider-

---

62. David du Plessis, the first Pentecostal chair, died in 1987. Jerry L. Sandidge, the Pentecostal Secretary, died in 1991. Justus du Plessis continued to chair the Pentecostal team in 1990 and 1991, but resigned from the dialogue in 1992. Longtime Pentecostal participants, Hugh Edwards of the Church of God of Prophecy, Bernice Gerard of the Pentecostal Assemblies of Canada, and Coleman Phillips of the International Church of the Foursquare Gospel all retired at the end of the Third Quinquennium.

63. This round included twelve Catholic theologians and thirty-one Pentecostals. Ten of the Pentecostals came as one-time observers. Of the thirty-one Pentecostals, twenty-three of them held advanced theological degrees, including twenty with doctoral degrees in theological disciplines — among them three denominational college presidents and one seminary president. The denominational leaders included Justus du Plessis (1990-92), Apostolic Faith Mission of South Africa; James Jenkins (1991-94), Church of God, Cleveland, TN; Steve Overman (1992-97), Foursquare; Coleman Phillips (1990-92), Foursquare; Raymond Pruitt (1994-96), Church of God of Prophecy; Chris Stathis (1991), Church of God of Prophecy; Vinson Synan (1991), International Pentecostal Holiness Church; Cees van der Laan (1991) and Huibert Zegwaart (1992-97), *Broederschap van Pinkstergemeenten* of the Netherlands. Five of these ecclesial representatives held advanced degrees.

64. This is acknowledged in "Evangelization, Proselytism and Common Witness," 68.

65. "Evangelization, Proselytism and Common Witness," 69-70.

able fear regarding whether the *koinonia* that they now recognized as existing between them was sufficiently capable of enabling the group to take on such seemingly intractable subjects. Still, the need to address these controversial subjects was supported quite forcefully by all but one of the Pentecostals and one Catholic, who had participated in the round on *koinonia*. As a result, the subjects of evangelization and proselytism would be placed at the heart of the fourth round of discussions.[66]

It is important to note that in the international Pentecostal-Catholic dialogue, the term "proselytism" has been reserved for actions taken by members of one Christian church that hurts another. As such, it has been viewed as a sin against the community of faith, a sin against other Christians, a sin against the church.[67] Sociologists, anthropologists, government leaders, secular media sources, and leaders of other religions often use the term "proselytism" to describe acts of "evangelization" as though these terms were synonymous.[68] This is not the way this term has been understood in this dialogue. This is an important point, for the blurring of the lines between evangelization and proselytism may ultimately hold significant consequences for the church as a whole; indeed, in some countries anti-proselytism and/or anti-conversion laws have already limited or eliminated any possibility for evangelistic outreach.[69]

---

66. The only two persons to voice opposition to taking up this subject were the Catholic Co-chair, Fr. Kilian McDonnell, OSB, and the Pentecostal Treasurer, Cecil M. Robeck, Jr. Justus du Plessis, the Pentecostal Co-chair, and Jerry L. Sandidge, the Pentecostal Secretary, were strongly in favor of the idea. In the end, they prevailed, but within one year, Jerry Sandidge had died, and within two years, Justus had retired. The task was thus left to Kilian McDonnell and Cecil M. Robeck, Jr., to complete. I have since wondered whether our ability to find common ground on the subject resulted from our shared fears that the subject was so fraught with dangers that it would bring an end to the dialogue altogether.

67. See Jacques Matthey, "Evangelism, Still the Enduring Test of Our Ecumenical — and Missionary — Calling," *International Review of Mission* 96, nos. 382-83 (July-October 2007): 356-57.

68. Unfortunately, this confusion seems to have gained credibility among some Christian churches and theologians in recent years. See, for example, Martin E. Marty and Frederick E. Greenspahn, *Pushing the Faith: Proselytism and Civility in a Pluralistic World* (New York: Crossroad, 1988). I view the proclamation of the gospel of Jesus Christ to people of other faiths as a form of evangelization and not of proselytism. Cf. "Evangelization, Proselytism and Common Witness," 97.

69. See, for instance, Allison Duncan, "Proselytism vs. Evangelism in India," accessed June 8, 2010 at www.globalengage.org/issues/articles/freedom/491-proselytism-vs-evangelism-in-india.html.

Within the Christian community, terms such as evangelization and proselytism are often treated in isolation from one another, and seldom is a civil discussion held between those who stand in opposition to one another. The charge of proselytism that Catholics frequently lodge against Pentecostals, especially in Latin America,[70] led the Pentecostal team to ask that the subjects of evangelization and proselytism be addressed in the fourth round of dialogue. The Pentecostals argued that what they were about was evangelization, not proselytism. At worst, they were evangelizing people who had been sacramentalized but who had never been properly evangelized.[71] The Catholics contended that Pentecostals were actually engaged in proselytism, not evangelization.[72] If any headway were to be made on the subjects of evangelization and proselytism, these terms and their limits needed to be described, illustrated, and defined *together.*

One of the major achievements in this dialogue is the level of candor that personifies the discussions. Dialogues are sometimes places where posturing occurs, where lines intended to separate or to mark out turf are set forth. With issues as difficult as the question of proselytism on the table, both teams quickly realized that the admission of guilt for their complicity in the problem was an important factor in arriving at the truth and in finding ways past their perceived impasse. The impasse would only be compounded by repeated denials and misrepresentations, made worse by each tradition measuring the motiva-

---

70. Alta/Baja California Bishops, "Dimensions of a Response to Proselytism," *Origins: CNS Documentary Service* 19, no. 41 (March 15, 1990): 666-69; John Paul II, "Opening Address to Fourth General Conference of Latin American Episcopate," *Origins: CNS Documentary Service* 22, no. 19 (October 22, 1992): 321, 323-32, especially Section 12, p. 326; Mac Margolis, "A Wave of Religious Revival Splits Brazil," *Los Angeles Times* (July 5, 1993): H6; Gary Haynes, "Brazil's Catholics Launch 'Holy War,'" *Charisma* 19, no. 10 (May 1994): 74-75.

71. This position seemed to gain some support from Thomas Weinandy, OFM Cap, "Why Catholics Should Witness Verbally to the Gospel," *New Oxford Review* 60, no. 6 (July-August 1993): 16, who noted that "[m]any contemporary Catholics possess no evangelistic fervor. One reason could be that they have little or no experiential knowledge of Jesus, and may even be ignorant of the basic Gospel message: that Jesus himself is the Good News. Perhaps they simply have not been fully transformed by the power and life of the Holy Spirit that comes through faith in Jesus, and thus are incapable of offering this new life to others."

72. Cf. R. W. Dellinger, "Evangelicals View Hispanic Evangelization Differently," *The Tidings* [Los Angeles, CA Archdiocesan newspaper] (July 8, 1994): 10-11.

tions and actions of the other by their own ideals.[73] Stereotypes were insufficient for making decisions.[74] In a number of places, then, confessions of misdeeds have been made.[75]

It would take eight years for the dialogue teams to explain how to distinguish between evangelization and proselytism, but the teams believed that it was critical that they spend this extra time needed to avoid misunderstanding. It was an important achievement for the dialogue to arrive at a clearly stated common understanding on such difficult subjects.[76] In the end, their work together enabled the dialogue to acknowledge "that God has charged all Christians to announce the Gospel to all people," that motivated by love for and obedience to Christ "proclaiming God's reconciliation of the world through Christ is central to the church's faith, life and witness,"[77] and that the message that "in Jesus Christ, the Son of God made man, who died and rose from the dead, salvation is offered to all humankind, as a gift of God's grace and mercy" lies at its very core.[78] Discussion focused on the ways and means of engaging in evangelization in keeping with a shared *koinonia,* including the role that culture plays in that process, the relationship between evangelization by word or proclamation and deed or social justice.

Clearly, the major point needing resolution was the acknowledgment of inappropriate forms of evangelization, in other words, proselytism. A failure to recognize one another as sisters and brothers or as Christians has contributed significantly to the problem. Thus, an appeal

73. "Evangelization, Proselytism and Common Witness," 75-79.

74. "Evangelization, Proselytism and Common Witness," 91-93.

75. "Evangelization, Proselytism and Common Witness," 19, 33, 62-64, 78, 81, 87, 89, etc. It should be noted that this has been a regular pattern in the dialogue since "Perspectives on *Koinonia,*" 38, 74-76, 80, 89, 103.

76. While it is the case that the Joint Working Group that coordinates work between the World Council of Churches and the PCPCU released its statement on proselytism before the dialogue released its report, the Joint Working Group received and incorporated into its report some of the findings of the dialogue to that point. Cf. "The Challenge of Proselytism and the Calling to Common Witness: A Study Document of the Joint Working Group between the World Council of Churches and the Roman Catholic Church, September 25, 1995," in William G. Rusch and Jeffrey Gros, eds., *Deepening Communion: International Ecumenical Documents with Roman Catholic Participation* (Washington, DC: United States Catholic Conference, 1998), pp. 583-95.

77. "Evangelization, Proselytism and Common Witness," 11, 16.

78. "Evangelization, Proselytism and Common Witness," 14 ("Evangelization in the Modern World," 27).

to existing *koinonia* provided the starting point for addressing the prose-lytism question.[79] The dispute emerges, in large part, because without agreement on the nature of the church, there is no common mind. As a result, we do not trust one another, we dismiss one another, we fail to recognize one another, and we fail to practice ethical behavior toward one another. The teams attempted to move beyond what they called the "lens of this disunity"[80] to a position of respect and love for one another. This began with a common declaration of the problem followed by an offering of reasons for existing conflict between Pentecostals and Catholics. With the stage now set, it was possible to define more clearly what constituted acts of proselytism. The achievement of this dialogue is that it may be the first such dialogue in which protagonists on both sides of the proselytism question sat together, reasoned together, and proposed solutions to the problem *together*. Issues such as intellectual laziness and dishonesty, willful misrepresentation of facts, the use of intimidation and force, manipulation, disrespect, unwarranted judgments of the other, competition, and the like were studied together, and both teams agreed on their inappropriateness when engaging in the evangelistic task.[81]

Two points that contributed significantly to the problem of proselytism were explored more fully. The first of these had to do with the fact that in some places, the Catholic Church has been the dominant church for centuries. In recent years, their hegemony has been challenged by Pentecostals who have begun evangelizing among them, without first establishing a relationship that takes seriously their existing bond of *koinonia* no matter how partial it might be. Without acknowledging this existing relationship, Pentecostals simply fished in the larger Catholic pond.[82] The second of these is related to the fact that when these Pentecostals began to "evangelize" among confessing Catholics, they did so because they did not fully recognize the marks of Christian faith and life that they expect to find in those who have truly heard and understood the gospel message.[83]

---

79. "Evangelization, Proselytism and Common Witness," 69.

80. "Evangelization, Proselytism and Common Witness," 78.

81. "Evangelization, Proselytism and Common Witness," 93.

82. I draw this image from Miroslav Volf, "Fishing in the Neighbor's Pond: Mission and Proselytism in Eastern Europe," *International Bulletin of Missionary Research* 20, no. 1 (January 1996): 26-31.

83. This situation is set up in "Evangelization, Proselytism and Common Witness," 68-79, especially 75.

Upon agreeing on the status and analyzing some of the reasons for these problems, the teams arrived at a common mind that would contribute to their resolution. The solution would begin with prayer and then move to conversation, which they believed would help to develop mutual respect.[84] It would require that both parties agree to condemn all proselytizing activities.[85] It would acknowledge the complicit roles of each party in the current state of affairs.[86] It would address the underlying factors that gave rise to past proselytizing activities.[87] And it would guarantee the right of all Christians to bear witness to their faith in Christ Jesus to whoever is willing to listen.[88]

This last decision was a challenge to both teams. For Catholics, it meant that Pentecostals would be free to "evangelize" Catholics, that is, to proclaim the gospel in a persuasive manner, "in such a way as to bring people to faith in Jesus Christ or to commit themselves more deeply to Him within the context of their own church." For Pentecostals, it meant limiting themselves to a kind of evangelization undergirded by genuine Christian love (1 Corinthians 13) that was never motivated toward their "own selfish ends by using the opportunity to speak against or in any way denigrate another Christian community, or to suggest or encourage a change in someone's Christian affiliation."[89]

By suggesting these ways to help settle some existing disputes between Catholics and Pentecostals related specifically to evangelization (which both parties agreed is essential to responsible Christian discipleship) and proselytism (which both parties agreed is reprehensible behavior that needs to be condemned), the teams went further to offer suggestions about possible ways in which Catholics and Pentecostals might be able to share a common witness to the reconciling love of God through Jesus Christ.[90]

---

84. "Evangelization, Proselytism and Common Witness," 79. See also 102.

85. "Evangelization, Proselytism and Common Witness," 82-84.

86. "Evangelization, Proselytism and Common Witness," 89.

87. "Evangelization, Proselytism and Common Witness," 91-92, 102-3, 110-16.

88. "Evangelization, Proselytism and Common Witness," 94.

89. "Evangelization, Proselytism and Common Witness," 94, 106-7. These actions raised questions regarding commitments to religious liberty such as have been expressed by the Catholic Church since at least 1948 with the publication of the *United Nations Declaration on Human Rights,* the *UN Declaration on the Elimination of All Forms of Intolerance and Discrimination Based on Religious Belief* (25 November 1981, Art. 1.1), and of course, by the Catholic Church since Vatican II through its *Declaration on Religious Liberty.*

90. "Evangelization, Proselytism and Common Witness," 117-30. Cf. Cecil M. Ro-

To say that the issues surrounding evangelization and proselytism and common witness are settled between Pentecostals and Catholics would be a gross overstatement. There has been push back on both sides even since the publication of this report. In countries where Catholics dominate and Pentecostals have occupied the margins, many Pentecostals are still not convinced that Catholics are sufficiently trustworthy for them to believe what Catholics have said in the report.[91] Pentecostals who are in constant contact with popular expressions of Catholicism — in places where the people seem not always to understand church teaching — still raise the argument that such Catholics may be properly sacramentalized but are essentially non-Christian and often unchurched, and they continue to defend their right to lead such individuals to Jesus[92] through means that the report does not support.[93] As a result many Catholics, especially Catholic leaders in Latin America, still speak of Pentecostals as a "sect" and in many instances remain unconvinced that Pentecostals are anything other than proselytizers and "ravenous wolves" who need to be marginalized. As a result, some Catholic leaders have interceded with the Pontifical Council to end the dialogue with Pentecostals.[94] Others have worked through more indirect means such as government legislation, to make life diffi-

---

beck, Jr., "Evangelization or Proselytism of Hispanics? A Pentecostal Perspective," *Journal of Hispanic/Latino Theology* 4, no. 4 (1997): 42-64, especially 56-64.

91. See, for instance, the untitled response to this document by Opal Reddin in *Pneuma* 12, no. 1 (1999): 81-84.

92. Cf. Terry Peretti, "Proclaiming the Gospel in Italy," *The Pentecostal Evangel* 4220 (March 26, 1995): 18, and Terry Peretti, "Learning from the Past, Looking to the Future," *The Pentecostal Evangel* 4220 (March 26, 1995): 19.

93. This is a pastoral problem readily recognized by the Catholic participants more than once in the dialogue. See "Perspectives on *Koinonia*," 60; "Evangelization, Proselytism and Common Witness," 62. It is becoming a problem for Pentecostals as well, as was later noted in "On Becoming a Christian," 55.

94. This fact is not widely publicized, but it has been the motivation behind such statements as Edward Idris Cardinal Cassidy, "Prolusio" [given at the Meeting of Representatives of the National Episcopal Commissions for Ecumenism, Rome, May 5-10, 1993] in *IS* 84 (1993/III-IV): 122. "We must be careful . . . not to confuse the issue [of sects and new religious movements] by lumping together under the term 'sect' groups that do not deserve that title. I am not speaking here, for instance, about the evangelical movement among Protestants, nor about Pentecostalism as such. The Pontifical Council has had fruitful dialogue and significant contact with certain evangelical groups and with Pentecostals. Indeed, one can speak of a mutual enrichment as a result of these contacts."

cult for those with whom they disagree and to bring about conformity to the older Catholic hegemony.[95] The road between us continues to be a bumpy one. Regardless of these continuing challenges, this document remains a major achievement, providing a high water mark on this subject of how to address the difficult issue of proselytism for the church as a whole. What is at stake now is its reception by the churches.

"On Becoming a Christian"

During the work on "Evangelization, Proselytism and Common Witness" one of the issues that was identified as a significant factor contributing to actions of proselytism involved the question of how it might be possible for members of either group more easily to recognize members of the other group as being fully Christian, and thus, not in need of further evangelization or proselytism. They observed that

> [a]n issue between Catholics and Pentecostals that relates to the problem of proselytism concerns the way a living faith is perceived in the life of an individual Christian or in a community. Through dialogue we have learned that Pentecostals and Catholics may have different ideas about who is "unchurched," different understandings of how living in a deeply Christian culture can root the Christian faith in someone's life. They may have different ideas of how to assess whether, or in what way, pastoral needs are being met in a Christian community or in a person's life. They may have different ways of interpreting whether or not a person can be considered an evangelized Christian.[96]

---

95. This situation has improved dramatically within the past decade, although accounts of such things have been documented as late as 1999 when the Catholic hierarchy in Chile opposed the passage of a law "granting legal equality to other churches." On this see Paul Freston, *Evangelicals and Politics in Asia, Africa and Latin America* (Cambridge: Cambridge University Press, 2001), p. 213. On similar issues see Brian H. Smith, *Religious Politics in Latin America: Pentecostal vs. Catholic* (Notre Dame: University of Notre Dame Press, 1998), pp. 60-64. Paul E. Sigmund, ed., *Religious Freedom and Evangelization in Latin America: The Challenge of Religious Pluralism* (Maryknoll, NY: Paulist Press, 1999), provides the best historical overview of the situation in a country-by-country format.

96. "Evangelization, Proselytism and Common Witness," 91. This point is picked up at the beginning of "On Becoming a Christian," 6.

In a sense, the fifth round of the dialogue addressed the issues raised in this paragraph. An attempt would be made to respond to these challenges by understanding "how an individual moves from his or her initial entry into the Christian life to being a fully active member of the church."[97] Five subthemes were chosen: (1) Conversion and Christian Initiation, (2) Faith and Christian Initiation, (3) Christian Formation and Discipleship, (4) Experience in Christian Life, and (5) Baptism in the Spirit and Christian Initiation.

One of the singular achievements of the fifth round of the Pentecostal-Catholic dialogue was the inclusion not only of the traditional biblical and theological discussions, but also the writings of the Fathers of the Church.[98] It may also be the first venue in which Pentecostal leaders have made a conscious effort to study the Fathers as their own "Fathers" in the faith. In earlier rounds, very little mention was made of the Fathers, and almost exclusively by members of the Catholic teams. In this round, the Fathers were included as early witnesses to the questions raised by both teams. Thus, alongside the biblical witness and later theological and pastoral reflections on the subjects, the insights of the Fathers were also studied. While Catholics grant the Fathers an authority that Pentecostals do not grant them, the dialogue partners on both teams found much in the Fathers that they affirmed together. Both teams were willing to grant the Fathers a "privileged" position in the church, though they did so on different bases. The Catholic team acknowledged the divine side in the work of the Fathers, suggesting that the Holy Spirit had inspired them in a unique way such that their teachings hold a special authority in keeping with Catholic tradition and in relation to the larger concept of "Word of God."[99]

In what must seem to be ironic to many, the Pentecostals played down the divine side, instead granting credibility to the human factors they found in the teachings of the Fathers. The Pentecostal team contended that the Fathers were no more or less inspired and no more or less pragmatic than are modern leaders in the church, that the decisions of the Fathers were best viewed in light of their pragmatism and context rather than as normative and universal, and that the Pentecos-

97. "On Becoming a Christian," 5.
98. "On Becoming a Christian," 8-13 and 275-77.
99. "On Becoming a Christian," 8-13, especially 9, as well as 185 and 266-70. Pentecostals typically view the Fathers and their decisions as more pragmatic and contextual than normative and universal.

tal reading of the Fathers was more consistent with the way the Fathers read themselves than the way subsequent generations of Catholics have come to read them.[100] For the Pentecostals, the "privileged" position of the Fathers had to do largely with their chronological proximity to Christ and the apostles. Yet, because it is easy to change over time, losing out on earlier acknowledged realities, the Pentecostals thought that a review of the Fathers might potentially offer restoration or corrections to contemporary thought and practice regarding Christ, the gospel, and the Christian life together.

As the teams worked their way through the subtopics of this round, both teams agreed that the works of the Fathers were worthy of careful consideration. Both teams were particularly encouraged by their piety and spirituality.[101] The Fathers were viewed as active participants in the process that would enable the credible transmission of the faith from their own generation to those who would follow them.[102] Participants viewed the Fathers as faithfully living out Christ's command to "Go . . . and make disciples" (Matt. 28:19-20),[103] and they saw the Fathers working within their various contexts to construct theological arguments that guaranteed consistency between them, ensuring that those who followed their leadership were of one mind. The Fathers reinforced the teachings of scripture, interpreting these teachings in fresh ways that were consistent with the original message but adaptable to the newest cultural contexts.[104] Both teams saw the Fathers adapting the message to the cultures in which they served, developing the concepts as well as the philosophical and theological frameworks that would ultimately communicate the truth to new audiences among whom they now ministered.[105] In the end, it must still be viewed as a major achievement that Pentecostals and Catholics have lifted up the Fathers *together,* granting them greater relevance to contemporary theological discussions between them than ever before.

---

100. See Cecil M. Robeck, Jr., "On Becoming a Christian: An Important Theme in the International Roman Catholic–Pentecostal Dialogue," *PentecoStudies: Online Journal for the Interdisciplinary Study of Pentecostalism and Charismatic Movements* 8, no. 2 (Fall 2008): 8.

101. "On Becoming a Christian," 267.

102. "On Becoming a Christian," 11.

103. "On Becoming a Christian," 12.

104. James A. Sanders, *Canon and Community: A Guide to Canonical Criticism* (Philadelphia: Fortress Press, 1984), p. 12.

105. "On Becoming a Christian," 12, 266.

As the subjects of conversion and of faith were brought into the discussion, the subject of baptism would be picked up once again, in keeping with a response to the suggestion made by one reviewer following the study of *koinonia*.[106] The Rite of Christian Initiation of Adults became a strong talking point with respect to the relationship between conversion, faith, and baptism for both teams.[107] Both parties agreed once again that conversion was "essential to salvation in Christ,"[108] although they differed at times on whether to emphasize the punctiliar or the processive nature of conversion.[109] They also agreed "that becoming a Christian is not comprehensible apart from faith," the kind of faith that "is a gifted response to God's revelation, involving an opening of the heart, an assent of the mind and actions which express our trust."[110]

For individuals to become a part of the church, both teams lifted up not only the necessity of conversion, faith, and baptism, but also the necessity of ongoing discipleship and Christian formation.[111] On this fact, there was broad agreement. Christian formation was viewed as a lifelong process, though how the life of discipleship, or the ways in which a Christian follows Christ may vary. Among these various discipleship paths, several were articulated: martyrdom, missions, the ascetic or monastic life, as well as the imitation of Christ in the daily life followed by most ordinary Christians.[112] The teams agreed that the role of the Holy Spirit in developing the life of Christian discipleship was strong, involving the transformation of the person.[113] It was also agreed that the formation of Christians begins by allowing the Word of God to form individual Christians together as the community of faithful, who gather together for fellowship, prayer, praise, and worship.[114]

The question of what role experience has in the Christian life was another major subject of discussion. The teams agreed that experience

---

106. Charles W. Gusmer, "A Review/Appreciation of 'Perspectives on *Koinonia,*'" *IS* 75 (1990-IV): 194.

107. "On Becoming a Christian," 27, 48-59, 76-96, 118, 127-32, 281.

108. "On Becoming a Christian," 25.

109. "On Becoming a Christian," 26-27, 189.

110. "On Becoming a Christian," 60.

111. "On Becoming a Christian," 97.

112. "On Becoming a Christian," 113-16.

113. "On Becoming a Christian," 117.

114. "On Becoming a Christian," 134-37.

was relevant to all the rest of the subjects under consideration,[115] and it became apparent that Pentecostals and Catholics share many important aspects of spiritual experience, including "the presence and power of the Spirit as well as contemplation, and mystical and active spiritualities."[116] As with other aspects of this study, Catholic and Pentecostal emphases differed at points. One of the places that experience was understood to play a major role was in the discussion of Baptism in the Holy Spirit.[117]

Although the role of experience in conversion and transformation yielded important shared observations, the dialogue teams did not find it possible to write a more definitive and integrated report on the subject. The difficult task of finding sufficient common ground and speaking to the subject together given the time constraints of the dialogue produced the most significant failure in the document. These separate accounts on the role of experience in conversion and the role of the experience of the community, while important, leave this segment of the paper open to criticism, though in comparing these accounts it should become apparent that more could have been done to find a broader consensus.[118]

Much of the disagreement on the role of experience in the Christian life seems to have had to do with what might be understood as measurable expectations of affective experiences. Both teams affirmed that "when the grace of the Holy Spirit touches the heart and mind, feelings and will of the individual in such a way that a person consciously encounters the Lord an authentic experience of God comes about."[119] Differences between the teams became apparent, however, when it came to claims about whether experience, especially affective experience, functions as a legitimate evidence or "assurance of salvation."[120] Both teams

---

115. "On Becoming a Christian," 141.

116. "On Becoming a Christian," 138.

117. "On Becoming a Christian," 141.

118. The section on "Experience in Christian Life" ran from paragraphs 138 to 191. The Pentecostal perspective is found in paragraphs 153-57 and 164-74, while the Catholic position is found in paragraphs 158-63 and 175-83. The teams did bring together some points of convergence in paragraphs 184-91, though it was clear that more work needs to be undertaken together, especially on the issue of discernment.

119. "On Becoming a Christian," 140.

120. The Pentecostal position is expressed in "On Becoming a Christian," 154-55, and 167, while the Catholic position is expressed in paragraph 178.

agreed that experience should not be viewed as an end in itself, but rather, as something calling for discernment.[121] As a result, the theme of discernment has been made a high-priority concern to be addressed in the sixth round of discussions, scheduled to begin in 2011.

If the issue of experience produced the most difficulty in the discussion, the subject of "Baptism in the Holy Spirit and Christian Initiation" produced some of its most substantive convergences[122] and the most substantive debate within the Catholic team.[123] The reason for substantial convergence may stem, in large part, from the fact that the Catholic Church has taken such an open and affirming position with respect to the activity of the Holy Spirit shared by Pentecostals and many Catholics who have identified with the Charismatic Renewal. The teams recognized from the beginning that they differed on issues related to "the meaning, significance, and timing of Baptism in the Holy Spirit,"[124] but they also affirmed that "the Holy Spirit has always been present in the church with grace, signs, and gifts."[125] They marked as their "most fundamental convergence" the "common conviction within both our communities that Baptism in the Holy Spirit is a powerful action of grace bestowed by God upon believers within the church."[126] They went on to note that their "sustained effort" to-

---

121. "On Becoming a Christian," 140 and especially 187.

122. This topic was included at the insistence of Fr. Kilian McDonnell, OSB, who served as the Catholic Co-chair at the beginning of this round of discussions. He had jointly authored Kilian McDonnell and George T. Montague, *Christian Initiation and Baptism in the Holy Spirit: Evidence from the First Eight Centuries* (Collegeville, MN: A Michael Glazier Book/Liturgical Press, 1991, 2nd rev. ed., 1994), 396 pp., in response to questions that had been raised in earlier rounds of the dialogue, and he asked to have the issue revisited as the dialogue discussed various aspects of becoming a Christian.

123. The discussion centered on the thesis that Fr. McDonnell championed, namely that the baptism in the Spirit is wrongly conceived if it is viewed as having only a role in private piety. It needs to be understood as part of community life, of public life and liturgy, and therefore it is constitutive of Christian life as a whole. Running counter to this position were Fr. Norbert Baumert, SJ, in Norbert Baumert, *Charisma — Taufe — Geisttaufe. Entflechtung einer semantischen Verwirrung* and *Charisma — Taufe — Geisttaufe: Normantivatät und persönliche Berufung* (Würzburg: Echter Verlag, 2001), 2 vols., and the German Catholic Charismatic Renewal, which argued that alongside the indwelling of the Spirit, it was possible to understand new outpourings of the Spirit such as might be understood as "occasional renewals."

124. "On Becoming a Christian," 192.

125. "On Becoming a Christian," 193.

126. "On Becoming a Christian," 260.

gether to study scripture and the patristic materials on this subject in order to gain greater clarity, in spite of internal diversity on both sides, amounted to "a step that is of no little significance, . . . considering the fact that our two communities together make up such a large portion of the worldwide Christian family."[127] Finally, the group affirmed and embraced together "the presence and exercise of charisms as an important dimension in the life of the church."[128] With these two large bodies making such affirmations, then, the dialogue can be said to have achieved a strong voice against the idea that the Holy Spirit has in some way ceased to work in the church through various charisms or means that were found to be so much a part of early Christian life.

One of the important achievements of the document, and hence of the dialogue, was the acknowledgment that the Holy Spirit has been active in both Pentecostal and Catholic churches, making it possible for mutual learning to take place. "Therefore," they concluded, "we are grateful that the renewal and outpouring of the Holy Spirit in the twentieth century has opened our hearts and minds to one another."

The Future of the Dialogue

Plans have been made to convene the sixth round of the international Pentecostal-Catholic dialogue in 2011. Because of the continuing concern expressed by a number of bishops from Latin America that Pentecostal churches should be placed in the category of "sect," the PCPCU has suggested and the Pentecostal steering committee has accepted that the next round of discussions build a solid academic base, so that it may provide theologically grounded pastoral answers to very real and sometimes difficult pastoral issues being raised in Latin America. With this process in mind, the theme of the sixth round will be "Charisms in the Church: Their Spiritual Significance, Discernment, and Pastoral Implications." The subthemes and studies will include (1) studies on our common ground with respect to charisms; (2) answers to the important questions of the "who," "what," and "how" of the discernment process; (3) the study of healing and suffering over against concerns re-

127. "On Becoming a Christian," 260.
128. "On Becoming a Christian," 262.

garding faith and presumption; and (4) explanations of what the gift of prophecy is and how it works.

The quest for the unity of the church is a quest that is rich with ecumenical and eschatological overtones. We are not simply seeking to return to some unknown past vision of the church reunited, but a future vision of the church united, in which denominations seem to play no further role. By focusing our attention on the past, we learn a great deal about what has not worked. By listening to the past, we learn the lessons of what can and should be avoided. But in the end, it is the future that pulls us relentlessly forward in this quest for unity, and the future is open to new visions even when we are not, simply because all too often we allow our past histories to control and limit our future together. Both Pentecostals and Catholics have much to learn from one another about the unity that we see portrayed when we study the myriads of peoples who surround the throne and stand before the Lamb in Revelation 7:9. This dialogue signifies one very important step along the journey to that point.

12 Pentecostal-Catholic International Dialogue: A Catholic Perspective

Ralph Del Colle

I. Setting the Stage

In order to appreciate the achievements of the international Catholic-Pentecostal dialogue it is important to contextualize the nature of this particular bilateral exchange. First, since its start in 1972, it has never been the expectation of this dialogue that its proximate goal would be organic unity between the Catholic Church and the many Pentecostal expressions of both church and faith. In fact, the ambiguity of whether Pentecostalism is a movement or an ecclesial expression has attended it since its beginnings at the turn of the last century. We can identify this as an antinomy in the relationship between the two traditions. In other words, the Catholic-Pentecostal dialogue is taking place between one of the most ecclesially focused traditions and one of the least. I will return to this theme, but the most immediate consequence is that the dialogue does not aim at "structural unity" but intends the fostering of "respect and understanding between the Catholic Church and Classical Pentecostal churches" (3).[1] This does not mean that the dialogue — now moving into a sixth phase scheduled to begin in mid-2011 — is unimportant. Granted that for some, the dialogues with the Orthodox, Anglicans, and Lutherans carry more weight because the goal of

---

1. Citations refer to the numbered paragraphs in the Reports and Vatican documents. This one is from the report of the fifth phase (1998-2006), titled "On Becoming a Christian: Insights from Scripture and the Patristic Writings with Some Contemporary Reflections." All may be found at the Centro Pro Unione website: http://www.pro.urbe.it/dia-int/pe-rc/e_pe-rc-info.html.

ecclesial unity is on the front burner; nevertheless, as former Catholic co-chair of the Catholic-Pentecostal dialogue, Kilian McDonnell, OSB, often stated, this is the most important dialogue. Without asking for agreement on that assertion I do want to identify several reasons that underscore the importance of this dialogue while also identifying more dialogical antinomies.

First, Catholicism and Pentecostalism represent the oldest and youngest expressions of Christian faith. Along with the Greek East and the Syriac Orient, the Latin West traces its ecclesial claims not just to the church of Jerusalem, but to the see of Rome founded in the first century and to the Petrine ministry that resides there. Although there were proto-Pentecostal movements in the nineteenth century and other contemporary charismatic ones, I will settle for the 1906 Azusa Street revival as the beginnings of the Pentecostal movement. Its fairly recent centenary bespeaks its youthfulness, which still combines a remarkable diversity with a truly global extension, something that rivals Catholicism. In some quarters, especially Latin America, this has led to unfortunate tensions between the two communities. If there is an antinomy here, it is between, on the one hand, historic tradition and the staid sacramental and juridical structures of the Catholic Church and, on the other, charismata as the basis for ecclesial life engendered as they are by the pneumatological and eschatological expectations of Pentecostal congregations and ministries. The former is not without its charismatic and mystical infusions, and the latter does not entirely discard ecclesiastical structure and dominical ordinances. Nevertheless, the antinomy holds, one which I will argue is a fruitful and creative one for both communions.

The second antinomy revolves around similar claims to the fullness of grace that each communion signifies. Pentecostals preach the "full gospel" in a distinctly restorationist perspective. Jesus is Savior, Baptizer in the Spirit, Healer, and Coming King — also Sanctifier in its Wesleyan-Holiness iteration. Catholics also claim to be the recipients of the fullness of divine grace that the risen Lord bestows as evidenced in this excerpt from the *Catechism of the Catholic Church*:

> In her subsists the fullness of Christ's body united with its head; this implies that she receives from him "the fullness of the means of salvation" which he has willed: correct and complete confession of faith, full sacramental life, and ordained ministry in apostolic succession. The Church was, in this fundamental sense, catholic on

the day of Pentecost and will always be so until the day of the Parousia. (*Catechism,* 830)[2]

Neither communion lacks in its sense of divine blessing that God bestows through Christ and the Spirit. Both identify with the apostolic imperative of Paul who reminded the Ephesians that he did not shrink from proclaiming to them the full counsels of God (Acts 20:27). Certainly we need not perceive this as a competition between these two traditions but as an exploratory vein to probe in dialogue.

Finally, the grace of the Pentecostal movement (using Catholic nomenclature) extends beyond classical Pentecostalism. The charismatic renewal in the historic churches, the nondenominational Charismatics (both independents and networks), and the significant influence of charismatic spirituality upon Messianic Judaism testify to the excessive or surplus nature of this grace.[3] As many Pentecostal ecumenists have observed: Pentecost cannot be confined to Pentecostalism. Without denying the primary influence of Classical Pentecostalism, one must evaluate the nature of this grace or experience vis-à-vis its various expressions and locations. Does it constitute ecclesial identity in an analogous manner to how, for example, the four marks of the church are historically essential for the Catholic Church (*Catechism,* 811-12)? Not incidentally, the Catholic Charismatic Renewal demonstrated how this grace was successfully and fruitfully integrated into the existing structures and faith of the *Catholica.* Another antinomy? In other words, do the charismata constitute the church or do they simply enliven and empower already-existing ecclesial structures? In order to answer this we now turn to themes and various phases of the international dialogue.

II. The Early Phases of the Dialogue

The five phases of the international dialogue have evolved from an engagement of a number of topics in the first two phases to focused attention on particular ones in the last three. This is not entirely unusual

---

2. All quotes from the Catechism are from the following edition: *Catechism of the Catholic Church: With Modifications from the Editio Typica* (New York: Doubleday, 1997).

3. Peter Hocken's point in his book *The Challenges of the Pentecostal, Charismatic and Messianic Jewish Movements: The Tensions of the Spirit* (Burlington, VT: Ashgate, 2009).

in ecumenical bilateral dialogues. The first and second phases (1972-76 and 1977-82) were characterized by this approach, with an important shift in Pentecostal representation taking place between the two. The first phase, as the title of its report signals, included "Leaders of Some Pentecostal Churches and Participants in the Charismatic Movement within Protestant and Anglican Churches."[4] The second phase decided that it "should be exclusively a conversation between classical Pentecostals and the Roman Catholic Church" in order "to more clearly focus the conversations" (6). It is not entirely evident whether the broader representation during the first phase significantly altered its final report from what would have been an exclusively classical Pentecostal account and interchange with Catholics. I will simply note several interesting notations among the topics covered during the first phase.[5]

Among the cluster of issues focused around "Baptism in the Holy Spirit" there is recognition that the reception of the Spirit in this event is distinct from that in conversion (12) and leads to "expanded openness and expectancy with regard to the Holy Spirit and his gifts" (16) but is not necessarily a sign of spiritual maturity (17). Nevertheless, the charisms that are the manifestations of the Spirit go "beyond the believer's natural ability" (15), require discernment (16 — but not to the extent of excluding charismatic manifestations), and are to be distinguished from mystical experiences, the latter being "more generally directed toward personal communion with God," while the former, though "including personal communion with God, are directed more to ministerial service" (17).

These are important distinctions, many of which were made in the early stages of the Catholic Charismatic Renewal, which, fortunately, was accompanied by no small amount of theological reflection. It is espe-

4. "Final Report: Dialogue between the Secretariat for Promoting Christian Unity and Leaders of Some Pentecostal Churches and Participants in the Charismatic Movement within Protestant and Anglican Churches, 1972-1976." The final reports from the first four phases have now been collected in the volume *Pentecostalism and Christian Unity: Ecumenical Documents and Critical Assessments,* ed. Wolfgang Vondey (Eugene, OR: Pickwick, 2010), p. 101. All further citations will only reference the paragraph numbers of the documents.

5. Topics covered included Baptism in the Holy Spirit, Giving of the Spirit and Christian Initiation, Baptism, Scripture and Tradition and Development, Charismatic Renewal in the Historic Churches, Public Worship, Public Worship and the Gifts, the Human Aspect, Discernment of Spirits, Prayer and Praise.

cially significant that this inaugural report was careful to ascribe both divine and human aspects to charismatic phenomena while at the same time not reducing them to the scope of scientific investigations. In other words, from a Catholic perspective there is an incipient recognition that grace does not discount nature while at the same time exceeding it. Even at the sacramental level the report notes that on the controverted issue of paedobaptism there is a recognition that "God's grace operates in advance of human awareness" (23). Again, at this early stage within the dialogue, common theological principles became matters of convergence even when the specific doctrinal disagreement remained unresolved.

The second phase revisited some of these issues.[6] Its section on faith and experience articulates a position amenable to Catholic sensibilities, and considering the absence of Protestant Charismatics in this phase, demonstrates a convergence between Catholics and classical Pentecostals.

> In . . . the Holy Spirit's manifestation in persons, he engages the natural faculties. In the exercise of the charisms, human faculties are not set aside but used. The action of the Spirit is not identical with the forces inherent in nature. (15)

Religious experience is also communal and embraces a conscious awareness of both the presence and absence of God (12), thus not excluding the formative influence of the cross in the Christian life (13).

Such irenic efforts also inform convergent statements on other issues, most notably on the subject of healing wherein the differences between the two traditions are sharper. Both affirm Jesus as healer and the exercise of healing ministry within the church. They even affirm that they "exercise reserve in making judgments about miraculous manifestations and healings" (34). Even though Catholics are more passive and Pentecostals more aggressive in regard to healing (35), and Pentecostals expect healing vis-à-vis situations of suffering "unless

6. The second phase covered the following topics: Speaking in Tongues, Faith and Experience, Scripture and Tradition, Exegesis, Biblical Interpretation, Faith and Reason, Healing in the Church, Community-Worship and Communication, Tradition and traditions, Perspectives on Mary (motherhood, veneration, intercession, her graces, virginity, immaculate conception, assumption), Ministry in the Church (including recognition), Apostolic Succession. "Final Report: Dialogue between the Secretariat for Promoting Christian Unity and Some Classical Pentecostals, 1977-1982."

there is a special revelation that God has some other purpose" (36), nevertheless, the divine will is preeminent and suffering for "some Pentecostals" as for Catholics can be a means of grace. The summary statement of convergence is quite remarkable.

> There are a number of areas where there is agreement between Roman Catholics and Pentecostals: the necessity of the cross, healing as a sign of the kingdom, healing of the total person, the involvement of the laity in prayer for healing, the expectation of healing through the Eucharist/Lord's Supper, and Christ as the healer. (40)

Disagreements about the relationship between scripture and tradition continue to exist and become prominent in the discussion about Mary, where Catholic beliefs and practices are rejected by Pentecostals for lack of biblical evidence.

> Classical Pentecostals, while recognizing that doctrinal development that is clearly based on scriptural evidence is not entirely absent from Pentecostal history, admit no doctrinal development with regard to Mary. (61)

Clearly, strong differences remain in reference to scripture and tradition, including Pentecostal caution about historical-critical method (23) even though there might be convergence between Catholic "Spirit-inspired exegesis" (24) and Pentecostal "pneumatic literal interpretation" (25). A similar and unusual convergence from the Pentecostal side is noted in reference to Mary's assumption.

> Pentecostals see a parallel between Mary's "assumption" and the Pentecostal understanding of the "bodily resurrection" or the "rapture of the church" (1 Thess 4:13-18, cf. esp. v. 17), but differ as to when this will take place for Mary. (76)

At the very least this illustrates creative theological engagement of commonalities amid persistent and most likely perduring disagreements.

The third phase of the dialogue (1985-89) was titled "Perspectives on *Koinonia*."[7] The theme of *koinonia* was taken up to continue the impli-

---

7. "Perspectives on *Koinonia:* Report from the Third Quinquennium of the Dialogue between the Pontifical Council for Promoting Christian Unity and Some Classical Pentecostal Churches and Leaders, 1985-1989."

cations of the discussion about Mary and the communion of saints in the previous round and the emergence of communion ecclesiology throughout the ecumenical movement. *Koinonia* was examined under five rubrics: the Word of God; the Holy Spirit and the New Testament Vision of *Koinonia;* Baptism; the Life of the Church; and the Communion of Saints. Again (as in the first phase) Pentecostals and Catholics can agree that interpretation of scripture requires the help of the Holy Spirit, but still disagree over the role that the Christian community plays in such discernment, specifically in regard to the role of a teaching office. However, Pentecostals acknowledge "God has given special gifts of teaching" (26) to the community, necessitating more discussion on the role of gifts and ministry/office from a pneumatological perspective.

Pentecostals and Catholics can unite around the "common experience of the Holy Spirit" (32) in their discussion of the second rubric, each with their particular emphasis. The Catholic communitarian dimension (the community as the temple of the Holy Spirit — 1 Cor. 3:16) and the Pentecostal personal one (the believer as temple of the Holy Spirit — 1 Cor. 6:19) are envisioned as complementary (33, 76), anticipating how this antinomy (often repeated in Catholic/Pentecostal discussions) can be a sign of future productive engagement. However, this does not resolve the issue of how each tradition perceives the visible unity of the church. Despite agreement "that the Holy Spirit is the Spirit of unity in diversity (cf. 1 Cor. 12:13ff.) and not the Spirit of division" (34), a telling statement demonstrates the incompatibility of their respective visions.

> Roman Catholics consider the establishment of denominations which result from the lack of love and/or divergence in matters of faith as departures away from the unity of the one church. . . . Pentecostals tend to view denominations as more or less legitimate manifestations of the one, universal church. (34)

This seems to be an incompatible divide except for a common affirmation that the visible and invisible dimensions of the church should not "be used to justify and reinforce separation between Christians" (35). How this might alleviate Catholic concern that the Pentecostal position is a justification of ecclesial divisions remains to be seen.

The rest of the document is rich in reflection and contains many affirmations by Pentecostals that are amenable to a Catholic perspective. Since Catholics and Pentecostals agree that faith must precede baptism (43), "some Pentecostals would even speak of baptism as a 'means of grace'" provided that the candidate for baptism has experienced conversion (50). In their respective emphases on (Catholic) sacramental and (Pentecostal) charismatic mediations of the Spirit, both agree that the freedom of the Spirit cannot be limited (68).

Finally, in regard to *koinonia* in the Life of the Church, differences are registered at both structural and existential levels, especially with reference to the mediation of grace through the sacraments. Pentecostals, for example, "do not accept the grace-conveying role of sacraments distinct from their function as a visible Word of God" (86), and "Pentecostals propose that presbyteral and/or congregational ecclesial models express better [as contrasted to the Catholic hierarchical model even 'within the context of collegiality' (87)] the mutuality or reciprocity demanded by *koinonia*" (87). Nevertheless, Pentecostals "recognize that the Spirit may work through ecclesial structures and processes" (88) and with Catholics "are troubled by the discrepancy between theology and practice of their own parishes and congregations" (89).

At issue is how the church mediates the grace of God and the further development of Pentecostal ecclesiology. An interesting insight is offered by Pentecostal appropriation of the Catholic notion of the church as "a kind of sacrament" or the more amenable language of the church as "a *sign* and an *instrument* of God's work in the world" (90, 93). Without the connection between authentic personal piety and ecclesial structures the possibilities of appropriation could not register within the Pentecostal imagination.

> In Pentecostal understanding, the church as a community is an instrument of salvation in the same sense in which each one of its members is both a sign and instrument of salvation. In their own way, both the community as a whole and the individual members that comprise it give witness to God's redeeming grace. (94)

III. Constructive Commentary

In order to deal adequately with these underlying ecclesiological issues let me take up this concern as it relates to the unity of the church in my own critical commentary. The unity of the church is a necessary prerequisite to perception of the veracity of the gospel (John 17:21). This is essential for the Catholic Church and is structured into the very nature of the church, not only juridically but sacramentally as well. The former in service of the latter is intended to provide the necessary pastoral governance so that the mystery of Christ's saving action and presence may be communicated in and through the sacramental acts of the church. Nor should this be understood as excluding other means of divine agency through various graces and gifts, most notably those that are charismatic and mystical in nature. One should not play one off against the other as if the Holy Spirit distributes charismatic gifts but not hierarchical gifts, or as if the exercise of a charism is pneumatological but not the priestly power to administrate the sacraments. Both can and should be understood within the joint-mission of Christ and the Holy Spirit through which trinitarian agency is registered in both the *Christus praesens* and the *Spiritus praesens*. Thus, for example, when the priest invokes the presence of the Holy Spirit upon the bread and wine in the eucharist through the prayer of epiclesis and utters the words of consecration from the Last Supper narrative, it effects the presence of Christ on the altar: body, blood, soul, and divinity as traditionally affirmed, e.g., by the Council of Trent. So too, however, the Holy Spirit can and does effect the presence of Christ's action through the counsel of a spiritual director or spiritual friend, a healing, a word of prophecy in a charismatic prayer meeting, a mystical grace, or founding charism of a religious order or lay ecclesial movement. In this manner the Holy Spirit is likened to the soul of the church (*Catechism*, 797).

I rehearse this because they all figure into the unity of the church under its one Lord enlivened by the one Spirit. Take, for example, when Pope John Paul II enunciated the contribution of the Catholic Church to the quest for Christian unity in his 1995 encyclical letter "On Commitment to Ecumenism," *Ut unum sint*.[8]

> The Constitution *Lumen gentium,* in a fundamental affirmation echoed by the Decree *Unitatis redintegratio,* states that the one Church of Christ subsists in the Catholic Church. The Decree on Ecumenism emphasizes the presence in her of the fullness

8. *Encyclical Letter "Ut Unum Sint" of the Holy Father John Paul II on Commitment to Ecumenism* (Boston: Pauline Books and Media, n.d.).

(*plenitudo*) of the means of salvation. Full unity will come about when all share in the fullness of the means of salvation entrusted by Christ to his Church. (*UUS*, 86)

Add to this the Petrine ministry; again, from John Paul II:

> Among all the Churches and Ecclesial Communities, the Catholic Church is conscious that she has preserved the ministry of the Successor of the Apostle Peter, the Bishop of Rome, whom God established as her "perpetual and visible principle and foundation of unity" and whom the Spirit sustains in order that he may enable all the others to share in this essential good. In the beautiful expression of Pope Saint Gregory the Great, my ministry is that of *servus servorum Dei*. This designation is the best possible safeguard against the risk of separating power (and in particular the primacy) from ministry. Such a separation would contradict the very meaning of power according to the Gospel: "I am among you as one who serves" (Lk 22:27), says our Lord Jesus Christ, the Head of the Church. (*UUS*, 88)

Note here that the Spirit sustains this ministry and the possibility that its power, i.e., the power of hierarchical jurisdiction, itself given by the Holy Spirit, may be separated from the service of this ministry in imitation of Christ. The realism of hierarchical and sacramental communion along with its pastoral exercise and implementation is in consideration. But as with all things in the church the maturation of ecclesial life including function and structure is in process as the "functioning of each part" contributes to growth into our head, Christ (Eph. 4:15-16).

I have laid out a portion of what Catholics consider to be essential for unity, "a unity constituted by the bonds of the profession of faith, the sacraments and hierarchical communion" (*UUS*, 9). In the framework of Catholic-Pentecostal dialogue what might the conjunction of hierarchical and charismatic gifts portend for both sides? Is it possible for the global Pentecostal movement to ever come to terms with this rather singular understanding of its ecclesial contribution to the quest for Christian unity? Let me suggest several possibilities, first from Pentecostals to Catholics.

As a diverse and variegated movement in which the multiplication of charismata is its signature, Pentecostals challenge the restriction or limitation of their exercise by ecclesiastical authorities. Nor should the arena of the outpouring of the Holy Spirit be confined within the walls of a particular ecclesial communion. Ironically, this has also proven to be true vis-à-vis charismatic outpourings beyond the walls of classical Pentecostalism. This has given rise to a Pentecostal/ Charismatic ecumenism, what in Catholic terminology we call *spiritual ecumenism*. In fact, I would argue that Catholics and Pentecostals agree that without communion in the Holy Spirit, a communion sustained by prayer, the possibilities for unity are considerably diminished. Our real but imperfect communion is constituted by a common baptism/ conversion in which the continual call to conversion is necessary for such progress. John Paul II stated it in these terms:

> Only the act of placing ourselves before God can offer a solid basis for that conversion of individual Christians and for that constant reform of the Church, insofar as she is also a human and earthly institution, which represent the preconditions for all ecumenical commitment. One of the first steps in ecumenical dialogue is the effort to draw the Christian Communities into this completely interior spiritual space in which Christ, by the power of the Spirit, leads them all, without exception, to examine themselves before the Father and to ask themselves whether they have been faithful to his plan for the Church. (*UUS*, 82)

Individual conversion and ecclesiastical reform are both in order. For Catholics this will entail supplication for and fidelity to the work of the Holy Spirit. Parish renewal and apostolic movements are as important as pastoral initiatives and discernment. The Pentecostal reception of this challenge is also significant. Let me pose it in the following terms.

The Pentecostal movement has to discover its ecclesial vocation. Granted all the historical circumstances of its genesis, its tendency to emphasize its movement origins, combined with the proliferation of denominational structures while independent congregations and loosely affiliated networks continue to flourish (including their stepchildren among nondenominational Charismatics), the ecclesial nature of the movement has yet to be determined. Two aspects of a distinctive Pentecostal ecclesiality need to be considered. First, is a charismatic ecclesiology sufficient to render the fullness *(plenitudo)* of the church, part of the mark of catholicity? Pentecostals and Catholics both claim fullness as we have already seen — *full gospel* proclaimed by Pentecostals, and Catholics locating such fullness in ecclesial structures. Can Pentecostals also embrace the sacramental and structural dimensions of the church and affirm their pneumatological inspiration? My concern is that without a move in this direction Pentecostals will remain satisfied with spiritual unity among believers without a corresponding visible instantiation of that unity.

The second dimension of Pentecostal ecclesiology is related. Since the advent of the charismatic renewal in the historic churches and the growth of nondenominational Charismatics, how do Pentecostals negotiate the charismatic distinctive as the basis for Pentecostal identity and ecclesiology? May I suggest that the significatory dimension of the charismata alerts the church catholic to charismata in their own communions and (perhaps a challenge for some Pentecostals) to a broader array of spiritual gifts than is sometimes the case? In other words, ordinary and extraordinary manifestations of the Spirit amplify the plenitude or fullness of grace and gifts that Christ bestows on the church.

The apostolicity of the church embraces fidelity to and the continuity of the apostolic faith. The communions differ significantly on this mark of the church although both adhere to its fundamental and foundational importance for ecclesial life. Both are concerned with what Catholics call the "deposit of faith" received from the apostles, with Catholics locating the guarantor of this tradition in the successors to the apostles in the College of Bishops. Pentecostals lay claim to the restoration of the full measure of apostolic faith and power as witnessed in Holy Scripture. Is it possible for a convergence between these competing views?

This partly has to do with the recognition of hierarchical ministries that I have already mentioned and that continue to reemerge in Pentecostal/Charismatic circles, especially in reference to the fivefold ministry of Ephesians 4:11: "And his gifts were that some should be apostles, some prophets, some evangelists, some pastors and teachers." But here I prefer to begin with the apostolate itself, a concept more amenable to Pentecostal sensibilities. This Catholic term is reflective of the missional dimension of the church, essential as it is for the church's identity. From the *Catechism of the Catholic Church:*

> The whole Church is apostolic, in that she remains, through the successors of St. Peter and the other apostles, in communion of

faith and life with her origin: and in that she is "sent out" into the whole world. All members of the Church share in this mission, though in various ways. "The Christian vocation is, of its nature, a vocation to the apostolate as well." Indeed, we call an apostolate "every activity of the Mystical Body" that aims "to spread the Kingdom of Christ over all the earth." (*Catechism,* 863)

And under the mark of catholicity:

> *The missionary mandate.* "Having been divinely sent to the nations that she might be 'the universal sacrament of salvation,' the Church, in obedience to the command of her founder and because it is demanded by her own essential universality, strives to preach the Gospel to all men": "Go therefore and make disciples of all nations, baptizing them in the name of the Father and of the Son and of the Holy Spirit, teaching them to observe all that I have commanded you; and Lo, I am with you always, until the close of the age." (*Catechism,* 849)

> *The origin and purpose of mission.* The Lord's missionary mandate is ultimately grounded in the eternal love of the Most Holy Trinity: "The Church on earth is by her nature missionary since, according to the plan of the Father, she has as her origin the mission of the Son and the Holy Spirit." The ultimate purpose of mission is none other than to make men share in the communion between the Father and the Son in their Spirit of love. (*Catechism,* 850)

Let me take up apostolate and mission under the rubric of evangelization. One cannot find a sector of contemporary global Christianity that is more eager for evangelism than Pentecostals. This has caused some tensions with Catholics, especially in Latin America, who have felt that Pentecostals often proselytize their own flocks. This was dealt with in the fourth phase of the international Catholic-Pentecostal dialogue (1990-97) under the title "Evangelization, Proselytism and Common Witness." The report received a warm welcome in ecumenical circles and was groundbreaking in many ways. I will leave it there except to make one comment. It has always seemed to me that vigorous Pentecostal evangelism should be met with vigorous Catholic evangelization, not among Pentecostals but within its own flock. To evangelize (and catechize) the sacramentalized is how I would put it. The legitimacy of Pentecostal evangelism does not exclude that, at times, they wrongfully misrepresent the Catholic tradition. The report certainly addresses this. And there is a legitimate distinction between proselytism and evangelization. However, I prefer more effective Catholic evangelization, more dialogue, and an accounting of our respective theologies of grace that inform perception and discernment of the other. I'll come to that momentarily. First, I turn to other aspects of the report of the fourth phase of dialogue, "Evangelization, Proselytism and Common Witness, 1990-1997."

IV. Fourth Phase with Constructive Commentary

As mentioned, this document has become a model for ecumenical reflection on the distinction between evangelization and proselytism. I will focus only on the relationship between evangelization and culture and evangelization and social justice. The following excerpt best represents their respective visions of the former.

> Pentecostals emphasize the changing of individuals who, when formed into a body of believers, bring change into the culture from within. Catholics emphasize that culture itself in its human institutions and enterprises can also be transformed by the gospel. (28)

Similar sentiments inform their reflections on evangelization and social justice, however, with the hope of learning from one another.

> We have come to realize that Pentecostals and Catholics have much to bring to one another with regard to social justice. While Catholics believe in the importance of personal faith, they also put great emphasis on the power of the gospel to change social structures. Pentecostals, on the other hand, have traditionally pursued social change at the individual and communal levels. Catholics wonder whether the Pentecostal theology of evangelization leaves them ill-equipped for engaging in social justice. Pentecostals believe that Catholics should take more seriously the importance of personal and communal transformation for promoting societal change. (61)

This dimension of the missional apostolate of the church is connected to spreading the kingdom of Christ over all the earth. This work of the church is not confined to explicit evangelization in the proclamation of the gospel, so that hearing the good news, a person comes to faith in Christ. It also includes a Christian and ecclesial praxis in which signs of the Kingdom are present through engagement with social and cultural issues and in the advocacy for social justice and the common good in the public square and the body politic. *Gaudium et spes* articulated the relationship between the kingdom of Christ and such activity. I quote substantially for the sake of our common memory.

> We do not know the time for the consummation of the earth and of humanity, nor do we know how all things will be transformed. As deformed by sin, the shape of this world will pass away; but we are taught that God is preparing a new dwelling place and a new earth where justice will abide, and whose blessedness will answer and surpass all the longings for peace which spring up in the human heart.
>
> Then, with death overcome, the sons of God will be raised up in Christ, and what was sown in weakness and corruption will be invested with incorruptibility. Enduring with charity and its fruits, all that creation which God made on man's account will be unchained from the bondage of vanity.
>
> Therefore, while we are warned that it profits a man nothing if he gain the whole world and lose himself, the expectation of a new earth must not weaken but rather stimulate our concern for cultivating this one. For here grows the body of a new human family, a body which even now is able to give some kind of foreshadowing of the new age.
>
> Hence, while earthly progress must be carefully distinguished from the growth of Christ's kingdom, to the extent that the former can contribute to the better ordering of human society, it is of vital concern to the Kingdom of God. For after we have obeyed the Lord, and in His Spirit nurtured on earth the values of human dignity, brotherhood and freedom, and indeed all the good fruits of our nature and enterprise, we will find them again, but freed of stain, burnished and transfigured, when Christ hands over to the Father: "a kingdom eternal and universal, a kingdom of truth and life, of holiness and grace, of justice, love and peace." On this earth that Kingdom is already present in mystery. When the Lord returns it will be brought into full flower. *(GS, 39)*[9]

9. Taken from the website of the Holy See: http://www.vatican.va/archive/

The key issue is the relationship between the kingdom of God and the better ordering of human society. Here there can be profitable conversation between our traditions to the benefit of the church catholic. And much is at stake.

Let me suggest some pointers in this conversation. The issue is pneumatological, how the Spirit is active in the church and in the world.[10] Surely, every Christian tradition can develop its own pneumatology. Even Pentecostals would agree that pneumatology is not their own preserve. In this case the question is how Catholic and Pentecostal pneumatologies interact dialogically vis-à-vis their respective understandings of grace. Pentecostal pneumatology, I would argue, commences as a charismology within the framework of the baptism of the Holy Spirit. Catholic pneumatology must account for sacramental, charismatic, mystical, and juridical mediations of pneumatic agency. Both lay claims to exist within the outpouring of the Holy Spirit at Pentecost. Theologians in both traditions have also attempted to identify the Spirit's working beyond the ecclesia. The Spirit acts in creation, the Spirit is present in culture and in other religions, and the Spirit promotes liberation.

My concern is: How are these various agencies of the Spirit the same or different? Is the Spirit's work in creation, culture, and politics the same as it is in the church and in Christian life? Charismata need not be confined to the church, but in the church they edify the body of believers. How do they function in the world, if they do? Are the workings of grace the same? If grace is operative among non-Christians, is it common grace or prevenient grace (*à la* Calvinist and Wesleyan traditions respectively), or on the same order as justifying or sanctifying grace? Or, should we make a strong distinction between nature and grace as Catholic scholastic theology has been wont to do?

One way to exploit these distinctions, which are worthy distinctions — the *ordo salutis* still has merit even as there is more emphasis these days on the *via salutis* — is to hold pneumatology and the theology of grace together in a corresponding relationship, not an identical

---

hist_councils/ii_vatican_council/documents/vat-ii_const_19651207_gaudium-et-spes _en.html.

10. This issue continually emerged in the International Dialogue Final Report between the World Alliance of Reformed Churches and Some Pentecostal Churches and Leaders (1996-2000), titled *Word and Spirit, Church and World* (especially nos. 19-21, 68-73, 88-95).

one. The Holy Spirit is the agent of grace but not grace itself. The same is true of the charismata or spiritual gifts. The Holy Spirit is the giver of gifts, not the gifts themselves although, indeed, they are pneumatic in character. Therefore, whatever graces or gifts are present outside of the church must correspond to the Spirit's work in the church, or more broadly speaking to the Spirit's agency in creation and redemption. The latter is the *telos* of the former. The problem is determining the relationship between the two. We can approach this from the perspective of the agency of the Spirit from above and from the reception of the Spirit from below.

I suggest that the manner in which we can speak of the agency of the Spirit in the world as compared to the church is by analogy. Parenthetically, I am moving back to a more ecclesiocentric approach to grace rather than the regnocentric approach of many. Take, for example, the gifts of the Holy Spirit. Our reception of spiritual gifts is the consequence of having received the gift of the Holy Spirit. The gift of the Holy Spirit is the fruit of the fullness of the Spirit. Catholics and Pentecostals share the affirmation of the reception of this gift in Confirmation and Baptism in the Holy Spirit respectively. Such is the down payment of what is to come, namely, the church present to the Lord at his parousia without spot or wrinkle (Eph. 5:27). Christ possesses a spousal relationship to the church, not to the world, and it is the church glorified that descends as the New Jerusalem on the foundation of the twelve apostles and the access of which proceeds through the gates of elect Israel (Rev. 21:9-14). This is the heart of the new heavens and new earth.

The analogy, therefore, is that whatever good happens in the world is related to the efficacy of the Spirit's grace within the church, where the gifts of the Spirit are received by faith (Gal. 3:2). Whatever developments take place in the world toward the common good and the fraternal ordering of society are analogous to the filial relation of the baptized/converted to the Father in Christ in the communion of the one, holy, catholic, and apostolic church. Pentecostals and Catholics need to stress that the bestowal of gifts and charismata are ordered to sanctification and Christian perfection, that is, the increase of grace in love. Likewise, the effects of the Spirit's work in the world are directed to the fraternal and gifted communion that constitutes the life of the church as the Body of Christ and the Temple of the Holy Spirit.

Much of this is evident in the developments that have marked the papal magisterium of Benedict XVI. From his first encyclical letter *Deus Caritas Est* (2005, henceforth *DCE*)[11] to the most recent one, *Caritas in Veritate* (2009, henceforth *CV*),[12] the Pope has chartered a course on the relationship between justice and love. "The just ordering of society and the state is a central responsibility of politics" (*DCE*, 28), and the primary and direct agent of this is the state, not the church. The church forms consciences and purifies reason and manifests love. Charitable works are the *opus proprium* of the church. The lay faithful are animated by this charity and even their political activity in the secular realm (their proper vocation) is lived out as social charity (*DCE*, 29). This does not deny that the "[c]hurch's social teaching argues on the basis of reason and natural law, namely, on the basis of what is in accord with the nature of every human being" (*DCE*, 28), the traditional Catholic approach to such issues.

In *Caritas in Veritate* Benedict takes a further step while preserving the analogous way of proceeding. He suggests (and it's quite remarkable in my view) that we promote an *"economy of gratuitousness and fraternity"* (*CV*, 38). This applies to the *"market,* the *State* and *civil society,"* all "redolent of the *spirit of gift"* (*CV*, 37). Is this just natural law and human reason? Benedict hedges only by way of analogy.

> The theme of development can be identified with the inclusion-in-relation of all individuals and peoples within the one community of the human family, built in solidarity on the basis of the fundamental values of justice and peace. This perspective is illuminated in a striking way by the relationship between the Persons of the Trinity within the one divine Substance. The Trinity is absolute unity insofar as the three divine Persons are pure relationality. The reciprocal transparency among the divine Persons is total and the bond between each of them complete, since they constitute a unique and absolute unity. God desires to incorporate us into this reality of communion as well: "that they may be one even as we are one" (John 17:22). The church is a sign and instrument of this unity. Relationships between human beings throughout history cannot but be enriched by reference to this divine model. In particular, *in*

11. *Encyclical Letter of the Supreme Pontiff Benedict XVI "God Is Love Deus Caritas Est"* (Boston: Pauline Books & Media, 2006).

12. *Encyclical Letter of the Supreme Pontiff Benedict XVI "Charity in Truth Caritas in Veritate"* (Boston: Pauline Books & Media, 2009).

the light of the revealed mystery of the Trinity, we understand that true openness does not mean loss of individual identity but profound interpenetration. This also emerges from the common human experiences of love and truth. Just as the sacramental love of spouses unites them spiritually in "one flesh" (Gen. 2:24; Matt. 19:5; Eph. 5:31) and makes out of the two a real and relational unity, so in an analogous way truth unites spirits and causes them to think in unison, attracting them as a unity to itself. The Christian revelation of the unity of the human race presupposes a *metaphysical interpretation of the "humanum" in which relationality is an essential element.* (*CV*, 54-55)

Why introduce this into Catholic-Pentecostal dialogue? Catholics and Pentecostals have antennas for the supernatural. In the effort to engage the world the temptation exists that the supernatural signatures of each tradition, sacramental and charismatic, might fade in the attempt to locate the *Spiritus praesens* in the secular and temporal realms. I am not saying that the Spirit is not present there. However, I am suggesting that such presence is directed toward what Catholics identify as the sanative and elevating work of the Spirit in grace. Promoting human relationality in all sectors of life is necessary, while analogous to the actual sharing in the triune life of God that is our sanctification and deification and the corporate maturation of the Body of Christ. Whatever prefigurations of the Kingdom are evident in the world are reflections of the consummation to come that is present in the church. Indeed we are called to sanctify the world and protect creation, but only as we are grounded in that new creation given efficaciously in baptism/conversion and nourished by the eucharist, the *Spiritus praesens* effecting the *Christus praesens,* head and members, the *Christus totus.* For "the God of our Lord Jesus Christ, the Father of glory . . . has put all things under his feet and has made him the head over all things for the church, which is his body, the fulness of him who fills all in all" (Eph. 1:17, 22-23).

V. Fifth Phase

I conclude with some very brief comments on the fifth phase of the dialogue (1998-2006), titled "On Becoming a Christian: Insights from

Scripture and the Patristic Writings with Some Contemporary Reflections."[13] This phase in many ways represents the maturation in the dialogue of some of the themes under discussion since the commencement of this bilateral relationship. One of the more important is the engagement of tradition, in this case, the Church Fathers, which certainly does not undermine that "the Bible is the highest authority" for the faith (13). Nevertheless, Pentecostals depart from a strict biblicism to the extent that they recognize that "the writings of these early Fathers . . . convey a close association between theology and pastoral concerns, and thus, they are aimed at doxology and devotion to God" (13). Therefore, the report examines both scriptural and patristic sources for the themes under discussion.

The first section of the document took up in detail the topic of conversion and Christian initiation, something already broached in the early phases of the dialogue. It continues to preserve a model of convergence that embraces diversity within unity.

> Catholics and Pentecostals generally agree that conversion involves both event and process, and recognize the need for ongoing formation. Both hold to a diversity of ways in which one is converted. Conversions may express varying characteristics, some more affectively oriented than others, some more cognitive, dramatic or volitional. (57)

Nevertheless, while both traditions "recognize conversion as the gift of God . . . they may not always agree about what constitutes a valid experience of conversion" (59).

Faith and Christian Initiation is the subject of Section II. Both sides agree on a definition of faith.

> Faith is a gifted response to God's revelation, involving an opening of the heart, an assent of the mind and actions which express our trust. (60)

---

13. "On Becoming a Christian: Insights from Scripture and the Patristic Writings with Some Contemporary Reflections. Report of the Fifth Phase of the International Dialogue between Some Classical Pentecostal Churches and Leaders and the Catholic Church (1998-2006)." All quotes and references are to the final draft of the document posted on the Centro Pro Unione website: http://www.pro.urbe.it/dia-int/pe-rc/doc/e_pe-rc_5-contents.html.

They also continue to maintain their divergent readings of New Testament texts as to whether they describe sacramental or nonsacramental modalities of grace (89). These may yet prove to be incompatible although they mutually share the evangelistic concerns at the heart of the gospel.

> Reflecting upon biblical and patristic perspectives about the relation of faith to becoming a Christian could allow Pentecostals and Catholics to affirm together that the church is a communion in faith whose nature is essentially missionary, impelling it to foster the profession of faith by each of its members and to invite into this communion of faith others who do not yet know the joy of believing in Jesus Christ. (96)

There is much convergence in Section III on Christian Formation and Discipleship, the reality of which is "enhanced in the growing experience of conversion and regeneration, and continues as new believers are called to live a mature Christian life in the community of faith, as empowered by the Holy Spirit" (98). Acts 2:42 ("They devoted themselves to the apostles' teaching and fellowship, to the breaking of bread and the prayers.") is the shared text for common affirmations, with both communions appreciating aspects of the other that they are presently assimilating.

> The Pentecostal imagination is formed by the manifestation of spiritual gifts amid the jubilant praise of those upon whom the Spirit has fallen. Yet many Catholics also have come to know the charismatic presence of the Spirit and Pentecostals are formed by their devout celebration of the Lord's Supper. (136)

Experience in Christian life — Section IV — deepens the reflections on faith and experience begun during the second phase of the dialogue. Both communions offer a rich account of the experiential tonality of each of their traditions and provide ample evidence that the following observation is true.

> We quickly discovered that some standard stereotypes of each of our traditions are too simplistic for any members of our communities to hold. For example, the superficial observation that Pentecostals largely live in their hearts and emotions while Catholic life

is solely determined by theological abstractions and outward rituals belies the profound way in which religious experience is important for us, both in regard to the common Christian faith that we
share and the differences that do distinguish us. (184)

After much inquiry and sharing between the two teams they confess in near poetic fashion that they have arrived in a very different
place.

> In the course of our dialogue we have come to realize that we have
> much more in common in our experience of the spiritual life than
> we expected. Mutual sharing and prayer have brought us to a deep
> appreciation of our common Christian experience. This includes
> both the affective and aesthetic dimensions of becoming a Chris-
> tian as vital, personal and transformative. Catholics and Pentecos-
> tals recognize that the thirst for salvation is at the same time a
> work of the Spirit and a human response. This level of experience
> continues after conversion in areas as diverse as family life, work,
> civic life and the promotion of justice and peace in society. (190)

The final section (V) examines the Pentecostal distinctive of Baptism in the Holy Spirit (initially raised during the first phase). The
main consideration for Catholics was how to interpret this Pentecostal
experience, especially in light of its reception by Catholics in the Charismatic Renewal. Is it the release of a sacramental grace, e.g., baptism
and confirmation, or an extra-sacramental grace bestowed on the
church analogous to charisms in new ecclesial movements? This question is left unresolved in the text,[14] but it is clear that this same grace is
present nonsacramentally at the origins and in the continuing growth
of the Pentecostal movement.

---

14. The text concludes: "Both interpretations attempt to be faithful to Catholic
tradition and both complement the charismatic experience with the church's theological and spiritual traditions. They both emphasize that the charismatic dimension is integral to the building up of the church and to the fullness of Christian life. Charisms,
free gifts of the Holy Spirit, whatever their character — sometimes it is extraordinary,
such as the gift of miracles or of tongues — . . . are oriented toward sanctifying grace,
and are intended for the common good of the Church. They are at the service of charity
which builds up the Church" (*Catechism*, 2003), 235.

VI. Conclusion

A fitting appraisal for this dialogue and, I think, for this account of it, is proffered in the conclusion of this Final Report. It portends the way forward that is consistent with the insights of Pope John Paul II in *Ut unum sint*. In order to advance the goal of ecumenism — namely, "making the partial communion existing between Christians grow toward full communion in truth and charity" (*UUS*, 14) — the pontiff, as we have already seen in part, stressed not only doctrinal dialogue (*UUS*, 18) but interior conversion (*UUS*, 15) and the primacy of prayer (*UUS*, 21). The Catholic-Pentecostal dialogue, to its credit, has internalized this exhortation.

> Since both of our traditions value the experience of grace as an important dimension of faith and spirituality we have come to appreciate the respective charismatic and mystical / liturgical emphasis of the Pentecostal and Catholic communities. We have also learned that one cannot simply divide these modalities of Christian experience between the two. Each has some experience of what has traditionally been prized by the other. This affords us another way forward in our dialogue, as "spiritual ecumenism" becomes more and more the basis for theological conversations. Most of all spiritual discernment alerts us to the providential possibilities that God offers in his freedom and grace towards us. (278)

May the Holy Spirit guide us. Our next topic in the sixth phase portends this, as we will discuss the topic of "Charisms in the Church: Their Spiritual Significance, Discernment and Pastoral Implications."

13 Evangelical-Catholic International Dialogue: Opening New Frontiers

Jeffrey Gros, FSC

One of the unexpected developments in Catholic ecumenism following the Second Vatican Council was the inception of a variety of dialogues with Holiness, Evangelical, and Pentecostal Christians. At the Council there were no formal representatives of Evangelical churches, though there were unofficial Pentecostal and Baptist guests who facilitated their communities' dialogue with the Catholic Church a few years later.

In this paper we will look at two texts, *The Evangelical–Roman Catholic Dialogue on Mission 1977-1984* (hereafter ERCDOM) and *Church, Evangelization, and the Bonds of Koinonia: A Report of the International Consultation between the Catholic Church and the World Evangelical Alliance 1993-2002* (hereafter WEA). These have very different histories and provenance, but both make important contributions to the theological ecumenical literature; they are historic in their own ways and rich resources for Catholic and Evangelical formation and local dialogue.

Before focusing on the two texts, a few background observations are necessary. First, Catholic-Evangelical relations were very delicate in the beginning and continue to be so, more from the Evangelical side than the Catholic side, because of historic tensions where there have been experiences of alienation or persecution. There are also hesitations in some Catholic communities where differentiation is difficult between anti-Catholic proselytizers, non-Christian groups, and the more open historic churches and some ecumenical Pentecostal and Evangelical groups.

Second, the majority of Christians from the Evangelical global subculture within Christianity are in Pentecostal, Baptist, and historic

Protestant communities with which the Catholic Church has other dialogues than those documented in these two texts.[1] Therefore, Pentecostals and ecumenically oriented Baptists are more likely to give attention to these specific dialogues, and use them for formation and theological renewal in their own traditions.[2] The Protestant and Anglican churches, whose evangelical members may be in these dialogues, are more likely to look to the specific dialogues with their churches than to these evangelical texts.

Likewise, evangelicals from the ecumenical churches who are in these dialogues, like Anglican John Stott and United Methodist Thomas Oden, may have other theological priorities than their own churches bring to their Catholic relations, and other experiences of Catholicism than their evangelical colleagues. For example, when Dr. Oden articulated that there should be no problem with Marian piety, and cited some of Charles Wesley's hymns, Latin American members of the evangelical dialogue voiced a very different point of view. Sometimes personalities in the evangelical movement bear a tenuous relationship with their own specific church tradition. For example, prominent Southern Baptists, like Billy Graham, Timothy George, Chuck Colson, or the late Carl F. H. Henry and R. G. Lee, have major evangeli-

---

1. Definitions of "evangelical" in the sense used in these two reports are notoriously imprecise, as noted in the ERCDOM text: "Yet all Evangelicals share a cluster of theological convictions which were recovered and reaffirmed by the 16th century Reformers. These include (in addition to the great affirmations of the Nicene Creed) the inspiration and authority of the Bible, the sufficiency of its teaching for salvation, and its supremacy over the traditions of the Church; the justification of sinners (i.e. their acceptance by God as righteous in his sight) on the sole ground of the sin bearing often called 'substitutionary' — death of Jesus Christ, by God's free grace alone, apprehended by faith alone, without the addition of any human works; the inward work of the Holy Spirit to bring about the new birth and to transform the regenerate into the likeness of Christ; the necessity of personal repentance and faith in Christ ('conversion'); the Church as the Body of Christ, which incorporates all true believers, and all of whose members are called to ministry, some being 'evangelists, pastors and teachers'; the 'priesthood of all believers,' who (without any priestly mediation except Christ's) all enjoy equal access to God and all offer him their sacrifice of praise and worship; the urgency of the great commission to spread the gospel throughout the world, both verbally in proclamation and visually in good works of love; and the expectation of the personal, visible and glorious return of Jesus Christ to save, to reign and to judge" (ERCDOM, Introduction, 1).

2. See, for example, Wolfgang Vondey, *Pentecostalism and Christian Unity: Ecumenical Documents and Critical Assessments* (Eugene, OR: Pickwick, 2010).

cal influence but their Convention belongs to neither the National Association of Evangelicals nor the Baptist World Alliance. Richard Mouw, president of Fuller Theological Seminary (the flagship evangelical seminary) and successor to David Hubbard, who was a participant in ERCDOM, is Reformed co-chair of the U.S. Reformed-Catholic dialogue and has a remarkable ecumenical history.

Thirdly, some evangelicals belong to churches with a clear ecclesiology and a commitment to the goal of the ecumenical movement as full communion in faith, sacramental life, and witness, including bonds of communion. Nevertheless, for the evangelical movement as a whole, identity is formed by mission and particular emphases within the Christian faith, and not ecclesiology. It is even more remarkable, as one long-time participant notes about the second of these two texts, that it "goes beyond [ERCDOM] as participants of the dialogue began to speak at some depth about the nature of the Church. In light of our respective histories it is almost more than one might have hoped for."[3]

Therefore, the *goal* of these two texts is "an exchange of theological views in order to increase mutual understanding and to discover what theological ground they hold in common" (ERCDOM, Introduction, 3), laying the groundwork for witness together. They are pioneering: ERCDOM because of (1) its foundation in two important texts *The Lausanne Covenant* [= LC], 1974, and Pope Paul VI's post-synodal exhortation *Evangelii nuntiandi* [= EN], 1975, (2) the methodology of the dialogue, and (3) the quality of its text; and WEA because of (1) earlier tensions, (2) the formal sponsorship of the conversation that produced the report, and (3) its convergence on the theology of the church.

The Two Texts

Early contacts between Evangelicals and Catholics, in the late 1960s, first occurred through the Bible societies in translation work together.[4]

---

3. Basil Meeking, "Comment on the Report: *Church, Evangelization, and the Bonds of Koinonia,*" in *IS* 113 (2003/II-III): 103.

4. John A. Radano, "International Dialogue between Catholics and Evangelicals since the Second Vatican Council," in Michael W. Goheen and Margaret O'Gara, eds., *That the World May Believe: Essays on Mission and Unity in Honor of George Vandervelde* (Lanham, MD: University Press of America, 2006), pp. 173-75.

Difficulties in these early encounters enabled the Secretariat (since the 1988 Pontifical Council) for Promoting Christian Unity at the Holy See to develop sensibilities and an understanding of what common ground needed to be created.

As the Catholic Church moved into the 1970s and beyond, it became possible to initiate conversations with these Christians, to begin the healing of memories, and to recognize the importance of speaking about religious freedom and proselytism, as a foundation for common witness. In addition to texts from these dialogues, interchanges of representatives at evangelical assemblies and at events sponsored by the Holy See have been stepping stones in enhancing this relationship. The Global Christian Forum has become another context for Catholic-Evangelical contacts.[5]

ERCDOM

The Secretariat for Promoting Christian Unity sponsored a conversation with an informal group of conservative evangelical Christians that produced *Evangelical–Roman Catholic Dialogue on Mission*.[6] The text has an unofficial and ad hoc character, and is the result of three sessions begun at Venice in 1977. It is offered as a record of a conversation and not an agreed statement.

Since this body of Christians has an important international presence, especially in mission and evangelism, these talks were a significant *early part of a long process*. It is in these groups, for example, that much of the historic anti-Catholicism has still to be overcome.[7] Likewise, it is here that the more aggressive evangelism, sometimes proselytism, is likely to take place relative to Catholics. So, even without formal representation, the process was significant, as the introduction notes:

5. See http://www.globalchristianforum.org/.

6. See http://www.prounione.urbe.it/dia-int/e-rc/doc/i_e-rc_ev-cath.html. See also Basil Meeking, "Introductory Note," in William G. Rusch and Jeffrey Gros, eds., *Deepening Communion: International Ecumenical Documents with Roman Catholic Participation* (Washington, DC: US Catholic Conference, 1998), pp. 425-26.

7. See William M. Shea, *The Lion and the Lamb: Evangelicals and Catholics in America* (New York: Oxford University Press, 2004). Stephen Bevans, "What Catholics Learn from Evangelical Mission Theology," *Missiology* 23, no. 2 (April 1995): 155-64.

> . . . the evangelical movement has a broad spectrum, which includes evangelical denominations (both within and outside the World Council of Churches), evangelical fellowships (within mainline, comprehensive denominations), and evangelical parachurch agencies (specializing in tasks like Bible translation, evangelism, cross-cultural mission, and Third World relief and development), which accept different degrees of responsibility to the Church. (ERCDOM, Introduction, 1)

Participants on both sides were drawn from missiologists and theologians who could give an account of their own tradition, evangelical and Catholic, with accuracy to the heritage, but without polemic.

The text recognizes early on the agreement cited in the Lausanne Covenant and the Catholic Exhortation *Evangelii nuntiandi,* noting:

> . . . a measure of convergence in our understanding of the nature of evangelism, as the following quotations show: "To evangelize is to spread the good news that Jesus Christ died for our sins and was raised from the dead according to the Scriptures. . . . Evangelism itself is the proclamation of the historical biblical Christ as Savior and Lord . . ." (LC, no. 4). Again, witness must be "made explicit by a clear and unequivocal proclamation of the Lord Jesus. . . . There is no true evangelization if the name, the teaching, the life, the promises, the Kingdom and the mystery of Jesus of Nazareth, the Son of God, are not proclaimed" (EN, no. 22). (ERCDOM, Introduction, 2)

The text that was produced has no standing with any of the participants or with the Catholic Church, and its diffusion is purely individual, though it has become an important resource, particularly in dealing with areas of tension. However, it pioneered an important theological *innovation in bilateral conversations* sponsored by the Holy See. It takes as its starting point the *theme of mission,* and how the different theological emphases *serve mission,* rather than concentrating on the historic differences over scripture, tradition, initiation, and salvation. These themes are treated in how they serve the mission of the church, and how differences over them impede common witness to the gospel. This provided an incentive for evangelicals for whom institutional unity, theological agreement, and even the word "ecumenism" are often alienating. Therefore, as Archbishop Kevin McNamara notes, it shows "evidence of a new confidence on the part of Christians in discovering more clearly and affirming more knowledgeably where they differ and what remains to be accomplished before fully common witness to the Lord Jesus can be achieved."[8]

Much of the text lays out in irenic fashion differences that are still divisive, differences that are emphases within a common approach to the gospel truth, and distortions of one another that can be clarified and put aside as a result of this dialogue. It suggests that the overcoming of such differences can make common witness possible. The text covers the themes of revelation and authority, salvation and justification, the nature of mission including its social and interreligious aspects, response in the Holy Spirit, the church and the gospel, gospel and culture — all in the service of common witness.

I. The discussion of *authority* and scripture leads off the document because of its centrality in gospel witness and its importance in the faith of both evangelicals and Catholics on which mission is based. Dialogue participants agree that they "will not come to closer understanding or agreement on *any* topic if they cannot do so on *this* topic":

> We agree on the objectivity of the truth which God has revealed. Yet it has to be subjectively received, indeed "apprehended," if through it God is to do his reforming work. How then should our response to revelation be described? (ERCDOM, 1, 1; 1, 4 b)

The text caries an extended treatment of biblical interpretation, tradition, and the role of the church, as well as of the individual and community, and the idea of reform, all areas where there have been misinterpretations of one another in the past. Continuing differences are formulated clearly where they are not resolved.

It demonstrates a sense of penitential reverence in response to the urgency of God's call to common witness in a variety of cultural contexts:

> We all acknowledge the difficulties we experience in receiving God's Word. For as it comes to us, it finds each of us in our own social context and culture. True, it creates a new community, but this community also has its cultural characteristics derived both from the wider society in which it lives and from its own history which

8. Kevin McNamara, "A Review/Appreciation of the Document: *Evangelical–Roman Catholic Dialogue on Mission,*" *IS* 60 (1986, I-II): 98.

has shaped its understanding of God's revelation. So we have to be on the alert, lest our response to the Word of God is distorted by our cultural conditioning. (ERCDOM, 1, 4 b)

II. In outlining the nature of mission, differences on the theological relationship between the evangelizing and social mission of the church, and the role of *cultural sensitivity* have been particularly acute between these communities; therefore the recorded convergence is indeed dramatic:

We are agreed that "mission" relates to every area of human need, both spiritual and social. Social responsibility is an integral part of evangelization; and the struggle for justice can be a manifestation of the Kingdom of God. Jesus both preached and healed, and sent his disciples out to do likewise. His predilection for those without power and without voice continues God's concern in the Old Testament for the widow, the orphan, the poor and the defenseless alien.

In particular we agree:

a. that serving the spiritual, social, and material needs of our fellow human beings together constitutes love of neighbor and therefore "mission";
b. that an authentic proclamation of the good news must lead to a call for repentance, and that authentic repentance is a turning away from social as well as individual sins;
c. that since each Christian community is involved in the reality of the world, it should lovingly identify with the struggle for justice as a suffering community;
d. that in this struggle against evil in society, the Christian must be careful to use means that reflect the spirit of the gospel.

And:

We all agree that the aim of "indigenization" or "inculturation" is to make local Christians congenial members of the body of Christ. They must not imagine that to become Christian is to become western and so to repudiate their own cultural and national inheritance. The same principle applies in the west, where too often to become Christian has also meant to become middle class.

There are a number of spheres in which each Church should be allowed to develop its own identity. The first is the question of certain forms of organization, especially as they relate to Church leadership. Although Roman Catholics and Evangelicals take a different approach to authority and its exercise, we are agreed that in every Christian community (especially a new one) authority must be exercised in a spirit of service. "I am among you as one who serves," Jesus said (Luke 22:27). Yet the expression given to leadership can vary according to different cultures. (ERCDOM, 2, 3)

III. The authors are also able to face the contentious *soteriological issue* that was at the core of the Reformation division, justification and salvation, even beginning a discussion of the role of Mary and contemporary Latin American liberation theologies as they approach mission together:

We agree that what is offered us through the death and resurrection of Christ is essentially "deliverance," viewed both negatively and positively. Negatively, it is a rescue from the power of Satan, sin and death, from guilt, alienation (estrangement from God), moral corruption, self-centeredness, existential despair and fear of the future, including death. Positively, it is a deliverance into the freedom of Christ. This freedom brings human fulfillment. It is essentially becoming "sons in the Son" and therefore brothers to each other. The unity of the disciples of Jesus is a sign both that the Father sent the Son and that the Kingdom has arrived. Further, the new community expresses itself in eucharistic worship, in serving the needy (especially the poor and disenfranchised), in open fellowship with people of every age, race and culture, and in conscious continuity with the historic Christ through fidelity to the teaching of his apostles.

Roman Catholics draw attention to the three dimensions of evangelization which *Evangelii nuntiandi* links. They are the *anthropological,* in which humanity is seen always within a concrete situation; the *theological,* in which the unified plan of God is seen within both creation and redemption; and the *evangelical,* in which the exercise of charity (refusing to ignore human misery) is seen in the light of the story of the Good Samaritan.

We all agree that the essential meaning of Christ's salvation is the restoration of the broken relationship between sinful humanity and a saving God; it cannot therefore be seen as a temporal or material project, making evangelism unnecessary. (ERCDOM, 3, 5)

IV. The role of the Holy Spirit, baptism, and the nature of *conversion* are issues where the differences are carefully outlined, and the level of mutual understanding and agreement spelled out. The nature, role, and mission of the church are one of the most divisive issues. Important areas of agreement support common witness, even without agreement on ecclesiology:

> Both Evangelicals and Roman Catholics are conscious of past failure in their understanding of the Church. Roman Catholics used to concentrate on the Church as a hierarchical institution, but now (since Vatican II) see it in new perspective by stressing the important biblical images such as that of the People of God. Evangelicals have sometimes preached an excessively individualistic gospel, "Christ died for me." This is true (Gal. 2:20), but it is far from the whole truth, which is that Christ gave himself for us "to purify for himself a people . . ." (Titus 2:14).
>
> Thus both Roman Catholics and Evangelicals agree that the Church as the Body of Christ is part of the gospel. That is to say, the good news includes God's purpose to create for himself through Christ a new, redeemed, united and international people of his own.[9] (ERCDOM, 5, 1)

V. The culmination of the report is the theological conviction that *common witness* is not only possible, but *demanded* by the common faith that is shared and the mission to which we are called as Christians:

> We who have participated in ERCDOM III [this text only represents those present at the last of the three meetings] are agreed that every possible opportunity for common witness should be taken, except where conscience forbids. We cannot make decisions for one another, however, because we recognize that the situation varies in different groups and places. In any case, the sad fact of our divisions on important questions of faith always puts a limit on the common

---

9. McNamara notes this ecclesiological emphasis as one of the most important breakthroughs in this text, "A Review/Appreciation of the Evangelical–Roman Catholic Dialogue on Mission," *IS* 60, p. 99.

witness which is possible. At one end of the spectrum are those who can contemplate no cooperation of any kind. At the other are those who desire a very full cooperation. In between are many who still find some forms of common witness conscientiously impossible, while they find others to be the natural, positive expression of common concern and conviction. (ERCDOM, Conclusion)

WEA

This second dialogue, resulting in the 2002 text, "Church, Evangelization, and the Bonds of *Koinonia*," is truly historic because "for the first time these meetings were sponsored by international bodies on both sides: the *World Evangelical Alliance* and the *Pontifical Council for Promoting Christian Unity*" (Preamble). It was not at all clear when this particular set of conversations began in 1990 that a text would emerge.[10]

The conversations were begun because the World Evangelical Fellowship (now Alliance) in 1987 issued "A Contemporary Evangelical Perspective on Roman Catholicism"[11] in response to protests from some southern European evangelical associations who objected to the presence of Roman Catholics, especially a member of the staff of the Secretariat for Promoting Christian Unity from the Vatican, at their 1980 international assembly in England. Catholics found this text theologically inaccurate, and therefore a set of meetings was begun, where clarifications and points of view were exchanged, initially with no plan for a statement.[12] At the 1999 meeting the group felt that there was sufficient theological convergence after almost a decade of meetings that drafting could be attempted. The next three meetings made it possible to produce this text.

The size, the cultural and historical differences are noted, and the gradual rapprochement is recorded. The first part of the text focuses on ecclesiology, through the lens of *koinonia*, a biblical term that has proved to be fruitful in the ecumenical movement. In the context set by common reflection on this ecclesial perspective, differences on proselytizing, religious freedom, and common witness are taken up in the second part.

---

10. See http://www.prounione.urbe.it/dia-int/e-rc/doc/e_e-rc_report2002.html.

11. World Evangelical Fellowship, "A Contemporary Evangelical Perspective on Roman Catholicism," *The Evangelical Review of Theology* 10, nos. 4 and 11, no. 1 (1986).

12. "Justification, Scripture and Tradition: World Evangelical Fellowship–Roman Catholic Dialogue," *The Evangelical Review of Theology* 21, no. 2 (April 1997).

The purpose of the dialogue is duly circumscribed:

> The purpose of these consultations has been to overcome misunderstandings, to seek better mutual understanding of each other's Christian life and heritage, and to promote better relations between Evangelicals and Catholics. . . . It is a study document produced by participants in this consultation. The authorities who appointed the participants have allowed the report to be published so that it may be widely discussed. It is not an authoritative declaration of either the Catholic Church or of the World Evangelical Alliance, who will both also evaluate the document. (Preamble)

Care is taken to be clear that differences are articulated with no compromise. In fact, due to Evangelical caution, over a year passed between the finalization of the text in 2002 and its publication.

I. Common *biblical understandings of "fellowship"* provide a theological consensus within which Catholic and Evangelical emphases and differences can be articulated. The text's focus on the Trinitarian character of ecclesial communion is a particularly important theological development beyond the ERCDOM text, following the theology of wider ecumenical conversations:

> For both Evangelicals and Roman Catholics communion with Christ involves a transformative union whereby believers are "*koinonia* of the divine nature and escape the corruption that is in the world by lust" (2 Pet 1:4). Catholics tend to interpret *koinonia* in this passage to mean a participation in the divine life and "nature," while Evangelicals tend to interpret *koinonia* as covenant companionship, as it entails escaping moral corruption and the way of the world. . . . (no. 5)

> Catholics believe that sacraments are Christ's instruments to effect the transformative union with the divine nature (1 Cor 12:12-13, where they see water-baptism, and 10:16-17, Eucharist). In passages such as these they hear other (Catholics would say deeper), more sacramental and participatory connotations in the word "*koinonoi*" than are expressed by the word "fellowship." Many Evangelicals consider the sacraments to be dominical means of grace or "ordinances" which are "visible words" that proclaim (*kataggellete*, 1 Cor 11:26) or are signs and seals of the grace of union with Christ —

grace to be received and enjoyed on the sole condition of personal faith. (no. 6)[13]

In the light of these beliefs, the report explains differences in understanding the communion of saints; the relationship of sacraments, sanctification, and justification; and the eschatological character of *koinonia*.[14] The introduction of the eschatological perspectives helps them understand how they can collaborate on the way to the Kingdom: "Catholics and Evangelicals should look to a deeper communion in this world, even if they disagree . . . on the means by which this might be achieved, and on the extent to which it can be realized prior to the return of Christ" (no. 9).

The text goes on to elaborate processes in history whereby the two communities have moved to a more positive evaluation of other Christians and, consequently, of one another. However, the text continues to articulate caution here for Evangelicals:

> Evangelical attitudes to the Roman Catholic and Orthodox churches differ widely. Some Evangelicals are praying, talking, studying Scripture and working with these churches. Others are strongly opposed to any form of dialogue or cooperation with them. All are aware that serious theological differences between us remain. Where appropriate, and so long as biblical truth is not compromised, cooperation may be possible in such areas as Bible translation, the study of contemporary theological and ethical issues, social work and political action. We wish to make it clear, however, that common evangelism demands a common commitment to the biblical Gospel (*Manila Affirmation* 9). (Citing Lausanne, 1989, 292) (no. 19)

The scripture, the apostolic faith as articulated in the classical creeds, the gospel call to conversion and the disciplined life, and responsibility

---

13. See Meeking, "Comment on the Report: *Church, Evangelization, and the Bonds of Koinonia,*" *IS* 113 (2003): 105.

14. The eschatological issue was raised by the evangelical theologian and co-chair of the WEA dialogue in his earlier evaluation of the Catholic response to BEM. He proposed that Catholic ecclesiology identified the fullness of *koinonia* too easily with its own present reality, without sufficient attention to the eschatological fullness, which holds all of our pilgrim communities under judgment. George Vandervelde, "Vatican Ecumenism at the Crossroads? The Vatican Approach to Differences with BEM," *Gregorianum* 69, no. 4 (1988): 689-711.

to witness and service in the world all characterize the uniting bonds of communion that bind Catholics and Evangelicals in Christ. The modern pilgrimage toward greater toleration, mutual understanding, and consequent ecclesial recognition is recounted.

Catholics and Evangelicals have theological differences on the visibility of the church, which lead to different emphases on the personal and the institutional dimensions of *koinonia* and the disciplines that flow therefrom. This discussion of differences has led to a surprising theological convergence:

> Catholics and Evangelicals experience a convergence in the understanding of the way that order and discipline serve the *koinonia* of the church. Catholics have begun to reemphasize the importance of the personal in understanding the church. Evangelicals show an increasing appreciation of visible expressions of unity in the life of the church beyond the bounds of their own denomination. Such a convergence in our understanding of biblical *koinonia* offers promise for a continuation of the dialogue. (no. 41)

The first part of the text, devoted to a theology of the church, ends with an exhortation to go beyond the history of alienation, to a new future:

> . . . It is not possible to reverse history, but it is possible to prepare for a different future. (no. 43)

> We realize the need for a spirit of repentance before God because we have not made sufficient efforts to heal the divisions that are a scandal to the Gospel. We pray that God grant us a spirit of *metanoia*. We need to continue to study and face issues which have separated us. We need to examine also the practices that uncritically continue the biases of the past. (no. 44)

> Could we not ask ourselves whether we sufficiently understand the levels of unity that we already share? (no. 45)

II. The *second section* of the text outlines views on *evangelization/ evangelism, resolving old tensions, repentance/conversion, religious freedom, and common witness,* all in the light of the *koinonia* discussion that was elaborated in part one. This is a particularly important section, since, historically, tensions between Catholics and Evangelicals have emerged from different theological approaches to mission, charges of proselytism, and the lack of religious freedom in some Catholic countries. On religious freedom, WEA is more articulate than ERCDOM, building on intervening dialogues and situating mission and freedom in the context of ecclesiology.

While Catholics and Evangelicals differ on their emphases within the gospel mission, they affirm together that "every Christian has the right and obligation to share and spread the faith" (no. 48). Both also affirm that "the real *koinonia* we already share gives rise to our mutual concern to view conjointly the issues of religious freedom and proselytism that have divided us. We believe that the two issues of religious liberty and proselytism must not be treated as totally separable areas but must be firmly linked and considered jointly as related concerns, seen in the context of the meaning of evangelization and the possibility of common witness." From an extended discussion of this common basis the text goes on to identify "repentance, conversion and commitment, in which we commit ourselves to the convergence that has already begun in our life together" as issues for substantive reflection (no. 56).

In this section themes of repentance, conversion, and commitment are key, laying the groundwork for a spirituality of dialogue and common witness (nos. 57-81).

On the basis of this shared faith, the authors of this text challenge their own communities to face the sensitive issues of mission and religious freedom in new ways:

> We repent of unworthy forms of evangelization which aim at pressuring people to change their church affiliation in ways that dishonor the Gospel, and by methods which compromise rather than enhance the freedom of the believer and the truth of the Gospel. (no. 69)

> . . . The bonds of *koinonia* imply that Christians in established churches protect the civil rights of the other Christians to free speech, press and assembly. At the same time, the bonds of *koinonia* imply that the other Christians respect the rights, integrity and history of Christians in established churches. Tensions can be reduced if Christians engaged in mission communicate with one another and seek to witness together as far as possible, rather than compete with one another. (no. 71)

Since Evangelicals believe their church to be catholic, and Catholics believe their church to be evangelical, it would seem that our future task is to recognize better the aspects that each of us emphasizes in the others' view as well. (no. 72)

In the discussion of religious liberty, the Evangelicals and the Catholics involved in this dialogue reiterate their commitment to common theological principles and modes of evangelism, drawing on earlier dialogues. They reaffirm together their commitment to the rights of all, not just Christians. They assert "that human rights should be interpreted and exercised within the framework of Scripture teaching and of rigorous moral reasoning. Due regard must be had for the needs of others, for duties towards other parties, and for the common good. Human rights language, also, must guard against being turned into narcissism, self-assertiveness and ideology" (no. 78).

The text ends with a firm conviction and biblical call:

. . . to the extent conscience and the clear recognition of agreement and disagreement allows, we commit ourselves to common witness. (no. 80)

We conclude this report by joining together in a spirit of humility, putting our work, with whatever strengths and limitations it may have, in the hands of God. Our hope is that these efforts will be for the praise and glory of Jesus Christ. (no. 81)

Conclusions

Pope John Paul in his 1995 encyclical *Ut unum sint* encouraged Catholics to make the results of these dialogues a "common heritage." These two texts are particularly important in (1) teaching missiology; (2) preparing pastoral agents for dealing with fellow Christians in their communities, especially in Latin America and the U.S. Hispanic community; and (3) providing the basis for local dialogues, especially marriage preparation.[15] They have also generated a renewed interest in ecclesiology among evangelical scholars.

15. See Thomas Rausch, ed., *Catholics and Evangelicals: Do They Share a Common Future?* (Downers Grove, IL: InterVarsity Press, 2000). Stephen Bevans, "What Catholics Learn from Evangelical Mission Theology," *Missiology* 23, no. 2 (1995): 155-64.

1. Missiology

ERCDOM is particularly useful in teaching missiology in both Catholic and Evangelical contexts since it can be used as an ecumenical commentary on the *Lausanne Covenant* and *Evangelii Nuntiandi*. Furthermore, in a Catholic context it can illustrate how *Ad Gentes* of the Second Vatican Council is beginning to be received in both the ecumenical and Catholic development. It also demonstrates a different methodology from the confessional bilateral or from unreflective approaches to collaboration.[16]

WEA is useful, for Catholics, in helping to demonstrate how important is the Vatican II affirmations of *Dignitatis Humanae* on Religious Freedom to the renewed understanding of the church as *koinonia*, and in its ecumenical relations and approach to evangelization. For evangelicals, it can help to correct misunderstandings and often unfortunate experiences of the Catholic Church. I think this dialogue and other ecumenical contacts are among the stimuli that have increased the interest in ecclesiology among Evangelicals.[17]

I have found these two texts particularly useful in teaching ecclesiology in both Catholic and ecumenical contexts, giving a sense of relevance to the issues under consideration and acting as bridges to how various issues of church, mission, and culture are seen differently. They have the potential for creating the basis for common witness.

2. Catechesis

The results of these dialogues are important contributions to Catholic catechesis, especially in countries where Catholics predominate. In

16. See Steven Bevans, SVD, and Jeffrey Gros, FSC, *Evangelization and Religious Freedom: Ad Gentes, Dignitatis Humanae* (New York: Paulist Press, 2008).

17. See, for example, George Vandervelde, "The Challenge of Evangelical Ecclesiology," *Evangelical Review of Theology* 27, no. 1 (January 2003): 4-26; Amos Yong, "The Marks of the Church: A Pentecostal Re-Reading," *Evangelical Review of Theology* 1, no. 26 (January 2002): 45-67; Miroslav Volf, "The Nature of the Church," *Evangelical Review of Theology* 1, no. 26 (January 2002): 68-75; Veli-Matti Kärkkäinen, *An Introduction to Ecclesiology: Ecumenical, Historical and Global Perspectives* (Downers Grove, IL: InterVarsity Press, 2002); and John H. Armstrong, *Your Church Is Too Small: Why Unity in Christ's Mission Is Vital to the Future of the Church* (Grand Rapids: Zondervan, 2010).

places like Spain and Colombia, a first evaluation of the Council by the local bishops was that it would not influence their situation in society and relationship to Christian minorities. On the other hand, Council fathers from Catholic countries, like Cardinals Rossi of Brazil and Silva of Chile were clear on the catechetical revolution that would be necessary to hand on the Catholic faith in a context that now affirmed the liberty of all persons in matters of belief. Even these visionary leaders did not realize how necessary this catechesis of freedom, life in a pluralist society, and ecumenical commitment would become, as evangelical Protestantism began to mushroom in the 1970s to the present.

Within the Latin American Catholic Church there is still no consensus on ecumenical priorities, the approach to an inevitable religious pluralism, or the advocacy of the religious rights of all citizens, for example in matters of education or marriage. With popular religion as the primary bearer of Catholic identity for many in Latin America, including U.S. Hispanic Catholics, catechesis becomes an important challenge for Catholic ecumenical progress.[18] These texts are particularly important for training catechists in communities of new immigrants from majority Catholic countries in Eastern Europe and Latin America.

To this catechetical task, these evangelical dialogues are an irreplaceable contribution to Catholic ecumenical formation, and education for pluralism and religious freedom. These relationships were not predicted in the Council, are very fragile, and least known where they are most needed: in the evangelical Protestant community, and in Catholic contexts where Catholics are a majority — with a memory of hegemonic times in which religious freedom was not at the center of the Catholic agenda.

3. Local Dialogues

Local institutions like Fuller Seminary in Pasadena, California or Catholic universities where evangelicals have had their training, like Leuven in Belgium, created the condition of possibility for some of these dialogues. The dialogue of truth builds on the dialogue of love — the shar-

---

18. See Thomas Rausch, "Ecumenism and America's Hispanic Christians," *Origins* 36, no. 3 (June 1, 2006): 41-45. Ricardo Ramírez, "Bringing Ecumenism to Hispanic Christians," *Origins* 22, no. 3 (May 28, 1992): 40-44; "The Crisis in Ecumenism among Hispanic Catholics," *Origins* 24, no. 40 (March 23, 1995): 660-66.

ing of faith, of hopes for common witness, can only develop where personal, spiritual relationships are nurtured.

Similarly, the reception of the results of these dialogues will not be seen in actions of the churches, but in the resources they provide for healing of memories, mutual understanding, and common witness. In places like Los Angeles, Chicago, St. Paul, Boston, Springfield, Philadelphia, and other communities around the world, a rich Catholic-Evangelical bonding has occurred in situations where dialogue, common prayer, and common witness are possible. A number of formal and informal but unofficial exchanges have made an immeasurable contribution to the reception of these initiatives.[19]

As Evangelicals and Catholics continue to marry one another, these texts are resources for couples and their pastors as they prepare for a life of dialogue, mutual understanding, and witness in an interchurch family. For young Catholics who come to faith in an evangelical, Pentecostal, or charismatic experience, these reports will help them clarify and differentiate their faith, strengthen their Catholic convictions, and deepen their ecumenical appreciation of fellow Christians.

We can join with the members of WEA dialogue (no. 81) in praying:

> "Now to Him who is able to do immeasurably more than all we ask or imagine, according to his power that is at work within us, to him be glory in the church and in Christ Jesus throughout all generations, forever and ever! Amen" (Eph 3:20-21).

And hope that the vision of ERCDOM continues to expand:

> At the same time we hope that dialogue on mission between Roman Catholics and Evangelicals will continue, preferably on a regional or local basis, in order that further progress may be made towards a common understanding, sharing and proclaiming of "the faith which was once for all delivered to the saints" (Jude 3). We commit these past and future endeavors to God, and pray that by "speaking the truth in love, we are to grow up in every way into him who is the head, into Christ" (Eph 4:15). (ERCDOM, Conclusion)

19. See, for example, Charles Colson and Richard John Neuhaus, eds., *Evangelicals and Catholics Together: Toward a Common Mission* (Dallas: Word, 1995), and *Your Word Is Truth* (Grand Rapids: Eerdmans, 2002). See http://www.firstthings.com/simpleSearch.php?offset=0&mySqlSearchCriteria=%22A+Statement+of+Evangelicals+and+Catholics+Together%22.

14 Disciples of Christ–Roman Catholic International Commission for Dialogue: Sharing the Fruits

Margaret O'Gara

The Disciples of Christ–Roman Catholic International Commission for Dialogue has been both rewarding and surprising in its breakthrough insights and the rich experiences it has provided for participants. I have been a member of this dialogue since 1983 and I am happy to share with you some of its distinctive characteristics and achievements.

A Distinctive Partner in Dialogue

This dialogue has a special character among the others because of the unique position held by the Disciples of Christ. On the one hand, since they participate in what one of our agreed statements calls a "protestant [sic] ethos," they share such Protestant emphases as the proclamation of the Word, the obligation of "each individual's conscience" to come to a judgment "as it is bound by the gospel," and responsibility for the personal appropriation of the Word of God, emphasized by believer's baptism.[1] On the other hand, because the Disciples movement actually emerged as a break from Protestant churches in the nineteenth century, "it had nothing to do with a deliberate break from the Roman Catholic Church and lacked the memories of sixteenth- and seventeenth-century

---

1. Disciples of Christ–Roman Catholic International Commission for Dialogue, "The Church as Communion in Christ (1983-92)" [hereafter CCC], *Mid-Stream* 41 (2002): 96-114; no. 6.

controversies."[2] And Disciples broke away from the Presbyterian tradition precisely over Disciples' commitment to the centrality of the eucharist in the church's life and to the unity among Christians which the eucharist symbolizes and effects. Hence their distinctive convictions have much in common with those of the Roman Catholic Church, which also "proclaims that it has a specific mission for the unity of the world, and affirms that this unity is signified and given by the eucharistic communion," and "teaches that the restoration of unity among all Christians is linked with the salvation of the world."[3]

Nevertheless, participants in our dialogue were keenly aware of the significant differences between us in history and style. Because Disciples believed that creeds, confessions, and doctrinal teachings in the Presbyterian Church had been keeping Christians from the eucharist and hence undermining the unity of the church, their tradition rejected such instruments of confession. In their place they set the baptism of believers and the weekly celebration of the eucharist, which they understood to be commanded by the New Testament. To understand the perspective of Disciples, then, their Catholic conversation partners could not look up Disciples' confessional statements in books or study their lengthy volumes of doctrinal disputes, because Disciples had been formed precisely in opposition to such traditions. Instead Catholics were required to spend lots of time examining the Disciples' actual traditions of biblical exegesis and theological interpretation, experiencing the dynamism of their weekly eucharistic celebrations, and talking for long hours about actual practices, precedents, and viewpoints that govern Disciples' community life. Gradually we came to the conviction that our shared commitment to the unity of the church and the centrality of the eucharist expressed "a very profound communion in some of the most fundamental gifts of the grace of God."[4]

I want to make one last point about the atmosphere of the dialogue. If you remember that the Stone-Campbell movements that launched the Disciples only began in the early 1800s, you realize that the last thirty years of dialogue with the Roman Catholic Church actually form a significant percentage of the life history of this church. Many times my Disciples colleagues made clear that they sought to

2. CCC, no. 8.
3. CCC, no. 8.
4. CCC, no. 8.

shape and reshape their own tradition through engagement with the ecumenical movement and in particular the Roman Catholic Church. At times it almost seemed as though Disciples were asking Catholics to suggest ways forward for their tradition that would be most fruitful, most at the service of the church's unity. The service of unity was, after all, precisely why they had emerged as a movement in the first place! The fluidity of Disciples' theology today and its openness to direction and advice hence also contributed to the dialogue's distinctiveness.

In the four phases of official dialogue between Disciples of Christ and the Roman Catholic Church since 1977, our four agreed statements have affirmed many of the central teachings also held in other bilateral dialogues: the saving work of Jesus Christ offered to all humankind, the doctrine of the Trinity, the church as communion in Christ, baptism as the initiation into Christ's life in the church, the eucharist as sign and instrument of unity in Christ, etc. I will not repeat our agreements on these common ecumenical themes. Instead, I will focus on two areas where our agreements have been distinctive — even surprising — and can contribute something original to the further tasks that lie before us. These two areas are: (1) teaching authority within the church; and (2) the eucharist.

Teaching Authority within the Church

On the question of teaching authority, it seemed at first glance that differences between the two church traditions were irreconcilable. While Roman Catholics emphasized continuity in the history of the church's teaching, Disciples had been formed by breaking from the Presbyterian tradition; they believe that "some discontinuities in the life of the Church have been necessary for the sake of the Gospel."[5] Where Roman Catholics trust creeds, confessions, doctrinal teachings, and the structures of episcopal authority, Disciples are distrustful of these parts of Christian tradition and are "readily critical of some developments in the history of the Church."[6] While Catholics wondered "how Disciples, with an apparent lack of structure and creedal formulations, have handed on the Gospel," Disciples were not sure that the

5. CCC, no. 11.
6. CCC, no. 15.

"more elaborate hierarchical structure" of the Roman Catholic Church with "its apparent emphasis on uniformity" could give believers "sufficient freedom in conscience."[7] At first, the notion that such differences between Disciples and Catholics could be overcome seemed "nearly incredible."[8]

Despite these differences, we found real convergence about teaching authority in the church. Believing that the eucharist sets us in communion with God and with each other and gives us a foretaste of the end times, members believe as well that the church "must live in the memory of its origins, remembering with thanksgiving what God has done in Christ Jesus."[9] Living in this memory means, for both church traditions, being in continuity with the witness of the apostolic generation. The church "is founded on their proclamation"[10] and both traditions "share an intention to live and teach in such a way that, when the Lord comes again, the Church may be found witnessing to the faith of the apostles."[11] Both Disciples and Roman Catholics believe that they maintain continuity with the apostolic witness by preserving the memory of the apostolic teaching and by proclaiming and living it anew.[12] Such remembering, proclaiming, and witnessing are made possible by the Holy Spirit, who acts especially in the eucharist to make Christ present. This commitment of the two traditions to live in memory of the apostolic teaching is highlighted by their central emphasis on the frequent celebration of the eucharist, where "the essential elements of Christian faith and life are expressed."[13]

We readily agreed that proclamation of God's Word takes place as a "living tradition of scriptural interpretation and prayer" through which all generations of Christians are linked.[14] We agreed as well that the memory of apostolic teachings is served by the canon of the scriptures, councils of the church, and creeds, all developed under the Holy

---

7. Disciples of Christ–Roman Catholic International Commission for Dialogue, "Receiving and Handing on the Faith: The Mission and Responsibility of the Church (1993-2002)" [hereafter RHF], *Mid-Stream* 41 (2002): 51-79; no. 1.4.

8. CCC, no. 17.

9. CCC, no. 25.

10. CCC, no. 26.

11. CCC, no. 27.

12. CCC, no. 27.

13. CCC, no. 30.

14. RHF, no. 2.4.

Spirit's guidance.[15] It was easy to understand that the setting of the canon "was at the same time an act of obedience and of authority"[16] and that the canon is closely linked to the church's unity. "Because it is held in common by Christians, the Bible holds Christians together with one another as they read and proclaim the same Word of God received from the Church of the apostles."[17] But more surprising were agreements on councils and on declarations of the faith, since the Disciples had emphasized their history of suspicion toward such instruments. We found more agreement about the first seven ecumenical councils than previously seen, since both Disciples and Roman Catholics "recognize the first seven councils as authentic gatherings of the Church able to speak in the name of the whole Church."[18] The councils were conscious of Christ's presence and their service of the gospel, and they defined the mystery of the triune God received in Christ. Furthermore, the councils of bishops, seen as succeeding the apostolic community, wished to serve the scripture; their definitions "clarified and made explicit the main affirmations of the Scriptures."[19] In addition, Disciples now regard these early councils as part of God's providential ordering of the church, and "the Disciples' tradition has never held the theological positions condemned by the early ecumenical councils."[20] Members write, "To the extent that they have accepted the decisions of those councils, Disciples have acknowledged their authority."[21] This interesting statement reveals the method often used in our discussions: to elicit the actual practice of the Disciples and its implicit meaning when set in relationship with the more explicit, articulated positions held by Roman Catholics.

Of course, early Disciples were famously critical of confessions of faith used as tests of fellowship at the Communion Table, though the main targets of their criticism were not the Apostles' or Nicene creeds but rather Reformed confessions such as the Westminster Confession and the Secession Testimony.[22] So Disciples have preferred New Testa-

15. RHF, no. 3.1.
16. RHF, no. 3.6.
17. RHF, no. 3.10.
18. RHF, no. 3.13.
19. RHF, no. 3.13.
20. RHF, no. 3.15.
21. RHF, no. 3.15.
22. RHF, no. 3.16.

ment confessions of faith, and "they emphasize the dependence of conciliar creeds on the New Testament."[23] But today in fact both Roman Catholics and Disciples use the central teachings of the first seven councils when judging new ideas or practices, while not necessarily affirming the "world view or conceptual structure" of their formulations.[24] In fact, both agree that some formulations may need reformulation at a later time for clarity, and the members agree that councils "demonstrate that sometimes the Church finds such restatement necessary precisely in order to remain in continuity with the faith it has received."[25]

While agreeing that the pilgrim church is affected by both finitude and sin in its remembering of the gospel, the members also were able to reach significant breakthroughs about God's assistance to the church in its teaching. They are agreed "that the Holy Spirit sustains the Church in communion with the apostolic community because Christ promised that the Spirit 'will teach you everything and remind you of all that I have said to you' (John 14:26 NRSV)." They write that "the Spirit guides the Church to understand its past, to recall what may have been forgotten, and to discern what renewal is needed for the Gospel to be proclaimed effectively in every age and culture."[26] The Holy Spirit helps the church to adopt fresh understandings or practices precisely in order to maintain continuity with the apostolic tradition and to preach the gospel in different contexts and circumstances.[27] The church is even given "a foretaste of the transformation" it will know fully in the future.[28] Through all of this — "the Holy Spirit guarantees that the Church shall not in the end fail to witness faithfully to the divine plan" — members agree.[29] This is a striking convergence.

The Holy Spirit gives a variety of charisms to the church that enable it to maintain continuity with apostolic tradition: everyday charisms for living the gospel, teaching children the faith, caring for the poor and needy, as well as charisms for especially vivid witness to the gospel. Among all of these complementary charisms is "a particular

23. RHF, no. 3.16.
24. RHF, no. 3.17.
25. RHF, no. 3.17.
26. CCC, no. 36.
27. CCC, no. 37.
28. CCC, no. 38.
29. CCC, no. 37.

charism given to the ordained ministry to maintain the community in the memory of the Apostolic Tradition," serving to "actualize, transmit, and interpret with fidelity the Apostolic Tradition."[30] While the whole church is called to hold fast to the gospel, the ordained ministry in each tradition is understood to have "the charism for discerning, declaring and fostering what lies in the authentic memory of the Church."[31]

The participants in the dialogue do acknowledge clearly many differences in emphasis in the exercise of teaching authority by ordained ministers in the two churches today. While Roman Catholics retain the episcopal office, including a Petrine ministry, the Disciples emerged from those traditions "which at the Reformation rejected episcopacy as the Reformers knew it in the Roman Catholic Church."[32] Participants in the dialogue recognize the tendency of the Catholic members to emphasize unity and continuity of church teaching, while Disciples members easily identify with those who disagree with the teaching of the church of their day out of obedience to the Word of God as they discern it. Disciples notice the tendency of the Roman Catholic teaching office today to articulate an increasingly large number of positions on new challenges and even make "decisions binding on the conscience of Roman Catholics,"[33] while Disciples' ordained ministers provide less official teaching "when a question is under debate" and do not give binding teachings through their assemblies.[34] Dialogue members point out that Disciples and Roman Catholics differ in the weight they give in teaching to the truths of revelation, theological arguments about them, the authority of the teachers, and reception by the whole church.[35] Yet both agree on the basic dynamics of the ordained ministers within the church: the "discernment of the authentic meaning of the revealed Word belongs to the whole community" while being "called and empowered by the Spirit to teach the Word of God" is the charism given to the ordained ministry.[36] This is another striking convergence.

30. CCC, no. 44.
31. CCC, no. 45.
32. CCC, no. 45.
33. RHF, no. 4.12.
34. RHF, no. 4.13.
35. RHF, no. 4.16.
36. RHF, no. 4.9.

Eucharist

It is interesting that the early discussions of the eucharist in our dialogue linked it with memory. Drawing on the idea of living in memory of the apostolic generation, Disciples of Christ and Roman Catholics easily agree that the Holy Spirit "keeps alive the sense of the faith in the whole community, and lavishes a variety of *charisms* that enable it to live in the memory of Jesus Christ." And they add, "In the Eucharist especially, the Spirit makes Christ present to the members of the community."[37] In early discussions, we emphasized the centrality of the eucharist for each of our traditions and its communal character. The eucharist is understood as "an act through which a divine reality otherwise more or less hidden emerges and is made present," revealing the good news of salvation — that Jesus Christ reconciles humanity to the Father.[38] We also emphasized that "the unity of the Church is accomplished" at the eucharistic table, and added: "Thus, precisely because the celebration of the Eucharist is the climax of the Church's life, disunity among Christians is felt most keenly at the Eucharist; and their inability to celebrate the Lord's Supper together makes them less able to manifest the full catholicity of the Church."[39]

I should observe that this lament was not limited to words, but is experienced keenly every day of our weeklong dialogues. When the Roman Catholic team members gather for daily morning eucharist, the majority of the Disciples participants are with us as well, never receiving communion during the Catholic celebrations but always wishing to. (When the Disciples' eucharist was celebrated during our sessions, the Roman Catholics were in the same position of attending without receiving communion.) Perhaps because it occurred every single day of our meetings and early in the morning — when most of us were barely awake — the silent witness of the Disciples to the pain of our division at the table of the Lord's Supper created a powerful spiritual testimony that urged us back to the table of dialogue again and again to search for a way forward.

In our most recent phase we addressed the eucharist as our major topic for the first time in an agreed statement. From this statement, I

---

37. CCC, no. 28.
38. CCC, no. 30.
39. CCC, no. 32.

will focus on our surprising agreements about the sacrificial aspect of the eucharist and Christ's real presence.

As early as 1982 in the first agreed statement, baptism is tied to the eucharist. Members note that "the oneness achieved in grace in baptism should find manifestation and completion in the *anamnesis* (memorial/remembrance) of the sacrifice of Christ for all humanity at the table of the one Lord."[40] Fuller discussions of the sacrificial character of the eucharist for the most recent statement yielded a surprising amount of agreement. While Disciples had "received and made their own, without much debate, the Reformers' rejection of sacrificial interpretations of the eucharist,"[41] they joined Roman Catholics in affirming the biblical recovery of *anamnesis*. For Roman Catholics, this recovery work gave Roman Catholic theology a tool to correct some misinterpretations of the Council of Trent "that gave the impression of a new oblation repeated daily during the eucharistic celebration."[42] For Disciples, "the recovery of the biblical meaning of memorial helps to prevent misunderstanding this term as simply mental recall, even though the Reformers themselves avoided this misunderstanding. . . ."[43] We have different emphases but a basic convergence.

We found more agreement on the sacrificial interpretation of the eucharist than we had anticipated, noting similarities between many official Disciples statements on the eucharist and the language of the *Catechism of the Catholic Church.*[44] One summarizing paragraph offers a good example of this insight, where we cite first from a 1998 Disciples document[45] describing the remembering at the eucharist as " 'not merely a recollection of something long gone and hence remote from us, but a re-presentation which makes what is past a vivid and lively reality here and now. Jesus Christ himself with all he has accomplished

40. Disciples of Christ–Roman Catholic International Commission for Dialogue, "Apostolicity and Catholicity (1977-1982)" [hereafter AC], *Mid-Stream* 41 (2002): 80-95; no. 32.

41. Disciples of Christ–Roman Catholic International Commission for Dialogue, "The Presence of Christ in the Church, with special reference to the Eucharist (2003-2009)" [hereafter PCCE]: *IS:* in press, no. 51.

42. PCCE, no. 52.

43. PCCE, no. 52.

44. PCCE, no. 55.

45. Commission on Theology of the Council on Christian Unity [Disciples of Christ], "The Church for Disciples of Christ: Seeking to Be Truly Church Today," ed. Paul A. Crow, Jr. and James O. Duke (St. Louis: Christian Board of Publication, 1998).

for us and for all creation is present in this *anamnesis.*'"[46] This citation is followed by one from the 1994 *Catechism of the Catholic Church*[47] which explains that the eucharistic memorial "is not merely the recollection of the past events but the proclamation of the mighty works by God for men" so that "when the Church celebrates the Eucharist, she commemorates Christ's Passover, and it is made present: the sacrifice Christ offered once for all on the cross remains ever present."[48] The text continues from the *Catechism*'s explanation of a quotation from the Council of Trent, explaining that the eucharist is a sacrifice "'because it *represents* (makes present) the sacrifice of the cross, because it is its *memorial* and because it *applies* its fruit.' . . ."[49] The section concludes with the dialogue's agreement that "the Eucharist is the sacrament of the sacrifice of Christ. Although the once-for-all sacrifice of Christ on the cross cannot be repeated, Christians in the celebration of the eucharist are drawn into the movement of Christ's self-offering."[50]

Even more surprising to me was the breakthrough agreement on the issue of Christ's real presence in the eucharist. While Disciples of Christ readily use the language of Christ's real presence in the eucharist, early Disciples criticized the language and teaching about transubstantiation as "unnecessarily metaphysical,"[51] just another source of "divisive controversies over a mystery" that had been given a variety of understandings in the history of the church.[52] Furthermore, the philosophical atmosphere of Scottish Common Sense realism in which the earliest Disciples were reared understood "what Aquinas described as 'accidents' . . . to constitute the real, and what he described as 'substance' . . . as an unnecessary abstraction. In this different philosophical framework, then, transubstantiation was taken to mean almost the opposite of what Aquinas had intended."[53]

But in our discussions, Roman Catholics explained the intention of the concept of *transubstantiation:* defending the mystery of Christ's real presence while opposing materialist misunderstandings as well as

46. PCCE, no. 55.
47. *Catechism of the Catholic Church* (Collegeville, MN: Liturgical Press, 1994).
48. PCCE, no. 55.
49. PCCE, no. 55.
50. PCCE, no. 56.
51. PCCE, no. 37.
52. PCCE, no. 36.
53. PCCE, no. 37.

those that reduce Christ's presence to a mere sign or figure.[54] I can still remember the discussion with my Disciples colleagues when some of them heard for the first time that Aquinas used the term *transubstantiation* in part to counter materialist views of the presence: they had believed Catholics were obligated to hold to just such views by the idea of transubstantiation. Disciples affirmed easily that "the ultimate significance of the bread and wine in the eucharist is not to be explained by their physical characteristics alone. Thus they affirm the mystery of Christ's presence in the eucharist, which makes receiving the bread and wine a true communion in his body and blood."[55] While Disciples "would not readily use the term" *transubstantiation* and have emphasized different moments in the mystery of Christ's presence than Catholics, we were able to agree that both of us "affirm the mystery of Christ's real presence in the eucharist, especially in the bread and wine; we both oppose reductionist understandings that see Christ's presence as simply materialist or figurative." We added that we had "reached some real convergence on this topic through the elimination of mutual misunderstandings, though we also recognize many remaining differences."[56]

Conclusion

The dialogue with the Disciples of Christ has yielded a surprising number of achievements. In this paper I have highlighted two of them: agreements about teaching authority within the church and about eucharist.

What can the ecumenical movement learn from this dialogue with a small worldwide church that emerged out of American movements for renewal and has entered into the free church stream of churches? I will mention four areas of learning.

First, we can be reminded again of the variety of ways in which Christians testify to their beliefs. While creeds and confessional statements are important sources to understand another tradition, dialogue with the Disciples forced me to become more attentive to many other sources where beliefs are witnessed: liturgical practice, biblical ex-

54. PCCE, no. 41.
55. PCCE, no. 42.
56. PCCE, no. 45.

egesis, preaching, communal decision making, the words of hymns, the style of pastoral care, the priorities of congregational budgets, the catechetical formation of children and adults, seminary education, and theological discussions. Using these as my sources sometimes lengthened the time it took me to understand what my Disciples colleagues thought, but the end result was reliable and broadening. In this way the Disciples of Christ–Roman Catholic dialogue can be a helpful model for the work that still lies ahead of the whole ecumenical movement in a more thorough engagement with churches in the free church tradition.

Secondly, large old churches like my own should be attentive in extending hospitality to partner churches like the Disciples when we dialogue with them. It is easy for large churches like the Roman Catholic Church to use our rich theological and doctrinal traditions as the only yardstick by which to measure the smaller, in some ways weaker, partner churches. But this would be a mistake, since it risks losing their distinctive gifts to the ecumenical movement and overlooking the sources that keep them vibrant communities of faith.

Third, in our dialogue we found that "paradoxically, some of our differences spring from the ways we have understood and pursued Christian unity."[57] For example, Disciples "refused to make creeds the definitive faith in order to promote unity and communion among Christians," while the Roman Catholic Church "holds to the creeds and the Petrine ministry for the same purpose."[58] Yet we found that our "commitment to Christ and . . . fellowship in the Gospel are the same. There is already a unity of grace which in some measure is present, bearing fruit, which is disposing us for visible unity and urging us to move ahead to it."[59] The intensity of the commitment to unity helps us understand why each of us might choose such different instruments in its pursuit, and it puts those differences in perspective.

Fourth, the dialogue with Disciples has yielded contributions in all five of the areas that Walter Kasper's *Harvesting the Fruits* lists as "questions for further discussion."[60] In the area of symbolic theology, where a "theology based on the binding creeds or confessions" might

57. AC, no. 9.
58. AC, no. 9.
59. AC, no. 59.
60. Walter Kasper, *Harvesting the Fruits: Aspects of Christian Faith in Ecumenical Dialogue* (New York and London: Continuum, 2009), nos. 106-11.

be necessary,[61] the Disciples help us see how such a theology could be based on the actual lived acceptance of the teaching of the historic creeds, even when that acceptance is reformulated or takes other forms. As we noted, "To the extent that they [Disciples] have accepted the decisions of those councils, Disciples have acknowledged their authority."[62] On the question of fundamental hermeneutical problems, the Disciples of Christ–Roman Catholic dialogue has contributed a major set of insights about how a free church that rejected dogmatic formulas and magisterial structures can today reappropriate Tradition and the meaning of a magisterium in a changed place and time. In our discussions on the freedom of conscience in its relationship to the teaching of the community, we explored an anthropological issue not yet widely discussed in other ecumenical dialogues. Our discussions on the church as communion in Christ add further dimensions to the topic of the sacramental nature of the church and underline the continuing strong commitment by both churches to the same goal of our dialogue as "neither unity on the basis of the lowest common denominator, nor peaceful coexistence, nor uniformity, but visible full communion in faith, sacramental life, apostolic ministry and mission according to the image of the unity of Father, Son and Holy Spirit within the Holy Trinity."[63] And our agreements on the eucharist as the sacrament of unity, the sacrament of the real presence of Christ, and the sacrament of his once-for-all sacrifice make some breakthroughs in eucharistic discussions that have not been reached elsewhere in ecumenical work.

With such fruits as these produced in our dialogue, it is a privilege to be called into the harvest.

---

61. Kasper, *Harvesting the Fruits,* no. 107.
62. RHF, no. 3.15.
63. *Harvesting the Fruits,* no. 110.

15 The Joint International Commission for Theological Dialogue between the Catholic Church and the Orthodox Church

Ronald G. Roberson, CSP

Prelude

The origins of the international Orthodox-Catholic dialogue can be traced back to the warming of relations that took place between the two churches in the 1960s. From the Catholic perspective, the convocation of the Second Vatican Council — at which Orthodox observers played a significant role behind the scenes — heralded a greater appreciation of Orthodoxy. A positive evaluation of the Orthodox is found in the Council documents, including a favorable assessment of their many legitimate traditions that are different from Latin practice, and an unqualified recognition of the validity of Orthodox sacraments. From the Orthodox perspective, the third pan-Orthodox conference (Rhodes 1964) encouraged the local Orthodox churches to engage in studies preparing for an eventual dialogue with the Catholic Church.

Both sides realized, however, that before any fruitful theological dialogue could take place, there would have to be an increase in confidence and trust between Orthodox and Catholics. This would be accomplished through a "dialogue of charity," marked by historic encounters and symbolic gestures that began in January 1964 with the meeting between Pope Paul VI and Patriarch Athenagoras of Constantinople in

Portions of Ronald Roberson's essays in this book originally appeared as "The Dialogues of the Catholic Church with the Separated Eastern Churches," in *U.S. Catholic Historian* 28 (Spring 2010): 135-52, issue on "Ecumenism," reprinted with permission by the editor of *U.S. Catholic Historian*.

Jerusalem. In a common declaration issued by them simultaneously in Rome and Istanbul on December 7, 1965,[1] the mutual excommunications of 1054 were lifted and "erased from the memory" of the church. In 1967 the Pope and Patriarch exchanged visits in Rome and Istanbul.

In the midst of this historic shift in relations, the Pope and Patriarch increasingly began to refer to their respective sees as "sister churches." Patriarch Athenagoras used the term in reference to the Church of Rome as early as 1962, and Pope Paul VI responded with a similar reference to Constantinople as a sister church in 1963. The concept was fleshed out on the Catholic side in Paul VI's brief *Anno ineunte* of July 25, 1967. In that text, the Pope stated that churches are "sisters" by virtue of their common participation in the mystery of divine love, specifically in the sacraments of Baptism, Eucharist, and Holy Orders. "And now," the Pope wrote, "after a long period of division and mutual misunderstanding, the Lord is enabling us to discover ourselves as 'sister churches' once more, in spite of the obstacles which were once raised between us."[2]

International Dialogue Established

This more positive atmosphere made possible the establishment in 1976 of a joint commission to prepare for an official dialogue. In 1978 it submitted a document[3] to the authorities of both churches in which it recommended that the goal of the dialogue be clearly defined as the re-establishment of full communion. It proposed a methodology according to which the dialogue would concentrate first on the many areas that the two churches have in common, establishing a firm theological foundation with a new theological language that would enable them at

---

1. *TOMOS AGAPIS Vatican-Phanar 1958-1970* (Rome and Istanbul, 1971), pp. 278-94.

2. "*Anno Ineunte*," in E. J. Stormon, SJ, ed., *Towards the Healing of Schism* (New York: Paulist Press, 1987), pp. 161-63. For a discussion of the use of the term "sister churches" in the context of Catholic-Orthodox relations, see Michael A. Fahey, SJ, *Orthodox and Catholic Sister Churches: East Is West and West Is East* (Milwaukee: Marquette University Press, 1996).

3. For an English translation of the French original text, see "Plan to Set Underway the Theological Dialogue between the Roman Catholic Church and the Orthodox Church," in John Borelli and John Erickson, eds., *The Quest for Unity: Orthodox and Catholics in Dialogue* (Washington, DC: USCCB, and Crestwood, NY: St. Vladimir's Seminary Press, 1996), pp. 47-52.

a later stage to address effectively the more divisive issues. The commission recommended that the sacraments be considered first, especially as they relate to ecclesiology.

The official announcement of the beginning of the theological dialogue was made jointly by Pope John Paul II and Patriarch Dimitrios I in Istanbul on 30 November 1979. This new "Joint International Commission for Theological Dialogue between the Catholic Church and the Orthodox Church" was to include bishops and theologians in equal numbers from both churches, the Orthodox side including representatives from all of the autocephalous and autonomous churches.

The First Ten Years

The first plenary session took place on the Greek islands of Patmos and Rhodes in 1980. This was an organizational meeting that unanimously adopted the plan for dialogue set forth in the 1978 document and chose initial themes for examination. Cardinal Johannes Willebrands, President of the Vatican's Secretariat for Promoting Christian Unity, and Archbishop Stylianos of Australia (Ecumenical Patriarchate) were named as co-presidents.[4]

Over the next eight years, the commission met five more times and adopted three common documents on foundational theological themes. In Munich in 1982, the text "The Mystery of the Church and of the Eucharist in the Light of the Mystery of the Holy Trinity"[5] was adopted. In Bari, Italy, the document "Faith, Sacraments and the Unity of the Church"[6] was finalized in 1987. At the Orthodox monastery at Valamo, Finland, in 1988 a third common document was adopted, titled "The Sacrament of Order in the Sacramental Structure of the Church, with Particular Reference to the Importance of the Apostolic Succession for the Sanctification and Unity of the People of God."[7] At Valamo it was agreed that the next area of study would be conciliarity

---

4. Cardinal Willebrands (d. 2006) was succeeded in 1989 by Edward Idris Cardinal Cassidy and in 2001 by Walter Cardinal Kasper; Archbishop Stylianos was succeeded by Metropolitan John [Zizioulas] of Pergamon as Orthodox Co-President at the Ninth Plenary in 2006.

5. *IS* 49 (1982/II-III): 107-12.

6. *IS* 64 (1987/II): 82-87.

7. *IS* 68 (1988/III-IV): 173-78.

and authority in the church. A draft text on this topic was later prepared for the sixth plenary, which was scheduled to be held in Freising, Germany, in June 1990.

The Impasse over "Uniatism"

During the two years before the Freising meeting, however, the unfolding of events prevented the commission from considering the text that would be prepared. The Valamo meeting had taken place on the eve of the 1989 collapse of the communist regimes in Eastern Europe. This event, happy as it was, caused a major crisis in Catholic-Orthodox relations because of the reemergence of Eastern Catholic churches that had been suppressed by the communists. Ugly confrontations arose between Eastern Catholics and Orthodox over Eastern Catholic property that had been confiscated by the communist authorities decades earlier and given to the Orthodox. All this dovetailed with longstanding Orthodox grievances arising from the process leading to the creation of some Eastern Catholic churches that the international commission refers to as "uniatism."

In view of what was happening in Eastern Europe, the Orthodox delegation at Freising insisted that the question of the origin and present status of the Eastern Catholic churches be the only topic of discussion. Under the circumstances it was only possible to issue a brief statement[8] at the end of the meeting, recognizing that the problem had to be dealt with urgently, and calling for a full-scale study of the issue.

This took place at the seventh plenary session in June 1993, held at the Balamand Orthodox School of Theology in Lebanon. The dialogue commission adopted a common document titled "Uniatism, Method of Union in the Past, and the Present Search for Full Communion."[9] It hinges on two central affirmations: on one hand, "the method which has been called uniatism" is rejected because it is "opposed to the common tradition of our Churches." And on the other hand, it unequivocally affirms that the Eastern Catholic churches "have the right to exist and to act in response to the spiritual needs of

8. For the text in French translation, see "Relations entre les Communions," *Irénikon* 63 (1990): 218-21.
9. *IS* 83 (1993/II): 96-99.

their faithful." It called upon Eastern Catholics to participate in the dialogue at all levels. The document also rules out all forms of proselytism between Catholics and Orthodox, affirming that salvation is available in either church.

The Balamand document was the first attempt to deal with this extremely delicate question, and therefore a major step forward. Pope John Paul II and Patriarch Bartholomew of Constantinople supported it as a step in the right direction. But on the local level reactions were mixed. In Greece, the Orthodox Church condemned the Balamand document and called for the abolition of the Eastern Catholic churches as the only solution to the problem. In Romania, the document was approved by the Holy Synod of the Romanian Orthodox Church, but rejected out of hand by the country's Greek Catholic bishops. It was only in Ukraine that Balamand gained support from both Eastern Catholics and Orthodox.

In any case, the Orthodox side insisted that, since there was no consensus regarding Balamand, the same topic would have to be treated in more depth before the commission could return to its theological agenda. After many delays, the Joint Coordinating Committee met at Ariccia, near Rome, in June 1998 and produced a draft text titled "The Ecclesiological and Canonical Implications of Uniatism." The eighth plenary session was then scheduled to take place at Mount St. Mary's College/Seminary in Emmitsburg, Maryland, hosted by Cardinal William Keeler, the Archbishop of Baltimore, in June 1999. But in March 1999 the meeting was again postponed when it became clear that some of the Orthodox would be unable to travel to a country participating in the NATO bombing of Serbia. The plenary finally took place from July 9 to 19, 2000.

The only text that came out of the Emmitsburg meeting was a Joint Communiqué, issued on July 19, 2000.[10] It notes that the documents previously issued about uniatism had met with strong opposition in some quarters, and that it had been necessary to make another attempt to reach agreement on this "extremely thorny question." Then comes the key paragraph:

> The discussions of this plenary were far-reaching, intense and thorough. They touched upon many theological and canonical ques-

10. *IS* 104 (2000/III): 147-48.

tions connected with the existence and the activities of the Eastern Catholic Churches. However, since agreement was not reached on the basic theological concept of uniatism, it was decided not to have a common statement at this time. For this reason, the members will report to their Churches who will indicate how to overcome this obstacle for the peaceful continuation of the dialogue.

Clearly an impasse had been reached at Emmitsburg on the question of the status of the Eastern Catholic churches, and six years would pass before the dialogue would meet again. During the intervening period, great efforts were made to create the conditions under which the dialogue could resume. In a certain sense, this was a reintensification of the "dialogue of love" that had been forged by Pope Paul VI and Patriarch Athenagoras, and that had never ceased even after the theological dialogue had begun.

For his part, Pope John Paul II repeatedly called for a resumption of the dialogue as the only way to resolve the outstanding issues, most notably when receiving delegations from the Ecumenical Patriarchate, especially on the feast of Saints Peter and Paul each June.[11] He and Patriarch Teoctist of Romania called for a resumption of the dialogue in the Common Declaration they signed during the Patriarch's visit to Rome on October 12, 2002.[12] The Pope also took some unilateral measures to express his esteem for the Orthodox, including the return of the Kazan icon of the Mother of God to the Russian Orthodox Church in August 2004,[13] the return of the relics of Saints John Chrysostom and Gregory Nazianzen to the Ecumenical Patriarchate in November 2004,[14] and the turning over of a church in Rome to the local Greek Orthodox community in June 2004.[15] Perhaps most importantly, the Pope's visit to Athens in May 2001 provided an opportunity to improve relations with the Orthodox Church of Greece and to ask forgiveness for the injustices of the past.[16] Exchanges of lower-level delegations

11. See for example Pope John Paul II's speech to the delegation from the Ecumenical Patriarchate on June 28, 2003, when he thanked the Patriarchate for its efforts to coordinate the continuance of the dialogue, which he described as "indispensable for our growth in unity." *IS* 113 (2003/II-III): 61.

12. *IS* 111 (2002/IV): 204-5.

13. *IS* 116 (2004/III): 121-26.

14. *IS* 117 (2004/IV): 148-54.

15. *IS* 116 (2004/III): 110.

16. *IS* 107 (2001/II-III): 62-66.

with the Church of Greece took place later, as well as a similar exchange with the Serbian Orthodox Church.[17] The Pope's visit to Bulgaria in 2002 included encounters with the Bulgarian Patriarch and the Holy Synod.[18] Taken together, these events increased the sense of trust among the Orthodox regarding the intentions of the Catholic Church towards them.

On the Orthodox side, Ecumenical Patriarch Bartholomew vigorously advocated a resumption of the dialogue. In the years following the Emmitsburg meeting, the Ecumenical Patriarchate sent out a delegation to visit the various autocephalous Orthodox churches to discuss ways of restarting the dialogue. The discussions these delegations had with high-ranking Orthodox hierarchs led to a consensus that the issue of uniatism could not be resolved without addressing the underlying theological questions, especially relating to primacy in the church. Thus there was general agreement among the Orthodox that the commission needed to return to its theological agenda, always keeping in mind that uniatism would still be addressed again at a later stage.[19] This made possible a meeting of the Inter-Orthodox Commission of the Theological Dialogue with the Catholic Church at the Ecumenical Patriarchate on September 12, 2005, where a decision was made to continue the dialogue.[20] Another important development that should not be overlooked was the appointment during this period of the prominent Orthodox theologian Metropolitan John (Zizioulas) of Pergamon as Orthodox Co-Chairman of the dialogue.

The Belgrade Turning Point

All this served as preparation for the Ninth Plenary Session of the international dialogue, which finally took place in Belgrade from Sep-

17. *IS* 112 (2003/I): 12-13.

18. *IS* 110 (2002/III): 152-58.

19. This effort by the Ecumenical Patriarchate to achieve a consensus among the Orthodox churches regarding the continuation of the dialogue with the Catholic Church was described in some detail in an Aide-Memoire issued by the Romanian Orthodox Patriarchate in March 2003. See *SEIA Newsletter on the Eastern Churches and Ecumenism* 91 (April 30, 2003): 9-10.

20. See the brief report in *Service Orthodoxe de Presse* 301 (September-October 2005): 23-24.

tember 18 to 25, 2006, hosted by the Serbian Orthodox Church.[21] This meeting was a crucial turning point in the dialogue's history.

First, the representation of the Orthodox churches was almost complete, demonstrating the effectiveness of the Ecumenical Patriarchate's efforts to increase participation. At Emmitsburg, the Orthodox churches of Jerusalem, Serbia, Bulgaria, Georgia, and the Czech and Slovak Republics were not represented, and the churches of Alexandria, Antioch, Russia, Cyprus, Poland, and Finland each sent one representative instead of the allotted two. At the previous meeting in Balamand in 1993, the Orthodox churches of Jerusalem, Serbia, Bulgaria, Georgia, Greece, and Czech and Slovak Republics were not present, and the churches of Poland, Albania, and Finland sent only one representative. As a result, Orthodox representation was severely compromised.

By contrast, at Belgrade all of the autocephalous and autonomous churches were represented by two members each, except for the churches of Antioch and Finland, which sent one representative, and the Bulgarian Orthodox delegation, which was not present due to illness. This much more ample representation of the Orthodox churches at Belgrade was a very positive sign.

Second, at Belgrade the dialogue was able to overcome the Emmitsburg impasse on the topic of uniatism, and return to the theological agenda that had been set out in the 1978 plan for the dialogue. The course of the dialogue since 1990 has revealed the wisdom of the original plan, and shown that the departure from the plan because of events in Eastern and Central Europe had led to a dead end. The status of the Eastern Catholic churches cannot be resolved without first dealing with the theological questions that lie at the heart of the division between Orthodox and Catholics: Does the fact of their full communion with other churches throughout the world place any limitations on the independence of local or national churches? If there must be such limitations, what are they? What kind of authority, if any, must be held by the local church that serves as the center of the universal communion in order for that church to fulfill its role? It is questions such as these that must be answered before the problem of uniatism can be resolved.

21. "Joint International Commission for the Theological Dialogue between the Roman Catholic Church and the Orthodox Church: Belgrade, Serbia, 18-25 September 2006," *IS* 122 (2006/II): 69-71.

Thus the mere fact that the international commission was able, at long last, to consider the text originally prepared sixteen years earlier for the 1990 Freising meeting was an enormous step forward. It was finally able to begin to tackle the underlying theological questions that made agreement on the issue of uniatism impossible.

Unfortunately, there was not enough time to finish work on the document in Belgrade. And there were some ominous signs in the public statements of Bishop Hilarion Alfeyev, one of the Russian Orthodox delegates, after the meeting. He expressed serious reservations about the draft text's treatment of the role of the Ecumenical Patriarchate among the Orthodox churches and the methodology of the dialogue.[22] Those comments foreshadowed a clash among the Orthodox that took place at the Tenth Plenary meeting, which was held in Ravenna, Italy, from October 8 to 14, 2007.

Breakthrough in Ravenna

Orthodox representation at Ravenna was still strong: the Bulgarians were not in attendance again, and also the Russians, whose absence will be examined below. The great accomplishment at Ravenna was that the dialogue was able to finish work on the draft that had been prepared for Freising in 1990. The document was finalized on October 13 and released to the public on November 15, 2007.

The full title of the Ravenna document is "Ecclesiological and Canonical Consequences of the Sacramental Nature of the Church: Ecclesial Communion, Conciliarity and Authority."[23] Its main purpose is to reflect on how the institutional aspects of the church visibly express and serve the mystery of *koinonia*. It takes as its starting point the relationship between the one Father and the other two hypostases within the Holy Trinity. And so it looks at the relationship of the one and the many at all levels of the church: local, regional, and universal. In each case, it is

22. "Bishop Hilarion Voices His Protest to Cardinal Kasper against Procedure at the Orthodox-Catholic Dialogue," *Europaica* 106 (October 4, 2006).

23. *Origins* 37, no. 24 (November 22, 2007): 382-87. For a Catholic evaluation of the Ravenna document, see Paul McPartlan, "The Ravenna Agreed Statement and Catholic-Orthodox Dialogue," *The Jurist* 69 (2009): 749-65. For an Orthodox perspective, see Kallistos Ware, "The Ravenna Document and the Future of Orthodox-Catholic Dialogue, *The Jurist* 69 (2009): 766-89.

a matter of the one primate and the authority he must have in order to ensure unity among the many. This was a challenge both to Catholics, who have tended to downplay the importance of the regional level, and to the Orthodox, who have downplayed the universal level.

Perhaps the most significant section of the document is where it treats the relationship between the one and the many at the universal level. Their conclusions regarding the primacy of Rome is found in these two paragraphs:

> 43. Primacy and conciliarity are mutually interdependent. That is why primacy at the different levels of the life of the Church, local, regional and universal, must always be considered in the context of conciliarity, and conciliarity likewise in the context of primacy. Concerning primacy at the different levels, we wish to affirm the following points: 1. Primacy at all levels is a practice firmly grounded in the canonical tradition of the Church. 2. While the fact of primacy at the universal level is accepted by both East and West, there are differences of understanding with regard to the manner in which it is to be exercised, and also with regard to its scriptural and theological foundations.

> 44. In the history of the East and of the West, at least until the ninth century, a series of prerogatives was recognized, always in the context of conciliarity, according to the conditions of the times, for the protos or kephale at each of the established ecclesiastical levels: locally, for the bishop as protos of his diocese with regard to his presbyters and people; regionally, for the protos of each metropolis with regard to the bishops of his province, and for the protos of each of the five patriarchates, with regard to the metropolitans of each circumscription; and universally, for the bishop of Rome as protos among the patriarchs. This distinction of levels does not diminish the sacramental equality of every bishop or the catholicity of each local Church.

These conclusions caused quite a stir in some Orthodox circles, and the Romanian Orthodox Church, for example, even issued clarification on its website to insist that the Orthodox had not accepted the Roman primacy at Ravenna.[24] Important as it was, however, the status of the

24. "Explanations of the Romanian Orthodox Church Concerning the Papal Primacy," *Religious Life* (Bucharest) 722 (November 22, 2007).

Ravenna document among the Orthodox was compromised by the decision of the Russian Orthodox delegation to walk out of the meeting as soon as it began, and the Moscow Patriarchate's subsequent criticism of the text.

The problem at Ravenna was that for the first time, the Ecumenical Patriarchate of Constantinople invited the autonomous Orthodox Church of Estonia to send a delegation to the dialogue. In order to understand why this was a problem, it is necessary to look back briefly at the history of Orthodoxy in Estonia during the last century. The predominantly Protestant Estonians came under Russian rule in the eighteenth century. Soon an Orthodox community developed there, under the auspices of the Russian Orthodox Church. Since the Russian Orthodox Church in Russia was being persecuted by the Bolsheviks, after Estonia received its independence in 1918 the Orthodox Archbishop of Estonia asked the Patriarchate of Constantinople to receive his church into its jurisdiction as an autonomous church. This was accomplished by means of a Patriarchal and Synodical Tomos of the Ecumenical Patriarchate in 1923.

This arrangement continued until 1940 when the Soviet Union annexed Estonia and incorporated the Orthodox in that country back into the Russian Orthodox Church. The leadership of the autonomous church went into exile. Fifty years later, when Estonia regained its independence in 1991, there was a segment of the Orthodox in the country that wanted to return to the interwar relationship with Constantinople. There were extended but fruitless negotiations between Constantinople and Moscow. Then in 1996 Constantinople unilaterally reestablished its church in Estonia by "reactivating" the 1923 Tomos against Moscow's wishes.

In response, Moscow broke relations with Constantinople and removed the Ecumenical Patriarch from the diptychs, which is tantamount to schism in the Orthodox world. A few months later, however, the two sides reached an agreement that provided for a double jurisdiction in Estonia: a Russian Orthodox diocese alongside the autonomous church linked to Constantinople. (The Russian jurisdiction is by far the larger with about 150,000 faithful; the autonomous church has about 18,000.)

This was only a temporary solution of the problem, since the Moscow Patriarchate still does not recognize the legitimacy of the Estonian autonomous church. Moreover, a decision had been made by the Russian Orthodox bishops in 2000 not to participate in meetings or conferences where delegates from the autonomous Estonian Church were present. This is why, when the Russian delegation learned that the Estonians were in Ravenna, they strongly protested. When Constantinople refused to cancel the invitation they had extended to the Estonians, the Russians walked out.[25]

After the Ravenna meeting, there was an exchange of heated recriminations between Moscow and Constantinople. Fortunately this internal Orthodox dispute was resolved in October 2008 when, at a meeting of the Primates of the Orthodox Churches at the Ecumenical Patriarchate, it was decided to limit Orthodox participation in the dialogue with the Catholic Church to the fourteen autocephalous Orthodox churches. This meant that the autonomous Estonian Church would not be represented at future meetings, and also the exclusion of the autonomous Orthodox Church of Finland, which had participated in the dialogue since the beginning.

In the meantime, the coordinating committee of the international dialogue met on the island of Crete in the fall of 2008. It produced a draft text on the next theme for study that had been determined at the Ravenna meeting: "The Role of the Bishop of Rome in the Koinonia/Communion of the Church in the First Millennium." This draft was considered at the plenary session that took place in Paphos, Cyprus, in October 2009. All the autocephalous Orthodox churches were represented at the Cyprus plenary except the Bulgarian Orthodox Church. The commission was not able to finish work on the text, and scheduled a further plenary session in Vienna, Austria, in September 2010.[26]

The North American Dialogue

Alongside the international dialogue, the work of the North American Orthodox–Catholic Theological Consultation should also be noted.[27]

---

25. "Bishop Hilarion Alfeyev: 'An Inter-Orthodox Problem,'" *Europaica* 130 (October 21, 2007). Metropolitan John [Zizioulas] of Pergamon explained Constantinople's position in "Progress in Dialogue with Catholics, Says Ecumenical Patriarchate," *Asia News,* October 19, 2007.

26. E. Fortino, "Per cattolici e ortodossi l'appuntamento è a Vienna," *L'Osservatore Romano,* January 18, 2010, p. 7.

27. In 1997 the Canadian Conference of Catholic Bishops officially joined the dia-

No other national or regional Catholic-Orthodox dialogue in the world today is as vital as this one. This is due in part to the fact that Catholics and Orthodox live together side by side in North America largely free of the ethnic tensions that complicate relations in Europe, and intermarriage is frequent. Also, since both groups are minorities in America, neither side feels threatened by the influence of the other in secular society.

The original initiative to begin a national dialogue came from the Orthodox side. After a positive Catholic response, the first meeting took place in Worcester, Massachusetts, on September 9, 1965. The dialogue made a number of groundbreaking statements in the early years, and from 1980 to 1990 it assumed a kind of "symphonia" with the international group, offering reflections on upcoming topics and critiques of documents produced.[28]

During the years when the international dialogue was not meeting because of the impasse over uniatism, the North American group refocused its efforts, and issued four important common texts on key topics in Orthodox-Catholic relations. It made a strong appeal in 1998 in support of a proposal to adopt a common date for Easter. It issued a courageous statement on baptism in 1999 that argued that Catholics and Orthodox should formally recognize the validity of each other's baptism. In 2000 it issued a statement called "The Ministry of Reconciliation" that affirmed the importance of the ecumenical movement and specifically the dialogue between our Catholic and Orthodox churches. And in 2003 it finalized an agreed statement titled "The Filioque: A Church-Dividing Issue?" in which it reviewed the history of this long-divisive question and recommended that all the churches return to the original form of the Creed, without the *filioque*. Since that time the North American dialogue has been studying the question of conciliarity and primacies in the church, and hopes soon to release an agreed statement on what a future reconciled Catholic and Orthodox Church might look like, including the way in which the ministry of the bishop of Rome might be exercised in relation to the Eastern churches.

---

logue; at that time the name was changed from the "United States" to the "North American" Theological Consultation.

28. For an overview of the work of the U.S. dialogue during these years, see R. Roberson, "The Dialogue between the Catholic Church and the Orthodox Church in the United States," *One in Christ* 27 (1991): 166-84.

In addition to the theological consultation, a Joint Committee of Orthodox and Catholic Bishops has met annually since 1981. More pastoral in its orientation, the Joint Committee has issued statements on ordination, mixed marriages, the situation in Eastern Europe, and an overall assessment of the Catholic-Orthodox relationship. Composed of seven bishops on each side, the Committee provides not only for an exchange of information but also the building up of personal working relationships that have been beneficial for all involved.[29]

Conclusion

The international dialogue between the Catholic and Orthodox churches was established by Patriarch Dimitrios I and Pope John Paul II in 1979 with a great sense of hope that the obstacles preventing the reestablishment of full communion could be overcome. This was now possible, they said in their Joint Declaration,[30] because the dialogue of charity had "opened up the way to better understanding of our mutual theological positions and, thereby, to new approaches to the theological work and to a new attitude with regard to the common past of our churches. This purification of the collective memory of our churches is an important fruit of the dialogue of charity and an indispensable condition of future progress." The crisis in relations between the two churches that resulted from the end of communism in Europe revived many unpleasant collective memories, and required a revitalization of the dialogue of love in order to begin to purify them as well. In fact, I think it's safe to say that Catholic-Orthodox relations have finally started to improve after the long impasse following the end of European communism in 1989.

All of this illustrates once again how extremely important it is to keep talking to one another, especially at times when new tensions arise. As Pope John Paul II recalled in his 1995 encyclical *Ut unum sint,* "It is necessary to pass from antagonism and conflict to a situation where each party recognizes the other as a partner. When undertaking

29. All the agreed statements produced by the North American dialogue and the Joint Committee of Orthodox and Catholic Bishops, as well as press releases issued about specific meetings, are posted on the website of the United States Conference of Catholic Bishops at http://www.usccb.org/seia/orthodox_index.shtml.

30. *IS* 41 (1979/IV): 25-26.

dialogue, each side must presuppose in the other a desire for reconciliation, for unity in truth. For this to happen, any display of mutual opposition must disappear. Only thus will dialogue help to overcome division and lead us closer to unity" (no. 29). I think this is precisely what has been happening between Catholics and Orthodox in the last couple of years.

But it is precisely full communion that remains the Holy Grail of the Orthodox-Catholic dialogue. No one knows when that day will come, but there is reason to think that there is some light on the horizon, and we must remain hopeful that the Lord's will for us will be realized. As Pope Benedict XVI and Patriarch Bartholomew put it so well in their Common Declaration in November 2006, "The Holy Spirit will help us to prepare the great day of the re-establishment of full unity, whenever and however God wills it. Then we shall truly be able to rejoice and be glad."

16 Two Phases of Baptist–Roman Catholic International Theological Conversations

Susan K. Wood, SCL

1. The Conversation Partners

The Baptist and Catholic conversation partners differ in scale, polity, ecumenical goals, and doctrinal and ecclesial commitments. Nevertheless, conversations between the two communities have borne significant fruit since the initial conversations in 1984.

The Baptist World Alliance (BWA), formed in 1905, is a worldwide fellowship of Baptist believers comprising 188 member bodies, called conventions or unions, counting 37 million baptized believers.[1] The Catholic Church has approximately 1.14 billion members in the world, approximately 17 percent of the total population, making it the largest Christian community and the second largest religion after Islam.[2]

Denton Lotz,[3] former Secretary General of the Baptist World Alliance, comments that while Baptists are eager to cooperate with other Christians in mission and evangelism, Baptists' congregational polity makes them wary of structural integration. Recent emphases on "mis-

---

1. Baptist World Alliance, http://bwanet.org/bwa.php?site=Resources&id=19, accessed May 26, 2010.

2. Matthew Bunson, "Where Are Today's Catholics?" *Our Sunday Visitor Newsweekly,* December 13, 2009, http://www.osv.com/tabid/7621/itemid/5709/In-FocusWhere -in-the-world-are-todays-Catholics.aspx, accessed March 6, 2011.

3. Denton Lotz (b. 1939) was General Secretary of the Baptist World Alliance 1988-2007.

sion and doctrine" sound divisive to Baptists, with the result that they are hesitant to join calls for structural unity or doctrinal unity.[4]

On the other hand, Catholics seek unity in faith as a priority. They identify visible unity as the ecumenical goal and consider the bond of initial unity established in baptism to be oriented towards "a complete profession of faith, a complete incorporation into the system of salvation as Christ himself willed it to be, and finally, complete integration into eucharistic communion.[5]

Baptist commitments include religious freedom for all, separation of church and state, open communion, and emphasis on the local congregation of believers. While Vatican II reemphasized the local church, Catholics have a strong sense of the church universal.

Denton cites Morgan Patterson's summary of the "Baptist way": (1) the essence of the Christian faith is spiritual, personal, and voluntary; (2) the scriptures are uniquely inspired and authoritative; (3) the church is composed of committed believers; (4) salvation is provided by the grace of God and is available to everyone through repentance and faith; (5) all believers are priests, with no intermediary other than Christ himself; (6) the scriptures command the observance of two ordinances, baptism and the Lord's Supper, which are understood to be basically symbolic in meaning; (7) baptism is properly performed by the biblical mode of immersion; (8) the authority for the administration of the church is in the hands of the congregation; (9) religious freedom should be given to all to enable each person to respond to the leadership of the Holy Spirit; (10) the separation of church and state best guarantees liberty of conscience for every citizen.[6]

One may get an idea of some of the differences between the two traditions by comparing the Catholic positions to this enumeration of "the Baptist way." Catholics (1) give priority to the community of faith, which precedes the faith of an individual believer; (2) agree with Baptists on the inspiration and authority of scripture, but say that an authentic interpretation of the word of God has been "entrusted to the living teaching office of the church alone";[7] (3) consider the church to be composed of all the baptized, some of whom are infants and chil-

4. Denton Lotz, "Baptists," *DEM2*, p. 99.

5. *Unitatis redintegratio*, 22.

6. Lotz, "Baptists," *DEM2*, pp. 98-99.

7. Vatican II, *Dei Verbum: Dogmatic Constitution on Divine Revelation*, November 18, 1965 [= *DV*], no. 10.

dren; (4) agree with Baptists that the gift of salvation is offered to everyone and that it must be received in faith, although there would be differences in terms of how explicit that faith needs to be, for Catholics hold to the possibility of salvation for non-Christians;[8] (5) agree that all the baptized belong to the common priesthood, but hold that the ministerial priesthood differs from the priesthood of the baptized "essentially and not only in degree";[9] (6) have a sacramental system of seven sacraments in which the two foundational sacraments are baptism and the eucharist; sacraments are believed to be both signs and effective means of the grace they signify; (7) agree that baptism "is performed in the most expressive way by triple immersion in the baptismal water," but also accept the practice of pouring the water over the candidate's head;[10] (8) hold that the authority for the governance of the church is in the hands of the magisterium, that is, the bishops in union with the bishop of Rome; (9) understand that the human person has a right to religious freedom, meaning that "everyone should be immune from coercion by individuals, social groups and every human power so that, within due limits, no men or women are forced to act against their conviction nor are any persons to be restrained from acting in accordance with their convictions in religious matters in private or in public, alone or in association with others."[11] Nevertheless, they hold that "while the religious freedom ... has to do with freedom from coercion in civil society, it leaves intact the traditional catholic teaching on the moral obligation of individuals and societies towards the true religion and the one church of Christ."[12]

2. History of the Conversations

The Commission on Baptist Doctrine and Interchurch Cooperation of the Baptist World Alliance and the Vatican Secretariat for Promoting Christian Unity sponsored the first international conversations between our two bodies from 1984 to 1988. The Pontifical Council for Pro-

8. *LG,* no. 16; *Nostra Aetate.*

9. *LG,* no. 10.

10. *Catechism,* no. 1239.

11. Vatican II, *Dignitatis Humanae: Declaration on Religious Liberty,* December 7, 1965 [= *DH*], no. 2.

12. *DH,* no. 1.

moting Christian Unity (PCPCU) wished to proceed immediately to a second phase of formal dialogue, but that was not then feasible for the Baptist World Alliance. The North American Mission Board of the Southern Baptist Convention had announced in 2001 the end of its formal conversations with the U.S. Catholic community. The Southern Baptist Convention then ended its membership in the BWA in 2004.

In the absence of formal dialogue, a series of informal two-day consultations between representatives of the BWA and the PCPCU were held: in 2000 (Rome), 2001 (Buenos Aires, representing the Latin American region), 2003 (Rome, representing the European region), and 2004 (Washington, D.C., representing the North American region). Sixteen years after the conclusion of the first phase of dialogue, the PCPCU and the BWA agreed to organize a second phase of international conversations, which began in 2006 and concluded in December 2010.

According to BWA spokesman Eron Henry, BWA talks with Roman Catholics and other Christian groups aim to fulfill the mission goals of uniting Baptists worldwide, to lead in world evangelism, to respond to people in need, to engage in the defense of human rights and religious freedom, and to promote theological reflection.[13] However, they especially are seen as aiding in the promotion of human rights and religious freedom where Baptists are a minority and experience discrimination.

3. First Phase of International Conversations (1984-88)

The final report on the first round of international conversations, "Summons to Witness to Christ in Today's World," identified these goals for the conversations: to come to a mutual understanding of certain convergences and divergences between the Baptist and Roman Catholic world confessional families, to establish relations and maintain a channel of communication through conversation for mutual as well as self-understanding, to identify new possibilities as well as to clarify existing difficulties in regard to a common witness in view of the current world situation and the mandate of Christ to proclaim the gospel, and to address existing prejudices between our two world con-

---

13. Mark Kelly, "BWA-Catholic Dialogue Reaches Midpoint," http://www.bpnews .net/bpnews.asp?id=27333, accessed May 25, 2010.

fessional families.[14] The challenge of ecumenical conversation between these two bodies is perhaps most evident by what is missing in these stated goals. No mention is made of growth towards full visible unity or full communion. As John A. Radano's report observes, "there is no clear sense in which unity is a goal."[15]

The topics discussed in this first round included "Evangelism/ Evangelization: The Mission of the Church," "Conversion/Disciple-ship, Aspects of Witness to Christ," "The Church as *Koinonia* of the Spirit," and specific issues standing in the way of improving common Christian witness, namely proselytism and restrictions on religious freedom.

Areas of agreement between Baptists and Catholics include "God's saving revelation in Jesus Christ, the necessity of personal commitment to God in Christ, the ongoing work of the Holy Spirit and the missionary imperative that emerges from God's redemptive activity on behalf of humankind."[16] Baptists and Catholics share a common faith in Jesus Christ as the revelation of God whom we come to know in the scriptures.[17] Both traditions affirm the inseparability of the person and work of Christ, whom God raised up and in whose name we are saved.[18] Baptists and Catholics were able to conclude in that conversation:

> Discussion of our witness to Christ has revealed that our two communions are one in their confession of Jesus Christ as Son of God, Lord and Savior. The faith in Christ proclaimed in the New Testament and expressed in the first four ecumenical councils is shared by both of our churches. Our discussion uncovered no significant differences with regard to the doctrine of the person and work of Christ, although some did appear with regard to the appropriation of Christ's saving work. We believe that this communion of faith in

14. Baptist–Roman Catholic Dialogue, "Summons to Witness to Christ in Today's World: A Report on Conversations 1984-1988," Atlanta, July 23, 1988, in *GA II*, p. 373.

15. Pontifical Council for the Promotion of Christian Unity, "Report by Mons. John A. Radano: Catholic Baptist Relations," http://www.vatican.va/roman_curia// pontifical_councils/chrstuni/eccl-comm-docs/rc_pc_chrstuni_doc_20070123_cattolici -battisti_en.html, accessed May 24, 2010.

16. "Summons to Witness," no. 2.

17. "Summons to Witness," no. 5.

18. "Summons to Witness," no. 6.

Christ should be stressed and rejoiced in as a basis for our discussions of other areas of church doctrine and life, where serious differences may remain.[19]

"*Koinonia* of the Spirit" was found to be a helpful description of a common understanding of the church.[20] Discussion of the various biblical passages related to *koinonia* led the delegations to conclude: "(1) that in and through Christ God has laid down the foundation of the church, (2) that *koinonia* both between God and human beings and within the church is a divine gift, and (3) that the Spirit effects the continuity between the church and Jesus."[21]

The conversations identified a number of major differences between Baptists and Catholics with regard to these themes. Catholics affirm that sacred scripture and sacred tradition "flow from the same divine wellspring" with the result that "the church does not draw her certainty about all revealed truth from the holy scriptures alone."[22] Thus for Catholics the ecumenical creeds are normative both for the individual believer and for subsequent church life, while for Baptists scriptures alone are normative, even though the Christological faith expressed by the first four ecumenical councils is shared by both traditions.

Conversion and discipleship are expressed differently by the two ecclesial communions. Baptists emphasize the initial experience of personal conversion wherein "the believer accepts the gift of God's saving and assuring grace." Thus it is primarily an act of personal faith and acceptance of Jesus as Lord and Savior. Subsequent baptism, entry into the church, and a life of faithful discipleship are testimony to that prior gift.[23] For Catholics, too, baptism is consequent upon faith, although in the case of infants, the community professes faith on behalf of the child. For Catholics baptism is the sacrament of rebirth by which a person is incorporated into Christ. They speak of the need for a life of continual conversion. Both Baptists and Catholics, however, stress the need for unbelievers and the unchurched to hear and live the message of salvation expressed in the scriptures.[24]

---

19. "Summons to Witness," no. 11.
20. "Summons to Witness," no. 19.
21. "Summons to Witness," no. 20.
22. *DV,* no. 9.
23. "Summons to Witness," no. 18.
24. "Summons to Witness," no. 55.

Baptists and Catholics understand the church in different ways. For Baptists, the church refers primarily "to the local congregation gathered by the Spirit in obedience and service to God's word."[25] Baptists have sought "to avoid development of structures which would threaten the freedom of individuals and the autonomy of local congregations."[26] Catholics view the church as a community of faith, hope, and charity established by Christ. The church, a complex reality analogously compared to the mystery of Christ, is comprised of both a human element with hierarchical organs and a divine element such that the church can be called the mystical body of Christ.[27] For Catholics the *koinonia* experienced in the local congregation "is simultaneously a *koinonia* with the other local congregations in the one universal church."[28] They discern the Spirit's activity in the institutional bonds of hierarchical ministry that unite congregations within dioceses presided over by bishops and in the unity of dioceses within the whole church presided over by the bishop of Rome.

Baptists and Roman Catholics have historically differed over the relation of the church to civil authority and on the question of religious liberty, although the Second Vatican Council's Declaration on Religious Liberty affirms the human person's right to religious freedom and states that "no one is to be forced to act in a manner contrary to his or her own beliefs."[29]

Finally, Baptists and Catholics differ regarding the possibility of salvation within non-Christian religions. While affirming that all salvation is through Christ, Catholics affirm the possibility of salvation for non-Christians who "seek God with a sincere heart, and, moved by grace, try in their actions to do his will as they know it through the dictates of their conscience."[30] Baptists, while not having issued any major statement on salvation for non-Christians, frequently interpret such texts as Acts 4:12 and John 14:6 in the narrow sense.

Challenges to common witness include a contemporary negative understanding of "proselytism," understood as the use of "methods that compromise rather than enhance the freedom of the believer and

---

25. "Summons to Witness," no. 23.
26. "Summons to Witness," no. 48.
27. *LG,* no. 8.
28. "Summons to Witness," no. 48.
29. *DH,* no. 2.
30. *LG,* no. 16.

of the gospel."[31] Today the term is used to refer to the "attempts of various Christian confessions to win members from each other."[32] Baptists and Catholics were able to agree both on what should characterize Christian witness and on those negative aspects to be avoided. Positively, witness reflects the spirit of love and humility and respects the full freedom of individuals to make personal decisions while permitting individuals and communities to bear witness to their own religious convictions. The negative aspects of witness, including every form of coercion, pressure, enticement, or unfavorable comparisons of the two communions should be avoided.

Areas identified as needing continued exploration include the different views and uses of theological authority and method; the different ways in which the *koinonia* of the Spirit is made concrete in the church; the relationship between faith, baptism, and Christian witness; the nature of faith; and the nature of the sacraments, called "ordinances" by most Baptists. Finally, devotion to Mary emerged as a challenge to common witness because for Baptists it seems to compromise the sole mediatorship of Jesus and because the Marian doctrines such as the immaculate conception and the assumption seem to have little explicit grounding in the Bible.[33]

4. Second Phase of International Conversations (2006-2010)[34]

While there were some reservations by some Baptist conventions in South America during the 1980s about engaging in conversation with Roman Catholics because of what they judged to be a hostile environment for Baptist witness to the gospel, by July 2006 Dr. Denton Lotz, General Secretary of the Baptist World Alliance, was able to report that these conventions would approve renewed conversations with Catholics.[35] A number of informal regional conversations addressed the is-

31. "Summons to Witness," no. 31.

32. "Summons to Witness," no. 33.

33. "Summons to Witness," no. 56.

34. Reflections that follow represent the main areas of discussion during this second phase, which has now been completed. The fullest picture of its results will be found in its official report when that is published in the near future.

35. Minutes of the Decision Meeting, BWA General Council/Annual Gathering, Mexico City, July 7, 2006 as printed in *Baptist World Alliance Annual Gathering, Accra, Ghana, July 2-7, 2007* (Falls Church, VA: Baptist World Alliance, 1977), p. 52.

sues in a provisional way. For instance, in December 2003 a meeting in Vatican City discussed papers on the "Joint Declaration on the Doctrine of Justification" on the part of Catholics, Lutherans, and Methodists in addition to papers on the Petrine ministry, responding to John Paul II's encyclical, *Ut unum sint.* The Baptists at this meeting said that Petrine ministry would need to be discussed in future conversations within the wider topic of "oversight in the church." In 2004 in Washington, D.C., papers were presented on the themes of baptism and the Blessed Virgin Mary. A paper by Timothy George argued that evangelicals should give the same honor to Mary that she receives in scripture and the early church.[36] Susan Wood's paper on baptism noted the normativity of adult baptism for the Catholic understanding of that sacrament because of the faith and conversion of life it presupposes. She cited the Decree on Ecumenism of the Second Vatican Council, that "Baptism is oriented toward complete profession of faith."[37]

The steering committee preparing for the second phase of conversations thought that a relationship of "a shared life of discipleship" might be approached by tackling the issues identified as needing continued exploration under the overarching theme of "The Word of God in the Life of the Church: Scripture, Tradition and *Koinonia.*" The aim was neither organic unity nor a united church structure, but the goal of becoming more clearly one as prayed by Jesus in John 17:23. The goals for the second phase of conversations express a clearer commitment to unity in biblical terms, although they still do not speak of "visible unity" or "full communion." The goals of the second phase were to increase mutual understanding, appreciation, and Christian charity towards one another, to foster a shared life of discipleship within the communion of the triune God, to develop and extend a common witness to Jesus Christ, and to encourage further action together on ethical issues, including justice, peace, and the sanctity of life.

Where the first phase focused on the theme of witness relating to mission, the second phase tackled some of the thorny doctrinal issues identified as areas of divergence in the first phase. The conversations

36. Timothy George, "The Blessed Virgin Mary in Evangelical Perspective," in Denton Lotz, ed., *Papers Delivered at Meeting of North American Baptist Theologians and the Pontifical Council for Promoting Christian Unity,* Washington, DC, December 10-11, 2004 (n.p.).

37. Susan Wood, "Baptism and the Church," in Lotz, ed., *Papers,* 48-49.

identified both significant agreements between Baptists and Catholics and remaining differences. Too often differing traditions focus on their differences while they overlook real commonalities that require no compromise of deep-seated convictions because they are grounded in a shared scriptural heritage and belief in Christ. The agreements reached on the interpretation of scripture and tradition, on Mary, on the meaning of baptism, and on the origin and purpose of the church all relate to a common confession of Christ as Lord and Savior and the narrative of that salvation in the Bible.

The Authority of Christ in Scripture and Tradition

In the first meeting of the second phase of conversations Baptists and Catholics were able to identify a striking convergence on the nature of scripture as the inspired Word of God and its central place in the life of the church. Baptist participants positively assessed the value of tradition and its relation to scripture, and Catholic participants manifested a critical approach to tradition in its relation to scripture. This was possible by understanding both the written scriptures and tradition as witnesses that stand under the Word of God, which assumes various forms in the world through preaching, the canonical scriptures, baptism and the eucharist, the events of God's action in history, and in the witness of faithful believers.

Baptists and Catholics accept the canonical books of the Bible as humanly written under the inspiration of the Holy Spirit and given to the church by God. Both traditions affirm the need for an ecclesial reading of Sacred Scripture requiring a christocentric interpretation of both the Old and New Testament. For both, scripture possesses authority for faith and practice. Both Baptists and Catholics affirmed a "Chalcedonian hermeneutic," acknowledging both the divine and human authorship of the scriptures.

The Relation of Scripture and Tradition

Catholics discerned in the Baptist participants an appreciation of the value of tradition in the church's efforts to embody the teachings of the scriptures in the contemporary world. Baptists saw in the Catholic participants a willingness to listen to various voices in the church including not only those of Pope and bishops, but also those of theologians and the laity, to discern what is truly authoritative in the tradition. While sensibilities regarding the relationship between scripture and tradition still differ, this movement on the part of each made it possible for both to articulate common understandings on a number of points.

First, both traditions realized that the Bible itself is the written embodiment of a living tradition and that both the Bible and tradition issue from the self-revelation of the triune God in Christ. Catholics and Baptists were able to distinguish apostolic tradition, transmitted by the apostles, from ecclesiastical traditions. Only the former is normative in the formation of the canonical scriptures and the life of the church. Both agree that tradition must always stand under the correction of scripture. Both agree that public revelation ends with the death of the last apostle, although both affirm that God continues to speak to his people today in the acts of reading the scriptures and proclamation of the gospel.

In spite of these significant common affirmations, differences remain. Catholics have been wary of the dangers of a private interpretation of scripture. They reserve the authoritative interpretation of the scriptures to the teaching office of the church exercised by the bishops in communion with the bishop of Rome. Baptists, on the other hand, maintain that a local congregation of believers has the responsibility and freedom to interpret the Bible under the rule of Christ and the guidance of the Holy Spirit. Catholics consider tradition to be the dynamic transmission of revelation in words and deeds. Baptists associate some of this same dynamism with the activity of preaching.

Sacraments/Ordinances

The second meeting addressed the subjects of sacraments/ordinances and Baptism and the Lord's Supper/eucharist as visible Words of God in the *koinonia* of the church. The delegations addressed the notions of sacrament and ordinance in their respective traditions. The first difficulty the delegates faced was one of terminology. Catholics and some Baptists share the language of sacrament for baptism and the eucharist/Lord's Supper. Although some Baptists are recovering an earlier

Baptist sacramentalism, most (but not all) Baptists continue to speak of these acts of worship as "ordinances." Regardless of the language used, however, both agree that sacraments/ordinances are signs through which God acts, and thus are visible signs of invisible grace. Baptists and Catholics agree that sacraments/ordinances originate from and are ordained by Christ and that they function as tangible and visible words of God. Since Baptists affirm that Christ promises to meet his disciples in baptism and the Lord's Supper, they do not regard ordinances as merely empty symbols even though they may disagree among themselves regarding the manner of Christ's presence. Both Catholics and Baptists acknowledge the sovereign freedom of God with respect to sacraments/ordinances and the necessity of freedom and faith for their graced reception.

Baptist language also differs from that of Catholics regarding the relationship between the sacrament and grace. Where the *Catechism of the Catholic Church* says that "[b]y the action of Christ and the power of the Holy Spirit they [sacraments] make present efficaciously the grace that they signify,"[38] Baptists would prefer to say, "By the power of the Holy Spirit Christ offers the grace that the sacraments signify."

Different understandings of how sacraments confer grace have traditionally divided Baptists and Catholics. Baptists regard Catholic teaching on sacramental efficacy *ex opere operato* (meaning "by the work worked" or "by the very fact of the action's being performed") as infringing on the freedom of God and as asserting that sacraments confer grace in and of themselves. Catholics, however, do not regard this as an automatic account of sacramental efficacy, but as an account that protects the objectivity and primacy of God's own action in the sacraments with respect to the minister's actions. The reception of sacramental grace also depends on the disposition (*ex opere operantis,* "from the work of the person working") of the person receiving it. This personal response, however, does not give objective validity to the sacraments. While Baptists continue to be uncomfortable with the Catholic teaching on *ex opere operato* and also with the idea that sacraments themselves "confer grace," a fuller understanding of Catholic teaching on these matters corrected past misunderstandings.

---

38. *Catechism,* no. 1084.

Susan K. Wood, SCL

Baptism

In spite of their divisions regarding the Catholic practice of infant baptism, Baptists and Catholics share much in their respective doctrines of baptism. Both traditions teach its trinitarian and Christological foundations. Both baptize in response to Christ's command in Matthew 28:19-20. Both believe that in baptism we share in the life, death, and resurrection of Christ, that we are made adoptive daughters and sons of the Father, members of the body of Christ, and temples of the Holy Spirit. Both affirm that we enter into the common priesthood of all believers and share in the mission of God through the power of the Spirit. Both agree that baptism, rightly understood, is to be received only once, although most Baptists do not regard infant baptism to be truly baptism. Both agree that in baptism we are baptized into one body (1 Cor. 12:13) and are thereby united with other Christians, although Baptists differ among themselves on the relationship between baptism and church membership.

In spite of these agreements, significant differences continue to divide Baptists and Catholics, and differences exist among Baptists. Some Baptists hold that baptism is only a sign of a salvation that has already happened, identifying "baptism in the Spirit" with that earlier moment of regeneration. For them Spirit-baptism always precedes water-baptism. Other Baptists place baptism within a whole process of being transformed by the grace of God and so can identify baptism in water as a baptism in the Spirit that deepens the reception of the Spirit given at the moment of conversion. Similar qualifications apply to the relationship between baptism and forgiveness of sin and new birth. While all Baptists agree that the images of baptism are expressive of new birth, there is disagreement about the extent to which baptism actually effects new birth.

While both Catholics and Baptists affirm the necessity of faith for baptism, Baptists require that every baptism includes a personal confession of faith by those baptized. Baptists only baptize believing disciples at an age when those baptized are able to share in God's mission in the world. Catholics, on the other hand, baptize infants, allowing the community to profess faith for an infant if the parents have the intent to raise the child in the faith of the church. The infant must later receive Christian teaching and grow in faith with the assistance of the whole ecclesial community.

Baptists and Catholics agree that initiation into Christ and the church is a larger process than the act of baptism itself. Both speak of initiation as a "journey" inclusive of evangelization, conversion, profession of faith, water baptism in the name of Father, Son, and Spirit, reception of the gifts of the Spirit, Christian formation, a life of discipleship, and participation in God's mission in the world.[39] It is easier for Baptists and Catholics to reach agreement on the processes of initiation taken as a whole than it is for them to affirm a "common baptism." The notion of a "common baptism" encounters the impasse of the Baptist practice of only baptizing a believing disciple upon a personal and public profession of faith, and the Catholic practice of baptizing infants.

Eucharist/Lord's Supper

Both Baptists and Catholics celebrate the eucharist/Lord's Supper in obedient response to Jesus' command "Do this in memory of me." Both structure their respective services around Jesus' practice of taking bread, breaking it, blessing it, and giving it to his disciples. Both traditions pray in thanksgiving to the Father *(eucharistia),* remember the death and resurrection of the Son *(anamnesis),* and call upon the Holy Spirit to make real Christ's presence *(epiclesis),* although they may differ regarding in how strong a sense they understand this to occur. Catholics believe that the eucharist makes sacramentally present the once-for-all sacrifice of Christ which the church sacramentally offers with Christ. Baptists, however, prefer to speak of the eucharist as a "sacrifice of praise and thanksgiving." They distinguish between Christ's self-offering and their sharing in this self-offering. Rather than praying to the Holy Spirit to transform the gifts of bread and wine, they pray to the Holy Spirit for help in making an act of remembrance and in using the signs of bread and wine to bring them into closer fellowship with Christ and each other. Both traditions believe that Christ is present through the eucharist/Lord's Supper, al-

39. For Baptists, see *Dialogue between the Community of Protestant Churches in Europe (CPCE) and the European Baptist Federation (EBF) on the Doctrine and Practice of Baptism,* Leuenberg Documents 9 (Frankfurt am Main: Otto Lembeck, 2005), pp. 19-22; *Pushing at the Boundaries of Unity: Anglicans and Baptists in Conversation* (London: Church House Publishing, 2005), pp. 31-57. For Catholics see *Catechism,* no. 1229.

though they may differ as to the manner of this presence. For both Baptists and Catholics this celebration is both a sign and a cause of unity (1 Cor. 10:16f.), which enjoins on those present the responsibilities for fellowship and communion *(koinonia)*, worship of God *(leiturgia)*, and service to others *(diakonia)* until Christ comes and God's reign is complete.

Mary in the Communion of the Church

The third meeting was devoted to a study of Mary in the communion of the church, first examining Mary in the light of scripture and the early church and her role and titles as Virgin mother, handmaid of the Lord, *Theotokos*, the hearer of the Word, the daughter of Zion, and witness to the cross, resurrection, and Pentecost. Then Mary was studied in the light of ongoing tradition, in relation to Christology and ecclesiology, addressing the development of doctrine represented in the Catholic doctrines of the perpetual virginity of Mary and the papal definitions of the Immaculate Conception and the Assumption. Finally, Mary was discussed in relationship to contemporary issues of inculturation and spirituality. This included "local identities" of the Blessed Virgin Mary, the relation of culture to scripture and tradition, the distinction and confusion between intercessions and mediation and between devotion and worship, Marian issues in feminism, and the relationship between Mary and the sanctity of life.

Baptists and Catholics affirm the scriptural witness to Mary, mother of the Savior, although they disagree regarding how certain claims about Mary on the part of Catholics have the warrant of scripture, both in the accounts of Mary in the New Testament and in a typological reading of the Old Testament. Baptists do not find a scriptural basis for Catholic beliefs about her perpetual virginity, immaculate conception, and bodily assumption. Nor do Baptists pray to Mary invoking her intercession, since they fear that this could detract from the unique glory and intercession of Christ. Nevertheless, with Catholics they pray *with* Mary and affirm that, as a "hearer of the Word," she offers Christians a model of discipleship and is a representative figure of the church. Both Baptists and Catholics agree that the various inculturations of Marian devotion are subject to correction by the gospel. Mary is always first and foremost a witness to Christ.

The Ministry of Oversight

The fourth meeting addressed oversight and primacy in the ministry of the church. Themes included the notion of oversight in relation to scripture and tradition, local and universal *episkopē*, and the contemporary developments of the Petrine office, including the ministry of unity as outlined in Pope John Paul II's ecumenical encyclical *Ut unum sint*. Participants also heard papers presenting overviews of both Baptist and Catholic ecclesiology.

The Koinonia of the Church

An agreement on the communion of the church led to discussion of the relationship between the local church and the church universal. Both delegations were able to agree on the mutual existence and coinherence of the local and universal church, although an asymmetry exists between the two traditions. Catholics identify the local church as the "particular church" or diocese. For them the ministry of the bishop, who witnesses to the continuity of the church with its apostolic origins, is essential for the identity of the local church. Baptists define the local church as a congregation of believers, joined together through faith and baptism, where the Word of God is preached and the Lord's Supper is celebrated. They understand the office of ministry to be exercised by the minister(s) called by the members of a local congregation to serve among them. Both Catholics and Baptists consider their respective ministry of oversight to be apostolic since it continues the witness of the apostles and bears the responsibility of enabling the congregation or the particular church to stand in the apostolic tradition of faith.

For Baptists, Christ rules in the midst of the local congregation, which has the right to call its own ministry, to celebrate the sacraments, and to order its own life under Christ free from any external human or ecclesial authority. This freedom "under the rule of Christ," is not the same thing as autonomy, a concept Baptists did not use as a description of the local church until the end of the nineteenth century. Nor is it to be identified with the individualistic freedom of the Enlightenment.

Neither Catholics nor Baptists consider the universal church as an accumulation of local churches. For both, the local church, in communion with other local churches, embodies and manifests the church universal. The church is never a voluntary association of individual believers, but is constituted and gathered by Christ through the action of the Spirit.[40]

For both Catholics and Baptists, all ministry flows from the ministry and authority of Christ. Oversight *(episkopē)* in the church serves the good order of the whole church and enables it to share in the ministry of Christ as prophet, priest, and king. For Catholics this office is fulfilled in the ministry of a bishop who serves in apostolic succession.[41] Baptists, on the other hand, emphasize a form of communal oversight, although some early Baptist Confessions speak of a personal *episkopē* in the form of "offices" expressed in the two offices of pastor and deacon.[42] Baptists and Catholics agree that even though *episkopē* serves a particular local church, it also serves the church universal. Catholics emphasize the collegial character of the college of bishops, which they consider to be a successor to the "college" of the apostles.[43] For Catholics, the collegiality of bishops expresses visibly and personally the communion of particular churches within the church universal. The one church is both understood to be a communion of churches and is concretely realized in each local church.[44] That is, the particular church is the specific place where the church universal is manifested and encountered, although this universality is manifested only in the communion of the local church with the other particular churches.

Baptists and Catholics believe that *episkopē* serves the unity of the church and is exercised at local, regional, and worldwide levels by a variety of ministries.[45] Baptists stress the freedom of the local congrega-

40. *The Baptist Doctrine of the Church* (1948), in Roger Hayden, ed., *Baptist Union Documents 1948-1977* (London: Baptist Union of Great Britain) states: "Such churches are gathered by the will of Christ and live by the indwelling of his Spirit. They do not have their origin, primarily, in human resolution."

41. *LG,* no. 20.

42. The London Confession (1644), art. XLIV, in William L. Lumkin, ed., *Baptist Confessions of Faith,* rev. ed. (Philadelphia: Judson Press, 1959), 168.

43. *LG,* no. 19.

44. See *LG,* no. 23.

45. For a Baptist understanding of *episkopē* see the Report of the International Conversations between the worldwide Anglican Communion and the Baptist World Alliance, *Conversations around the World 2000-2005,* the Anglican Communion office, 2005,

tion under the rule of Christ, even while it remains connected to other congregations in a covenantal relationship, while Catholics tend to emphasize the unity of the church universal, while at the same time recognizing the diversity of local churches. In addition to promoting unity, *episkopē* bears responsibility for keeping the community in apostolic faith and for preserving and promoting true doctrine.

Despite what Baptists and Catholics can affirm in common, major differences exist between Baptists and Catholics regarding *episkopē*. For Catholics the ministry of the bishop is essential to the structure of the church. By "divine institution" bishops take the place of the apostles as pastors of the church.[46] Differences on *episkopē* at the worldwide level center on whether the individual ministry of the papacy is necessary in order to fulfill Christ's will for the unity of the whole church and how such a ministry might be exercised. While agreement on a universal ministry is not on the immediate horizon, intermediate steps might demonstrate the value of such a ministry. For instance, the Pope might initiate collaboration by Christian leaders and their communities in addressing common ethical and theological questions of our time. While Catholics remain committed to the ministry of the bishop of Rome, joint reflection on a universal ministry responds to John Paul II's invitation to reflect on the exercise of a universal ministry so that this ministry might "accomplish a service of love recognized by all concerned."[47] Such reflection also invites Baptists to reevaluate their traditional views of the papacy. Both sides acknowledge past failures and divisiveness related to this topic as they seek to forge more irenic ecumenical relationships in the future.

Conclusion

Major differences between Baptists and Catholics result from divergent notions of authority, differing views on the development of doctrine, and differing views on the church. One of the challenges of dialogue is

---

nos. 70-71. Beyond the local church, *episkopē* is exercised by those who may be designated as "Regional Ministers" or "Union Presidents" or "Regional General Secretaries" of the Baptist World Alliance. Catholic *episkopē* is exercised by bishops in their own dioceses and by the bishop of Rome and college of bishops for the church universal.

46. *LG*, no. 21.

47. *UUS*, nos. 95-96.

that two streams of Baptist thought are represented in the conversation, one representing a Baptist sacramentalism and the other seeing ordinances as signs but not instruments of God's action in the lives of Christians. The ecumenical challenge is not only conversation with a partner from a different ecclesial tradition, but also conversation across the spectrum of difference within a tradition.

The first phase of conversations addressed commonalities and differences related to the practice of evangelism/evangelization. The second phase tackled the hard doctrinal issues that have traditionally divided the two traditions. A third yet unexplored area could be the meta-assumptions behind some of those remaining doctrinal differences: historical consciousness, the possibilities and limits of the development of doctrine, and those conditions necessary for an ecclesial tradition to teach authoritatively. To be appealing to Baptists, one would need to demonstrate that these seemingly more abstract and philosophical issues have an impact on mission and the preaching of the gospel.

Finally, both traditions are challenged to witness to Jesus Christ as Savior and Lord of all life in our contemporary Western culture. Baptists and Catholics have experienced united witness and action on ethical issues, including justice, peace, and the sanctity of life. One of the original purposes of the first phase of conversations was to heal misunderstandings and mutual mistrust. Although the ecumenical goal between Baptists and Catholics may not yet be full visible unity, there is a missional urgency for reconciliation in order that Baptists and Catholics may provide a united witness to common values in our world today. This is analogous to the need for a united witness recognized at the Missionary Conference at Edinburgh in 1910, the conference that initiated the ecumenical movement.

17 Catholics and Mennonites in Search of "the Spirit of Unity in the Bond of Peace"

Helmut Harder

Introduction

On October 17, 1998 fourteen persons chosen by the Mennonite World
Conference (MWC) and the Roman Catholic Church's Pontifical
Council for Promoting Christian Unity (PCPCU) gathered in a meeting
room at the MWC global offices in Strasbourg, France. This was a historic meeting — the first time since the great schism of the sixteenth
century that these two churches had ventured into church-to-church
dialogue. Understandably, the meeting room was charged with anticipation. It was also fraught with a degree of fear. How would the two
"sides" respond to each other? How would the discussion unfold and
develop over the projected five years of discourse? Would the two
groups grow still further apart, or would they find significant common
ground? The answer is hinted at in the title of the lengthy Report issued jointly in July 2003, after the group had met annually for six
weeklong sessions. The Report bears the title *Called Together to Be Peacemakers* (hereafter *Called Together*).[1]

    Called Together is divided into three sections, reflecting the recur-
ring threefold agenda that guided the dialogue. The first section,
"Considering History Together," identifies and discusses those historical events and movements that the dialogue group chose to revisit in

---

1. *Called Together to Be Peacemakers:* Report of the International Dialogue between
the Catholic Church and the Mennonite World Conference (1998-2003), in *IS* 113 (2003,
II/III): 111-48. (Also referred to throughout the paper as the Report.)

an effort to come to terms with the story of a difficult past. The second section, "Considering Theology Together," reports on the group's discussion of three theological themes: church, sacraments, and peace. The third section, "Toward a Healing of Memories," reflects progress made in seeking reconciliation.

The dialogue was given a threefold task: to share information about each other's churches; to gain an understanding of each other's positions on Christian faith; and to seek to overcome longstanding prejudices. This paper concentrates on the second of the three tasks, namely to foster a better understanding of each other's theological positions. But as the dialogue progressed over the five years, it became evident to this participant that we were achieving more than "a better understanding" of each other's theologies. Somewhat beyond initial expectations, we found ourselves also claiming significant agreement on fundamental Christian foundations of the faith.

This paper seeks to document that claim by drawing on the three theological themes discussed in the course of the dialogue: the nature of the church; theology of sacraments (baptism and the eucharist/ Lord's Supper); and peace theology. I will explore the extent to which, according to the Report, Catholics and Mennonites can affirm common theological foundations, and the extent to which they hold differing views. Underlying our discussion is the question of whether, given the foundations of faith to which each of our churches ascribes, it is warranted to claim that Catholics and Mennonites can indeed be one and the same body of Christ.

A. The Nature of the Church

Ecclesiology is an essential element of Christian theology for both Catholics and Mennonites.[2] Thus it seemed important that the dialogue begin by presenting their respective theologies of the church and then identifying similarities and differences. Significant theological agreement came to light in at least five areas, along with some notable differences.

2. Harold S. Bender, *These Are My People: The New Testament Church* (Scottdale, PA: Mennonite Publishing House, 1962); *Dogmatic Constitution on the Church (Lumen Gentium)*, in Marianne Lorraine Trouvé, ed., *The Sixteen Documents of Vatican II* (Boston: Pauline Books & Media, 1999), pp. 109-99.

1. Images of the Church in Common

The dialogue Report claims that "Catholics and Mennonites agree on conceiving the Church as the people of God, the body of Christ, and the dwelling place of the Holy Spirit, images that flow from the Scriptures."[3] Indeed, of the many possible images of the church that could be highlighted, both church groups identify these three as basic to their ecclesiologies. That said, the two churches differ in the way they give accent to these images. Catholics begin by drawing attention to their universal import, while Mennonites draw these images into the congregational context.

For Catholic ecclesiology, the people of God extends "to the ends of the earth"; the church is the body of Christ "in and for the world"; the temple of the Holy Spirit has to do with "the fullness of the whole world."[4] In *Lumen gentium* the three images are gathered into one global vision: "[T]he Church both prays and labors in order that the entire world may become the People of God, the body of the Lord and the temple of the Holy Spirit, and that in Christ, the head of all, all honor and glory may be rendered to the Creator and Father of the universe."[5]

For Mennonite ecclesiology, the church is first of all a congregation and a "family" of congregations. The body of Christ suggests commitment to Christ as a "body of believers," and commitment to "one another" in the name of Christ. Mennonites prefer the image of the "community" of the Holy Spirit, perhaps because the "temple" suggests a formidable edifice.[6] Mennonites plant their ecclesiological foothold in the church as the new community of disciples, declaring that "in God's people the world's renewal has begun."[7]

While these three biblical images suggest a reference to the Trinity, Catholic theologians have made more of the church's trinitarian basis than have Mennonites: "Catholics express the mystery of the Church in terms of the inner relation that is found in the life of the

---

3. *Called Together,* no. 93. For fuller Catholic and Mennonite explications of these three images, see *Called Together,* nos. 72-74, 84-86.

4. *Called Together,* nos. 72-74.

5. *LG,* no. 17, in Trouvé, pp. 141f.

6. *Called Together,* no. 86.

7. See Douglas Gwyn, George Hunsinger, Eugene F. Roop, and John Howard Yoder, *A Declaration on Peace: In God's People the World's Renewal Has Begun* (Scottdale, PA/Waterloo, ON: Herald Press, 1991).

Trinity, namely *koinonia* or communion."[8] Mennonite theology has always accepted the doctrine of the Trinity.[9] But the fruitfulness of a trinitarian basis for ecclesiology has only recently been explored.[10] The focus in these recent studies has also been on trinitarian *koinonia* as paradigm for the church community.

2. One Foundation: Jesus Christ

Both Catholics and Mennonites hold to the biblical word that Jesus Christ is the "cornerstone" (Eph. 2:20) and "foundation" (Eph. 2:21-22; 1 Cor. 3:11) of the church.[11] According to *Lumen gentium,* an understanding of Christ as the foundation of the church has its origin in the plan of God before the foundations of the world were laid, when the Son was already present with the Father.[12] Christ, as the church's foundation, is shrouded in prehistorical mystery. In the incarnation, according to Catholic theology, "the mystery of the holy Church is manifest in its very foundation, [namely] the Lord Jesus [who] set it on its course by preaching the Good News. . . ."[13]

From the beginning, Mennonites have affirmed the Christological basis of their ecclesiology. Menno Simons, the sixteenth-century Catholic priest turned Anabaptist, from whom the Mennonite churches derive their name, never tired of quoting 1 Corinthians 3:11 as a motto for the Anabaptist movement. At times he used this text to differentiate the Anabaptist understanding of "the church's one foundation" from what he caricatured as "the church of Antichrist."[14] Seen against this provocative background, it is altogether

---

8. *Called Together,* no. 75.

9. See Menno Simons, "A Solemn Confession of the Triune, Eternal, and True God, Father, Son, and Holy Ghost," in J. C. Wenger, ed., *The Complete Writings of Menno Simons, c. 1496-1561* (Scottdale, PA: Herald Press, 1956), pp. 487-98.

10. For example, see Fernando Enns, "Believers Church Ecclesiology: A Trinitarian Foundation and Its Implications," in Abe Dueck, Helmut Harder, and Karl Koop, eds., *New Perspectives in Believers Church Ecclesiology* (Winnipeg, MB: CMU Press, 2010), chapter 10.

11. *Called Together,* no. 94.

12. *LG,* no. 2, in Trouvé, p. 124.

13. *LG,* no. 5, in Trouvé, p. 126.

14. See Menno Simons, "Reply to Gelius Faber," in Wenger, ed., *The Complete Writings of Menno Simons,* pp. 739-43.

striking when today Mennonites and Catholics confess together that "Christ is Lord"!

3. One Apostolic Authority

Both Catholics and Mennonites hold to the primacy of scriptural authority for the church's teaching on faith and work. Both subscribe to the authority of the apostolic teaching, which has its basis and origin in the New Testament. The Catholic Church embraces tradition as the progressive authoritative historical vehicle whereby the scriptures are interpreted and guarded by the church throughout time and culture.[15] The ecumenical creeds form an indispensable part of authoritative tradition. The teaching office of the church, defined as the bishops in communion with the bishop of Rome, is entrusted, in the name of Christ, with the preservation and interpretation of sacred scripture and sacred tradition on behalf of the church.

Mennonites also take care to connect the apostolic teaching of the New Testament with the church. While Mennonite ecclesiology respects tradition for informing revelation, it is the living congregation that is entrusted with the hermeneutical task of interpreting the scriptures. The stage was set for this approach when, at the time of the Reformation, Mennonites broke with the papal authority of the Catholic Church and relied instead on the (local) community of the faithful, under the guidance of the Holy Spirit, to discern the word of the Lord in its contemporary context. Leaders are appointed for the various functions of ministry in the church. Yet all baptized believers are responsible for participating in the process of discerning God's truth and building up the body of Christ. Furthermore, it is the responsibility of the church at all levels, from local congregation to global communion, "to lead a holy life and to give honor to God by serving one another in the Church and in a needy world."[16] Faithfulness of all believers is an essential element in upholding the apostolic nature of the church.

Comparing the Catholic and Mennonite ways of linking apostolic faith with the church, one might depict the former as a "ground route" while Mennonites follow an "air route." Their differing ap-

---

15. *Called Together,* nos. 77, 83.
16. *Called Together,* no. 91.

proaches need not be considered church-dividing provided there is a sincere commitment to the apostolic faith even as the means whereby that end is attained may differ.

While there are significant differences between Catholics and Mennonites in the way leadership is structured and authority delegated, the dialogue partners agreed that "ministry belongs to the whole Church, and that there are varieties of gifts of ministry given for the good of all."[17]

4. One Lord, with Differing Structures

While Catholics and Mennonites lay claim to the same foundation and cornerstone for their churches, namely the foundation laid in Jesus Christ (1 Cor. 3:11; Eph. 2:20), their church structures differ. "For Catholics the visible Church of Christ consists of particular churches united around their bishop in communion with one another and with the Bishop of Rome as the successor of Saint Peter."[18] A hierarchical polity governs its affairs. The church has universal status, both geographically and in its envisioned embrace of "the unity of the whole human race."[19] The local churches "exist in and out of the one Church, [and are] shaped in its image."[20] It is evident that Catholics conceive the church "from above."

Mennonite ecclesiology approaches church structures "from below," beginning with particular congregations and assemblies of people: "[T]he primary manifestation of the Church is the local congregation and the various groupings of congregations variously named conferences, church bodies, and/or denominations."[21] A recent Menno-

---

17. *Called Together*, no. 100.

18. *Called Together*, no. 105.

19. *LG*, no. 1, in Trouvé, p. 123.

20. *Called Together*, no. 81. To be sure, there are innumerable local parishes, but these are linked firmly to each other in a hierarchy fortified by creed, liturgy, priestly accountability, and the like. While the one church and the particular churches "are interior to each other (perichoretic) . . . the unity of the Church has priority over the diversity of local churches, and over all particular interests" (no. 81).

21. *Called Together*, no. 105. This depiction is fortified by the Mennonite churches' attention to local congregational autonomy, voluntary membership, a covenant of faithfulness, grassroots leadership, a common calling to a "higher righteousness," the sole authority of scripture, simplicity, and the like.

nite confession of faith puts it this way: "The church exists as a community of believers in the local congregation, as a community of congregations, and as the worldwide community of faith."[22]

That said, dialogue participants looked beyond structural differences when they agreed that "the Church is a visible community of believers originating in God's call to be a faithful people in time and place . . . evidenced when, in word and deed, its members give public witness to faith in Christ."[23] Faithfulness to the gospel is not dependent on one structure over against another, but on devotion to the Lord, for "he himself is before all things, and in him all things hold together" (Col. 1:17).

5. One Missional Purpose

Catholics and Mennonites agree that the church exists to carry out God's mission in the world. For both, "the Church is a chosen sign of God's presence and promise of salvation for all creation."[24] The missional focus of the Catholic Church is expressed in the opening paragraph of *Lumen gentium,* which begins with the affirmation that "Christ is the Light of nations." The purpose of the church is "to bring the light of Christ to all men, a light brightly visible on the countenance of the Church."[25] Catholics emphasize the sign-character of the church's missional impact by speaking of the church as "the universal sacrament of salvation at once manifesting and actualizing the mystery of God's love for humanity."[26]

Mennonites express the missional task of the church less universally, but with the same missional spirit: "The church is called to witness to the reign of Christ by embodying Jesus' way in its own life and patterning itself after the reign of God."[27] The global emphasis in a

22. *Confession of Faith in a Mennonite Perspective* (Scottdale, PA/Waterloo, ON: Herald Press, 1995), "The Church of Jesus Christ," Article 9, 40.

23. *Called Together,* no. 97.

24. *Called Together,* no. 99.

25. *LG,* no. 1, in Trouvé, p. 123.

26. *GS,* no. 45, in Trouvé, p. 668.

27. *Confession of Faith in a Mennonite Perspective.* "The Church in Mission," Article 10, 42.

Mennonite missional statement is cast in terms of God's call "to direct its mission to people from all nations and ethnic backgrounds."[28]

We will return later to the question of whether Catholics and Mennonites are "on the same page" with their ecclesiologies. We turn now to the theme of sacraments and ordinances,[29] with particular reference to baptism and the Lord's Supper.

B. Sacraments

The theology and practice of sacraments represented a point of contention when, in the sixteenth century, the Anabaptists challenged medieval Catholic traditions. In a highly provocative move, they discounted paedobaptism and invited their followers to undergo the "true baptism" as practiced, in their view, by the first Christians. The Anabaptists baptized upon personal confession of faith alone. In their view, the Lord's Supper was, in the first place, a meal of remembrance, reminding the faithful of Jesus' sacrifice on the cross. No mysterious power is conveyed by way of these elements.

Today, centuries later, the two churches are revisiting their historic sixteenth-century differences over sacraments, and are asking whether their views might be more compatible than was held at the time.[30] This has led to the discovery of significant convergence in their mutual understanding of baptism and the Lord's Supper. We will briefly outline four areas in which the dialogue partners found themselves on common theological ground, but also with some difference of viewpoint.

1. Sacraments, a Participation in Christ

The Report states that, having compared their respective understandings of baptism and the Lord's Supper, Catholics and Mennonites are

28. *Confession of Faith in a Mennonite Perspective,* "The Church in Mission," Article 10, 43.

29. Mennonites prefer the term "ordinance" over "sacrament," although the latter term is used in some Mennonite confessions of faith. Mennonites recognized two ordinances, baptism and the Lord's Supper.

30. Mennonites rarely use the term "eucharist," but prefer the designations "Lord's Supper" or "communion."

in agreement "that Baptism and the Lord's Supper have their origin and point of reference in Jesus Christ and in the teachings of Scripture."[31] For Catholics the sacraments afford the believer the reality of participation in Christ — the fundamental encounter of the Christian with God through Jesus Christ.[32] The baptismal waters convey the grace of Christ to the recipient. Participation in baptism is a participation in the cleansing grace of Christ. When the eucharist is celebrated, Christ is "made really present under the species of bread and wine."[33] Participation in the eucharist is a participation in the body and blood of Christ. The fundamental encounter of the Christian with God through Jesus Christ comes by way of the sacraments of baptism and the eucharist.

Mennonites understand baptism as a public testimony of the believer's participation in Christ, while the Lord's Supper is a sign bearing witness to the church's participation in the body and blood of Christ. Mennonites focus on what the ordinances point to and signify. The act itself is symbolic, and in itself is in the nature of testimony. That said, Mennonite theology "does not dismiss the effectual power of the ordinance to bring change to the participants."[34] Indeed, while the Lord's Supper is, for Mennonites, a memorial and sign, the meal has the power to bring change into the life of the participants and of the community of faith, making them "one loaf together." However, Christ is present, "not in the elements as such, but in the context as a whole, including the communion of the gathered congregation."[35]

As is well known, the Anabaptist-Mennonite theology of sacraments emerged in the sixteenth century against the background of a severe criticism of what was perceived as the Catholic understanding of the time, namely that the mass transforms the bread and the wine into

---

31. *Called Together,* no. 128.

32. *Called Together,* nos. 112, 116.

33. *Called Together,* no. 138.

34. *Called Together,* no. 126. Mennonites do not employ the concept of "mystery" as does Catholic theology, which accentuates "the mysterious manner in which God has used the elements of his creation for his self-communication" (no. 112). Underlying the whole sacramental system is the "Paschal mystery [which] is the place where God reveals and grants salvation in symbolic acts and words" (no. 113). In contrast, there is something straightforward and "earthy" about the Mennonite understanding that differentiates it from the mystical experience surrounding the Catholic celebration of the eucharist.

35. *Called Together,* no. 126.

the actual body and blood of Christ, and thus the very elements effect the salvation of the recipient.[36] However, this severe critique cannot be sustained. On the Mennonite side there is today a renewed emphasis on the power of the presence of Christ known in the participant's partaking of the elements of bread and wine in the midst of the believing community.[37] At the same time, as Catholic participants in the recent Catholic-Mennonite dialogue pointed out, the Catholic position, as enunciated in Vatican II, speaks also of "the sacrament as a reality to be lived especially as the life of the Christian is linked to the Paschal mystery."[38] Furthermore, among the points of reference for understanding sacraments, Vatican II emphasized that "sacraments are linked to the whole of the Christian life, since there is a strong link between the sacramental celebration and the ethic of Christian living"; that is, "between the Word of God proclaimed, the Word of God celebrated and the Word of God lived that engages each Christian in their daily life."[39] Thus a renewed understanding of sacramental participation in Mennonite theology and a broadened emphasis on the relationship between sacraments and Christian discipleship draw Mennonites and Catholics toward each other in their understandings of the sacraments.

2. Sacraments Convey Grace

Catholics and Mennonites agree that baptism and the Lord's Supper are effective in communicating the grace of God to participants. Both churches celebrate baptism and the Lord's Supper as "extraordinary occasions of encounter with God's offer of grace revealed in Jesus Christ."[40] To receive the water of baptism and the elements of the Lord's Supper is to participate in the life, death, and resurrection of Jesus Christ, who was offered up for the redemption of the world.

Catholics hold that the very act of baptism cleanses the recipient

---

36. For example, see Menno Simons, "Foundation of Christian Doctrine" (1539), in Wenger, ed., *The Complete Writings of Menno Simons,* pp. 153-58.

37. For example, see John D. Rempel, "Toward an Anabaptist Theology of the Lord's Supper," in *The Lord's Supper: Believers Church Perspectives,* ed. Dale R. Stoffer (Scottdale, PA/Waterloo, ON: Herald Press, 1997), pp. 243-49.

38. *Called Together,* no. 113.

39. *Called Together,* no. 114.

40. *Called Together,* nos. 128, 133.

of original sin, and that the eucharistic bread and wine enact the miracle of grace in the believer. The sacraments proclaim the Word of God and seal the salvation of the individual. In the case of infant baptism, the benefits are bestowed upon the recipient in the hope that infants will eventually acknowledge and personalize the faith. Meanwhile, the faith is carried on their behalf by the church, into which they have been baptized.

Mennonites believe that in baptism the individual bears witness that he/she has repented of sin, has received the grace of God, and has been cleansed of all unrighteousness.[41] The Lord's Supper is primarily a meal reminding participants that Jesus Christ gave his life for sinners. That is, Mennonites do not view baptism and the Lord's Supper as the occasion for the bestowal of grace, but as a sign of grace received.

It becomes evident that the difference between a Catholic and a Mennonite has much to do with the *means* whereby grace is bestowed on the person and with the *timing* of grace received. While these differences are not unimportant, they need not be church-dividing. For both, the Christian is, in the end, a sinner saved by grace.

3. Sacraments Nourish the Body

Catholics and Mennonites embrace baptism and the Lord's Supper as "acts of the Church."[42] The sacraments are essential to the body-life of the church. Through baptism, believers are incorporated into the church, the body of Christ, and are assured of the gifts of the Holy Spirit. The Lord's Supper nourishes and sustains the life of the church and of its members in their communion with God and with one another. The community participates in the ritual as "corporate personality."

In both traditions the church takes care to ensure that the sacraments and ordinances are administered on behalf of the church by chosen ordained leaders. The traditions differ as to how accountability of leaders is assured. But the intent to appoint leaders to represent the church is the same. In Mennonite practice the ordination of pastoral leadership is regulated within each congregation or family of congregations, while in the Catholic tradition the universal church authorizes

41. *Called Together,* no. 121.
42. *Called Together,* no. 128.

and attends to priestly order. This is another means of upholding the connection between church and sacrament/ordinance.

4. Sacraments Invite Covenant-Making

Catholics and Mennonites hold in common that the sacraments offer "important moments in the believers' commitment to the body of Christ and to the Christian way of life."[43] For Catholics, "sacraments are linked to the whole of the Christian life, since there is a strong link between the celebration and the ethic of Christian living."[44] Even the baptism of infants is linked to Christian life, since on the occasion of baptism the parents and the church pledge to nurture the infant in the life of faith. The sacrament of confirmation gives occasion for the infant to "own" his/her baptism by way of a pledge of faithfulness. Since Vatican II, the Catholic Church has given greater attention to the integration of baptism, confirmation, and the eucharist, linking them together and naming them "The Sacraments of Christian Initiation."[45]

The Mennonite practice of baptism is reserved for youth and adults. Yet the children are not neglected. Most Mennonite congregations invite parents to bring their children to a service of dedication at which the children receive a pastoral blessing and the parents and congregation promise to nurture their children in the love of God.[46] The Mennonite ritual of baptism "provides a public sign to the congregation of a person's desire to walk in the way of Christ."[47] In baptism new believers give witness to the work of God and the Holy Spirit in their lives. They signify their commitment to follow Christ as his disciples. They

43. *Called Together,* no. 128.

44. *Called Together,* no. 114.

45. See *Catechism of the Catholic Church,* 2nd ed. rev. (Vatican City: Libreria Editrice Vaticana, 2000), nos. 1212-1405.

46. In 1539 Menno Simons wrote as follows concerning parents in relation to their children: "[Parents] train them in the love of God and in wisdom by correcting, chastising, teaching, and admonishing them, and by the example of an irreproachable life, until these children are able to hear the Word of God, to believe it, and to fulfill it in their works. Then is the time and not until then, of whatever age they may be, that they should receive Christian baptism, which Jesus Christ has commanded in obedience to his Word to all Christians, and which His apostles have practiced and taught" (Menno Simons, "Christian Baptism," in Wenger, ed., *The Complete Writings of Menno Simons,* p. 281).

47. *Called Together,* no. 121.

commit themselves to give and receive counsel in the congregation and to participate in God's mission. The Lord's Supper is not only about remembering, but includes renewal and recommitment to the way of the cross. The Supper serves as an occasion for renewal of baptismal vows.

The above summary reflects similarities as well as significant differences between Catholics and Mennonites on the theology and practice of baptism and the Lord's Supper. As we will show below (D.2 and D.3), recent theological reflection by both Catholics and Mennonites holds the promise of an increasing convergence of views.

C. Peace Theology

Dialogue participants anticipated from the beginning that peace theology would form an important component of their agenda. Over the past sixty years Mennonites have distinguished themselves in ecumenical circles as advocates for the peace witness.[48] When the Catholic representatives were asked why they desired to dialogue with the Mennonites, their first response was: "We want to learn from you what it means to be a peace church."

Did Catholics and Mennonites find themselves on common ground with respect to a theology of peace? If so, on what basis? To what extent? The title of the final Report of the dialogue, *Called Together to Be Peacemakers,* bears evidence of the importance of the theme of peace for the dialogue. It would be difficult to be peacemakers together if the respective peace theologies are not compatible. Indeed, Catholics and Mennonites found substantial convergence in their views on peace, as evidenced below. There were also differences and difficulties, as will be noted.

1. The God of Peace

It is of great significance that, in their dialogue on peace theology, Catholics and Mennonites base their commitment to peace on their

---

48. See Thomas D. Paxson, Jr., ed., *Ecumenical Engagement for Peace and Nonviolence: Experiences and Initiatives of the Historic Peace Churches and the Fellowship of Reconciliation* (Elgin, IL: Global Mission Partnerships, Church of the Brethren General Board, 2006).

understanding of the character of God as the God of Peace. The Report begins the section on "Our Commitment to Peace" with this telling statement: "Through our dialogue, we have come to understand that Catholics and Mennonites share a common commitment to peacemaking . . . rooted in our communion with 'the God of Peace' (Rom. 15:33)."[49] While Catholics point to the holiness of God, Mennonites focus on the love of God.[50] Both understand God as creating, restoring, and re-creating a peaceable kingdom where humankind and the environment are pervaded with God's shalom. Heading up a long list of convergences on a theology of peace, the dialogue Report states: "Mennonites and Catholics can agree that God . . . has destined humanity for one and the same goal, namely, communion with God's own self . . . , unity with one another through reciprocal self-giving . . . [and] peace with one another and with all humankind (2 Cor. 13:11; Rom. 12:18)."[51] A commitment to peace includes the obligation of God's people to live as committed caretakers, and not as exploiters, of the earth.

2. Rooted in Jesus Christ

According to the Report, Mennonites and Catholics base their peace witness in Christology. Both "understand peace through the teachings, life and death of Jesus Christ."[52] Together, Catholics and Mennonites point to such texts as Ephesians 2:14: "For he is our peace; in his flesh he has made both groups into one and has broken down the dividing wall, that is, the hostility between us . . . that he might create in himself one new humanity in place of the two, thus making peace."

Catholics and Mennonites agree on the intersection of soteriology and peace. The sacrificial death of Christ proclaims God's forgiving love for enemies. Jesus' way of the cross invites believers to walk in the way of peace, thereby participating in Jesus' ministry of salvation. Jesus' willingness to suffer and die rather than to retaliate and kill forged the way of salvation, making atonement for human sin "once for all" (1 Pet. 3:18), and "leaving [us] an example that [we] should follow in his steps" (1 Pet. 2:21).

49. *Called Together,* no. 145.
50. *Called Together,* no. 150.
51. *Called Together,* no. 172.
52. *Called Together,* no. 174.

3. Peace and Nonviolence

Catholics and Mennonites find themselves in agreement on a commitment to nonviolence.[53] A commitment to nonviolence has been central to a Mennonite theology of peace from the beginning. Mennonites emphasize that Christ's atoning death on the cross and his resurrection laid the foundation for peace with God, with one another, and also with the enemy. While in Catholicism there have always been voices that upheld nonviolence, recent decades have seen a momentous increased preference for nonviolence in response to sin and aggression. Under the inspiration of the late Pope John Paul II and earlier leaders, Catholics are increasingly calling the church to a radical peace stance[54] based not on "Christian realism," but on a principled pacifism.[55]

4. Peace and Ecclesiology

Participants in the dialogue, both Catholics and Mennonites, claim their churches to be *peace* churches and *peacemaking* churches.[56] As such, their churches intend to be a sign to the world of the peace of Christ, and a model to society of how to engage in peacemaking. The term "peace church" makes a statement about *being,* whereas the term "peacemaking church" is a statement about *doing.*

53. *Called Together,* no. 178.

54. In the context of the Catholic-Mennonite dialogue, the cogent insights of Fr. Drew Christiansen, SJ, provide a particularly encouraging impetus in this direction. See Rev. Drew Christiansen, SJ, "What Is a Peace Church? A Roman Catholic Perspective," unpublished paper prepared for the International Mennonite-Roman Catholic Dialogue, Thomashof, Karlsruhe, Germany, November 23-30, 2000. Fr. Christiansen points in particular to Pope John Paul II's encyclical letter, *Centesimus annus* (1991), which brought to a head a century of modern papal social teaching on peace and warfare. John Paul II writes: "No, never again war, which destroys the lives of innocent people, teaches how to kill, throws into upheaval even the lives of those who do the killing, and leaves behind a trail of resentment and hatred, thus making it all the more difficult to find a just solution of the very problems which provoked the war" (quoted in Report, no. 159).

55. As Fr. Christiansen points out, the tradition of Christian realism, which advocates the mobilization of power in the face of social life infected by sin, can be traced back from Augustine to twentieth-century theologians such as Reinhold Niebuhr, Paul Johnson, Michael Novak, and George Weigel. See Christiansen, "What Is a Peace Church? A Roman Catholic Perspective," p. 2.

56. *Called Together,* nos. 175-76.

Yet Mennonites and Catholics differ with respect to some aspects of their peace stance and activity. Mennonites claim to be pacifist, based on the model of the peaceful wing of the Anabaptists.[57] A prolific succession of Mennonite confessions of faith gives evidence of this persistent stance throughout post-Reformation history.[58] Historically, Mennonite confessions have called for a stance of nonresistance. In the twentieth century, nonresistance took the form of conscientious objection against war and alternate service.[59] Today many include a stance of nonviolent resistance to evil as a means of peacemaking. Meanwhile the primary emphasis among Mennonites is on building cultures of peace.[60]

The Catholic Church views the peace church stance as an ideal to which the church ought to aspire. Yet historically, as in the present day, Catholics have also faced the world of violence with a certain realism. The church respects those who, for conscience' sake, shun military service; yet the church also blesses those who take up arms under legitimate authority in circumstances where aggressive action is required for a "just" cause.[61] War is justified if, as a last resort, it serves

---

57. Menno Simons writes: "Seeing then that Christ Jesus is the Prince and the Lord of eternal peace, . . . none can be the recipient of His honor and good will, or be given a place in His kingdom save those who have the holy peace of God in their hearts. For His kingdom is the Kingdom of peace; it knows no strife, even as it is written in the prophets that in the kingdom of Christ and in His church they beat their swords into plowshares and . . . no more raise up their hands unto warfare" (Wenger, ed., *The Complete Writings of Menno Simons*, p. 1031).

58. For a compendium of Mennonite confessions of faith from the sixteenth century to the twentieth century, see Howard John Loewen, *One Lord, One Church, One Hope, and One God: Mennonite Confessions of Faith* (Elkhart, IN: Institute of Mennonite Studies, 1985).

59. *Called Together*, nos. 164-65. A recent statement of the Historic Peace Churches, which include the Mennonite churches, speaks for the Mennonite standpoint on military power: "The church's most effective witness and action against war comes . . . simply in the stand she takes in and through her members in the face of war. Unless the church, trusting the power of God in whose hand the destinies of nations lie, is willing to 'fall into the ground and die,' to renounce war absolutely, whatever sacrifice of freedoms, advantages, or possessions this might entail, even to the point of counseling a nation not to resist foreign conquest and occupation, she can give no prophetic message for the world of nations" (Gwyn et al., eds., *A Declaration on Peace*, pp. 74f.).

60. Alan Kreider, Eleanor Kreider, and Paulus Widjaja, *A Culture of Peace: God's Vision for the Church* (Intercourse, PA: Good Books, 2005).

61. *Called Together*, nos. 187-88.

to protect the innocent and vulnerable, and offers an opportunity for "peace in the making." Meanwhile, there are voices within the Catholic Church, including voices of recent pontiffs, that call for an end to warfare.[62]

We note, in concluding this section, that while there is considerable convergence between a Catholic and a Mennonite understanding and practice of peace, there are also some marked differences in their views. We consider these differences in D.4 below.

D. Concluding Considerations

A comparison of theological positions held by Catholics and Mennonites on ecclesiology, on the sacraments of baptism and the Lord's Supper, and on peace theology has revealed significant theological compatibility. Admittedly, the dialogue has not compared all aspects of Catholic and Mennonite theology. Nonetheless, based on church-to-church conversations to date, there is good reason to hope that a broad and fruitful exploration of Christian unity in essentials can develop between Catholics and Mennonites. Meanwhile there are also outstanding issues that require further discussion and debate. I conclude with four succinctly stated questions.

1. One Church?

Our review has shown that Catholics and Mennonites claim common ecclesiological ground in at least five important ways. First, we hold central biblical images of the church in common. Second, both claim Jesus Christ as the only foundation of the church. Third, we hold to apostolic authority as the basis for the church's teachings. Fourth, we affirm the church is a visible community of faithful believers meeting in time and place under the Lordship of Christ. And finally, both churches conceive and practice mission in accordance with the Great Commission of our Lord.

Do these ecclesiological agreements comprise sufficient basis upon which to claim that Catholics and Mennonites together bear wit-

---

62. *Called Together,* no. 159.

ness to the church as "one body"? Some interchurch efforts to find common ground focus on the lowest common denominator. Our search has taken us in the other direction, to common foundational claims. From this perspective, differences of structure and practice, while by no means incidental, tend to diminish in importance.

2. One Baptism?

The theology and practice of baptism has been a divisive issue from the beginning of the Anabaptist movement.[63] But in our day there appears to be a greater possibility for mutual understanding in this area. While Mennonite confessions of faith continue to hold to "believer's baptism," some (possibly many) Mennonite churches no longer require rebaptism for new members previously baptized as infants. In such situations the person's covenant of membership serves, in effect, as a confirmation of a previous baptism. Meanwhile the Catholic Church has clarified its thinking about baptism. Today adult baptism is considered normative, along with infant baptism. Also, the rite of infant baptism is linked resolutely with the sacrament of confirmation. The two sacraments together provide the seal of faith for the believer.

These shifts and emphases set the stage for a more favorable climate of acceptance between Catholics and Mennonites. It is noteworthy that, in some jurisdictions of the Catholic Church, Mennonite baptism has been declared acceptable for persons who desire to join the Catholic Church.[64]

---

63. What I mean by "a reasonable measure of agreement" is exemplified in the understanding reached between the Catholic Church and the Lutheran Church on the doctrine of justification. See John A. Radano, *Lutheran and Catholic Reconciliation and Justification* (Grand Rapids: Eerdmans, 2009), especially pp. 140f.

64. I draw this example from procedures applied in the Archdiocese of Winnipeg. The stipulation is that persons "converting" from Mennonite to Catholic must have been baptized 1) with water, and 2) in the name of the Father, the Son, and the Holy Spirit. Whether or not the person subscribes to the sacramental effect of baptism as a removal of sin is not addressed. Presumably the concern to avoid the appearance of a rebaptism takes precedence over the question of agreement with a full Catholic theology of baptism.

3. One Eucharistic Table?

The sacrament of the eucharist, that quintessential event in the life of the Catholic Church, continues to pose a formidable obstacle to unity vis-à-vis the other Christian churches, including the Mennonites. Why should this be so? As we have seen, in many respects Catholics and Mennonites take their stand on the same theological foundation concerning the Lord's Supper. One point at issue concerns the question of the nature of Christ's presence at the meal relative to the communion elements of bread and wine. For Catholics, Christ is made present in and through the elements. In Mennonite understanding, the elements are a sign pointing to Christ who is present at the meal. Both churches hold that, above all, the communion celebration assures the believer of the grace of Christ.

While differing perspectives on the Lord's Supper are not unimportant, they need not be church-dividing. On the contrary, is there not some room for gift-sharing around the one eucharistic table? *Among Mennonites there is a longing* for a more intensely spiritual experience of the presence of God in the sacrament than what the current Mennonite practice tends to afford. Some have experienced this presence particularly in ecumenical communion services and in services in their own congregations where recognizably "catholic" elements are sometimes included in the liturgy. There is a marked interest among Mennonite theologians to reclaim a stronger sense of the power of the sacraments, and of the link between the sacraments and the grace of God.[65]

At the same time, Mennonites have communion gifts to share with Catholics. This includes a rich tradition of mutual accountability and community-building in the context of the communion meal. Also, Mennonites build a strong link between the communion meal, along with foot-washing, and a life of servanthood and discipleship. The world is hungry not only for a sacramental experience shrouded in mystery and supported by exacting doctrine, but for the sacrament of sacrificial service to people who are hungry for the necessities of life. Such ministries are embodied in people whose lives are transformed by the sacrifice of

---

65. See, for example, Andrea M. Dalton, "A Sacramental Believers Church: Pilgram Marpeck and the (Un)mediated Presence of God," in Abe Dueck et al., *New Perspectives in Believers Church Ecclesiology*, pp. 223-36.

Christ and who represent his sacramental presence in the world.[66] Could a Mennonite theology of the sacraments help to enrich the renewed Catholic emphasis on the link between sacraments and ethics, on "the link between eucharist and justice, peace and reconciliation"?[67]

4. Peacemaking Together?

The title of the final Report issues the challenge to the two churches to offer the world a joint witness as peacemakers. The call has double strength. Not only could something practical be accomplished through cooperative peacemaking projects, but the visible act of drawing together intentionally in peace witness sends an unmistakable message about oneness in Christ. But is there sufficient agreement between Catholic and Mennonite theologies of peace for the two churches to engage one another in this way?

In recent decades Mennonite and Catholic *individuals* have increasingly worked side by side as peacemakers.[68] But the call of the dialogue goes a step further, calling for a peace witness *together as churches*. Time will tell if this is a sustainable possibility. It will depend in part on whether or not the two churches are willing to risk joint initiatives. It will also depend on whether the two churches can cooperate despite their current differences regarding the just war tradition. From a Mennonite standpoint, the historic and continuing support of Catholic theology for the just war theory poses a difficulty. For Mennonites, absolute nonviolence is not only highly preferable; it is the only way. To kill another human, whatever the attempt at justification, is against the way of Christ, and thus against the way of his disciples. In this matter, Mennonites are ready to disobey the state.[69] They

66. I am indebted to Alan Kreider, Professor of Church History at the Associated Mennonite Biblical Seminary, for some of the emphases in this paragraph. His unpublished paper titled "The Significance of the Mennonite-Catholic Dialogue: A Mennonite Perspective" was presented at the Catholic-Mennonite Symposium at Notre Dame University, South Bend, IN, July 30, 2007.

67. *Called Together*, no. 119.

68. E.g., *Christian Peacemaker Teams*, originating in the Mennonite Church, has active Catholic participation.

69. Nor do Mennonite churches appeal to some political entity, akin to the Vatican's diplomatic corps, to assist in the church's role as peacemaker. For an assessment, see Drew Christiansen, SJ, "Benedict XVI: Peacemaker," in *America* (July 16, 2007).

have also shown themselves ready to go to prison and to die rather than to kill.

But these differences need not pose obstacles to a joint peace witness since "we hold the conviction in common that reconciliation, nonviolence, and active peacemaking belong to the heart of the Gospel."[70] Mennonites are greatly encouraged by Catholic voices that continue to affirm this conviction. Most recently, on February 18, 2007, Pope Benedict XVI stated in his Angelus message that "[l]oving the enemy is the nucleus of the 'Christian revolution.'"[71] Mennonites ought to be willing to deliberate and work together with the Catholic Church in a spirit of *semper reformanda* and gift-sharing.

Conclusion

In the concluding session of the dialogue, the current title of the Report was proposed with some enthusiasm by Msgr. John A. Radano, Catholic co-secretary of the dialogue. His suggestion was readily received by the Mennonite delegates, whose participation in ecumenical initiatives over the past sixty years has sought to uphold the biblical challenge to "maintain the unity of the Spirit in the bond of peace" (Eph. 4:3).[72]

As *Called Together* claims, and as we have illustrated, "despite centuries of mutual isolation [Catholics and Mennonites] continue to share much of the Christian heritage which is rooted in the Gospel."[73] Our study has substantiated this claim, based on the themes chosen for the international dialogue. Even those views on which we have differences of opinion are in flux, hopefully toward a good end. Our study offers hope and encouragement for future ecumenical endeavors between our two churches.

Meanwhile, it is of great significance that after five years of conversation, the dialogue group issued a call for Catholics and Mennonites to be peacemakers together. The response to that call need not wait until every claim to unity is settled and every remaining question is satisfied.

70. *Called Together,* no. 179.

71. Accessed at www.catholicpeacefellowship.org/nextpage.asp?m=2308.

72. For a thumbnail summary of the first forty years of Mennonite participation in the modern ecumenical movement, see Gwyn et al., *A Declaration on Peace,* Appendix C, pp. 93-105.

73. *Called Together,* no. 8.

18 Oriental Orthodox–Catholic International Dialogue

Ronald G. Roberson, CSP

You know, I always have to roll my eyes when I hear talk about "the undivided church of the first millennium." The problem is, of course, that there was no such thing: there were plenty of divisions among Christians in the first millennium, and some of those divisions have persisted up to the present day. What I'm referring to are the churches that did not accept certain Christological teachings of the ecumenical councils of the fifth century. Today most of these churches are known as Oriental Orthodox. But there is also another church that had separated even earlier, known today as the Assyrian Church of the East. Most of this lecture will be devoted to our dialogue with the Oriental Orthodox, but at the end I will say a few words about our relationship with the Assyrians as well.

Here at the outset I'd like to point out that, from the Catholic perspective, the foundation of our new relationships with these churches was provided in the section of Vatican II's Decree on Ecumenism *(Unitatis redintegratio)* that referred to "The Special Position of the Eastern Churches" (nos. 14-18). It affirms the legitimate diversity represented by the eastern Christian traditions, and specifically recognizes the sacraments of these churches, including the eucharist and holy orders. Because of this, these churches "are still joined to us in closest intimacy" (no. 15). It goes on to recognize the power of these churches to govern themselves according to their own disciplines and calls for churchwide efforts to promote unity in a gradual way.

I. The Oriental Orthodox Churches

So again, by far the largest separate communion of churches today that resulted from the early Christological controversies is known as Oriental Orthodox. It is composed of six churches, each of which is fully independent and possesses many distinctive traditions. The Oriental Orthodox often refer to themselves as a "family" of churches, but this family has no administrative center, or any patriarch who claims even a symbolic primacy among them. They make up what I like to call a "flat communion."

The common element among these churches is their rejection of the Christological definition of the Council of Chalcedon (451), which taught that Christ is one divine hypostasis/person in two natures (one human and one divine), undivided and unconfused. The Oriental Orthodox adhere to a strong Alexandrian Christology and prefer the formula of St. Cyril of Alexandria, who spoke of Μία Φύσις τοῦ θεοῦ Λόγου σεσαρκωμένη (the one incarnate nature of the Word of God). But they also reject the classical monophysite position of Eutyches, who held that Christ's humanity was absorbed into his single divine nature. Even so, the Oriental Orthodox have often been referred to erroneously as monophysites in the past.[1] At different times they have also been called "Non-Chalcedonian," "Pre-Chalcedonian," "Ancient Eastern Churches," or "Lesser Eastern Churches."

For the sake of clarity it might be a good idea to briefly describe each of these six churches in a little more detail.

First, there is the Armenian Apostolic Church, which dates back to the early fourth century when the Armenian king adopted Christianity as the official religion of his country. Today the head of this church is His Holiness Karekin II, the Supreme Patriarch and Catholicos of All Armenians, who resides in Holy Etchmiadzin, near Yerevan the Armenian capital. But there is another Armenian Catholicos (of Cilicia) based in Antelias, a suburb of Beirut, Lebanon. It is administratively independent of the Catholicos in Armenia but they are in full communion with one another. These two Armenian Ap-

---

1. For a discussion of these Christological issues in a contemporary ecumenical perspective, see P. Gregorios, W. Nazareth, and N. Nissiotis, eds., *Does Chalcedon Divide or Unite? Towards Convergence in Orthodox Christology* (Geneva: World Council of Churches, 1981).

ostolic centers participate separately in the international dialogue. There are also Armenian Apostolic patriarchates in Istanbul and Jerusalem, both nominally dependent on the Catholicos in Armenia. Today the total membership of this church numbers around six million.

The Coptic Orthodox Church is most of what is left of the ancient patriarchate of Alexandria, which almost unanimously rejected the Christological teachings of the Council of Chalcedon. In the first millennium this church included most of the population of Egypt, but after the Arab invasions the church slowly declined and eventually became a minority. Its membership today is hotly disputed in Egypt; estimates run anywhere from five to ten million. Today it is by far the largest Christian church in the Middle East.

The Syrian Orthodox Church is descended from the half of the ancient patriarchate of Antioch that did not receive Chalcedon. Later known as the "Jacobite" church, its patriarch resides near Damascus; it is centered in Syria and Lebanon. It also includes a rather large church of Thomas Christians in southern India, the Malankara Syrian Orthodox Church. Total membership is around 1.7 million, 1.2 million of them in India.

Then there is the Ethiopian Orthodox Church, which is composed of about half the population of modern Ethiopia. Christianity became the state religion of Ethiopia in the fourth century, and appears to have arrived directly from Palestine in a form that was still strongly influenced by its Jewish roots. As a result, the Ethiopians observe a number of Jewish practices such as circumcision, kosher laws, and the Saturday Sabbath as well as Sunday. It was dependent on the Coptic Church until 1959 when it became fully independent. Membership is probably around 35 million.

Since Eritrea became independent from Ethiopia in 1993, there has also been a separate Eritrean Orthodox Church, which now numbers around 1.5 million members. The Eritrean government has severely curtailed the freedom of this church, deposing the legitimate patriarch and appointing a new one subject to the authority of a lay government minister. Because of this situation, the participation of the Eritrean Church in the dialogue has been sporadic.

And finally, there is the Malankara Orthodox Syrian Church in India. This group was part of the church dependent on the Syrian Orthodox patriarchate until early in the twentieth century when there was a split in the community. A minority stayed with the Syrian Patriarch, but the majority broke away to become a fully independent church that now participates in the dialogues in its own right. It now has around 2.5 million members.

So altogether these churches represent somewhere between 50 and 60 million Christians today. They are also the guardians of several ancient liturgical, theological, canonical, and spiritual traditions that make up an extremely rich patrimony. These Syriac, Alexandrian, and Armenian traditions are a great treasure for the entire Christian world.

Relations between Catholics and Oriental Orthodox have improved enormously since the Second Vatican Council. This came about initially as the result of official visits between Popes and heads of these churches, and semiofficial meetings of theologians sponsored by the "Pro Oriente" Foundation in Vienna, Austria.[2]

The most notable progress in this relationship has been in the area of Christology.[3] The work of the first two Pro Oriente meetings laid the groundwork for a historic Common Declaration signed by Pope Paul VI and Coptic Pope Shenouda III in 1973.[4] Avoiding terminology that had been the source of disagreement in the past, the declaration made use of new language to express a common faith in Christ. Since that time Popes and Patriarchs have repeatedly asserted that their faith in Christ is the same. In their 1984 Common Declaration, Pope John Paul II and Syriac Patriarch Ignatius Zakka I Iwas stated that past schisms and divisions concerning the doctrine of the incarnation "in no way affect or touch the substance of their faith" because the disputes arose from differences in terminology and culture. As a result of all this, it can be safely said that the different Catholic and Oriental Orthodox Christological formulas are no longer a reason for division.

---

2. The work of the first four Pro Oriente meetings in 1971, 1973, 1976, and 1978 was summarized in *Selection of the Papers and Minutes of the Four Vienna Consultations between Theologians of the Oriental Orthodox Churches and the Roman Catholic Church* (Vienna: Pro Oriente, 1988), 285 pp.

3. For Catholics there was already a long-standing conviction that the Christological dispute was essentially a question of terminology. This was officially expressed as early as 1951, when Pope Pius XII stated in his encyclical *Sempiternus Rex* that these Christians "verbis praecipue a recto tramite deflectere videantur" ("seem to depart from the right path chiefly in words"). *Acta Apostolicae Sedis* 43 (1951): 636.

4. The full text of all the Common Declarations signed by Popes and heads of Oriental Orthodox churches from 1970 through 2008 can be found in R. Roberson, *The Eastern Christian Churches: A Brief Survey* (Rome: Edizioni Orientalia Christiana, 2008), pp. 193-220.

It should be noted that both sides retained their traditional formulas, but there was a recognition that the same faith was being expressed by means of different formulas, properly understood. This is a principle of the very greatest importance for ecumenical relations.

Progress has also been made in the area of ecclesiology. Both sides clearly recognize each other as churches, and there have been agreements on the mutual recognition of each other's sacraments. In their 1984 common declaration, Pope John Paul II and the Syrian Patriarch even authorized their faithful to receive the sacraments of penance, eucharist, and anointing of the sick in the other church when access to one of their own priests was morally or materially impossible. Until the 2001 agreement with the Assyrian Church of the East, this was the only reciprocal agreement of this type that we had with any other church.

Because of the rather diffuse nature of the Oriental Orthodox communion, in the early decades after Vatican II the Catholic Church engaged each of these churches directly, sometimes through the establishment of bilateral dialogues. Such a dialogue between the Catholic Church and the Coptic Orthodox Church met regularly from 1973 to 1992.[5] In India, a dialogue with the Malankara Orthodox Syrian Church was established in October 1989, and another with the Malankara Syrian Orthodox Church in 1991; they continue to meet annually.[6] The dialogue with the Malankara Syrian Orthodox Church published an important agreed statement on mixed marriages in January 1994.[7]

In the meantime, a fifth Pro Oriente meeting in 1988 called for the establishment of an international dialogue between the Catholic Church and the Oriental Orthodox churches,[8] and preparations for

5. For a history of this dialogue by one of its Catholic members, see Frans Bouwen, "The Official Dialogue between the Catholic Church and the Coptic Orthodox Church," *One in Christ* 42, no. 1 (Summer 2008): 75-98.

6. See X. Koodapuzha and J. Panicker, eds., *Joint International Commission for Dialogue Between the Catholic Church and the Malankara Orthodox Syrian Church: Papers and Joint Statements 1989-2000* (Kottayam, 2001), 661 pp. The Malankara Orthodox Syrian Church is independent, while the Malankara Syrian Orthodox Church is autonomous but linked to the Syrian Orthodox patriarchate near Damascus.

7. "Agreement Between the Catholic Church and the Malankara Syrian Orthodox Church on Interchurch Marriages" and "Pastoral Guidelines on Marriages between Members of the Catholic Church and of the Malankara Syrian Orthodox Church," in *IS* 84 (1993/III-IV): 159-61.

8. "Fifth Ecumenical Consultation between Theologians of the Oriental Ortho-

such a dialogue began slowly to move forward. It was not until 2003 that a Joint Preparatory Committee was set up and met in Rome. At this meeting it was announced that the co-chairmen of the new International Joint Commission for Dialogue would be Metropolitan Bishoy of Damiette, General Secretary of the Holy Synod of the Coptic Orthodox Church, and Cardinal Walter Kasper, President of the Pontifical Council for Promoting Christian Unity. The Preparatory Committee also established rules of membership in the dialogue, a work plan and procedures, as well as a timetable for the Joint Commission's work. Altogether seven Oriental Orthodox churches participated, in view of the fact that the two Armenian Catholicosates are represented separately.[9]

The first plenary meeting of the Joint Commission took place in Cairo in January 2004, and it has been meeting annually since that time. At its sixth meeting, in January 2009, the Commission finalized its first agreed statement, titled "Nature, Constitution and Mission of the Church."[10] (You can make a case for saying that this is the first joint text by Catholics and Oriental Orthodox since the first council of Ephesus in 431!) It treats some fundamental themes in ecclesiology such as the relationship between the Trinity and the church, attributes of the church, bishops in apostolic succession, synodality and primacies in the church, and the church's mission. The text also outlines a number of areas that need further study, and will be considered at a future stage of the dialogue. At its seventh meeting in January 2010, the commission focused on the ways in which full communion was expressed between the Catholic and Oriental Orthodox churches before the division of the mid-fifth century.[11]

I have been a member of this dialogue since the second meeting in 2005, and in general the atmosphere at these meetings is very friendly. I think much of this is due to our history and that, for the most part, we have not had the direct confrontations with them that we have had

---

dox Churches and the Roman Catholic Church," *Wort und Wahrheit* Supplementary Issue Number 5 (July 1989): 151.

9. *IS* 112 (2003/I): 10-11.

10. "Nature, Constitution and Mission of the Church," *Origins* 38, no. 35 (February 12, 2009): 551-60.

11. See the report issued at the end of the meeting at http://www.vatican.va/roman _curia/pontifical_councils/chrstuni/anc-orient-ch-docs/rc_pc_christuni_doc_20100131 _meeting-antelias_en.html.

with the Eastern Orthodox. So on a gut level there is more trust, more openness to listen to the other side.

I would say that on a practical level, the greatest difficulty we encounter is the fact that the Oriental Orthodox are a very diverse group who sometimes do not know each other very well. So it is often difficult for them to express a common position on the topics under consideration. In fact, not long ago some voices in the Vatican opposed having a dialogue with the Oriental Orthodox as a group because they have such widely divergent theological positions and practices. One example would be their attitude towards Catholic baptism: the Armenian, Syrian, and Malankara Orthodox recognize Catholic baptism, but the churches in Africa — the Copts, Ethiopians, and Eritreans — receive Catholics into their church through rebaptism. Another is the question of mixed marriages, which the African churches do not allow under any circumstances. Ironically, in many ways their dialogue with the Catholic Church has also facilitated a dialogue among the Oriental Orthodox, helping them to achieve consensus on the issues at hand. And overall, I would say that this dialogue is very promising.

In the United States, a dialogue between the U.S. Conference of Catholic Bishops and the Standing Committee of Oriental Orthodox Churches (SCOOCH) was established in 1978, a full twenty-five years before the international Joint Commission was founded. It has brought together representatives of the Armenian Apostolic Church (Catholicosate of Etchmiadzin), the Coptic Orthodox Church, the Syrian Orthodox Church, the Malankara Syrian Orthodox Church, and the Ethiopian Orthodox Church. The U.S. jurisdictions of the Malankara Orthodox Syrian Church and the Armenian Apostolic Church (Antelias) do not participate because they are not members of SCOOCH. The U.S. dialogue published a statement on the "Purpose, Scope and Method" of the dialogue in 1980, and a brief statement on the eucharist in 1983. In 1995 the dialogue published a book on the relationship with a focus on mixed marriages.[12] It also issued an agreed text, in 1999, on the pastoral care of Oriental Orthodox students in Catholic schools.[13]

12. *Oriental Orthodox–Roman Catholic Interchurch Marriages and Other Pastoral Relationships* (Washington and New York: National Conference of Catholic Bishops and the Standing Conference of Oriental Orthodox Churches, 1995), 164 pp.

13. All the agreed statements of the U.S. Catholic–Oriental Orthodox dialogue, along with press releases about individual meetings, are posted on the website of the

The Catholic–Oriental Orthodox relationship has already made a major contribution to the ecumenical movement by providing an example of how past disagreements over verbal formulas can be overcome. This was not done by one side capitulating to the other, but by moving beyond the words to the faith that those words are intended to express. Catholics and Oriental Orthodox agree that by means of different words and different concepts, they express the same faith in Jesus Christ.

II. The Assyrian Church of the East

As I mentioned at the beginning of this lecture, the Assyrian Church of the East[14] is in a special situation. It is an ancient church of the East Syriac tradition that until relatively recent times was known simply as the Church of the East. It traces its origins to ancient Mesopotamia, and flourished for centuries as a minority within the Persian Empire. It also has an astonishing history of missionary activity in places as distant as China, Tibet, Mongolia, India, Japan, Sri Lanka, and Indonesia.[15] But these outlying communities disappeared by the fifteenth century, and soon the church was reduced to a small community of ethnic Assyrians in what is now eastern Turkey. Today the largest concentration of Assyrians is found in Iraq, where the community faces a very difficult if not catastrophic situation. Many have emigrated to other parts of the world, and the Patriarch (currently Mar Dinkha IV) resides in Chicago. There are about a half-million Assyrian Christians in the world today.

The Church of the East accepted only the first two ecumenical councils and not the third (the first council of Ephesus in 431), which condemned Nestorian Christology. Consequently the Church of the East has often been referred to as "Nestorian." But most scholars today

---

U.S. Conference of Catholic Bishops at: http://www.usccb.org/seia/oriental_orthodox .shtml.

14. General introductions to the Assyrian Church of the East include W. Baum and D. Winkler, *The Church of the East: A Concise History* (New York: Routledge Curzon, 2003), and Mar Bawai Soro, *The Church of the East: Apostolic and Orthodox* (San Jose, CA: Adiabene Publications, 2007).

15. J. Duncan, "The Nestorian Missions: The Spread of the Gospel in Asia from the V to the XV Centuries," *Centro Pro Unione Semiannual Bulletin* 75 (Fall 2009): 3-12.

would agree that this title is not fair to the Assyrians. Nestorius himself was never a member of their church, and his name is not mentioned in church documents of the fifth or sixth centuries. In fact, the church has asked that it not be called "Nestorian" because of the term's negative connotations.[16] The Church of the East always considered itself to be part of the wider church, but because of the political situation it could not participate in councils held within the Roman Empire. Indeed, it was isolated from the rest of the Christian world during most of its history.

Ecumenical relations between the Catholic Church and the Assyrian Church of the East took a decisive step forward on November 11, 1994, when Mar Dinkha IV signed a Common Christological Declaration[17] with Pope John Paul II in Rome. They declared that Catholics and Assyrians are "united today in the confession of the same faith in the son of God," and set aside the Christological disputes of the past. The declaration calls for broad pastoral cooperation between the two churches, especially in the areas of catechesis and priestly formation. It also established an official theological dialogue and charged it with overcoming the obstacles that still prevent full communion.

In the years following the Common Declaration, a warm relationship also developed between the Assyrian Church of the East and the Chaldean Catholic Church, its Catholic counterpart. Mar Dinkha IV and Chaldean Patriarch Raphael Bidawid met in Detroit in November 1996 and issued a joint patriarchal statement pledging to work for the reunification of their churches by forming a joint commission for unity that was to elaborate a common catechism, oversee the foundation of a seminary in the United States for both churches, and develop common pastoral programs.[18] On August 15, 1997, the members of the Holy Synods of the two churches signed a "Joint Synodal Decree for

---

16. Mar Bawai Soro and M. J. Birnie, "Is the Theology of the Church of the East Nestorian?" in *Syriac Dialogue: First Non-Official Consultation on Dialogue within the Syriac Tradition* (Vienna: Pro Oriente, 1994), p. 129. See also Sebastian Brock, "The 'Nestorian' Church: A Lamentable Misnomer," *Bulletin of the John Rylands University Library of Manchester* 78 (1996): 23-36.

17. "Common Christological Declaration Between the Catholic Church and the Assyrian Church of the East," *IS* 88 (1995/I): 2-3.

18. "Joint Patriarchal Statement of His Holiness Mar Raphael I (Bidawid) Catholicos Patriarch, His Holiness Mar Dinkha IV, Catholicos Patriarch, and Their Respective Delegations," *Eastern Churches Journal* 3, no. 3 (1996): 171-73.

Promoting Unity," which recognized that Assyrians and Chaldeans should accept their diverse practices as legitimate, formally implemented the establishment of an Assyrian-Chaldean Joint Commission for Unity, and declared that each side recognized the apostolic succession, sacraments, and Christian witness of the other. The text also spelled out the central concerns of both sides in the dialogue: while both churches wanted to preserve the Aramaic language and culture, the Assyrians were intent on preserving their freedom and self-governance, while the Chaldeans affirmed that the preservation of full communion with Rome was among their basic principles.[19]

In 2001 the Congregation for the Doctrine of the Faith (with the approval of Pope John Paul II) recognized the validity of the Anaphora of Addai and Mari, an ancient eucharistic prayer used by the Assyrian Church that does not have a coherent Institution Narrative.[20] Later in the same year the Pontifical Council for Promoting Christian Unity issued its "Guidelines for Admission to the Eucharist between the Chaldean Church and the Assyrian Church of the East," which approved sacramental sharing between the churches under some circumstances.[21]

The theological dialogue between Catholics and Assyrians made very good progress for several years, but relations have been going through a challenging period following the decision of the Assyrian Holy Synod in 2005 to suspend Mar Bawai Soro, the bishop in California who had been in charge of ecumenical relations. In May 2008 he was received into the Chaldean Catholic eparchy in San Diego along with a number of clergy and laypeople. The two churches remain committed to building closer relations, but because of tensions resulting from these recent events, the theological dialogue, which had almost finalized an agreed statement on the sacraments, has not met since 2004.

---

19. "Joint Synodal Decree of the Assyrian Church of the East and the Chaldean Catholic Church," *Eastern Churches Journal* 4, no. 3 (1997): 175-78.

20. On the significance of this decision, see Robert Taft, "Mass without the Consecration? The Historic Agreement on the Eucharist between the Catholic Church and the Assyrian Church of the East Promulgated 26 October 2001," *Centro Pro Unione Semiannual Bulletin* 63 (Spring 2003): 15-27. Taft considers this to be "the most remarkable Catholic magisterial document since Vatican II." His study also appeared in an abbreviated form as "Mass without the Consecration?" *America Magazine*, May 12, 2003.

21. *IS* 108 (2001/IV): 148-52.

Ronald G. Roberson, CSP

Conclusion

On May 11, 1970, immediately following a private audience with Pope Paul VI in the Vatican, Armenian Catholicos Vasken I spoke to a group of waiting Catholic and Armenian bishops. He said that he and the Pope, in his words, "have remembered, as if in a reawakening, that we have been brothers for the past two thousand years. O Lord, may this moment last eternally, for it is sublime!"[22]

This, I think, sums up in a few words what has been happening the past few decades between the Catholic Church and Oriental Orthodox churches. Painful memories have given way to a rediscovery of one another as brothers and sisters who profess the same faith. They have made dramatic progress towards reestablishing full communion in a process that should give all of us encouragement and hope.

22. "Visit to Rome of His Holiness Vasken I, Supreme Catholicos of All Armenians," *IS* 11 (July 1970/III): 9.

Contributors

S. Wesley Ariarajah, a Methodist minister from Sri Lanka, is currently Professor of Ecumenical Theology at the Drew University School of Theology. Before joining Drew in 1997 he served the World Council of Churches for sixteen years, first as Director of its Interfaith Dialogue Program and then as Deputy General Secretary of the Council.

Peter C. Bouteneff is Associate Professor in Systematic Theology at St. Vladimir's Orthodox Theological Seminary. From 1995 to 2000 he served as a staff member of the Commission on Faith and Order of the World Council of Churches. Afterwards he has served as member of the Special Commission on Orthodox participation in the WCC.

Ralph Del Colle, Associate Professor of Theology, Marquette University, served on the fifth phase of Pentecostal-Catholic International Dialogue and is now a member of the sixth phase. He has also served on the international informal conversations between the Catholic Church and the Seventh Day Adventists, and on the USA Reformed-Catholic Dialogue and the Evangelical-Catholic Dialogue.

Lorelei F. Fuchs, SA, research assistant for the National Council of Churches of Christ in the USA, is a member of the Methodist–Roman Catholic International Dialogue, of the Commission on Faith and Order of the World Council of Churches, and of the Commission on Faith and Order of the National Council of Churches.

Donna Geernaert, SC, Congregational Leader, Sisters of Charity (Halifax, Nova Scotia), participated in the International Anglican–Roman Catholic Commission on Unity and Mission. Its 2007 text "Growing Together in Unity and Mission" reviewed forty years of Anglican-Roman Catholic Dialogue. She has participated in Reformed-Catholic International Dialogue, Canadian Anglican-Catholic Dialogue, and Faith and Order (WCC).

Jeffrey Gros, FSC, Catholic Studies Scholar in Residence, Lewis University; Dean, Institute for Catholic Ecumenical Leadership, participated in the World Evangelical Alliance-Catholic International Dialogue. He served ten years as Director of Faith and Order, National Council of Churches of Christ USA, fourteen years as Associate Director, Secretariat for Ecumenical and Interreligious Affairs, USCCB.

Helmut Harder, Emeritus Professor of Theology, Canadian Mennonite University, Winnipeg, Canada, where he taught for thirty years, served also for nine years as General Secretary of Mennonite Church Canada. He was co-chairman of the International Catholic-Mennonite Dialogue, 1998-2003. He participates in Mennonite-Catholic dialogue in Winnipeg.

William Henn, OFM Cap, is Professor of Ecclesiology and Ecumenism at the Pontifical Gregorian University in Rome. As a member of the WCC's Commission on Faith and Order he has contributed to a number of its publications. He has participated also in the international Reformed-Catholic, Pentecostal-Catholic, and Baptist-Catholic dialogues.

Margaret O'Gara, holds the SSJT Chair in Systematic Theology at the Faculty of Theology, University of St. Michael's College, Toronto. She has served on the Disciples of Christ-Roman Catholic International Commission for Dialogue since 1983, the Lutheran-Roman Catholic International Commission for Unity, 1995-2007, the U.S. Lutheran-Roman Catholic Dialogue since 1994, and dialogues in Canada between Roman Catholics and Anglicans, 1977-93, and Evangelicals since 2008.

John A. Radano, Adjunct Professor, Seton Hall University, was staff member of the Pontifical Council for Promoting Christian Unity, Vatican City, 1984-2008. He served as co-secretary for the second and third phases of Reformed–Roman Catholic International Dialogue, and on international dialogues with Lutherans, Baptists, Mennonites, Pentecostals, Evangelicals, and as PCPCU liaison with Faith and Order.

Cecil M. Robeck, Jr., Professor of Church History and Ecumenics, Fuller Theological Seminary, has served on the Pentecostal-Catholic Dialogue since 1985, co-chairman since 1992. He has served as co-chair of the Joint Consultative Group between the World Council of Churches and Pentecostals, and of the World Alliance of Reformed Churches-Pentecostal Dialogue, and on the Commission on Faith and Order (WCC and NCCCUSA).

Ronald G. Roberson, CSP, Associate Director, Secretariat for Ecumenical and Interreligious Affairs, United States Conference of Catholic Bishops, Washington, D.C., is a member of the Catholic-Oriental Orthodox International Dialogue, and staffs the United States dialogues with the (Eastern) Orthodox and Oriental Orthodox Churches. He served on the staff of the Pontifical Council for Promoting Christian Unity, Vatican City, 1988-1992.

William G. Rusch, Adjunct Professor, Yale Divinity School, was ELCA Ecumenical Officer during its 1993 initiative regarding the inapplicability of sixteenth-century condemnations on justification to the Catholic Church and contributed to the LWF and PCPCU decision to develop a joint declaration on justification. He served on the USA Lutheran-Catholic Dialogue, and on Faith and Order, both WCC and NCCCUSA.

Mary Tanner, currently the President (for Europe) of the World Council of Churches, served as a member of the Faith and Order Commission of the World Council of Churches from 1975, and its Moderator, 1991-1998. As first General Secretary of the Church of England's Council for Christian Unity, she participated in ARCIC and other bilaterals. Queen Elizabeth named her a Dame of the British Empire in 2007.

Geoffrey Wainwright holds the Cushman Chair of Christian Theology at Duke University. Since 1986 he has been co-chairman of the Joint Commission between the World Methodist Council and the Roman Catholic Church. A member of the Faith and Order Commission of the World Council of Churches, 1976-1991, he chaired the final redaction of the Faith and Order text *Baptism, Eucharist and Ministry* (1982).

JARED WICKS, SJ, currently Writer in Residence, John Carroll University, taught at the Gregorian University School of Theology for twenty-five years. He took part in the third and fourth phases of the International Lutheran-Catholic Dialogue, 1986-2005, and in the drafting of the *Joint Declaration on the Doctrine of Justification*. He has also served on the USA Catholic-Lutheran Dialogue from 2005.

SUSAN K. WOOD, SCL, professor and chair, Department of Theology, Marquette University, served on the second phase of international Baptist-Roman Catholic conversations (2006-2010), and the fifth phase of the International Lutheran-Catholic Dialogue. She also serves on the USA Lutheran-Roman Catholic Dialogue and the North American Orthodox-Catholic Theological Consultation, and has participated in Faith and Order studies.

Index of Names

Index of Subjects and Major Themes

All Under One Christ (1980), 73, 78, 88

Anabaptist movement, 286, 290-91, 298, 300. *See also* Mennonite World Conference

Anglican Communion, xxi, 80, 123, 123n.2, 124, 126, 131, 135, 138, 139, 166n.9, 280n.45

Apostolicity. *See* Church

"Apostolicity and Catholicity" (2002), 244, 247

"Apostolicity of the Church" (2006), 66-73, 77, 79-92

Apostolic succession: in faith, 85; in ministry, 70-72, 82, 84-85, 91, 101-3, 117, 120, 149, 162, 196, 251, 280, 309, 313

Apostolic teaching, 83, 239, 287

Assyrian Church of the East, 304, 311-12

Baptism, 28, 32, 50, 68, 99, 103, 132, 148, 177-79, 190, 205, 213, 226, 228, 261, 265-66, 271, 273-77, 300; adult/infant baptism, 45, 176-77, 178, 199, 236-37, 272, 276-77; as basis of communion, 115, 124, 128, 244, 250; and experience of the Holy Spirit, 178; and faith, 119, 179, 190, 202, 269, 272; trinitarian formula for, 178. *See also* Baptism, Eucharist and Ministry

Baptism, Eucharist and Ministry (BEM), 28-32, 35-36, 40-41, 44-46, 48-49, 60, 83, 83n.17, 97, 118, 120, 162

Baptism in the Holy Spirit, 191-92, 198, 211, 216, 276

Baptist World Alliance, 172n.26, 220, 264, 266, 267, 271

Brighton Report (2001) "Speaking the Truth in Love," 100

Called to Be the One Church (2007), 34, 45

Called Together to Be Peacemakers (2003), 283

Catholicity. *See* Church

Chalcedon, Council of (451), 305, 306; Chalcedonian, 95, 273. *See also* Councils, historic ecumenical

Charismatic renewal: Catholic, 165, 167, 192, 197-98, 216, 235; Anglican, Orthodox, Protestant, or non-denominational, 173, 197, 198, 199, 205, 206

Charismatic gifts, 203, 204, 206

Charisms, 193, 198-99, 216, 241

Christology, 106n.5, 144, 278, 305, 307, 311. *See* Jesus Christ

272, 282; evangelization and social justice, 208-9; theology of peace, 284, 295-99, 302-3

Eucharist/Lord's Supper, 25, 58, 93, 127, 251, 265; Addai and Mari, Anaphora of, 313; *anamnēsis* (memorial/remembrance) and, 45, 119, 244-45, 277, 290; within *BEM*, 28, 32-33, 43-46, 50, 60; brings about unity, 115, 237, 243, 278; center of the Church's life, 68, 237, 239, 243; component of the goal of visible unity, 26, 28; convergences on, 129, 132, 145, 290; discussion of, 97, 100, 103, 243-46, 274-75, 277-78, 290-95, 301-2; *epiclesis,* 45, 203, 277; real presence of Christ in, 39, 45, 97, 119, 145n.9, 148, 239, 244-46, 248, 277-78, 291, 301-2; recognition of, 304, 308, 313; and reconciliation in society, 32, 301-2; and the sacrifice of Christ, 78, 97, 119, 244-45, 248, 277; "sister churches" and, 250; source of apostolic teaching, 239; transubstantiation, 245-46; trinitarian basis of, 137, 148. *See also Baptism, Eucharist and Ministry*

Eucharist (1978), 73, 78

Evangelical–Roman Catholic Dialogue on Mission (1984), 221-27

Evangelii nuntiandi, Apostolic Exhortation of Paul VI (1974), 220, 222, 225, 233. See also *Lausanne Covenant*

Evangelization, 3-4, 175, 180-87, 207-8, 218, 224-25, 230, 277, 282. *See also* Common witness; Mission; Proselytism; Religious freedom (liberty)

"Evangelization, Proselytism and Common Witness" (1998), 175, 180-87, 208-13

Experience, Christian, 97, 104, 108, 110, 156, 216-17

Facing Unity (1984), 73, 79, 80, 88

Faith, 7, 10, 14, 19, 23, 55, 57, 68, 70, 96, 100; and Christian initiation, 188, 214; expressed in creeds, 30, 47, 129,

229; full communion/unity in, 26, 34, 36, 39-40, 44-45, 103; justification in, 60-61, 63-64; revelation and, 100, 103; rule of, 67, 86. *See also* Apostolic succession; Baptism; Creeds

Faith and Order Commission, 10, 12, 16, 24, 26-37, 40-50

"Faith, Sacraments and the Unity of the Church" (Bari, 1987), 251

"Final Report" (1981, ARCIC), 124

Fellowship: Baptist World Alliance as fellowship of churches, 264; *BEM* helped bring churches into closer, 29; common biblical understanding of, 228; conciliar, 7; evangelical fellowships, 222; goal of World Council of Churches and Faith and Order is visible unity in eucharistic fellowship, 26, 33; life in communion includes deep fellowship, 117; as one translation of *koinonia,* 108, 111; WCC as a fellowship of churches, 6, 12, 17, 36, 59

Gaudium et Spes: Pastoral Constitution on the Church in the Modern World (7 December 1965), 46, 114, 209, 289n.26

Gift of Authority: Authority in the Church III (1999), 125

Gospel: accord on, 72; acknowledging what is truly of Christ, of the gospel, and thereby of the church in one another, 101, 121; and the apostolicity of the church, 68-69, 71-72, 78-79, 82-91; common Christian witness to, 222-23, 267; discernment of Gospel authenticity of any tradition takes place within the church, 42; Holy Spirit maintains the church in the truth of, 87, 241; and justification, 62-63; proselytism/unworthy forms of evangelism, as challenge to, 231, 270-71; reconciliation, non-violence, active peacemaking belong to the heart of, 303;